MACHIAVELLI AND EMPIRE

Mikael Hörnqvist challenges us to rethink the overall meaning and importance of Machiavelli's political thinking. *Machiavelli and Empire* combines close textual analysis of *The Prince* and *The Discourses* with a broad historical approach, to establish the importance of empire-building and imperial strategy in Machiavelli's thought. The primary context of Machiavelli's work, Hörnqvist argues, is not the mirror-for-princes genre or medieval and Renaissance republicanism in general, but a tradition of Florentine imperialist republicanism dating back to the late thirteenth century, based on the twin notions of liberty at home and empire abroad. Weaving together themes and topics drawn from contemporary Florentine political debate, Medicean ritual, and Renaissance triumphalism, this study explores how Machiavelli in his chancery writings and theoretical works promoted the longstanding aspirations of Florence to become a great and expanding empire, modeled on the example of the ancient Roman republic. Original and thought-provoking, this book makes a major contribution to our understanding of the Renaissance, and of the history of European ideas.

MIKAEL HÖRNQVIST teaches at the Department of the History of Science and Ideas at Uppsala University in Sweden.

IDEAS IN CONTEXT 71

Machiavelli and Empire

IDEAS IN CONTEXT

The books in this series will discuss the emergence of intellectual traditions and of related new disciplines. The procedures, aims and vocabularies that were generated will be set in the context of the alternatives available within the contemporary frameworks of ideas and institutions. Through detailed studies of the evolution of such traditions, and their modification by different audiences, it is hoped that a new picture will form of the development of ideas in their concrete contexts. By this means, artificial distinctions between the history of philosophy, of the various sciences, of society and politics, and of literature may be seen to dissolve.

The series is published with the support of the Exxon Foundation.

A list of books in the series will be found at the end of the volume.

MACHIAVELLI AND EMPIRE

MIKAEL HÖRNQVIST

PUBLISHED BY THE PRESS SYNDICATE OF THE UNIVERSITY OF CAMBRIDGE
The Pitt Building, Trumpington Street, Cambridge, United Kingdom

CAMBRIDGE UNIVERSITY PRESS
The Edinburgh Building, Cambridge, CB2 2RU, UK
40 West 20th Street, New York, NY 10011–4211, USA
477 Williamstown Road, Port Melbourne, VIC 3207, Australia
Ruiz de Alarcón 13, 28014 Madrid, Spain
Dock House, The Waterfront, Cape Town 8001, South Africa

http://www.cambridge.org

First published 2004

Printed in the United Kingdom at the University Press, Cambridge

Typeface Adobe Garamond 11/12.5 pt. *System* LaTeX 2ε [TB]

A catalogue record for this book is available from the British Library

Library of Congress Cataloguing in Publication data
Hörnqvist, Mikael.
Machiavelli and empire / Mikael Hörnqvist.
p. cm. – (Ideas in context ; 71)
Includes bibliographical references and index.
ISBN 0-521-83945-9
1. Machiavelli, Niccolò, 1469–1527. Principe. 2. Machiavelli, Niccolò, 1469–1527. Discorsi sopra la prima deca di Tito Livio. 3. Florence (Italy) – Foreign relations – 1421–1737. 4. Political science – Italy – Philosophy – History – To 1500. I. Title. II. Series.
JC143.M4H67 2004
320.1 – dc22 2004040761

ISBN 0 521 83945 9 hardback

To Justine, Véronique, and Shohreh

Contents

Acknowledgments

This project began as a doctoral dissertation in the Department of the History of Ideas at Uppsala University and has evolved into a book after a long process of restructuring and rethinking. It would have been impossible to follow this crooked path had it not been for the guidance and encouragement from good friends and respected colleagues.

The author wishes to thank Rolf Bagemihl, Alison Brown, Salvatore Camporeale, Lorenzo Casini, Gunnar Eriksson, Riccardo Fubini, Ken Gouwens, Stephen Greenblatt, James Hankins, Johan Köhler, Harvey Mansfield, John Najemy, Patricia Osmond, Marco Pellegrini, Mats Persson, and Quentin Skinner for their critical advice and support in this venture.

Institutional support has been received from the Department of the History of Science and Ideas at Uppsala University, the Kennedy School of Government at Harvard University, the Villa I Tatti: The Harvard University Center for Italian Renaissance Studies in Florence, and the Instituto Nazionale dei Studi sul Rinascimento in Florence.

I owe a special thanks to the many institutions that have provided financial support for this venture. I am particularly indebted to the Axel and Margaret Ax:son Johnson Foundation for the main source of funding without which the project would not have reached completion. Generous funding was also provided by the Swedish Research Council, the Knut and Alice Wallenberg Foundation, the Melville J. Kahn Fellowship Fund, the Swedish Institute, the Sweden–America Foundation, and the Wennergren Center Foundation.

My greatest debt is to my family, Justine, Véronique, and Shohreh. It is with pleasure and a sense of deep gratitude that I dedicate this book to them.

On the use of Machiavelli's texts

For the renditions of Niccolò Machiavelli's *Prince* in English, I have consulted the following translations to offer translations of my own:

The Prince, trans. W. K. Marriott (London: J. M. Dent & Sons, 1908).

"The Prince," in *The Portable Machiavelli*, eds. Peter Bondanella and Mark Musa (London:Viking Penguin, 1979), pp. 77–166.

The Prince, trans. Harvey C. Mansfield Jr. (Chicago: University of Chicago Press, 1985).

The Prince, eds. Quentin Skinner and Russell Price (Cambridge: Cambridge University Press, 1988).

For Machiavelli's *Discorsi sopra la prima deca di Tito Livio*, I have relied on Harvey Mansfield and Nathan Tarcov's translation in Niccolò Machiavelli, *Discourses on Livy* (Chicago: University of Chicago Press, 1996) with minor adaptations.

Unless otherwise stated, all other translations in the text are my own.

As a rule, Machiavelli's name has been omitted in the notes.

CHAPTER I

Another philosophy

> There is another philosophy that is better suited for political action, that takes its cue, adapts itself to the drama in hand, and acts its part neatly and well.
>
> Sir Thomas More

In Machiavelli's most famous comedy, *La mandragola* (1518), the desperately love-sick Callimaco asks his clever friend, Ligurio, for help in getting into bed with the beautiful Lucrezia, the childless and unhappy wife of Nicia, a wealthy merchant and "the simplest and most stupid man of Florence."[1] Ligurio, a former marriage-broker, who now is said to "make his living out of deceiving people," accepts the assignment.[2] Acting as something of a playwright in the play, at one point likening himself to a military captain giving orders to his troops before going into battle, Ligurio selects his cast, invents his plot, and sets it in motion. Busy attending to things big and small, he provides the other characters with motivations, reasons, and pretexts for their actions, and coaches and supervises their performances. When he first introduces Callimaco to Nicia, presenting him as a famous physician at the court of the king of France, he carefully constructs his friend's fictitious character, his *ethos*, so that it will impose itself on the merchant, and win his trust. Knowing that unlettered men like Nicia are easily impressed by people who have a knowledge of Latin, he encourages Callimaco to embellish his speech with a store of Latin stock phrases and maxims. Predictably enough, Nicia is taken in by the charade and comes to view Callimaco, alias the famous physician, as a man of great dignity and worthy of faith.

Nicia yearns for an heir, and on Ligurio's advice Callimaco persuades him that the most effective way of making his wife pregnant is to prepare

[1] Niccolò Machiavelli,"La mandragola" in *Opere*, vol. IV, ed. L. Blasucci (Turin: UTET, 1989), [hereinafter *La mandragola*], p. 119: [CALLIMACO]: "el più sciocco omo di Firenze."

[2] *La mandragola*, p. 124: [CALLIMACO]: "Io lo credo, ancora che io sappia ch'e' pari tuoi vivino di uccellare gli uomini."

her for the sexual act by giving her a magic concoction made of mandrake root. The only catch, Callimaco goes on to explain, is that the power of the drink is such that it will cause the death of the first man who has intercourse with her. The ever-resourceful Ligurio has a solution at hand, though. By exploiting Nicia's simplicity, and by playing on his emotions, his vanity, and his uncontainable desire for male offspring, he makes him accept the idea of having another man sleep with Lucrezia in his place. The plan is put into effect, and the play is brought to a climatic end as Nicia, acting as the unwitting, and ridiculously happy, accomplice in his own cuckolding, leads Callimaco, now disguised as a young street-singer, into his wife's bedroom in the false belief that the youth, after having made Lucrezia pregnant, will die of the potion she has been given for the purpose.

As this brief account makes evident, *La mandragola* is a comedy imbued with rhetoric. Perhaps, it could even be argued that the main theme of the play is the art of persuasion itself, and its conspiratorial use within the private sphere. Almost every scene of the play is staged as a scene of persuasion: Ligurio filling Callimaco with hope; Ligurio insinuating himself into Nicia's confidence; Ligurio tempting Father Timoteo, the cunning priest in the play; Father Timoteo and Lucrezia's mother, Sostrata, seeking to influence Lucrezia; Callimaco exhorting Nicia; Callimaco, in a soliloquy, talking sense to and inspiring courage in himself, and so forth. A detailed study could also be made of how Machiavelli throughout the play employs the traditional functions of classical rhetoric – reason (*logos*), character (*ethos*), and emotion (*pathos*) – for persuasive ends.

The rhetorical nature of *La mandragola* is also evident from the extent to which its characters are fashioned according to their different degrees of insight into the principles and the workings of rhetorical manipulation. Ligurio acts the master rhetorician, displaying an unerring sense for *kairos* – the rhetorical situation – that is, the circumstance, the place, the time, and the persons involved, and a great capacity for improvisation. He is an exemplary specimen of what Richard Lanham has called the rhetorical man, *Homo rhetoricus*. According to Lanham's definition, this is a type of person who conceives of himself as an actor on the public stage, and has a sense of identity that "depends on the reassurance of daily histrionic reenactment." His focus is on the local and the contemporary, and his motivations are of a "ludic" and "agonistic" nature. He is trained "not to discover reality but to manipulate it," and reality for him comes therefore to be "what is accepted as reality, what is useful."[3]

[3] Richard Lanham, *The Motives of Eloquence: Literary Rhetoric in the Renaissance* (New Haven: Yale University Press, 1976), p. 4.

Father Timoteo is a perceptive witness to Ligurio's performance and a fairly competent con-artist himself. Callimaco is capable of dissimulation and concealment when coached by Ligurio, and is also aware of the fact that appearances and false impressions can work the same effect on a person's state of mind as realities and true emotions. At the bottom of this hierarchy, we find the gullible and self-deceiving Nicia. In contrast to Father Timoteo, who, even though he realizes that Ligurio is taking him in, plays along in the intrigue, because he believes that it will serve the interest of his church, Nicia has no grasp of what Ligurio and his companions are up to. While he is generally aware that people have designs on each other and engage in intrigues,[4] he is totally incapable of comprehending the true nature of the role he is asked to play, believing as he does that the whole plot has been set up for his sake and for the purpose of giving him a child. In a sense, it could be claimed that the personal disaster Nicia brings upon himself is a direct consequence of his failure to read Ligurio and the other characters rhetorically, and his inability to grasp their intentions, and to see how they control his responses and actions by manipulating his emotions, his sense of commonplaces, and the shortcomings of his character. Nicia, in short, is a bad interpreter of Ligurio's and the other figures' rhetorical performances.

As a play about rhetoric and deception, *La mandragola* could be read as a reflection back on Machiavelli's best-known work, *The Prince* (1513). Ligurio's mastery of persuasion, deception, and staging, and his ability to exploit the weaknesses of others, give him – and his associates – within the private sphere a power over men that resembles the political power of the Machiavellian prince. Ligurio's manipulation of Nicia can be read as an illustration or enactment of Machiavelli's dictum in *The Prince* that great pretenders will always get the better of the simple and the obedient, and that the deceiver will "always find someone who will allow himself to be deceived."[5] This analogy is fairly obvious and has often been commented upon, but could Machiavelli's comedy contain a model or blueprint for how to read *The Prince* as well? Could it be that the Florentine, by laying bare in *La mandragola* the mechanisms of rhetorical manipulation, has given us clues and interpretative tools that, if properly understood and used, will allow us to dissolve the mysteries surrounding this, his most famous masterpiece? The current study is an attempt to explore this possibility by situating Machiavelli's intellectual and political project within the contexts of classical rhetoric and early Cinquecento Florentine politics. But before

[4] Cf. *La mandragola*, p. 126: [NICIA]: "io non vorrei che mi mettessi in qualche lecceto, e poi mi lasciassi in sulle secche."

[5] Niccolò Machiavelli, "Il principe," in *Opere*, ed. C. Vivanti (3 vols., Turin: Einaudi, 1997–), I [hereinafter *Il principe*], p. 166: "colui che inganna troverrà sempre chi si lascerà ingannare."

we can begin to approach this important chapter in the history of Western civilization, we need to gain a firmer understanding of the form of interpretation Nicia failed to develop in *La mandragola*; in other words, we need to find out what it means to read rhetorically.

MACHIAVELLI THE RHETORICIAN

Ever since the revival of rhetoric in the 1950s, the term "rhetorical reading" has been loosely employed to describe a form of textual interpretation that focuses on how the author seeks to provoke, control, and manipulate the responses of his readers. In his now classical *Rhetoric of Fiction* of 1961, Wayne Booth discusses at length, and with explicit reference to Aristotle's poetics, how authors of fiction employ character and emotion – *ethos* and *pathos* – to engage their readers ethically and emotionally in the narrative.[6] Later in the sixties, Edward Corbett defined rhetorical reading, or rhetorical criticism, as "that mode of internal criticism which considers the interaction between the work, the author, and the audience." According to Corbett, the chief interests of rhetorical reading are in "the *product*, the *process*, and the *effect* of linguistic activity, whether of the imaginative kind or the utilitarian kind . . . It is more interested in a literary work for what it *does* than for what it *is*."[7] More recently, Thomas Sloane has claimed that rhetorical reading can be distinguished from other forms of textual close analysis by the fact that it is founded on the assumption that "language reflects a speaker's design as he confronts an audience, who he assumes are not possessed of *tabulae rasa* but of minds filled with associations, conventions, expectations, which he must direct, control, or take advantage of."[8]

In Machiavelli criticism, the term rhetoric has until recently been used almost exclusively for denoting the final chapter of *The Prince*, where Machiavelli in an ardent, patriotic appeal addresses his Medicean readers, exhorting them to liberate Italy from the barbarians.[9] Commenting on the state of Machiavelli studies some twenty-five years ago, Eugene Garver

6 Wayne Booth, *The Rhetoric of Fiction*, 2nd edn (Chicago: Chicago University Press, 1983).

7 Edward P. J. Corbett, *Rhetorical Analyses of Literary Works* (Oxford: Oxford University Press, 1969), p. xxii.

8 Thomas O. Sloane, "Reading Milton Rhetorically," in *Renaissance Eloquence: Studies in the Theory and Practice of Renaissance Rhetoric*, ed. J. J. Murphy (Berkeley, CA: California University Press, 1983), p. 398.

9 For a typical example, see Ernst Cassirer, *The Myth of the State* (London: Oxford University Press, 1946), pp. 143–44: "It is true that in the last chapter his cool and detached attitude gives way to an entirely new note. Machiavelli suddenly shakes off the burden of his logical method. His style is no longer analytical but rhetorical."

observed that *The Prince* as a whole, despite all that had been written and said about the treatise, rarely, if ever, had been defined, or interpreted, as a work of rhetoric.[10] Incredible as this remark may sound to us today, there can be no denying that it carried a great deal of truth at the time.[11] This anomaly has been abundantly compensated for in recent years, which have seen a vast, and still-growing, flood of studies emphasizing the rhetorical character of Machiavelli's work and teaching. Today, it is taken more or less for granted that Machiavelli in his youth received a formal rhetorical training and that these studies constituted an important aspect of his intellectual formation.[12] The forceful, and often manipulative, rhetoric of his Chancery writings has been studied by Jean-Jacques Marchand, Giorgio Barberi Squarotti, and Anthony Parel.[13] Theodore Sumberg has offered a perceptive and subtle rhetorical reading of Machiavelli's *Esortazione alla penitenza*,[14] and the rhetorical *bravura* displayed in his comedies, embodied by the figure of Ligurio of *La mandragola*, has received penetrating treatment from Giulio Ferroni, Wayne Rebhorn, and Harvey Mansfield.[15] Several studies have attempted to define Machiavelli's views on rhetoric and his rhetorical view of politics in relation to the general tradition of classical and humanist rhetoric. John Stephens has argued that Machiavelli's realism,

[10] Eugene Garver, "Machiavelli's *The Prince*: A Neglected Rhetorical Classic," *Philosophy and Rhetoric* 13 (1980), p. 99.

[11] Kenneth Burke's oft-quoted discussion of Machiavelli's administrative rhetoric in *A Rhetoric of Motives* of 1950 had at the time received little attention from Machiavelli scholars. See Kenneth Burke, *A Rhetoric of Motives* (Berkeley, CA: California University Press, 1969), pp. 158–66. That Leo Strauss in *Thoughts on Machiavelli* of 1958 treated *The Prince* in part as a philosophical, in part as a rhetorical work, seems to have gone largely unnoticed, even by Strauss himself, who preferred to speak of the rhetorical level of the text in terms of the modern phenomenon of propaganda. See Leo Strauss, *Thoughts on Machiavelli* (Chicago: University of Chicago Press, 1958), pp. 172–73. Strauss also speaks (pp. 154 and 172) of Machiavelli as an unarmed captain engaging in spiritual warfare. On one occasion, he defines him (p. 45) as an artist who, in an artful way, uses examples that "are beautiful without being true." Cf. Harvey C. Mansfield, *Machiavelli's Virtue* (Chicago: University of Chicago Press, 1996), pp. xi and 4.

[12] On Machiavelli's education, see Robert Black, "Machiavelli, Servant of the Florentine Republic," in *Machiavelli and Republicanism*, eds. G. Bock, Q. Skinner, and M. Viroli (Cambridge: Cambridge University Press, 1990), pp. 71–99.

[13] Giorgio Barberi Squarotti, *Machiavelli o la scelta della letteratura* (Rome: Bulzoni, 1987), pp. 39–61; Jean-Jacques Marchand, *Niccolò Machiavelli: I primi scritti politici (1499–1512): Nascita di un pensiero e di uno stile* (Padua: Antenore, 1975); Anthony J. Parel, "Machiavelli's Notion of Justice: Text and Analysis," *Political Theory* 18 (1990): 528–44.

[14] Theodore A. Sumberg, *Political Literature of Europe: Before and After Machiavelli* (Lanham, MD: University Press of America, 1993), pp. 47–62.

[15] Giulio Ferroni, *"Mutazione" e "riscontro" nel teatro di Machiavelli* (Rome: Bulzoni, 1972); Wayne A. Rebhorn, *Foxes and Lions: Machiavelli's Confidence Men* (Ithaca: Cornell University Press, 1988); Harvey C. Mansfield, "The Cuckold in Machiavelli's *Mandragola*," in *The Comedy and Tragedy of Machiavelli: Essays on the Literary Works*, ed. V. B. Sullivan (New Haven: Yale University Press, 2000), pp. 1–29.

his popular way of thinking, and his method based on the "effectual truth" all have their origin in the works of Cicero.[16] Recently, Virginia Cox has argued that Machiavelli's advocacy of force and deception, conceptually as well as technically, draws on the pseudo-Ciceronian *Rhetorica ad Herennium*,[17] while Maurizio Viroli has traced elements deriving from classical rhetoric in his works.[18] Other scholars have inquired into how Machiavelli's view on rhetoric departs from that of his humanist predecessors. Special emphasis has here been given to the way in which Machiavelli extends the range of political persuasion by advocating a rhetorical use of means, such as visual displays, public rituals, sacrifices, threats, coercive action, and public executions, which traditionally had been precluded from the sphere of rhetoric.[19] Today it is also widely recognized that there exists a close analogy between the position Machiavelli, the author of *The Prince*, assumes in this work, and the role he prescribes for his princely reader: they are both innovators of new modes and orders, and they both use, or are expected to use, rhetorical deception and dissimulation to achieve their ends, the former within the sphere of discourse, the latter within that of political action.[20] In the light of this development, it is hardly an exaggeration to claim that the rhetorical approach in recent years has contributed to redirect and reshape the field of Machiavelli studies.

The present chapter contrasts the ideological readings of John Pocock and Quentin Skinner to the rhetorical approach. This discussion leads to a critical reexamination of Skinner's methodology and to a definition of the concept of rhetorical reading, which pretends to be more concise, and at the

[16] J. N. Stephens, "Ciceronian Rhetoric and the Immorality of Machiavelli's *Prince*," *Renaissance Studies* 2 (1988): 258–67. Cf. Marcia Colish, "The Idea of Liberty in Machiavelli," *Journal of the History of Ideas* 32 (1971): 323–51.

[17] Virginia Cox, "Machiavelli and the *Rhetorica ad Herennium*: Deliberative Rhetoric in *The Prince*," *Sixteenth Century Journal* 28 (1997): 1109–41.

[18] Maurizio Viroli, *Machiavelli* (Oxford: Oxford University Press, 1998), pp. 73–113.

[19] See for example Burke, *A Rhetoric of Motives*, p. 161; Ezio Raimondi, "Machiavelli and the Rhetoric of the Warrior," *Modern Language Notes* 92 (1977): 1–16; John D. Lyons, *Exemplum: The Rhetoric of Example in Early Modern France and Italy* (Princeton: Princeton University Press, 1989), pp. 47–63; Victoria Kahn, *Machiavellian Rhetoric: From the Counter-Reformation to Milton* (Princeton: Princeton University Press, 1994), pp. 19, 36, and 52; Mansfield, *Machiavelli's Virtue*, pp. 295–314.

[20] See for example Strauss, *Thoughts on Machiavelli*, pp. 70–84 and 154; Claude Lefort, *Le travail de l'œuvre Machiavel* (Paris: Gallimard, 1972), p. 356; Garver, "Machiavelli's *The Prince*," pp. 100–01 and 111–12; Thomas M. Greene, "The End of Discourse in Machiavelli's *Prince*," in *Literary Theory/Renaissance Texts*, eds. P. Parker and D. Quint (Baltimore: The Johns Hopkins University Press, 1986), pp. 68, 70, and 77; Kahn, *Machiavellian Rhetoric*, pp. 32–33; Lyons, *Exemplum*, pp. 36 and 47; Albert Russell Ascoli, "Machiavelli's Gift of Counsel," in *Machiavelli and the Discourse of Literature*, eds. A. R. Ascoli and V. Kahn (Ithaca: Cornell University Press, 1993), p. 238; Mansfield, *Machiavelli's Virtue*, pp. ix–xvi, 3–5, 60–61, 125, and *passim*. Wayne Rebhorn claims that Machiavelli, by describing his new prince as "a master of disguising his motives and acts by means of some 'colore' or other," defines him as "a master rhetorician"; see Rebhorn, *Foxes and Lions*, p. 114.

same time more classically oriented, than current definitions of the term. In order to make explicit the general assumptions underlying the present study, I will then give a brief sketch of the methodological framework within which my own reading of *The Prince* will be performed.

IDEOLOGICAL, DIALECTICAL, AND DECONSTRUCTIONIST READINGS

Before anything else is said, it must be recognized that there exists no such thing as a well-defined rhetorical approach to Machiavelli. The numerous studies of recent date focusing on the rhetorical dimension of his work, or being pursued from a rhetorical point of view, are simply too diverse and too incongruous to allow for such a labeling. To a large extent, this diversity can be put down to the strong theoretical and methodological influences the field has come to receive of late from a variety of scholarly disciplines and approaches, such as linguistics, semiotics, speech act theory, deconstruction, and post-structuralism. For our present purpose, though, the generic term rhetorical reading is sufficiently well understood, and yet broad enough, to allow us to describe a widespread, but far from uniform, tendency within contemporary Machiavelli research.

Since the rhetorical approach, which we have begun to outline here, in large part can be seen as a reaction to the ideological readings developed in the 1970s by John Pocock and Quentin Skinner, it would be appropriate to take their work as our point of departure. We will do so in two steps, beginning with Pocock and his critics, and then proceeding to a discussion of Skinner's methodology. Pocock's treatment of rhetoric in *The Machiavellian Moment* takes as its starting point a distinction, borrowed from Jerrold Siegel, between the philosophical outlook of the medieval schoolmen and the rhetorical mindset of the Renaissance humanists. In contrast to scholastic philosophy, which had aimed at establishing universal, timeless, and objective truth, Renaissance rhetoric was concerned with "persuading men to act, to decide, to approve" in social contexts "presupposing the presence of other men to whom the intellect was addressing itself." While philosophy subordinated particulars to universals, rhetoric was "invariably and necessarily, immersed in particular situations, particular decisions, and particular relationships."[21] According to Pocock, the intellectual outlook of the Florentine humanists, Machiavelli included, was not philosophical,

[21] J. G. A. Pocock, *The Machiavellian Moment: Florentine Political Thought and the Atlantic Tradition* (Princeton: Princeton University Press, 1975), pp. 58–59. On Pocock's approach to Machiavelli, see John H. Geerken, "Pocock and Machiavelli: Structuralist Explanation of History," *Journal of*

but predominantly and self-consciously rhetorical. Their main concern was with the active life of the citizen, and they conceived of language as "a means of action."[22] In the light of such declarations, one could have expected Pocock to treat *The Prince* and the *Discourses* as works of rhetoric, immersed in the political and social reality of interacting particulars. But instead, Pocock reads Machiavelli ideologically. *The Prince* is in his view a theoretical treatise, "inspired by a specific situation but not directed at it." The work presents us with "a typology of innovators and their relations with fortune," but its analysis is not undertaken "in the specific context of Florence." To what extent Machiavelli meant to "illuminate the problems faced by the restored Medici in their government of Florence" must therefore remain a matter of speculation.[23] How, then, are we to understand Pocock's claim that Machiavelli was a rhetorician, and not a political philosopher? Machiavelli's works were rhetorical, he seems to argue, because they aimed at reconstituting "a world of civic action" and bringing about a revival of the ancient ideal of citizenship.[24] In the political culture that was to result from this reform, we are led to believe, rhetoric and a rhetorical understanding of politics would have a fundamental role to play.[25] So in Pocock's final analysis, Machiavelli is a rhetorician or a champion of rhetoric, who does not write rhetorically, but longs for a time when human communication and civic action will yet again be possible.

Dissatisfied with Pocock's ideological and essentially unrhetorical reading, recent scholars have sought other trajectories to approach the rhetoric of Machiavelli's texts. In an unorthodox and highly demanding study, inspired

the History of Philosophy 17 (1979): 309–18; Vickie B. Sullivan, "Machiavelli's Momentary 'Machiavellian Moment': A Reconsideration of Pocock's Treatment of the *Discourses*," *Political Theory* 20 (1992): 309–18; Paul A. Rahe, *Republics Ancient and Modern: Classical Republicanism and the American Revolution* (3 vols., Chapel Hill: University of North Carolina Press, 1992); Rahe, "Situating Machiavelli," in *Renaissance Civic Humanism Reconsidered*, ed. J. Hankins (Cambridge: Cambridge University Press, 2000), pp. 270–308; Mark Bevir, "Mind and Method in the History of Ideas," *History and Theory* 36 (1997): 167–89; Kahn, *Machiavellian Rhetoric*, pp. 6–8 and 243–48.

22 J. G. A. Pocock, "Machiavelli and Guicciardini: Ancients and Moderns," *Canadian Journal of Political and Social Theory/Revue canadienne de théorie politique et sociale* 2 (1978): 93–109; quote from p. 97.

23 Pocock, *The Machiavellian Moment*, p. 160. Pocock's discussion of the *Discorsi* is pursued along similar lines. The work is thus said to contain a typology of modern and ancient republics defined according to how they manage, or have managed, to cope with change and historical contingency. Presenting himself as a political analyst, operating "at a higher level of theoretical generality" (p. 186) than his contemporaries, Machiavelli already from the outset makes it clear that he will pay no particular attention to his native Florence, since the city fails to qualify as a true republic, having had an unfree beginning under the Romans and having never been able to achieve "stability of either dominion or liberty" (pp. 186–87).

24 Pocock, "Machiavelli and Guicciardini," p. 97; cf. Pocock, *The Machiavellian Moment*, p. 193.

25 In Pocock's view, the *Discorsi* constitutes an analysis in general terms of the republic's quest for liberty, stability, and power, and of the conditions of active citizenship and participatory politics.

by semiotics, Russian formalism, and French post-structuralism, Michael McCanles argues that Machiavelli in *The Prince* combines a nondialectical and a dialectical form of discourse. On the surface of the text, McCanles claims, the work seems to be aspiring to a nondialectical mode of discourse characterized by differentiality between binary pairs, analyticity, noncontradiction, and well-formedness. But this closed and one-dimensional form of speech is adopted by Machiavelli only to demonstrate how nondialectical discourse, "despite itself," is bound to fall under "the regulation of a dialectical model."[26] By confronting his reader with discursive slides, conceptual slippages, and dissolving distinctions, Machiavelli seeks to impart a "competence in a discursive practice that allows one to think and speak dialectically, that is, to understand how differentially paired terms not only exclude each other but also imply each other."[27] The aim of this pedagogical project, McCanles maintains, is to make the reader aware of the dialectical structure governing human discourse and human action in general.[28] Having come to grasp "the logic that weaves words into texts, which is identical with the logic that weaves events into enterprises," the reader of *The Prince* will abandon the noxious and self-defeating nondialectical mode of proceeding and adopt a dialectical mode of thinking and acting instead.[29]

The contrast between a nondialectical and a dialectical mode of discourse and action, McCanles establishes, bears a close resemblance to Eugene Garver's and Victoria Kahn's distinction between ideological and rhetorical, or dialectical, politics. Reading Machiavelli in relation to the humanist rhetorical tradition and the reception of Machiavelli among later Renaissance rhetoricians, Kahn argues that the Florentine writer adopts a "rhetorical view of politics" and employs rhetorical devices to criticize the traditional ideological approach to politics.[30] Following the lead of McCanles, she argues that Machiavelli by "showing the reader how to think rhetorically – on both sides of a question – about notions such as imitation, virtue and the good . . . exposes the ideological nature of all such positive terms."[31] The pedagogy of *The Prince* aims at educating the reader's "practical judgment," understood as his capacity to deliberate about particulars "within the contingent realm of fortune."[32] By recreating on the discursive level "the practical problem of judgment" the prince will encounter in political life, Machiavelli seeks to "engage the reader in a critical activity" which will help him to develop this specific quality.[33] For Kahn, Machiavelli's

[26] Michael McCanles, *The Discourse of* Il Principe (Malibu, CA: Undena, 1983), p. 110.
[27] Ibid., p. 84. [28] Ibid., pp. 107 and 109. [29] Ibid., p. 110; cf. ibid., pp. 18 and 39.
[30] Kahn, *Machiavellian Rhetoric*, p. 19. [31] Ibid.
[32] Ibid., p. 20; cf. p. 59. [33] Ibid., pp. 31–33.

rhetorical view of politics is not ideologically neutral, but closely linked to his preference for republics over principalities. Already in *The Prince*, she argues, "the superiority of republics emerges out of a rhetorical and dialectical analysis of principalities."[34] In the *Discourses*, the political success of the ancient Roman republic is seen by Machiavelli as "a consequence of its ability to conduct its politics rhetorically and dialectically."[35] But since a rhetorical approach to politics can be adopted by princes as well as by republics, Kahn claims that Machiavelli's work is reducible to neither an ideological reading nor a one-sided republican theory.

Also in Garver's view, *The Prince* is a text that teaches political prudence to its readers by "presenting its own argument as an example of prudent action which forces the reader to engage in prudential activity."[36] The work problematizes the relation between rules and cases, discourse and action, writer and reader, and encourages the new prince to imitate Machiavelli's discursive argument in his extradiscursive action.[37] *The Prince* and the *Discourses* are rhetorical works because their aim is "to initiate political discourse, not just discourse *about* politics but talk and texts which embody commitments by the speaker and aim at practical consequences."[38]

In contrast to McCanles, who views the discourse of *The Prince* as being completely self-referential, save for the dedicatory letter and the final chapter, Kahn and Garver both claim to offer rhetorical readings of Machiavelli's work. Garver is aware of the fact that *The Prince* "has an author and some readers, a purpose and an intended effect,"[39] and elaborates on a distinction borrowed from speech-act theory between illocutionary acts and prelocutionary effects. In a brief aside, he defines the intended prelocutionary effects posited by the work's "dramatic framework" to be the author's attempt to obtain employment for himself, and the future unification of Italy through the agency of the reader.[40] But this distinction seems only to serve the purpose of isolating the discursive aspects of the text from its extradiscursive implications and aims. Kahn, on her part, argues that Machiavelli's work "needs to be read and analyzed rhetorically,"[41] and claims that what she herself is proposing is "a rhetorical analysis"[42] of *The Prince* and the *Discourses*. But what she in reality offers, it seems to me, is an analysis of Machiavelli's general teaching of how to conceive of politics in rhetorical instead of ideological terms. She demonstrates how he conveys

[34] Ibid., p. 19. [35] Ibid., p. 52.

[36] Eugene Garver, *Machiavelli and the History of Prudence* (Madison: University of Wisconsin Press, 1987), p. 50.

[37] Ibid., pp. 50–51. [38] Ibid., p. 54; cf. p. 57. [39] Ibid., p. 51.

[40] Ibid., p. 56. [41] Kahn, *Machiavellian Rhetoric*, p. 243. [42] Ibid., pp. 6 and 16–17.

this wisdom by employing various rhetorical strategies, it is true, but she has nothing to say about how his speech is adapted to suit his implied audience, the time, the place, and the circumstances. Since rhetorical speech, by definition, is an intended, adapted, and addressed form of discourse, a rhetorical approach to texts must be based on a recognition of the relational, historically contingent, and often interested, status of language and human communication. The general level of analysis adopted in these pedagogical readings simply does not allow for such considerations.[43]

The dialectical reading has also been criticized for taking too affirmative and optimistic a view of Machiavelli's intellectual project. Thomas Greene claims in a tightly argued article that Machiavelli's scientific pretensions in *The Prince*, based on general truths and fundamental rules, are gradually withdrawn in the course of the work, and replaced by a discourse characterized by indeterminacy and uncertainty.[44] Analyzing the various stages of this "progressive capitulation,"[45] Greene registers how tangled generalizations,

43 The basically unrhetorical character of McCanles's, Garver's, and Kahn's dialectical, or pedagogical, approach is evident from how they treat the question of the implied audience of *Il principe*. Here, McCanles is a special case since his stated objective (*The Discourse of* Il Principe, p. x) is to "capture and articulate" his own experience of reading *Il principe*, which at one point prompts him to posit (p. 124) an "ideal" reader, whose understanding of "the discursive model" of *Il principe* goes beyond both Machiavelli's own and his intended reader's understanding of the text. Kahn is notoriously vague in her comments on the implied reader of Machiavelli's work, referring to him at times as "the prince," and at others as some kind of general student of politics. See Kahn, *Machiavellian Rhetoric*, pp. 19–20, 31–33, 41, and 59. Garver is more elaborate in this regard, claiming (*Machiavelli and the History of Prudence*, p. 55) that Machiavelli in *Il principe* is addressing both a princely reader and "the internally specified audience of Lorenzo [de' Medici] and the indefinite public." Challenging the notion that the work contains some form of esoteric teaching, he argues (p. 52) that Machiavelli by refusing "to separate what the prince is supposed to make of the text from how the unspecified wider audience is to interpret it, refuses to allow an interpretation that finds two meanings and attributes them to what just happens to be a single expression in *The Prince*." Instead, Garver maintains, the teaching of the work is available to princes and subjects alike; while it instructs the prince how to manipulate his subjects, it provides the subjects with the means of unmasking his deceptive strategies. The major problem with this view is that it assumes that Machiavelli wrote *Il principe* and the *Discorsi* with the express intention of having the works published and disseminated among a wider audience (p. 55: "*The Prince* and the *Discourses* are designed to be overheard as well as heard, publicized as well as read"). As far as I know, there is neither any internal, nor any circumstantial, evidence to support this contention. On the contrary, everything we know about the circulation of these works prior to Machiavelli's death in 1527 suggests that he made no arrangements for, and took no interest in, their publication. On the manuscript and early publication history of Machiavelli's work, see Adolph Gerber, *Niccolò Machiavelli: Die Handschriften, Ausgaben und Übersetzungen seiner Werke im 16. Und 17. Jahrhundert* (Turin: Bottega d'Erasmo, 1962). For contemporary Florentine readings of Machiavelli's work, see Carlo Pincin, "Machiavegli e altri," in *Florence and Venice: Comparisons and Relations*, eds. Sergio Bertelli Nicoloi Rubinstein, and Craig Hugh Smyth (2 vols., Florence: La Nuova Italia, 1980), II, p. 97; J. N. Stephens and H. C. Butters, "New Light on Machiavelli," *English Historical Review* 97 (1982): 54–69, esp. 61–62; Vivien Gaston, "The Prophet Armed: Machiavelli, Savonarola, and Rosso Fiorentino's *Moses Defending the Daughters of Jethro*," *Journal of the Warburg and Courtauld Institutes* 51 (1988), p. 224.

44 Greene, "The End of Discourse," p. 70.

45 Ibid.

imploding concepts, circular arguments, contradictions, and a general breakdown of analysis begin to make their way into the work. Since Machiavelli, unwilling to purge his text from its mythical element, refuses to take notice of this intellectual disaster, the treatise fails to perform its function as an advice-book for princes, and comes in the end to act out "its own version of the prince's failure."[46]

Elaborating on Greene's deconstructionist interpretation, and taking issue with the dialectical reading of McCanles, John Najemy presents his own version of Machiavelli's self-defeating discourse in *The Prince*. According to Najemy, Machiavelli seeks initially to establish political discourse as an isolated and detached form of speech "uncontaminated by the ambiguities and deceptions inherent in the way people generally and normally speak."[47] This quest for discursive and epistemological autonomy is duplicated on the political level, where the new prince, if he follows Machiavelli's advice, is promised security and "the power to impose [his] own will on the world."[48] Towards the end of the work, Najemy maintains, the fantasies of a stable language, of a pristine, limitless, and unmediated knowledge, and of political autonomy are unmasked as Machiavelli's discourse collapses under the burden of its own pretensions.

A similar concern with discursive and princely autonomy and the mythical element of Machiavelli's theory governs Andrew Mousley's analysis of *The Prince*.[49] Like Greene and Najemy, Mousley claims that Machiavelli's attempt to present useful and effective advice to the work's princely reader ends with failure; and like them, he strongly emphasizes the author's effort to impose a single reading on his implied reader. This rhetorical strategy, Mousely argues, is at work already in the dedicatory letter, which establishes "the text's exclusivity of readership" and proclaims "the way the book is to be read and used."[50] The fact that Machiavelli "seems to be writing confidentially, for the sole benefit of a single reader/ruling elite," has, in Mousley's view, the effect of "channelling potentially diverse readings and uses of the text towards a single reading, a single use."[51] But like all such closed and one-dimensional texts, *The Prince* cannot succeed in fixing its own position vis-à-vis the reader. Mousley detects instances when multiple meanings, "contradictory messages," and "destabilising alternative

[46] Ibid., p. 74. Cf. Barberi Squarotti, *Machiavelli o la scelta*, pp. 144–49.

[47] John, M. Najemy, *Between Friends: Discourses of Power and Desire in the Machiavelli–Vettori Letters of 1513–1515* (Princeton: Princeton University Press, 1993), p. 194.

[48] Ibid., p. 197.

[49] Andrew Mousley, "*The Prince* and Textual Politics," in *Niccolò Machiavelli's* THE PRINCE*: New Interdisciplinary Essays*, ed. M. Coyle (Manchester: Manchester University Press, 1995), pp. 151–73.

[50] Ibid., p. 153. [51] Ibid., p. 154.

perspectives" exert pressures on the monolithic text. In fact, Machiavelli himself contributes to this undoing by "effectively refusing the reader access to any single, totalising technique."[52] The conflicting perspectives conveyed by Machiavelli's use of "'literary' devices" and various rhetorical strategies are to be seen as a failure, since they contradict one of the explicit aims of the book, namely, "to expunge the 'literary', to remove 'politics' from the realm of speculation and interpretation."[53]

The deconstructionist reading takes a radical position on the crucial question of who is in control of the rhetorical, or discursive, movement of the text.[54] According to Greene, Najemy, and Mousley, the discursive slippages, failed examples, contradictions, and conceptual collapses occurring in Machiavelli's texts have not been planted there by their cunning author, but are the inevitable consequences of the text's – of any text's – inherent tendency to turn in on itself, simultaneously asserting and negating what it asserts. Therefore, their approach can hardly be defined as rhetorical, since it denies Machiavelli both a rhetorical intention and the kind of command of the text that we normally associate with rhetorical speech.

SKINNER'S METHODOLOGICAL APPROACH

While the dialectical and the deconstructionist readings, in their different ways, draw attention to the shortcomings of the ideological Pocockian approach, they both fail to address the fundamental question of how Machiavelli's work rhetorically engages and interacts with its intended audience.[55] The same criticism can be leveled against Maurizio Viroli's treatment of Machiavelli's rhetoric. In contrast to John Trinkler and Albert Ascoli, who view *The Prince* as a piece of deliberative oratory, Viroli reads the work as an example of the epideictic or demonstrative genre.[56] According to him,

[52] Ibid., p. 160. [53] Ibid., p. 169.

[54] We will return to this issue in chapter 7 when we consider the argument of *Il principe* chapter 25 in more detail. The possibility to choose, or to control, deconstruction is explicitly denied by Paul de Man: "There is no escape from [deconstruction], for the text also establishes that deconstruction is not something we can decide to do or not to do at will. It is co-extensive with any use of language," *Allegories of Reading: Figural Language in Rousseau, Nietzsche, Rilke, and Proust* (New Haven: Yale University Press, 1979), p. 125.

[55] See note 43 above.

[56] The theory of classical rhetoric divided oratory into three different genres, defined on the basis of their objectives and their intended audiences: deliberative or political, forensic or judicial, and epideictic or demonstrative. In Aristotle's paradigmatic definition, the aim of deliberative oratory, addressed to the ruler or the political assembly, either urges to or deters from action. Forensic speaking addresses a judge or a jury in a law court and has as its goal either to prosecute or to defend somebody. The aim of epideictic rhetoric, delivered primarily at public festivals or funerals, is to shape public opinion

Machiavelli seeks in this work to "redescribe as vices the actions that other theorists on state matters qualify as virtues but are in fact leading to the loss of the state, and redefine as virtues those actions that are considered to be vices but do in fact lead to the preservation of the state."[57] In chapters 15 through 18 of the work, the Florentine is thus said to offer "a set of advice on the typical rhetorical issue of praise and blame."[58] Viroli's assignment of *The Prince* to the demonstrative genre explains why he, in a chapter entitled "The Power of Words," has disappointingly little to say about Machiavelli's more contingent and political aims in writing the work.

Viroli's definition of the rhetorical discourse of *The Prince* needs to be understood within the context of Quentin Skinner's methodological approach, on which his study heavily depends. Since Skinner's influence on recent Machiavelli scholarship has been considerable, and since the present study partly adheres to, and partly departs from, his mode of reading, a more detailed discussion of Skinner's approach to political discourse in general and Machiavelli's work in particular is presented here. As we will see, Skinner's methodology also warrants our interest because of the way it brings to light the difference between the ideological and the rhetorical approaches to Machiavelli, which will be a major concern in this study.

In an authoritative article, included in *Meaning and Context: Quentin Skinner and his Critics*, James Tully divides Skinner's interpretative model into five different steps.[59] Since steps three through five, which deal with how ideologies are formed, diffused, challenged, and changed, and with

by giving either praise or blame to somebody or something. On the rhetorical genres, see Aristotle, *Rhetoric* 1358a–b. John Trinkler sees Machiavelli's manifest concern with utility as a clear sign of the deliberative genre : John F. Trinkler, "Praise and Advice: Rhetorical Approaches in More's *Utopia* and Machiavelli's *The Prince*," *Sixteenth Century Journal* 19 (1988): 187–207, esp. 198. Albert Ascoli claims that one of the work's aims is "the implementation of a plan for dramatic action . . . designed to resolve [the] ever-worsening political crisis" of the Italian peninsula: "Machiavelli's Gift of Counsel," p. 220. But given Trinkler's and Ascoli's emphasis on the deliberative aspects of *Il principe*, they have disappointingly little to say about the work's political and strategic aspects.

57 Viroli, *Machiavelli*, pp. 92 and 94–95. For Viroli's explicit claim that *Il principe* belongs to the demonstrative genre, see p. 202n.

58 Ibid., pp. 94–95.

59 James Tully, "The Pen is a Mighty Sword: Quentin Skinner's Analysis of Politics," in *Meaning and Context: Quentin Skinner and his Critics*, ed. J. Tully (Cambridge: Polity Press, 1987), pp. 7–16. Skinner's methodology and reading of Machiavelli are also discussed in the other essays collected in *Meaning and Context*. See also Mark Hulliung, *Citizen Machiavelli* (Princeton: Princeton University Press, 1983), pp. 230–31 and 242–46; Erik Åsard, "Quentin Skinner and his Critics: Some Notes on a Methodological Debate," *Statsvetenskaplig Tidskrift* 90 (1987): 101–16; Wayne R. Newell, "How Original is Machiavelli?" *Political Theory* 15 (1987): 612–34; Bevir, "Mind and Method"; Rahe, "Situating Machiavelli"; Kari Palonen, *Quentin Skinner: History, Politics, Rhetoric* (Cambridge: Polity Press, 2003). In private conversation with the present author, Skinner has attested the validity of Tully's presentation of his methodological approach. A broad collection of Skinner's articles are available in *Visions of Politics* (3 vols., Cambridge: Cambridge University Press, 2002).

how ideological change becomes established and normative, are of limited interest for our present purpose, we will here focus on the two initial steps in Tully's account. The first regards the relationship between the individual text and its ideological context. It is centered on the question: "what is or was an author doing in writing a text in relation to other available texts which make up the ideological context?"[60] In concrete terms, this means that to grasp the intended, or illocutionary, force of Machiavelli's *Prince*, the work needs to be located in an explanatory context consisting of other works *de regimine principium*, and the linguistic, conceptual, and epistemological conventions governing contemporary humanist writings on government. An examination of how Machiavelli's text contributes to, and challenges, the basic assumptions underlying the established genre will enable us to determine the extent to which it was "accepting and endorsing, or questioning and repudiating or perhaps even polemically ignoring, the prevailing assumptions and conventions of political debate."[61] To put the matter differently, what Skinner here is asking us to do is to read the individual work from the point of view of the tradition and its conventions.[62]

The principal merit of this proceeding is that it allows us to determine the precise relationship between an individual text, or a specific statement, and the ideological context in which it occurs. My debt to Skinner's method on this point will be obvious. The current study contains frequent references to ideological conventions and to contexts of various kinds. Chapter 2, for example, reexamines the Florentine patriotic tradition and the importance Florentine writers attributed to the concepts of liberty and empire. This discussion serves then as the general ideological framework for the rest of the study. In chapter 3, the focus will be on how Machiavelli's treatment and use of the example of the ancient Romans changed over the years. It will here be argued that Machiavelli's open endorsements of, oblique references to, and silences on the Roman model must be understood in relation to the general context of contemporary Florentine political debate. As we shall see, the example of the ancient Romans was at the beginning

60 Tully, "The Pen," pp. 7–8.

61 Quentin Skinner, *The Foundations of Modern Political Thought* (2 vols., Cambridge: Cambridge University Press, 1978), I, p. xiii.

62 For a reader steeped in the commonplaces, beliefs, and values of the mirror-for-princes genre, Machiavelli's discussions in *Il principe* of the need to check the power of fortune, of the prince's chief objective being the pursuit of honor, glory and fame, and of the ruler's need to provide for his own security would have appeared perfectly traditional, while his emphasis on military affairs, his rejection of humanist education, and his flexible definition of virtue would have stood out as original contributions to, or departures from, the conventions. See Skinner, *The Foundations*, I, pp. 118–38.

of the Cinquecento viewed with extreme skepticism, if not outright hostility, within the *reggimento*, the Florentine ruling class. Being well aware of this opposition, Machiavelli adapted his speech to fit this general opinion. This discussion of Machiavelli's flexible use of the Roman example will in the subsequent chapters provide the background for our discussion of Machiavelli's political and rhetorical project.

The second step in Skinner's approach deals with the relationship between the individual text and its practical context, and with the author's intention as political actor. Its principal aim is to determine what an author is doing in composing his text "in relation to available and problematic political action."[63] The text is now studied as a piece of political activity, as "a political manoeuvre,"[64] responding to and seeking to affect the conditions and the problems of contemporary political life. This emphasis on authorial intention and on speech as political action seems to invite some form of rhetorical reading, and a view of the political text as an intended, adapted, and addressed form of speech. It may also induce us to believe that the political point of the text has something to do with how it addresses a particular audience at a particular place and time, and for a particular purpose. But this is not what Skinner and Tully have in mind when speaking of the political point and the practical context of a work. For within the Skinnerian methodological framework the political point of a given text consists in how it interacts with, manipulates, and reshapes the ideological and linguistic conventions conditioning this action, and not in how it seeks to influence contemporary political action itself. This distinction is of central importance, since it allows us to see why Skinner's approach must be defined as ideological rather than as rhetorical.[65] The fact that the rhetorical purpose with which Skinner invests the political texts he studies is limited to how they interact with the available ideological codes and linguistic conventions of the day, means that their relation to the more immediate context of political action, which is the principal subject of deliberative rhetoric, is excluded from his interpretative model. So when Skinner calls for a study of "the links between political theory and practice," what he really intends is an inquiry into how political texts *indirectly* affect the practical sphere of politics, by manipulating and redescribing the conventions, categories,

[63] Tully, "The Pen," p. 8. [64] Ibid., p. 10.

[65] Charles Taylor criticizes Skinner's methodological approach for leaving aside questions regarding the truth or the validity of the ideas and the ideologies under study, see Charles Taylor, "The Hermeneutics of Conflict," in *Meaning and Context*, pp. 218–28. The criticism advanced here, by contrast, concerns Skinner's lack of attention to the rhetorical level of discourse. This is to say that the ideological form of reading practiced by Skinner takes place at an intermediary level between the philosophical level, to which attention is called by Taylor, and the rhetorical level, emphasized in the current study.

and concepts regulating how political action is defined and legitimized, not into how a given text seeks to influence practical politics *directly* through various forms of rhetorical persuasion and deliberative speech.[66]

Although Skinner as a rule remains within the limits set by this interpretative framework, there are in his theoretical work interesting openings towards a different kind of reading, and in his eloquent defense of the need to understand intellectual texts within their historical context, he comes close to articulating the premises for a more rhetorical form of textual analysis. Any statement, he argues in an article originally published in 1969, "is inescapably the embodiment of a particular intention, on a particular occasion, addressed to the solution of a particular problem, and thus specific to its situation in a way that it can only be naive to try to transcend."[67] Even if it would be wrong to claim that Skinner's empirical writings in general, and his treatment of Machiavelli in particular, have been informed by this radical emphasis on the particularity of the rhetorical situation, there are moments in his investigations when this rhetorical perspective is allowed to break out of the methodological constraints of his normally ideological mode of interpretation.

A most telling example occurs when Skinner comments on the oblique strategies Machiavelli uses to draw attention to the Florentine context of *The Prince*. Since this statement offers a good introduction – or starting point – to my own interpretative approach and reading of Machiavelli, it is worth quoting at length:

> although [Machiavelli] has taken care to present his argument as a sequence of neutral typologies, he has cunningly organized the discussion in such a way as to highlight one particular type of case, and has done so because of its local and personal significance. The situation in which the need for expert advice is said to be especially urgent is where a ruler has come to power by Fortune and foreign arms. No contemporary reader of *The Prince* could have failed to reflect that, at the point when Machiavelli was advancing this claim, the Medici had just regained their former ascendancy in Florence as the result of an astonishing stroke of good Fortune, combined with the unstoppable force of the foreign arms supplied by Ferdinand of Spain. This does not imply, of course, that Machiavelli's argument can be dismissed as having no more than parochial relevance. But it does appear that he intended his original readers to focus their attention on one particular time and place. The place was Florence; the time was the moment at which *The Prince* was being composed.[68]

66 See Skinner, *The Foundations*, I, p. xiii.

67 Skinner, "Meaning and Understanding in the History of Ideas," in *Meaning and Context*, p. 65.

68 Quentin Skinner, *Machiavelli* (Oxford: Oxford University Press, 1981), p. 24. Cf. Skinner, "Introduction," in Niccolò Machiavelli, *The Prince*, eds. Q. Skinner and R. Price (Cambridge: Cambridge University Press, 1988), p. xii.

By drawing attention to Machiavelli's implied audience and to his rhetorical *here and now*, this comment seems to give us reason to question whether the practical political context of a given text can be as narrowly defined as Tully's presentation of Skinner's method suggests. But such moves into the realm of contingency, where "particular intention[s]" are played out on "particular occasion[s]," and where solutions to "particular problem[s]" are proposed or promoted, are far from common in Skinner's empirical studies.[69] However, as an isolated instance in his analysis of *The Prince*, the quoted passage is of great interest because of the light it throws on the inherent limitations of his methodology.

If we are to create "a history of political theory with a genuinely historical character," as is Skinner's stated objective, we need to acknowledge that the practical and political context of a given text is much broader than the normative vocabularies and ideological conventions regulating political action.[70] While it might be sufficient for an ideological, or modestly rhetorical, reading to consider the text in relation to a general audience devoted to, or familiar with, the conventions and values endorsed or challenged by the text, it can plausibly be argued that such a reading does not exhaust the political point, or intention, of a rhetorical work like Machiavelli's *Prince*. Since the political context at any moment in history is immensely complex and diverse, there can be no practical limit to what the author might do, openly or obliquely, in addressing the political society of his day. He might, for example, support or challenge proposed policies, give advice on war and peace, warn against dangers, exhort to, or deter from, action, and so forth. The range of political action open to an author who wishes to radically change, modify, or otherwise influence the practical and political context in which he operates can simply not be confined to the manipulation and reshaping of ideological and linguistic conventions. In the case of *The Prince*, for example, it would be interesting to know more about how Machiavelli adapted his discourse to fit the deliberative context of local Florentine politics, but this is an aspect of the work about which Skinner and Viroli have nothing, or little, further to say.

To conclude, by positing a hybrid form of reading, hovering somewhere between the rhetorical and the ideological levels of interpretation – the analysis of how the author is addressing the practical and political context

[69] Florence and the Medici here immediately disappear out of sight in Skinner's analysis, to reappear only briefly in the course of his discussion of the militia. See Skinner, *Machiavelli*, pp. 32–33. Skinner's treatment of *Il principe* in this study (pp. 34–41) follows the general outline established in *The Foundations* and ends with a discussion of Machiavelli's view of the princely virtues and vices.

[70] Cf. Skinner, *The Foundations*, I, pp. xi–xiii; Tully, "The Pen," p. 11.

by manipulating the available ideological conventions – Skinner's own work, and Tully's presentation of his methodology, threaten to confuse the distinction between the two modes. This means that we, in order to access the rhetorical level of the text, where we can expect to find its "political point" and the various rhetorical strategies negotiating the relationship between the author and his audience, need a broader, more open and inclusive form of contextualism, and a type of reading that pays more attention to particulars and to the rhetorical movement of the text.[71] The present study will be based on such a double methodological approach. It contends that political and literary texts need to be considered both as integral and relatively autonomous objects of study and as discursive strategies participating in, or relating to, the general modes of representation and the various forms of cultural transaction available at that particular moment in time. In the following section we shall take a closer look at some of the philosophical and political assumptions underlying the rhetorical approach to the spoken and written word.

THE PHILOSOPHICAL VS. THE RHETORICAL APPROACH

In the preceding sections we have contrasted rhetorical reading with various forms of ideological, dialectical, and deconstructionist interpretations. However, probably the best way to explain wherein the rhetorical approach consists is by comparing it with its philosophical counterpart. We will here therefore return to the classical distinction between philosophy and rhetoric, which we first encountered in our discussion of Pocock's ideological treatment of Machiavelli's work.[72] In Chaim Perelman's definition, philosophical discourse is "discourse addressed to reason." As a rule, the Belgian scholar contends, the philosopher pays little attention to the particular nature of his audience, demanding instead that "the reader make an effort of purification, of ascesis, in order to be better able to have access to

[71] Cf. Mikael Hörnqvist, "The Two Myths of Civic Humanism," in *Renaissance Civic Humanism Reconsidered*, ed. J. Hankins (Cambridge: Cambridge University Press, 2000), pp. 130–31.

[72] See above pp. 7–8. On the historical quarrel between philosophy and rhetoric, see George A. Kennedy, *The Art of Persuasion in Greece* (Princeton: Princeton University Press, 1963), esp. p. 15; Jerrold E. Siegel, *Rhetoric and Philosophy in Renaissance Humanism: The Union of Eloquence and Wisdom* (Princeton: Princeton University Press, 1968); Brian Vickers, "Rhetorik und Philosophie in der Renaissance," in *Rhetorik und Philosophie*, eds. H. Schanze and J. Kopperschmidt (Munich: Wilhelm Fink, 1989), pp. 121–25; Chaim Perelman, *The New Rhetoric and the Humanities: Essays on Rhetoric and its Applications* (Dordrecht: Reidel, 1979), pp. 43–51; Nancy S. Struever, *The Language of History in the Renaissance: Rhetorical and Historical Consciousness in Florentine Humanism* (Princeton: Princeton University Press, 1970), pp. 5–39; Lanham, *The Motives of Eloquence*, pp. 1–33.

the truth."[73] This formative aspect of philosophical speech is particularly evident in the classical and the humanist literature on the education of the ruler. The general aim of this immensely influential genre, which includes works like Plato's *Republic*, Aristotle's *Politics*, and Cicero's *De Officiis*, is to shape genuinely ethical individuals by encouraging virtuous action and deterring from wickedness. The basic assumption underlying the educational program set forth in these works is that the political virtues – justice, prudence, fortitude, temperance – are necessary for creating a stable and lasting regime. In the late Middle Ages and the Renaissance, moral concerns of a related kind came to dominate the advice-books *de regimine principum*, also known as mirror-for-princes, and the formal orations on justice addressed to republican magistrates.

In this literature, the edifying portrait of the good ruler is painted in the fairest colors. In a letter to Francesco of Carrara, the ruler of Padua, Petrarch gives a vivid account of the shaping power generally attributed to the image of the virtuous prince:

> And I want you to look at yourself in this letter as though you were gazing in a mirror. If you see yourself in what I am describing (as no doubt you will quite often), enjoy it . . . On the other hand, if sometimes you feel that it is difficult for you to meet the standards I describe, I advise you to put your hands to your face and polish the countenance of your great reputation written there, so that you might become more attractive, and certainly more illustrious, as a result of this experience.[74]

Petrarch's description helps us to see why the mirror-for-princes must be defined not as a rhetorical, but as a philosophical, or didactic, genre. Here, it is the reader, the prince, who is expected to adapt himself to the model prince presented in the text, and not the other way around. Since the ideal prince and the values he represents are considered to exist on a universal, if not transcendental, level, which the individual prince is expected to strive for, and to arrive at, by modeling himself after his example, originality and diversity did not become hallmarks of the genre.[75]

The success of the mirror-for-princes genre was guaranteed as long as the princely reader accepted its premises and identified with the idealized

73 Perelman, *The New Rhetoric*, pp. 46–47.

74 Francesco Petrarch, "How a Ruler Ought to Govern his State," in *The Earthly Republic: Italian Humanists on Government and Society*, eds. B. G. Kohl and R. G. Witt (Philadelphia: University of Pennsylvania Press, 1978), pp. 41–42.

75 On the mirror-for-princes genre in general, see Allan H. Gilbert, *Machiavelli's Prince and its Forerunners*: The Prince *as a Typical Book* de regimine principum (Durham, NC: Duke University Press, 1938); Skinner, *The Foundations*, I, pp. 113–38.

image presented to him. It is an axiom in this literature that just rule is not only in accordance with the divine will and Aristotelian ethics, but also in the personal interest of the individual ruler. By ensuring him the love of his people, it argues, righteous rule reinforces his position and contributes to rendering his state stable and prosperous. But suppose that a ruler begins to question these assumptions, and to suspect that the noble principles of classical ethics and Christian piety may, perhaps, after all not be conducive to effective rule and the pursuit of power and glory. What if the princely reader came to align himself with the figure of Trasymachus, who in Plato's *Republic* had claimed that wickedness and immorality actually pay off, and that there is no justice above the rule of the strongest? Such a ruler would be defined as a tyrant according to the classical taxonomy; but this would be merely to name the problem, not to provide a solution to it.

This was a political and ethical dilemma that most fourteenth- and fifteenth-century humanists tended to evade, by investing virtue itself – Christian and Aristotelian virtue – with the persuasive powers Roman orators traditionally had reserved for rhetorical speech. Had not Plato, the "prince of philosophers," Petrarch asks, with his teaching of virtue been able to win over Dionysius, the tyrant of Syracuse; and had not Euripides done the same with regard to Archelaus, the king of Macedonia? In Petrarch's eyes, these two examples show that "talent and eloquence" can soften an "unbending, tyrannical spirit" and moderate "barbaric excess."[76] The persuasive power of virtue is so great, he suggests, that even the most vicious of tyrants must yield to it. In his contribution to the mirror-for-princes genre, Giovanni Pontano claims that virtue is "the most splendid thing in the world," more splendid even than the sun, since "the blind cannot see the sun," whereas "even they can see *virtus* as plainly as possible."[77] By holding up a model of virtue for the prince, the potential tyrant, the political counselor could steer him away from vice and lead him onto the right path.

But not all humanists were as optimistic about the inherent persuasiveness of virtue. According to Leonardo Bruni, not all men are susceptible to reason and to a teaching based on the attractiveness of virtue. There are those, he claims, whose sight is so darkened by vice that they mistake seeming goodness for the real thing, and side with tyrants and commit robbery, fraud, adultery, and other similar crimes merely "to satisfy their lusts." If these men were to wake up and regain their senses, they "would

[76] Francesco Petrarch, *Fam.* III.22; English translation in Francesco Petrarca, *Rerum Familiarium Libri I–VIII*, trans. A. S. Bernardo (Albany: State University of New York Press, 1975), p. 169.

[77] Quoted from Skinner, *The Foundations*, I, p. 121.

realize their error and be themselves the first to despise it." But in Bruni's view it was beyond human power to "pluck out of them their lust and their diseased minds and pour into them the mind and judgment of a good man."[78] In Matteo Palmieri's *Vita civile* we encounter a similar view. Since the teaching of virtue is not equally effective on all men, Palmieri argues, it should be reserved for those who are receptive to it. For the others, the wicked, who cannot be persuaded to avoid evil out of love of virtue, and who are immune to reproach, he envisages a regime of restraint designed to inspire "fear of punishment."[79]

How should one then deal with the wicked and the uncorrectable? And what was one to do if the ruler himself began to show signs of immorality? One available strategy was to turn one's back on politics, and on mundane affairs in general, and to adopt a posture of stoic aloofness. This is the position taken by the figure of Genipatro in Leon Battista Alberti's dialogue *Theogenius*,[80] and by Raphael Hythlodaeus in Thomas More's *Utopia*. Although Hythlodaeus, the well-traveled utopian philosopher, is said to have many good and radical proposals for how to reform contemporary society, he categorically refuses to enter the service of worldly princes out of the conviction that no one will listen to his advice. The political adviser, he argues, must be true to himself, for if he starts to accommodate to the perverse customs of the court, he is bound to lose his integrity and end up becoming a mere marionette in the hands of the prince and his entourage: "Either they will seduce you, or, if you keep yourself honest and innocent, you will be made a screen for the knavery and madness of others. Influencing policy indirectly! You wouldn't have a chance."[81]

In *Utopia*, the classical dispute between philosophy and rhetoric is reenacted in the dialogue between Hythlodaeus, impersonating the role of the philosopher, and the figure of Morus, Thomas More's own alter ego, assuming the part of the rhetorician. To better appreciate the conflicting premises underlying their respective positions, we need to take a closer look at how rhetorical and philosophical speech differ in their ways of approaching their audiences, before turning to consider Morus's response to Hythlodaeus's challenge.

While philosophical speech, to use Perelman's words, is "discourse adressed to reason," rhetorical speech is always addressed to specific

[78] *The Humanism of Leonardo Bruni: Selected Texts*, eds. G. Griffiths, J. Hankins, and D. Thompson (Binghamton: Center for Medieval and Early Renaissance Studies, 1987), p. 282.
[79] Matteo Palmieri, *Vita civile*, ed. G. Belloni (Florence: Sansoni, 1982), pp. 66, 91, and 107.
[80] Leon Battista Alberti, *Opere volgari* (3 vols., Bari: Laterza, 1960–73), II, pp. 76–77.
[81] Thomas More, *Utopia*, trans. R. M. Adams (New York: Norton, 1992), pp. 26–27.

audiences in particular times and places. As a consequence, the rhetorical man may agree with Hythlodaeus, the philosophical man, that rhetorical persuasion is superfluous in communication between virtuous and enlightened men,[82] governed by reason, or *logos*, but go on to contend that an open and straightforward form of speech should not be used in all circumstances, or extended to all kinds of people. Assuming that human discourse never evolves in a social or cultural vacuum, he holds that the orator should pay special attention to the specific character of his intended audience. In Aristotle's view, here speaking as a rhetorician, the orator should, when fashioning his speech, take into consideration factors such as age, habits, social status, wealth, aspirations, and political constitution or ideological point of view.[83] Cicero similarly claims that "one must not speak in the same style at all times, nor before all people, nor against all opponents, nor in defence of all clients."[84] Therefore, the orator should be, in the words of the figure of Antonius in *De Oratore*, "a man of sharpness, ingenious by nature and experience alike, who with keen scent will track down the thoughts, feelings, beliefs and hopes of his fellow-citizens and of any men whom on any issue he would fain win over by his word."[85] Quintilian argues in a similar vein that the art of rhetoric cannot be reduced to a coherent system of rules, since "most rules are liable to be altered by the nature of the case, circumstances of time and place, and by hard necessity itself."[86] Throughout the *Institutio Oratoria*, Quintilian attaches great importance to the personal character of the judge, the principal audience of forensic oratory: "I should also wish, if possible, to be acquainted with the character of the judge. For it will be desirable to enlist their temperaments in the service of our cause, where they are such as are like to be useful, or to mollify them, if they are like to prove adverse, just according as they are harsh, gentle, cheerful, grave, stern, or easy-going."[87]

[82] See for example, Francesco Petrarch, *Fam.* IX.11; English translation in Francesco Petrarca, *Letters on Familiar Matters: Rerum Familiarium Libri IX–XVI*, trans. A. S. Bernardo (Baltimore: The Johns Hopkins University Press, 1982), p. 30.

[83] Aristotle, *Art of Rhetoric* 2.12–17; English translation in *The Art of Rhetoric*, trans. H. C. Lawson-Tancred (London: Penguin, 1991), pp. 172–79.

[84] Cicero, *Orator* 123, trans. H. M. Hubbell (Cambridge, MA: Harvard University Press, 1939), p. 399.

[85] Cf. Cicero, *De Oratore* 1.51.223; English translation in *De Oratore*, trans. E. W. Sutton and H. Rackham (2 vols., Cambridge, MA: Harvard University Press, 1942), I, p. 159. Antonius goes on: "He ought to feel the pulses of every class, time of life, and degree, and to taste the thoughts and feelings of those before whom he is pleading or intending to plead any cause." Renaissance literature from Machiavelli to Shakespeare is replete with such streetwise figures, Ligurio of *La mandragola* and Iago of Shakespeare's *Othello* being two of the most striking examples.

[86] Quintilian, *Institutio Oratoria* 2.13.2; English translation in *The Institutio Oratoria of Quintilian*, trans. H. E. Butler (4 vols.,Cambridge, MA: Harvard University Press, 1920–22), I, p. 291.

[87] Quintilian, *Institutio Oratoria* 4.1.17, trans. II, p. 15; ibid., 5.12.11, II, p. 303.

Renaissance humanists were equally sensitive about the particularity of their audiences. Coluccio Salutati expresses the classical view, when in a private letter he complains about his addressee's lack of rhetorical training: "You are badly instructed in the art of organizing a speech according to the nature and condition of the listener."[88] A similar criticism is to be found in Poggio Bracciolini's dialogue *On Avarice*, where the figure of Cencio Romano pours scorn over the oratorical shortcomings of the mendicant preachers of the day: "So they have learned by heart certain set speeches that they are wont to speak in all places. Sometimes they speak before the ignorant of recondite and obscure matters that the audience cannot understand."[89] Erasmus elaborates on this theme when setting forth the principles of effective letter-writing: "When we have perceived what affects each person, we shall put these things constantly before him, amplifying them deliberately: honours, for instance, for the ambitious man, reward for the greedy, a peaceful existence for an old man, and likewise for the rest; conversely, whatever we have found to be most despised must be put forward brutally and insistently."[90]

The difference between the philosophical and the rhetorical approach emerges most clearly when the speaker, or the author, in a political context is faced with the task of addressing an audience of ignorant or wicked men. On such an occasion, the philosophical man has two basic options: either he could seek to educate his audience by informing them about the attractive and edifying nature of virtue; or he could choose to follow Hythlodaeus's example and turn his back on political affairs, seeking refuge in contemplation and inner withdrawal.

But for the rhetorical man there exists a third possibility as well: rhetorical manipulation by direct or indirect means. This was an aspect of persuasive speech to which classical theorists paid particular attention. In *De Oratore* Cicero argues that emotional delivery should be used to influence "the ignorant and the mob" since rational arguments often are beyond their comprehension. Quintilian takes this argument a step further, when he claims that the orator who addresses "an ignorant audience," or speaks "before popular assemblies, of which the majority is usually uneducated," often must dispense with the honorable in the name of expediency. In his

88 Coluccio Salutati, "Letter to Caterina di messer Vieri di Donatino d'Arezzo," in *The Earthly Republic*, eds. Kohl and Witt, p. 116.
89 Poggio Bracciolini, "On Avarice," in *The Earthly Republic*, p. 244.
90 Erasmus, *Collected Works of Erasmus*, vol. XXV: *Literary and Educational Writings III: De Conscribendis Epistolis Formula/De Civilitate*, ed. J. K. Sowards (86 vols. to date, Toronto: University of Toronto Press, 1985), p. 81.

effort to lead a hostile, or wicked, judge to serve the cause of justice, the orator should therefore, in Quintilian's view, be prepared to substitute falsehood for the truth, and to employ concealment, deception, and emotional appeals for persuasive ends.[91]

Renaissance humanists, faced with the task of giving advice to wicked rulers, tended to take a similar view. In seeking to persuade Hythlodaeus to change his mind and to place his experience and his wisdom in the service of the princes of Europe, the figure of Morus in *Utopia* argues that there are other, more oblique ways of influencing those in power:

> You must strive to influence policy indirectly, handle the situation tactfully, and thus what you cannot turn to good, you may at least – to the extent of your powers – make less bad. For it is impossible to make all institutions good unless you make all men good, and that I don't expect to see for a long time to come.

Although the counselor at times might be able to influence his prince through an open and direct form of speech, Morus contends, he could not expect this strategy to serve his purposes on all occasions.[92] To make his advice more effective, he will have to free himself of the rigid, universalist attitude of traditional philosophical discourse, embodied by Hythlodaeus, and, to quote Morus, adopt "another philosophy that is better suited for political action." To ingratiate himself with the prince, and to gain a position of influence by his side, the counselor should adapt himself "to the drama in hand," and act his part "neatly and well."[93] As Thomas More – like Guicciardini, Castiglione, Montaigne, Machiavelli, and other sixteenth-century humanists with experience of political affairs – was well aware, there existed a time-honored and well-tried technique for this indirect and oblique form of persuasion. It is to this method we shall turn when in the next section we focus on the rhetorical use of *ethos* and *pathos*, character and emotion.

[91] Quintilian, *Institutio Oratoria* 2.17.19–20, I, pp. 333–35. Cf. ibid., 1.11.18, I, p. 191; 2.17.27, I, p. 327; 6.1.7, II, pp. 385–87; 6.1.31–33, II, p. 403; 5.14.35, II, p. 369.

[92] Counselors who governed their rulers were far from unheard of at the time. In connection to the Italian campaign of Charles VIII of France in 1494, the Florentine chronicler Piero Parenti reported that the king was controled (*menata*) by his counselors, who used him as a front man, or a mask (*maschera*), for their own purposes: "E veramente giudicato fu che la persona propria del Re da' malvagi suoi governatori menata fussi, e' quali per maschera l'usassino, e a mangerie sotto tale coverta attendessino," Piero di Marco Parenti, *Storia fiorentina* (Florence: Olschki, 1994), I, p. 155. Similarly, the Venetian ambassador to England in 1515, Sebastian Giustinian, claimed in his *relazione* that the person his employers should seek to influence was not the king, Henry VIII, but the real ruler of the country, his counselor, Cardinal Wolsey, Thomas More's mentor and predecessor as Lord Chancellor. On Giustinian's mission to England, see Rawdon Brown, *Four Years in the Court of Henry VIII* (2 vols., London: Smith, Elder & Co., 1854).

[93] More, *Utopia*, p. 25.

ETHOS

In the view of classical theorists, medieval manuals on *ars oratoria*, and Renaissance humanists, an orator should know how to use the three main functions of oratory, the so-called *officia oratoris*: to instruct his audience through rational argument (*logos* or *ratio*), to win its benevolence through self-representation and the projection of an appealing moral character (*ethos*), and to arouse its emotions (*pathos*) in order to move it to action.[94] While rhetoric shared the first function, reason, with the philosophical disciplines of logic and dialectic, the other two, character and emotion, belonged to it exclusively. In the words of Coluccio Salutati, logic "acts on the intellect with compelling force by means of reasoning" and aims at illuminating the mind "to an intellectual conviction," while rhetoric also "acts upon the will," and strives to create a "willing attitude" among the hearers. While logic "proves in order to teach," rhetoric "persuades in order to guide."[95] In the following, we will concentrate on the two functions that distinguish rhetorical speech from philosophical discourse: the classical theorists' advice on how the orator should establish his *ethos*, or moral character, and on how he should arouse and manipulate the emotions, or *pathos*, of his audience.

Cicero and other Roman writers on rhetoric treat character and the securing of the hearers' goodwill extensively in their discussions on the exordium.[96] In *De Inventione*, Cicero distinguishes between two different kinds of exordium: introduction (*principium*) and insinuation (*insinuatio*). While the introduction consists in an open and direct address aimed at rendering the audience attentive, receptive, and kindly disposed, the insinuation should be employed only under special circumstance, and primarily when the speaker has reason to suspect that the audience is hostile towards him or his case. On such occasions, when a straightforward approach is likely to be ineffective, or even counterproductive, the orator is advised to

94 Jakob Wisse, *Ethos and Pathos from Aristotle to Cicero* (Amsterdam: Hakkert, 1989). Cf. George Kennedy, *A New History of Classical Rhetoric* (Princeton: Princeton University Press, 1994), pp. 4–5; Rita Copeland, *Rhetoric, Hermeneutics, and Translation: Academic Traditions and Vernacular Texts* (Cambridge: Cambridge University Press, 1991), pp. 152–54; Wayne Rebhorn, *The Emperor of Men's Minds: Literature and the Renaissance Discourse of Rhetoric* (Ithaca, NY: Cornell University Press, 1995), p. 84.

95 Quoted from *Humanism and Tyranny: Studies in the Italian Trecento*, ed. E. Emerton (Gloucester, MA: P. Smith, 1964), p. 358.

96 Before the translation of Aristotle's *Rhetoric* into Latin, Roman rhetoricians tended, when discussing the authority projected by the speaker, to use the term *dignitas* instead. See Kennedy, *A New History*, p. 126.

use dissimulation and concealment to insinuate himself, and his argument, into the minds of his hearers.[97]

Most Roman rhetoricians agree that, regardless of whether the orator chooses the direct or the indirect approach, it is essential that he in the exordium avoids drawing attention to the calculated and rhetorical nature of his speech. Cicero recommends in *De Inventione* that a casual style and plain words should be used in this part of the speech in order to prevent the presentation from appearing excessively clever.[98] In the dialogue *Brutus*, he extols Antonius for his ability to steal himself into the minds of his hearers by giving an air of casualness, while in reality being extremely well prepared: "His memory was perfect, there was no suggestion of previous rehearsal; he always gave the appearance of coming forward to speak without preparation, but so well prepared was he that when he spoke it was the court rather that often seemed ill prepared to maintain its guard."[99] Elaborating on this point, Quintilian argues that an orator performing at a court of law should give "no hint of elaboration in the *exordium*, since any art that the orator may employ at this point seems to be directed solely at the judge." Instead, he should conceal his eloquence, "avoid anything suggestive of artful design," and make everything "seem to spring from the case itself rather than the art of the orator."[100]

Although most Roman rhetoricians hold that a good *ethos* can be more easily established if the speaker actually possesses the qualities conducive to a good reputation, they are not foreign to the idea that an artful appearance of virtue and integrity can serve the same purpose. Commenting in *Brutus* on the manners of the Roman orator Scaurus, Cicero argues that he "conveyed the impression not only of experience and wisdom, but of that quality which holds the secret of success, trustworthiness." Scaurus had been endowed with this character by nature, but as Cicero informs us, there are books in circulation that give advice on how to acquire the appearance of trustworthiness and other commendable qualities artificially.[101] With reference to Aristotle, Quintilian claims that "the strongest argument in support of a speaker is that he is a good man," but he is quick to add

[97] Cicero, *De Inventione* 1.15.20–1.17.25; trans. H. M. Hubbell (Cambridge, MA: Harvard University Press, 1949), pp. 42–50. Cf. *Ad Herennium* 1.3.5–1.7.11; trans. H. Caplan (Cambridge, MA: Harvard University Press, 1954), pp. 10–20.

[98] Cicero, *De Inventione* 1.18.25, p. 53. Cf. *Ad Herennium* 1.6.11, p. 21.

[99] Cicero, *Brutus* 139–40; text in *Brutus and Orator*, trans. G. L. Hendrickson and H. M. Hubbell (Cambridge, MA: Harvard University Press, 1962), p. 122.

[100] Quintilian, Institutio Oratoria 4.1.56–57, II, p. 37; and 4.2.126, II, p. 119. Cf. ibid., 4.1.9, II, p. 11.

[101] Cicero, *Brutus* 112, p. 100.

that "to seem good is also of value."[102] Elsewhere, he teaches that the mere appearance of possessing a certain virtue can have the same persuasive effect as the actual possession of it.[103]

On the basis of these observations, what can be said about Machiavelli's self-representation, or *ethos*, in *The Prince*? Since it is generally acknowledged that one of the Florentine's principal aims in composing the work was to obtain employment with the Medici, and to promote himself in the role of Medicean counselor, we might expect him to attempt to create a favorable *ethos* in the eyes of his Medicean readers. Although many scholars have in passing commented on this aspect of the work, no one has to the best of my knowledge noted how closely Machiavelli's self-promotional campaign follows Cicero's teaching on the *insinuatio*. In *De Inventione*, which we have commented on above, the Roman orator recommends four different strategies for capturing the goodwill of a hostile, or indifferent, audience. To achieve this end, the speaker should first of all draw attention to his good actions and good services, modestly and discreetly. Secondly, he should take the sting out of the charges brought against him and counteract the suspicions of dishonorable conduct that might attach to his person by responding to these accusations in advance. Thirdly, he should make his listeners aware of the misfortunes and the hardships he is suffering. And finally, he should adopt a deferential and subservient tone when beseeching and entreating his auditor.[104]

Beginning with Cicero's first point, Machiavelli, in the dedicatory letter to Lorenzo de' Medici accompanying *The Prince*, draws attention to his own actions and good services, by stating that the advice contained in the treatise is based on his "knowledge of the actions of great men, learned by me through long experience of modern affairs and continual study of ancient history," and acquired "in so many years, and with much difficulty and danger for myself."[105] He alludes to his own person again in chapter 3, where he relates a conversation he had in 1500 in Nantes with the cardinal of Rouen over the differences between Italian and French warfare and statecraft. We are allowed to witness Machiavelli in action also in chapter 7, where he presents himself as Cesare Borgia's confidant during his mission to the Roman curia back in 1503. Machiavelli reenters the stage implicitly in chapter 23, as he relates a speech by Bishop Luca Rinaldi, ambassador

[102] Quintilian, *Institutio Oratoria* 5.7.9, II, p. 303.

[103] Ibid., 6.2.18, II, p. 427.

[104] Cicero, *De Inventione* 1.16.22, p. 44.

[105] *Il principe*, dedication, p. 117: "la cognizione delle azioni delli uomini grandi, imparata da me con una lunga esperienza delle cose moderne e una continua lezione delle antiche . . . in tanti anni e con tanti mia disagi e periculi."

of Emperor Maximilian of Habsburg, which he had the privilege of listening to during his legation to the imperial court in 1508. It should be transparently clear that Machiavelli in these passages, by referring, with humility, as Cicero had advised, to his own actions and services, is establishing his credentials as political adviser and engaging in a campaign of self-promotion.

Following Cicero's second recommendation – to anticipate the charges one is facing and to counter the bad reputation attaching to one's name – Machiavelli seeks in chapter 20, in a long, and rather acrobatic, apology for those who at the beginning of a new regime are regarded with suspicion, to cleanse himself of the stigma with which he has been branded. Princes, and new princes in particular, he claims, "have often found that men whom they had regarded with suspicion in the early stages of their rule prove more reliable and useful than those whom they had trusted at first." This is especially true with respect to those "who were hostile to him in the early stages of his regime, but who were insufficiently powerful to maintain their position without help." With studied indirectness and without bringing up his own name, Machiavelli explains why this category of men – to which he himself undoubtedly belongs – is likely to become the new prince's most reliable servants: "They are constrained to serve him faithfully, because they are well aware how necessary it is for them to act in such a way as to cancel his initially unfavourable view of them. Thus he will always find them more useful than those who, because they feel very secure in their positions, tend to neglect his affairs."[106]

Thirdly, Cicero had recommended that the speaker should expand on the bad luck that had befallen him and draw attention to the adversities he is experiencing. Following this advice, Machiavelli in the concluding lines of the dedicatory letter famously complains about his bitter fate. If Lorenzo from the summit of his power were to cast a glance down toward the lowly place where Machiavelli dwells, he would learn how "undeservedly" the former Secretary is enduring the cruelty of "a great and continuous misfortune."[107] The humble tone of this entreaty reflects Cicero's fourth

[106] *Il principe* 20, pp. 177–78: "Hanno e' principi, et praesertim quegli che sono nuovi, trovata piú fede e piú utilità in quelli uomini che nel principio del loro stato sono suti tenuti sospetti, che in quelli che erano nel principio confidenti . . . quelli uomini che nel principio d'uno principato sono stati inimici, che sono di qualità che a mantenersi abbino bisogno di appoggiarsi, sempre el principe con facilità grandissima se gli potrà guadagnare: e loro maggiormente sono forzati a servirlo con fede, quanto conoscono essere loro piú necessario cancellare con le opere quella opinione sinistra che si aveva di loro. E cosí el principe ne trae sempre piú utilità, che di coloro che, servendolo con troppa sicurtà, straccurano le cose sua."

[107] *Il principe*, dedication, p. 118: "indegnamente sopporti una grande e continua malignità di fortuna."

and final piece of advice – to express one's pleas and requests with a humble and obliging attitude. Machiavelli also adopts this posture when explaining why it need not be a sign of presumption (*prosunzione*) if "a man of very low and humble condition dares to discuss and lay down rules about princely government."[108] According to him, no one is better equipped to understand the people than a prince, and conversely, no one is more fit to judge the character of princes than a man of the people, that is, a man like himself.

As this brief survey demonstrates, Machiavelli labors in *The Prince* to construct his *ethos* along the lines established by Cicero in his discussion of the *insinuatio* in *De Inventione*. This calculated use of *insinuatio*, which is most evident in the dedicatory letter, but continues to play an important role throughout the work, suggests that the feelings Machiavelli expresses towards the intended readers of the treatise, the Medici, should not be taken at face value, but instead be seen as belonging to a rhetorical strategy firmly rooted in classical rhetorical theory. This observation raises the important question of the appropriate context for understanding the emotional appeals made in *The Prince* in general. If it is true, as has recently been argued, that Machiavelli "composed all his political works, and above all *The Prince*, in the manner of the rhetorician following the rules illustrated by the Roman masters of rhetoric,"[109] one could assume that the emotive force of these texts would be best explained by situating them within the context of classical rhetoric, rather than in relation to Romantic, or post-Romantic, notions about expressive subjectivity and unconscious motivations, as has traditionally been done. This gives us reason to attend to the third function of rhetoric, *pathos*.

PATHOS

In sharp contrast to Aristotle, who condemns appeals to the emotions when seeking to influence a judge at a court of law,[110] the Roman rhetoricians view *pathos*, and the vehement style associated with it, as the most important and the most genuinely rhetorical of the *officia oratoris*. According to Cicero, emotional manipulation is the most powerful and effective means by which an orator can bend the wills of men and move them to action.[111] The principal virtue of the orator consists, he claims, in the capacity to

[108] Ibid.: "se uno uomo di basso e infimo stato ardisce discorrere e regolare e' governi de' principi."
[109] Viroli, *Machiavelli*, p. 73.
[110] Aristotle, *Art of Rhetoric* 1.1.5, p. 5; and 1.2.5, p. 17. Cf. Kennedy, *A New History*, p. 103.
[111] Cicero, *De Oratore* 2.41.178, 1, p. 324. Cf. George Kennedy, *The Art of Rhetoric in the Roman World 300 BC–AD 300* (Princeton: Princeton University Press, 1972), pp. 219–20.

arouse "men's hearts to anger, hatred, or indignation," and to recall "them from these same passions to mildness and mercy."[112] As Quintilian was to point out later, Cicero himself had on many occasions at the Roman law courts and in the political assemblies demonstrated how an orator by appealing to the emotions can impose his will on an audience and secure the desired outcome of his case.[113] Commenting on Aristotle's misgivings about this form of persuasion, Quintilian argues that even those who view "susceptibility to emotion as a vice, and think it immoral that the judge should be distracted from the truth by an appeal to his emotions and that it is unbecoming for a good man to make use of vicious procedures to serve his ends," could not deny that "appeals to emotion are necessary if there are no other means for securing the victory of truth, justice and the public interest."[114] Since judges, at least the judges of Quintilian's court room, are no epitomes of goodness or justice, the orator must be prepared to stir their emotions, to shape and transform them, and to compel them to "weep with them or share their anger" in order to "lead [them] to do justice."[115]

According to Quintilian, orators had for a long time been employing special methods for simulating emotions and giving them an appearance of reality. This view receives confirmation in Cicero's *De Oratore*, where the figure of Antonius protests that a skillful orator has no need of such devices, since his ability to treat the proofs and the arguments of the case in a persuasive way allows him "to dispense with all make-believe and trickery."[116] Although he assures us that the feelings he has inspired in his audience always have been produced by his own emotional reaction to the facts of the case, Antonius insinuates in passing that there exists a "loftier art" (*maior ars*) for counterfeiting emotions.[117]

While *De Oratore* does not explicitly endorse the view that dissembled emotions may serve the same purpose as the display of one's true sentiments, Quintilian, by contrast, sets out to disclose the secret principles of this practice. Since the feigning of strong emotions such as grief, anger, and indignation easily can backfire and cause ridicule, Quintilian argues, the orator should use art to give an authentic and natural appearance to the feelings he displays: "if we wish to give our words the appearance of sincerity, we must assimilate ourselves to the emotions of those who are genuinely so

[112] Cicero, *De Oratore* 1.12.53, I, p. 41.

[113] See for example Quintilian, *Institutio Oratoria* 4.1.21, II, p. 17.

[114] Ibid., 6.1.7, II, pp. 385–87.

[115] Ibid., 2.17.27, I, p. 327; 6.2.1–6.2.6, II, pp. 417–21. Cf. ibid., 6.2.6, II, pp. 419–21: "because passion forestalls the sense of sight, so the judge, when overcome by his emotions, abandons all attempt to enquire into the truth of the arguments, is swept along by the tide of passion, and yields himself unquestioning to the torrent."

[116] Cicero, *De Oratore* 2.46.191, I, p. 335.

[117] Ibid., 2.46.189, I, p. 333.

affected, and our eloquence must spring from the same feeling that we desire to produce in the mind of the judge." This frame of mind can be achieved, he claims, by a sophisticated form of auto-suggestion. By producing visions, or hallucinations, before his inner eye, the orator can substitute fantasy and imagination for real experience, enabling him to place the facts of the case so vividly before the eyes of his auditors that they afterwards will believe they have had a first-hand experience of them.[118] In this artful and deceptive way, the orator may transmit his feigned emotions to the audience. Both will then be moved, but in contrast to his hearers, the orator will know that his emotions are not authentic, but artificially produced.[119]

Turning to Machiavelli's work, we can see how this general pattern is reproduced in Ligurio's rhetorical performance in *La mandragola*. A master at arousing and swaying the emotions of others, Ligurio employs in the play methods similar to those described by Quintilian, when stirring the other characters to hope, fear, desire, and compassion. First, he succeeds in persuading the listless Nicia, who jealously watches over his wife and rarely leaves Florence, to take her to the baths in the countryside for an improvised encounter with Callimaco. Informing Callimaco about their interview, he relates how he finally managed to work up and inflame Nicia's desire: "I have heated him up (*ce l'ho riscaldato*)," he says, "and at the end he told me that he was willing to do anything."[120] Next, Ligurio attends to the overly passionate Callimaco, who has begun to despair about his chances of getting into Lucrezia's bed. In a state of agitation, Callimaco exclaims: "I need to try something, be it something great, something dangerous, something harmful or something infamous. It is better to die than to live like this."[121] Ligurio calls for moderation: "Don't say that, put a restraint on that impulsive spirit of yours."[122] By claiming that he shares his friend's desire to see the plan succeed, owing to an occult affinity between their bloods, Ligurio manages to cool Callimaco down. At this point, the plot undergoes a comical reversal: from now on, it is the impatient Nicia, the future cuckold, who needs cooling down, and the enamored Callimaco who must be spurred on towards sexual conquest.

At a first glance, it may be difficult to see what bearing these comical and rhetorical maneuverings have on the discourse of *The Prince*. To judge

[118] Quintilian, *Institutio Oratoria* 4.2.25–4.2.32, II, pp. 430–36.

[119] On Renaissance accounts of the rhetorical techniques of producing emotions in an audience, see Rebhorn, *The Emperor of Men's Minds*, pp. 86–89.

[120] *La mandragola*, p. 123: "Pure, io ce l'ho riscaldato, e mi ha detto infine che farà ogni cosa."

[121] Ibid.: "A me bisogna tentare qualche cosa, sia grande, sia periculosa, sia dannosa, sia infame. Meglio è morire che vivere così."

[122] Ibid.: "Non dire così, raffrena cotesto impeto dell'animo."

by the dedicatory letter, where Machiavelli states his intention to write in a simple and straightforward manner, the treatise was not conceived from a rhetorical point of view:

I have not embellished this work by filling it with rounded periods, with high-sounding words or fine phrases, or with any of the other beguiling artifices or superfluous ornaments which most writers employ to describe and embellish their subject matter; for my wish is that, if it is to be honoured at all, only the variety of the matter and the gravity of the subject should make it acceptable.[123]

This statement, it would seem, supports the traditional claim that Machiavelli in *The Prince* aspires to treat politics from an analytical, objective, and scientific, or proto-scientific, perspective.[124] But as has frequently been pointed out, denunciation of rhetoric is itself a conventional rhetorical trope and should therefore not automatically be taken at face value.[125] As we have seen, the classical theory of rhetoric taught that the orator, especially in the exordium, should take care to conceal the rhetorical and manipulative nature of his speech. Approximately at the same time as Machiavelli composed *The Prince*, Baldesar Castiglione coined the term *sprezzatura* to name a commonly practiced technique by means of which a courtier may "conceal all art and make whatever is done or said appear to be without effort and almost without any thought about it." Castiglione's explicit source of inspiration is "certain most excellent orators in ancient times who . . . tried to make everyone believe that they had no knowledge whatever of letters; and dissembling their knowledge, they made their orations appear to be composed in the simplest manner and according to the dictates of nature and truth rather than of effort and art."[126] Is Machiavelli adopting a similar posture when he maintains that in his *Prince* "the variety of the matter and the gravity of the subject" – *la materia* and *il subietto* – will speak plainly for themselves without superfluous embellishments or rhetorical enhancements? Is, in other words, his claim to a natural, objective, and matter-of-fact form of speech in reality a strategy to conceal the rhetorical and cunningly deceptive nature of his text? As we shall see later in the

[123] *Il principe*, dedication, pp. 117–18: "La quale opera io non ho ornata né ripiena di clausule ample o di parole ampullose e magnifiche o di qualunque altro lenocinio e ornamento estrinseco, con e' quali molti sogliono le loro cose descrivere e ornare, perché io ho voluto o che veruna cosa la onori o che solamente la varietà della materia e la gravità del subietto la facci grata."

[124] See for example Leonardo Olschki, *Machiavelli the Scientist* (Berkeley, CA: The Gillick Press, 1945); Cassirer, *The Myth of the State*.

[125] It could also be argued that Machiavelli in the quoted passage is only rejecting a particular kind of rhetoric, the ostensible and high-flown eloquence of the mirror-for-princes literature.

[126] Baldesar Castiglione, *The Book of the Courtier*, trans. C. S. Singleton (New York: Anchor Books, 1959), pp. 43–44.

course of our discussions of chapters 19 and 25 of *The Prince*, there are good grounds for mistrusting Machiavelli's earnestness on this point.

THE DUAL TEXT AND THE EMPHATIC READER

As our survey of the oratorical use of *ethos* and *pathos* has shown, a rhetorical understanding of a speech, or a text, must, in order to accommodate the contrasting viewpoints of the orator and his implied audience, be dual in character. It also teaches that these two perspectives stand in a hierarchical relationship to each other. While the intended audience's point of view, its intellectual response, and emotional reactions constitute an integral aspect of the speaker's, or the author's, conception of the rhetorical situation, the uninformed listener, or reader, will, by definition, remain ignorant of the rhetorical strategies being imposed on him. In his dialogue *Brutus*, Cicero highlights this duality when comparing the trained expert's and the uninformed multitude's ways of perceiving and judging rhetorical speech. Conceding that an orator who speaks effectively and wins the assent of the general public must be approved by the specialist as well, Cicero claims that the trained orator, in contrast to the unwittingly moved hearer, will be able to recognize, judge, and explain the reasons behind the orator's failure or success.[127] In cases where rhetorical dissimulation and concealment are employed, it goes without saying, the distinction between these two audiences – the expert and the ignorant – is of paramount importance. On such occasions, the speech, or the text, will be not one, but two, assuming different characteristics depending on the point of view from which it is considered.

In Machiavelli's comedy *La mandragola*, we are allowed to witness at close quarters how this rhetorical duality is produced, maintained, and exploited to great comical effect. By employing a set of literary strategies of ancient origin, Machiavelli places us, his audience, in a privileged position, which enables us to see how Ligurio and his co-conspirators manipulate and dupe the credulous and unsuspecting Nicia. As a consequence, Machiavelli comes in the play to demystify the rhetorical and manipulative approach to human communication that Ligurio, the model rhetorician, embodies. Plays like Machiavelli's *Mandragola* and Shakespeare's *Othello*, to mention just two of the most striking examples, teach us that things look very different depending on which side of the rhetorical manipulation we stand on, whether we are deceivers, dupes, or perceptive bystanders.

[127] Cicero, *Brutus*, 184–87, 200, and 219–20, pp. 157–59, 171, and 187–89.

If applied to Machiavelli's *Prince*, this observation is bound to have far-reaching consequences for our understanding of what the former Secretary is doing, or trying to do, in this work. As we saw at the beginning of this chapter, there exists in *La mandragola* a hierarchy of perceptions, from that of the master manipulator Ligurio at the one extreme, to that of the naïve and gullible Nicia at the other. An intermediary position communicating between the two is taken by the astute and perceptive bystander-participant Father Timoteo, the priest in the comedy, who plays along in Ligurio's plot to serve the interest of his church. While Ligurio, as the playwright in the play, on a more general level can be seen to represent the principle of authorial intention and Nicia that of the implied audience, Father Timoteo offers a critical and demystifying view of the rhetorical transaction taking place in the play. This is also to say that the priest occupies an interpretative position from which the authorial intention governing a rhetorical performance like that of Ligurio, or a rhetorical text such as *The Prince*, can be studied with regard to how it controls, or seeks to control, the reaction of its implied audience.

However, to be able to participate in this way, as part bystanders, part manipulated readers, in a rhetorical performance like that of *The Prince*, we need to resurrect the much discredited dramatic, or emphatic, aspect of the hermeneutic tradition. Since rhetorical speech and texts aim at creating rhetorical effects in an intended hearer or reader, they call for an emphatic form of interpretation based on identification either with the work's intended audience (as in the case of *The Prince*), or with the characters of the play (as in *La mandragola*). To uncover the authorial intention, or intentions, at work in the rhetorical text, we therefore need to submit to its seductive power and to allow ourselves to be governed by its arguments and manipulative strategies. Cicero likens the listener's ear to a wind instrument, and Renaissance rhetoricians who picked up on this metaphor compared the hearer's emotion to the vibrating strings of a lyre.[128] If we draw out the implications of these musical metaphors, it is only after we have let ourselves be transformed into the willing instruments of the manipulative author that we can begin to glimpse the hidden meaning of his work. In other words, to see where the text is trying to lead us, we must let ourselves be led, or played on.[129]

[128] Ibid., 192 and 200, pp. 162–64 and 170; Rebhorn, *The Emperor of Men's Minds*, p. 88.

[129] This, I would argue, is also how we normally, unreflectingly and imperfectly, read and interpret texts that we consider to be rhetorical, that is, intended, addressed, and adapted to the circumstances. It is also how we instinctively react when we in our daily lives enter into rhetorical situations where others are trying to control or manipulate our intellectual or emotive responses. What is that person

A rhetorical reading of this kind requires an open and receptive mind. It demands that we provisionally suspend our own views, judgments, and doubts, and allow ourselves to be molded into the implied reader of the text. The elicited responses the text provokes may not be in accordance with our inclinations, but if we, for some personal, moral, or ideological reason, resist identification and manipulation, we cannot expect to arrive at a true understanding of the authorial intention behind the rhetorical strategies contained in the text. On the most basic level, it is a matter of allowing the rhetorical text to force itself into our minds and to engage our sensibilities.

To exemplify, if we are to understand what Machiavelli's *Prince* does, or attempts to do, to a princely reader in general, and to Lorenzo de' Medici and the Medici family in particular, we must seek identification with the work's Medicean readers and read the treatise with a view to how it was intended to be used by them. But at the same time as we let the text act upon us in this immediate, concrete, and naïve way, we must take a step back and carefully register the effect it has upon us. Our subordination to the author should, in other words, be a feigned form of submission, allowing us to engage in a double act of empathic reading and demystification.

This, I would argue, is also how Father Timoteo, the priest in *La mandragola*, reads Ligurio. Having under false pretenses been introduced to Nicia by the former marriage-broker, the friar stops to reflect on the role he has been asked to play in his scheme:

> Ligurio, that scoundrel, came and told me that first story to try me out. "If the friar agrees to the first little scheme," he must have said to himself, "it'll be all the the easier to talk him into the second; while if he doesn't agree to the first, we won't tell him about the second at all. There'll be no risk of his babbling out our real plans, and if he blabs the imaginary ones it won't matter." He had me there, I admit; but there's some good in it for me as well.[130]

On the basis of this observation, Father Timoteo decides to play along in the plot, fully conscious of the fact that he has been duped into it,

up to? we ask. Why, so out of the blue, is he, or she, so kind to me? Surely, there must be some ulterior motives for him, or her, acting in this way . . . And we start to inquire. This is also to say that none of us can pretend to be a stranger to the kind of mind game Machiavelli, the author of *Il principe*, invites us to participate in.

[130] *La mandragola*, pp. 142–43: "Questo tristo di Ligurio ne venne a me con quella prima novella per tentarmi, acciò se io li consentivo quella, m'inducessi più facilmente a questa; se io non gliene consentivo, non mi arebbe detta questa, per non palesare e' disegni loro senza utile, e di quella che era falsa non si curavono. Egli è vero che io ci sono stato giuntato; nondimeno questo giunto, è con mio utile." Here I have used Bruce Penman's free translation; see *Five Italian Renaissance Comedies*, ed. B. Penman (London: Penguin, 1978), p. 37.

accepting the role Ligurio has assigned to him. This, I would submit, is how we should read Machiavelli's *Prince*: projecting ourselves into the implied princely reader of the work while keeping a critical distance. Father Timoteo's dual mode of interpreting Ligurio's rhetorical manipulations provides us, in other words, with a model for understanding the sophisticated rhetorical transaction taking place in *The Prince* and allows us to approach Machiavelli's deceptive rhetoric from within the work. Our first point of identification, then, should be not with the author of *The Prince* or the work's intended Medicean reader, but with Father Timoteo, the model reader created for us in retrospect by Machiavelli himself.

In this introductory chapter we have offered a theoretical framework for a rhetorical reading of Machiavelli's work in general, and of *The Prince* in particular. We have for this purpose elaborated on Quentin Skinner's methodological approach, and explored the dual nature of rhetorical speech as theorized by such classical orators as Cicero and Quintilian. To open up what I perceive to be a hitherto unexploited potential for rhetorical analysis buried within Skinner's interpretative model, I have distinguished between two different levels of reading: on the one hand, an ideological level, focusing on the relationship between the particular text and the ideological vocabularies and the systems of representation available at the time; on the other hand, a rhetorical level that addresses the text's engagement with, and embeddedness in, the local and historically contingent political and practical context of interacting particulars. While Skinner's empirical studies have been concerned mainly, if not entirely, with the former of these two levels, the present study focuses on the latter, and on the relationship between the two levels.

Our reasons for adopting this approach are not merely methodological. The interpretation of *The Prince* we shall present in chapters 3 through 7 will be based on the assumption that Machiavelli's main concern in composing this work was the application of his general principles *here and now*, that is, in Florence at the beginning of the Cinquecento. But to understand what was at stake in this heroic, but ill-fated, enterprise, we need to go back and reexamine the patriotic Florentine context Machiavelli's work participates in, comments on, and challenges. This will be the principal theme of the next chapter.

CHAPTER 2

The republic's two ends

> A city that lives free has two ends – one to acquire, the other to maintain itself free.
>
> Niccolò Machiavelli

The Renaissance idea that the Republic had two ends – one internal, centered around the classical concept of liberty (*libertas*), and one external, aspiring to acquisition of dominion (*imperium*), material goods, greatness, and glory – went back to the revival of Roman republicanism in the fourteenth century. During the early Trecento Roman historians, primarily Livy and Sallust, began to exert a profound influcncc on the intellectual life of the Italian city-states. In Livy's history of Rome, republican theorists encountered the fullest and most detailed history of the Roman republic ever written. Livy relates how Rome rose from her obscure and humble beginnings to become the ruler of the world, and how the early kingship developed into a strong and vigorous republic based on citizenship, liberty, the common good, simple and austere mores, piety towards the ancestral gods, and an ardent and uncompromising pursuit of personal glory.[1] From Sallust was derived the notion that republican government, expansionism, and imperial authority were not merely compatible but closely related and mutually supportive phenomena.[2] The idea that freedom-loving republics

[1] The enormous impact of Livy on Italian Renaissance thought is attested to by the fact that at least four of the major works of the period, Petrarch's *Africa* and *De Viris Illustribus*, Bruni's *Historiae Florentini Populi*, and Machiavelli's *Discorsi sopra la prima deca di Tito Livio*, are all based on Livy.

[2] On Sallust's importance for Italian intellectuals from the Trecento up to Machiavelli, see Quentin Skinner, "Machiavelli's *Discorsi* and the Pre-humanist Origins of Republican Ideas," in *Machiavelli and Republicanism*, eds. G. Bock, Q. Skinner, and M. Viroli (Cambridge: Cambridge University Press, 1990), pp. 121–41; reprinted in a slightly altered version as Skinner, "The Vocabulary of Renaissance Republicanism: A Cultural Longue-durée?" in *Language and Images of Renaissance Italy*, ed. A. Brown (Oxford: Clarendon Press, 1995), pp. 87–110; Patricia J. Osmond, "Sallust and Machiavelli: From Civic Humanism to Political Prudence," *Journal of Medieval and Renaissance Studies* 23 (1993): 408–38; Osmond, "Princeps Historiae Romanae: Sallust in Renaissance Political Thought," *Memoirs of the American Academy in Rome* 40 (1995): 101–43; Benedetto Fontana, "Sallust and the Politics of Machiavelli," *History of Political Thought* 24 (2003): 86–108.

are more acquisitive and more vigorous than monarchies and principalities underlies his widely read *Bellum Catilinae*, where Rome's exceptional growth under the republic is contrasted to her more hesitant progress under the kings and the stagnation and decline that followed her loss of liberty.

Inspired by their reading of Aristotle, Cicero, and these Roman historians, medieval theorists of communal self-government began to view the life enjoyed under a free republican form of government as distinct from the servitude experienced under the corrupt and tyrannical rule of a prince or *signore*.[3] In order to provide an ideological defense against the aspirations of the emperor, the Pope, the aggressive principalities emerging in northern Italy, and the ever-present threat of internal tyranny, apologists for the Italian city-states during the Dugento and the early Trecento came with increasing frequency to invoke the term liberty (*libertas* or *libertà*). Employed in the dual meaning of political independence and republican self-rule, the concept constituted – together with other classically inspired values like the common good, justice, greatness, peace, civic concord, and the pursuit of virtue – the cornerstone of the new republican ideology that began to develop at the turn of the fourteenth century.

But *libertas*, or *libertà*, was a complex term in the political vocabularies of the day. On the one hand, it was used in a juristic context to denote a negative form of liberty, the right to live one's life free from external interference under the protection afforded by the law. This form of liberty was compatible with both princely and republican rule. On the other hand, the term was employed by vernacular poets and humanists within a civic context, where it was given a more positive meaning, signifying the independence and self-rule of the Republic and the citizen's right to participate in the government of the city. Used in this way, liberty came to be seen as an exclusive property of the Republic, which at times was also referred to as a *vivere libero*, *vivere politico*, or *vivere civile*. On a purely theoretical and ideological level, the contest for supremacy in the chaotic political landscape of Trecento Italy could therefore be said to oppose two well-defined ideologies based on two distinct sets of values. Whereas a prince or a monarch traditionally was conceived of as ruling over friends (*amici*), assisting him in his government, and subjects (*sudditi*), who were allowed passively to enjoy the protection afforded by the laws and the stewardship of their ruler,

3 Although Cicero's most ambitious political work, *De Re Publica*, was lost during the period, its thought was available to Renaissance readers through countless references in Augustine's *Civitas Dei* and through Macrobius's extensive and immensely influential commentary on the sixth book of the work, also known as the *Somnium Scipionis*, Scipio's Dream. See Macrobius, *Commentary on the Dream of Scipio*, trans. W. H. Stahl (New York: Columbia University Press, 1952).

republics like the Florentine took pride in their self-rule, free way of life (*vivere libero*), and collective form of government.

But matters were complicated to a considerable degree by the fact that only a minority of the inhabitants living within the territory controled by an Italian republic could call themselves citizens and enjoy the special prerogatives that went with that designation. In Florence, one of the most popular and broadly based republics of the day, approximately 3,000 of the city's total of 20,000 male inhabitants were qualified to hold public office at the beginning of the fifteenth century.[4] This meant that republics, like princes, ruled over subjects who lacked the privileges and positive rights that full citizenship carried. In the case of Florence, the subjects of the republic could be divided into two principal categories: on the one hand, the disfranchised workers living within the city proper; on the other, the people of the dominion, which traditionally was divided into the countryside (*contado*) and the outlying district (*distretto*). To this second category belonged also the inhabitants of subject cities like Pistoia, Arezzo, and Pisa after they had been brought under Florentine control.[5]

By the middle of the fourteenth century, when the Florentine republic began to emerge as an imperialist state in its own right aspiring to Tuscan hegemony, the terms *libertas* and *libertà* were often coupled with the concepts *imperium* and *signoria*, denoting dominion over internal or external subjects. A Florentine document from 1353 states, for example: "Signory and liberty, for mortal men nothing is more dear, nor more welcome than these two things."[6] The proclamation reflects the prevailing attitude of the day. Internal liberty enjoyed by free citizens under a republican form of government and external growth and acquisition of foreign lands were conceived of by most Florentines not as contradictory, but as complementary

[4] See Nicolai Rubinstein, "Oligarchy and Democracy in Fifteenth-Century Florence," in *Florence and Venice: Comparisons and Relations*, eds. Sergio Bertelli, Nicolai Rubinstein, and Craig Hugh Smith (2 vols., Florence: La Nuova Italia Editrice, 1979–80), 1, p. 107.

[5] On Florence's rule of the *contado* and the *distretto*, see Giorgio Chittolini, *La formazione dello stato regionale e le istituzioni del contado: secoli XIV e XV* (Turin: Einaudi, 1979); Chittolini, "The Italian City-State and its Territory," in *City-States in Classical Antiquity and Medieval Italy*, eds. A. Molho, K. Raaflaub, and J. Emlen (Stuttgart: Franz Steiner Verlag, 1991), pp. 589–602; Guidubaldo Guidi, *Il governo della città-repubblica di Firenze del primo Quattrocento, vol. III: Il contado e distretto* (Florence: Olschki, 1981); Marvin B. Becker, "The Florentine Territorial State and Civic Humanism in the Early Renaissance," in *Florentine Studies: Politics and Society in Renaissance Florence*, ed. N. Rubinstein (London: Faber and Faber, 1968), pp. 109–39; Athanasios Moulakis, *Republican Realism in Renaissance Florence: Francesco Guicciardini's* Discorso di Logrogno (Lanham, MD: Rowman and Littlefield, 1998), pp. 59–67. See also the articles included in *Florentine Tuscany*, eds. W. J. Connell and A. Zorzi (Cambridge: Cambridge University Press, 2000).

[6] Quoted from Jerrold E. Siegel, "'Civic Humanism' or Ciceronian Rhetoric? The Culture of Petrarch and Bruni," *Past and Present* 34 (1966), p. 24.

concepts. Since the republic, understood as a community of free men, ruled over internal subjects in a legally binding relationship of domination and submission, there was basically nothing incongruous in its desire to extend its *imperium* and to incorporate more lands and more subjects in its dominion. Imperialism was not an external or additional element to the republican ideology. It was an integral and essential aspect of the tradition. Freedom, for some, entailed oppression or control of others.

Ever since the publication of Hans Baron's seminal work *The Crisis of the Early Italian Renaissance* in 1955, scholarly orthodoxies have come to conceive of Florentine republicanism as identical to an ideology of liberty.[7] In order to relate this ideology to the historical context in which it is alleged to have originated, the image of the Florentine republic as a small and vulnerable city-state, bravely and courageously defending her independence and republican liberty against an outside world of powerful predatory states, has been forged. Whereas Baron, who called this embryonic form of liberalism civic humanism, claimed that the ideology was born in Florence around 1402 in the immediate aftermath of the Republic's protracted war against Giangaleazzo Visconti of Milan, Quentin Skinner and, later, Maurizio Viroli have demonstrated that this development had been initiated far back in the Dugento in city-states all around Italy. While these scholars have contributed greatly to our understanding of medieval and Renaissance republicanism, they have, however, to my mind, come to distort the tradition by overemphasizing its domestic, self-contained, and polis-oriented side. As a consequence, they have paid little attention to its imperialist aspects, and at times even argued that the republican liberty promoted by Florentine pre-humanists and humanists was purely defensive in character.[8] Although this was a perspective that prevailed among the *ottimati* at the turn of the Cinquecento, it does not reflect the dominant tendency within the tradition. In this chapter, we will instead argue that most Florentine republicans from the Dugento to the early Cinquecento, through a strong and intensely felt identification with the ancient Roman republic, came to

7 Hans Baron, *The Crisis of the Early Italian Renaissance: Civic Humanism and Republican Liberty in an Age of Classicism and Tyranny* (Princeton: Princeton University Press, 1966).

8 Studies adopting this perspective are Quentin Skinner, *The Foundations of Modern Political Thought* (2 vols., Cambridge: Cambridge University Press, 1978), 1, pp. 3–189; Maurizio Viroli, *From Politics to Reason of State: The Acquisition and Transformation of the Language of Politics 1250–1600* (Cambridge: Cambridge University Press, 1992), pp. 2–177; Viroli, *For Love of Country: An Essay on Patriotism and Nationalism* (Oxford: Clarendon Press, 1995), pp. 21–40. For a related criticism of this approach, see Mark Hulliung, *Citizen Machiavelli* (Princeton: Princeton University Press, 1983), pp. 3–30; William J. Connell, "Republican Territorial Government: Florence and Pistoia, Fifteenth and Early Sixteenth Centuries," Ph.D dissertation, University of California, Berkeley, 1989.

regard Florence as destined for imperial greatness and hegemonial rule over Tuscany, Italy, and, on occasions, even the entire world.

To the best of my knowledge no comprehensive study has been devoted to this aspect of the Florentine tradition. C. C. Bayley has studied the history of the Florentine wars and the tradition of humanist thought on the militia, but his study is not informed by an interest in the ideological side of the development.[9] John Pocock's scholarly efforts within the field have chiefly been devoted to the republican quest for stability in a world dominated by fortune, which he regards as the dominant theme of Florentine republicanism.[10] Donald Weinstein has focused mainly on the religious side of the tradition, and in so doing established a fundamental link between the Trecento chronicles, the popular prophecies of the Quattrocento, and the teaching of Savonarola, centered on the notion of the Myth of Florence. But while his scholarship is invaluable for the early part of Florence's republican development, Weinstein has not related his findings to the republican ideology of the civic humanists, or to Machiavelli's political theory.[11]

Such a link is suggested by Mark Hulliung, who should be given credit for his attempt to reorient scholarly attention from Florentine republican liberty to republican imperialism. But Hulliung's study, it is fair to say, is marred by a lack of sustained textual analysis, and a general neglect of the historical context, and has not had a major impact on the field.[12] Richard Trexler, in his monumental, and truly fascinating, *Public Life in Renaissance Florence*, touches upon several themes which are important for this tradition, but his research has been oriented more towards the ritualistic and behavioral aspects of the Florentine Renaissance, and less towards the intellectual culture of the period.[13] Whereas the works of Weinstein, Hulliung,

[9] C. C. Bayley, *War and Society in Renaissance Florence: The* De Militia *of Leonardo Bruni* (Toronto: University of Toronto Press, 1961).

[10] J. G. A. Pocock, *The Machiavellian Moment: Florentine Political Thought and the Atlantic Tradition* (Princeton: Princeton University Press, 1975).

[11] Donald Weinstein, *Savonarola and Florence: Prophecy and Patriotism in the Renaissance* (Princeton: Princeton University Press, 1970), esp. pp. 27–66. On the civic humanists, Weinstein remarks (p. 35): "As much as civic humanism may have reshaped and intensified the historical consciousness of the Florentines, it did not terminate their disposition to look at themselves in the light of prophecy. Florentine civic humanism developed on the established base of popular and patriotic traditions, and humanist classicism and the older *volgare* culture grew not merely side by side, but in a mutually influential relationship." Weinstein ends this brief aside with a reference to Baron's *Crisis*. To the best of my knowledge, Weinstein's only comments on Machiavelli are in "Machiavelli and Savonarola," in *Studies on Machiavelli*, ed. M. P. Gilmore (Florence: Sansoni, 1972), pp. 253–64.

[12] Hulliung, *Citizen Machiavelli*. The same criticism can be levied against Warman Welliver's *L'impero fiorentino* (Florence: La Nuova Italia, 1957).

[13] Richard C. Trexler, *Public Life in Renaissance Florence* (Ithaca: Cornell University Press, 1994).

and Trexler are invaluable for the insights they give into the darker sides of the Florentine Renaissance, they do not offer a comprehensive treatment of the city's republican imperialist tradition.

Other scholars, notably Charles Davis, Marvin Becker, Gene Brucker, Ricardo Fubini, and Lauro Martines, have illuminated important parts of the development on which we have begun to focus, but since their research has been limited chronologically, or dominated by other concerns, they do not provide the continuum or the center of attention necessary to perceive the tradition.[14] Nicolai Rubinstein's extensive investigations into Florentine republicanism and constitutional history have highlighted many of the aspects of the process we are about to sketch, but the emphasis of his work has been on republican liberty rather than on republican acquisition and imperialist aspirations.

Recent research by Randolph Starn, John Najemy, Victoria Kahn, Alison Brown, and James Hankins has been informed by a decidedly more skeptical, and ideologically less naïve, view of Florentine republicanism.[15] Emerging from these studies is a republican ideology conceived largely as a rhetorical construct designed partly to conceal, partly to remedy the breach existing between what Starn has called the republic of interest and the republic of principles.[16] But even if these scholars have developed a perspective on the Florentine republican tradition that closely resembles the one we will adopt in this chapter, their work does not provide the general outline of the imperialist side of Florentine republicanism from the early days of the commune to Machiavelli that we propose to present here, however briefly

[14] See primarily Charles T. Davis, *Dante's Italy and Other Essays* (Philadelphia: University of Pennsylvania Press, 1984); Marvin B. Becker, *Florence in Transition* (2 vols., Baltimore: The Johns Hopkins University Press, 1967–68); Gene A. Brucker, *The Civic World of Early Renaissance Florence* (Princeton: Princeton University Press, 1977).

[15] Randolph Starn and Loren Partridge, *Arts of Power: Three Halls of State in Italy, 1300–1600* (Berkeley, CA: University of California Press, 1992), esp. pp. 11–59. Recent articles by John M. Najemy include "The Dialogue of Power in Florentine Politics," in *City-States in Classical Antiquity and Medieval Italy*, ed. Molho et al., pp. 269–88; "The Republic's Two Bodies," in *Language and Images of Renaissance Italy*, ed. Brown, pp. 237–62; "Civic Humanism and Florentine Politics," in *Renaissance Civic Humanism Reconsidered*, ed. J. Hankins (Cambridge: Cambridge University Press, 2000), pp. 75–104. Victoria Kahn contrasts the rhetoric of Machiavelli to the more confined form of eloquence pursued by the civic humanists in *Machiavellian Rhetoric: From the Counter-Reformation to Milton* (Princeton: Princeton University Press; 1994), pp. 15–59 and 243–48. Alison Brown surveys how the term *imperio* in the course of the Quattrocento began to be employed in Florence to denote the Florentine state: see "The Language of Empire," in *Florentine Tuscany*, ed. Connell, pp. 32–47. James Hankins offers a balanced evaluation of Baron's work, a survey of recent Bruni scholarship, and many valuable observations on Florentine republicanism in "The 'Baron Thesis' after Forty Years and some Recent Studies of Leonardo Bruni," *Journal of the History of Ideas* 56 (1995): 309–38; and in "Rhetoric, History, and Ideology: The Civic Panegyrics of Leonardo Bruni," in *Renaissance Civic Humanism*, ed. Hankins pp. 143–78.

[16] Starn and Partridge, *Arts of Power*, pp. 45 and 58.

and imperfectly. In providing the ideological and patriotic context, which Machiavelli's work draws on and partially challenges, we shall pay special attention to Florence's Roman legacy and to how the concepts of liberty and empire were used and combined in the Florentine patriotic tradition. These fundamental themes will be elaborated on when we turn in the following chapters to consider Machiavelli's work in more detail.

THE CITY ELECT AND ROME'S DAUGHTER

The claim to a Roman descent had been an integral part of the Florentine tradition from the very outset. According to the oldest extant chronicle of the city, the thirteenth-century *Chronica de Origine Civitatis*, Florence had been founded during the reign of Julius Caesar "from the flower of Roman manhood." At her foundation, the city had been given a plan modeled on that of the imperial mother city, and, as a token of her privileged status within the empire, the colony had received the name "little Rome" (*parva Roma*).[17] By the middle of the Dugento, the aggressive and self-assertive attitude of the Florentines had begun to catch the eyes of their neighbors. Addressing the Florentine people in 1260 after the battle at Montaperti, where the Florentine militia had been routed by the Ghibellines of Siena, Friar Guittone of Arezzo appealed to the Florentines' sense of pride and patriotism: "O queen of towns . . . where is now your pride and your greatness (*grandessa*), who almost appeared as a new Rome, since you were striving to subject the whole of the world? And truly, the Romans had no greater beginnings than you, nor did they achieve more in so short a time."[18] The ties between Florence and her great ancestor were loudly proclaimed at the turn of the fourteenth century, when an inscription was placed on the recently erected Communal palace, the present-day Palazzo Vecchio, celebrating Florence as the leader of Tuscany, a city enjoying good fortune and full of wealth, and a fearful warring nation comparable to triumphant Rome.[19]

Bombastic claims such as this, which continued to be advanced in the course of the Trecento, had, of course, no or little foundation in the political

[17] Weinstein, *Savonarola and Florence*, pp. 36–37; Nicolai Rubinstein, "The Beginnings of Political Thought in Florence: A Study of Mediaeval Historiography," *Journal of the Warburg and Courtauld Institutes* 5 (1942): 198–227.

[18] Quoted from Rubinstein, "The Beginnings of Political Thought," p. 213: "O reina de le cità . . . ov'è l'orgoglio e la grandessa vostra, che quazi sembravate una novella Roma, volendo tutto suggiugare el mondo? E cierto non ebbero cominciamento il Romani più di voi bello, nè in tanto di tempo più non feciero . . ."

[19] Ibid., p. 213.

realities of the day. At this time the territory controled by the Florentine commune corresponded broadly with the extension of the diocese, its outlook was still parochial and its power too limited to pose a serious threat to neighboring cities like Pisa, Lucca, Siena, or Arezzo. This was a period not of expansion, but of consolidation, as is indicated by the ambitious campaign at the turn of the Trecento to build a belt of fortified administrative centres, so-called new towns, along the commune's eastern borders.[20] This grandiose scheme, the principal aim of which was to establish Florentine authority in the outlying part of the territory and to eradicate the power base of the local barons, marks the birth of the Florentine territorial state, but does not allow us to talk about an expansive Florentine empire at this point in history.

The inflated claims made on behalf of the commune at the time should instead be seen in relation to the role Florence was aspiring to within the Guelf league. Florentine Guelfism had emerged in the course of the Dugento, when the bitter struggle between Guelfs and Ghibellines, the supporters of the Papacy and the Holy Roman Empire respectively, divided Italy. Resting upon an amalgam of Christian, patriotic, and civic notions and ideals, mainly vernacular in expression, and imbued with strong popular sentiment and Francophile sympathies, the Guelf ideology began to assume the status of the Florentine commune's official ideology at the turn of the Trecento.[21] Florentine intellectuals of the day conceived of their city as a living creature invested with a millenarian role in the great design of divine providence, and as the champion of city-state independence and communal liberty in the face of imperial and signorial aggression. Her future destiny was understood within the frameworks of both sacred and secular history: on the one hand, she was celebrated as the Elect Nation destined to become the center of a spiritual revival and the rebirth of the Church; on the other, she was hailed as the "daughter of Rome" and seen as the future ruler of a great and glorious empire.[22]

Giovanni Villani's *Cronica*, begun early in the Trecento, constitutes the principal example of Florentine self-representation from this period. The idea of composing the chronicle, Giovanni relates, had come to him during his pilgrimage to Rome in the Holy Year of 1300. Walking among the ruins of the Eternal city and reflecting upon the possibility that Florence

[20] See David Friedman, *Florentine New Towns: Urban Design in the Late Middle Ages* (Cambridge, MA: The MIT Press, 1991).

[21] On Florentine Guelfism, see Diane Finiello Zervas, *The Parte Guelfa, Brunelleschi and Donatello* (Locust Valley, NY: J. J. Augustin, 1987).

[22] See Weinstein, *Savonarola and Florence*, p. 35.

one day would also be reduced to this deplorable state, he decided to follow the examples of Livy and Sallust, whose histories had preserved the Roman name in spite of the destruction of the city.[23] To establish a Roman legacy for Florence, Giovanni rehearsed the traditional myth of Florence as Rome's daughter, but he made an important innovation with regard to the thirteenth-century *Cronica*, by attributing the second founding of the city not to the Romans, but to Charlemagne. Motivated by Florence's strong orientation towards France at the time, this refashioning of the city's early history served to bolster her developing republican ideology as well. If we are to believe Giovanni, Charlemagne had not only refounded Florence, but also granted the city her communal liberties and her right to self-rule. Following the restoration, a republican government had been set up along Roman lines with a Senate and two elective consuls. But while he insisted on the historical bond linking Florence to her Roman past, Giovanni did not endorse the bellicose aspects of the tradition.[24] Opposing, on religious grounds, the republic's aggressive and expansionist foreign policy, he came to attribute Florence's defeat by Pisa in 1341, and her loss of Lucca the year after, to God's wrath against the city's insatiable appetite for territorial acquisition.[25]

It has been claimed that this negative attitude towards territorial expansion was typical of the time, and that there were no signs during the first half of the Trecento of an emerging imperialist ideology in Florence. Warlike activity outside the city walls, Donald Weinstein informs us, "was generally justified as a defense of Guelphism – that is, of domestic republicanism, civic virtue, and service to the cause of the Church."[26] This observation is largely confirmed by Quentin Skinner's important survey of the republican values articulated in the writings of the so-called *dictatores*, the trained rhetoricians affiliated with the Italian universities and the chanceries of the city-states.[27] Until the beginning of the Trecento the term greatness (*grandezza*), which the pre-humanists frequently used to denote the highest aspiration of a city-state, had been understood almost exclusively within an

[23] See ibid., p. 40; Hans Baron, *In Search of Florentine Civic Humanism: Essays on the Transition from Medieval to Modern Thought* (2 vols., Princeton: Princeton University Press, 1988), I, p. 48.

[24] Donald Weinstein argues (*Savonarola and Florence*, pp. 40–41) that the greatness of Florence in Giovanni Villani's eyes consisted in "a composite of her wealth, her republican institutions, her culture, and her charitable and pious citizenry."

[25] Weinstein, *Savonarola and Florence*, p. 40n. But at the same time as he extolled peace, Giovanni Villani could rebuke the civic leaders of Florence for their lack of military virtue, and remind them of the fact that Julius Caesar had brought Rome military success by personally leading his army; see Bayley, *War and Society*, p. 15. On Giovanni Villani's complex view of the Luccan warlord Castruccio Castracani, see Louis Green, "The Image of Tyranny in Early Fourteenth-Century Italian Historical Writing," *Renaissance Studies* 7 (1993), p. 346.

[26] Weinstein, *Savonarola and Florence*, p. 41.

[27] Skinner, "Machiavelli's *Discorsi*."

Augustinian context, as a state of perfect peace, tranquillity, and concord. At the turn of the fourteenth century a decisive change can be observed within the tradition. Inspired by their reading of Sallust's *Bellum Catilinae*, the theorists of communal self-government began to regard an excessive attachment to peace as conducive to corruption and factionalism, and to hold that wars waged for the sake of liberty were lawful and justifiable. But according to Skinner, the writers of the tradition continued to condemn military aggression and to insist that in order to be legitimate, war must be fought in self-defense.

But these pacifist views and ideological niceties did little to prevent or to hamper Florentine expansion. Towards the middle of the Trecento, the city entered a series of aggressive wars resulting in the acquisitions of Colle Valdelsa in 1338, Prato and Pistoia in 1351, San Gimignano in 1354, and Volterra in 1361. As a rule, these campaigns were justified on the grounds that they were carried out for the sake of territorial security and to protect Florentine and Tuscan liberty in the face of Milanese aggression, but in reality, we have reason to believe, their aim was the subjugation of the surrounding cities and the establishment of Florentine hegemony in Tuscany.[28]

One of the witnesses to this process was Matteo Villani, who continued to write on his brother Giovanni's chronicle after the latter's death in the plague in 1348. In the Manichean world-view of Florentine Trecento Guelfism, to which Matteo whole-heartedly subscribed, Guelf liberty under papal overlordship was contrasted to Ghibelline tyranny and imperialism.[29] For Matteo, the liberty of the Italian city-states did not depend upon the German emperors, but went back to antiquity when the Italian peoples had enjoyed the status of free cities within the Roman empire. In contrast to foreign nations, who had been tributaries and subjects of Rome,[30] the Italian communes had "participated in the citizenship and the liberty of the Roman people." According to Matteo, Roman ancestry and love of liberty were not an exclusive Florentine inheritance, but a legacy the Arno city shared with other ancient cities such as, for example, Perugia, Siena, Pisa, and Volterra.[31]

But Matteo's view of Florentine liberty and expansionism was wrought with ambiguity. On the one hand, he criticized in the spirit of his brother the Florentine authorities' use of deception (*inganno*) in their foreign relations,

[28] To legitimate their expansion, the Florentines also often claimed that they were saving their new subjects from domestic or foreign tyrants. See, for examples, Nicolai Rubinstein, "Florentina Libertas," *Rinascimento*, n.s. 2 (1986), p. 8; and Brucker, *The Civic World*, p. 304.

[29] See for example Matteo Villani, *Cronica* VIII.24.

[30] Ibid., IV.77.

[31] See for example ibid. III.1 and IV.77.

and condemned their war-mongering and rapacity; on the other, he did not question the legitimacy of Florence's acquisition of the neighboring communes. The subjugation of Colle Valdelsa, a hilltop town halfway between Florence and Siena, is a case in point. The Colligiani had recovered their liberty and their self-rule after the expulsion of the Duke of Athens from Florence in 1443. But according to Matteo, they soon became so beset by internal strife that they could no longer maintain their liberty. When it became known that one of the factions had begun to negotiate "with powerful and great neighbors in order to make themselves tyrants,"[32] the other party took to arms, and fighting erupted in the city. At this point, the Florentines sent out troops to restore order in the town. Realizing that their internal divisions prevented them from opposing the Florentines, "who had been sent there for their own good," the Colligiani put down their arms and opened the gates to let the neighbors in. Convened in a general council, they came to the conclusion that it was to "the common benefit of their commune" to seek the protection of the Florentines, and they deliberated, "unanimously and concordantly," that the Comune of Florence should be allowed, for all time to come, to assume the guardianship of the city. In Matteo's tendentious account, the role of the Florentines is thus made to seem altruistic and disinterested, although there can be little doubt that their actions in reality were motivated by their strong desire to regain possession of the rebellious neighbor. The same justificatory rhetoric governs Matteo's narrative of how the Florentines shortly afterwards stepped in and restored unity and order in San Gimignano, Pistoia, and Prato.[33]

As a devoted Guelf, Matteo viewed Florentine foreign policy within the general context of papal aspirations for world hegemony and universal peace.[34] But by the middle of the Trecento the traditional political orientations and mental routines of medieval thought had begun to erode. The ties uniting the members of the Guelf league were weakening, and Florentine chroniclers and poets expressed concerns over the fact that Florence no longer could rely on the support of her former allies, the Avignon pope and the Angevin dynasty of Naples. In this new political landscape, infused with doubts and uncertainties, and dominated by the aggressive Visconti *signori* of Milan, who were laying claims to large parts of central Italy, it

[32] Matteo Villani, *Cronica con la continuazione di Filippo Villani* (2 vols., Parma: Fondazione Pietro Bembo/Guanda, 1995), I, p. 83: "cominciarono a setteggiare e a volere cacciare l'uno l'altro, e alcuna parte trattava coll'aiuto di potenti e grandi vicini d'essere tiranni."

[33] Ibid., I, pp. 85, 142, 188–89, and 411.

[34] According to Weinstein (*Savonarola and Florence*, p. 42): "Matteo [Villani] thought of Guelfism as the party of piety, of liberty, and of Latinity, the bulwark against the tide of German barbarism which was threatening to engulf the free cities of Italy."

was clear that the republic would have to search for new political loyalties and a new ideological identity.

It is against this background that the renewed importance Florentines towards the end of the Trecento came to attach to the notion of *libertas* and the city's Roman legacy should be understood. In the context of the traditional Guelf ideology, the liberty (*libertas*) of the individual commune had been seen as subordinate to the *libertas* of Christendom at large. Expansionism in the name of Guelf *libertas* was conducted primarily for the sake of the *Respublica Christiana*, secondly for the Papacy, and only thirdly for the commune itself. On the basis of this reasoning, Matteo Villani could in the middle of the Trecento complain about the Church's unwillingness to assist Florence in spite of the many acquisitions the republic had made in her name.[35] But after the breakdown of the Guelf league, this traditional notion of liberty lost much of its meaning. Matters were brought to a head during the War of the Eight Saints (1375–78), which saw Florence openly defying papal leadership and claiming the status of the champion of liberty against tyranny, Good against Evil, and true Christianity against its perverted form embodied in the Roman Church.[36] In the patriotic poetry, religious writings and political debates of the 1370s and 1380s, Florentines rehearsed their city's elect status as the blessed center of the future Christian *renovatio* and the eternal daughter of Rome, and prophesied that Florence would emerge as the new leader of Italy, bringing renewal, peace and *libertas* in her train. Under such proclamations, the republic took it upon herself to defend the sacrosanct liberties of Arezzo (acquired in 1384), Montepulciano (annexed in 1390), Perugia, Bologna, and other cities allegedly under threat from the advancing Visconti dukes of Milan.

In the so-called *missive*, the republic's official correspondence, composed by Coluccio Salutati during his tenure as chancellor from 1375 to his death in 1406, Florence was frequently represented as the champion of Italian liberty opposing foreign domination and domestic tyrants.[37] In his letters to other free communes, Salutati often appealed to love of liberty and to the principle of republican self-government as a common cause uniting

[35] Weinstein, *Savonarola and Florence*, p. 42.

[36] Becker, *Florence in Transition*, II, pp. 201–04; Weinstein, *Savonarola and Florence*, pp. 42–43.

[37] On the *missive* in general, see Ronald G. Witt, *Coluccio Salutati and his Public Letters* (Geneva: Librairie Droz, 1976); Peter Herde, "Politik und Rhetorik in Florenz am Vorabend der Renaissance," *Archiv für Kulturgeschichte* 47 (1965): 141–220; Herde, "Politische Verhaltenweisen der Florentiner Oligarchie, 1382–1402," in *Geschichte und Verfassungsgefüge: Frankfurter Festgabe für Walter Schlesinger*, ed. K. Zernack (Wiesbaden: Steiner, 1973), pp. 156–249; Daniela De Rosa, *Coluccio Salutati: Il cancelliere e il pensatore politico* (Florence: La Nuova Italia, 1980). On Salutati, see also Robert Black, "The Political Thought of the Florentine Chancellors," *Historical Journal* 29 (1986): 991–1003.

all free city-states in their defense against princely or signorial aggression. Writing to the Sienese at a time when the Visconti were aspiring to greater dominion in central Italy, Salutati sought to establish such a bond between the two republics:

> If you wish, as is your duty, to leave your old enemy [i.e. Milan], who pretends to be a friend and protector only in order to be able to command you . . . and to return to the friendship of your old, true and eternal brothers in order to defend together with us your liberty and that of the others, as was the custom of your ancestors, we are ready to embrace you.[38]

It is tempting to see in passages such as this confirmation of Baron's thesis that the civic humanists, and Salutati among them, supported the idea of creating a system of independent city-states in central Italy. But such a reading of the *missive* ignores the rhetorical and strategic aspects of Salutati's invocations of Italian liberty, and the hidden motives we have reason to believe were concealed behind the Florentines' claim to Italian and Tuscan leadership. The implications of Salutati's appeals to the common cause and the Florentines' protestation of goodwill were rarely lost upon the city's neighbors, who had learnt from hard-won experience to view Florentine motives with suspicion. On this particular occasion the Sienese, who were anxious to curb Florentine influence in neighboring Montepulciano, currently under Sienese jurisdiction, saw little reason to accept the Florentine embrace and to decline the Milanese offer of assistance.

In his public letters, Salutati also contributed to strengthening and deepening the city's Roman identity by inserting quotations and examples from classical authors, and by drawing close parallels between the Florentine republic and her ancient Roman forebear. The Roman idea that love of liberty and the pursuit of empire are not only compatible, but closely interrelated, is a frequent theme in the *missive*. Addressing the peoples of Cesena, Spoleto and Recanati, for example, Salutati argued that the servitude in which the Italian peoples presently found themselves was particularly humiliating given "the Italic race's" innate desire for liberty, which in the past had inspired it to "obtain liberty at home after innumerable victories," and to "exercise empire over the whole world."[39] In Salutati's laudatory account of the Italian peoples' Roman past, which constitutes a continuous feature in the *missive*, empire abroad comes to appear as a natural extension of liberty at home rather than as a betrayal of the values of the *res publica*. According to him the ancient Romans had acquired their world-wide empire by fighting for their own liberty and by defending their allies and confederates. In an inspired moment he even went on to claim

[38] Quoted from De Rosa, *Coluccio Salutati*, p. 103.

[39] Quoted from ibid., p. 92.

that it was "the desire for liberty alone that brought forth the empire, the glory and all the dignity of the Roman people."[40]

THE MILANESE WARS

Towards the end of the Trecento, Roman civic ideals and *exempla* were being invoked in patriotic, religious and political contexts in Florence with a frequency suggesting that the emerging humanist culture by now had come to gain a foothold in the city. Volgare poets like Fazio degli Uberti, Franco Sacchetti and Braccio Bracci celebrated Florence's greatness by comparing her to ancient Rome, though within a pronouncedly Christian framework. Bracci, a Tuscan serving at the court of Bernabò Visconti of Milan, in 1375 praised the Florentines after the republic had entered a league with the Lombard city. Florence had been favored by God to such an extent, he claimed, that each of her children had come to resemble Cato. The city had restored liberty to life and even surpassed the achievements of the ancient Romans: "Rome never did what you are doing, / But held her provinces subject, / While you raise them from their servitude."[41]

Twenty years later when the two powers were at war, contending for supremacy in central Italy, these compliments were substituted by a bitter propaganda war, in which humanists, literary men and patriotic poets on either side made frequent appeals to Roman history, military might and greatness.[42] In a poem from 1397, celebrating Florence's victory at Governale, Bruscaccio of Rovezzano drew a close parallel between the Florence–Milan conflict and the Second Punic War. Bruscaccio urged Florence, the champion of liberty, Italian unity and peace, to seize the opportunity history offered her:

> You are Rome and the Duke is Hannibal.
> If you will, transmit
> To the people the light of freedom in their state.
> This rejected dog
> Ought to be destroyed; it will please God.
> And peace for all of Italy will follow.[43]

[40] Quoted from Ronald G. Witt, "The Rebirth of the Concept of Republican Liberty," in *Renaissance Studies in Honour of Hans Baron*, eds. J. A. Tedeschi and A. Molho (Florence: Sansoni, 1970), p. 196.

[41] "Roma non fece mai quel che tu fai, / Ma tenne le provincie soggiogate, / E tu da servitu tutte le trai" (quoted from Weinstein, *Savonarola and Florence*, p. 50).

[42] For a survey of this ideological battle with many documents relating to the debates, see Antonio Lanza, *Firenze contra Milano: Gli intellettuali fiorentini nelle guerre con i Visconti (1390–1440)* (Rome: De Rubeis, 1991).

[43] "Voi siete Roma, e Anibàle è il Duca. / Se volete riluca / Liberamente il popol loro stato, / Questo can rinneghato / Convien che ssie disfatto, ch'a dDio piace, / E seguiranne a tutta Ytalia pace" (quoted from Weinstein, *Savonarola and Florence*, p. 53).

To the same period belongs Giovanni Gherardi's *Dolce mia patria, non ti incresca udirmi*, which was written in reply to an anti-Florentine poem by the Sienese author Simone Serdini, also known as il Saviozzo. With the explicit aim of exhorting his Florentine compatriots to emulate the virtues of their Roman ancestors, Gherardi offers a Roman hall of fame, similar to the one found in Petrarch's *De Viris Illustribus*:

> You are of this ancient and sacred blood
> which runs through your divine members,
> and gives you the Roman soul and kinship.
> There is not a heart so proud, so hard and bitter
> that it does not tremble or soften if it remembers;
> trembling does still the world in wonder.
> Open your mind and raise your eyes:
> See Brutus, Publicola and Camillus,
> Horace, Cincinnatus and Scipio,
> Marcellus, Fabius and Cato,
> Torquatus and Africanus, divine to view,
> Fabricius and more than a thousand in this choir,
> who nothing else than liberty treasure.[44]

In these verses, swelling with patriotic pride, the defense of Florentine liberty and the celebration of the Roman republic's greatest conquerors come together to bolster the essential link between Florentine republicanism and the quest for empire.

On the Milanese side the banners were flown by Antonio Loschi, the leading humanist at the Visconti court, and a personal acquaintance of Salutati, his main adversary in the dispute. Sometime around 1395, Loschi wrote an anti-Florentine pamphlet in which he challenged the Florentines' right to call themselves the champions of Italian liberty as well as their longstanding claim to a direct Roman descent. During the following decade, a series of Florentine intellectuals and humanists took it upon themselves to refute Loschi's allegations, among them Salutati, Cino Rinuccini, the teacher of rhetoric at Santa Maria in Campo, and Leonardo Bruni, Salutati's brilliant disciple and future successor as the republic's chancellor. What was at stake in this paper war, the Florentine responses reveal, was Florence's right to

[44] Giovanni Gherardi, "Canzona morale di patria e di libertade," text in Lanza, *Firenze contra Milano*, pp. 205–07, vv 105–17: "Tu sse' pur di quel sangue antico e sacro,/ e tiello ancor[a] per le divine membra,/ che tti diè l'alma Roma in sua famiglia./ Non è sì fero cor[e], duro, né acro/ che non trema o dolcisca se 'l rimembra;/ tremane il mondo ancor per maraviglia./ Apri la mente e alza su le ciglia:/ vedrai Bruto, Publicola e Camillo,/ Orazio, Cincinato e Scipïone,/ Marcel[lo], Fabio e Catone,/ Torquato e ll'African[o], divo e vedello,/ Fabrizio e più di mille in questo coro,/che libertà sol vollon per tesoro."

exercise dominion over subject cities, while continuing to claim to be the defender of Italian liberty.

In his reply to Loschi, *Invectiva in Antonium Luschum Vicentinum* (*c.* 1403), Salutati opposed the Milanese's claim that the subjects of the Florentine republic were suffering under the tyrannical yoke of the Tuscan city. The subject cities in the Florentine dominion, he assured, were quite satisfied to enjoy the sweet liberty of living under the law and being protected by it:[45]

> [Are you saying] that Florentine subjects, whom our city has established and made or snatched and taken back from the hands of tyrants have been suffocated by tyranny or despoiled of their ancient dignity? Those who were either born with us in liberty or recalled to the sweetness of liberty from the distress of a wretched servitude? Do they long to throw off a yoke they do not have, or exchange the sweet restraints of liberty (*dulce libertatis frenum*) – which is to be free from arbitrary power and live according to the law (*iure vivere legibusque*) to which everyone is subject – for the tyrannical yoke of your lord, as you pretend to believe?[46]

The definition of liberty Salutati offers here is not the positive participatory form of freedom which has traditionally come to be identified with Florentine republicanism. Salutati does not concede the subjects of the Florentine dominion the liberty of self-government and political participation. The juristic understanding contained within the term *iure vivere* only in practice means that Florentine subjects have the privilege of living under Florentine laws instead of under those of the duchy of Milan.

In Salutati's view, Florence's Roman heritage and love of liberty gave the city a natural right to dominion and lordship over Tuscany and the rest of the peninsula. While the Florentines, who were Roman citizens by both blood and legal right, had received their love of liberty as a divine gift and gradually acquired the habit of hating servitude, the Milanese and the Lombards lived under the deception that "the highest liberty and the inestimable dignity" were to obey the unrestrained will of a tyrannical patron like the Visconti duke. To live under the constraints of law appeared to them as "a grave yoke and a horrendous servitude." Whether or not they would be able to rise to liberty, now that ancient virtue was being revived under Florentine auspices, only time could tell. The outcome would depend entirely, Salutati argued, on whether they would prove themselves to belong

45 *Invectiva Lini Colucii Salutati in Antonium Luschum Vicentinum*, ed. D. Moreni (Florence, 1826). The essential part of the text has been published in *Antologia della letteratura italiana, vol. II: Il Quattrocento e il Cinquecento*, ed. A. Asor Rosa et al. (Milan: Rizzoli, 1966), pp. 50–54. My references are to this latter edition (henceforth cited as Salutati, *Invectiva*).

46 Salutati, *Invectiva*, p. 52.

to the servile Lombard race of transalpine origin, or to "the glorious Gallic race" which formerly had inhabited Cisalpine Gaul and had been imbued with the freedom-loving Italic spirit. In the latter case also the Lombards would be able to claim a place of privilege within the new emerging political order based on liberty and Florentine hegemony.[47] Needless to say, it does not take much to read the traditional paradigm of Roman imperialism into Salutati's defense of Florentine republicanism and expansionism in the *Invectiva*.

Loschi's challenge was also met by Cino Rinuccini, who in his *Risponsiva alla Invettiva di messer Antonio Lusco* celebrated Florence as the defender and head of Italy's liberty.[48] According to Rinuccini, there had at all times existed a fundamental difference between the ends of Florentine and Milanese politics. While the Visconti had always acted like tyrants in relation to their own city and to foreign lands, the Florentines had not only defended their own freedom but also treated their subject peoples in a just and fair manner. Referring to Florence's recent purchase of Arezzo from the French, which in reality had been one of the factors provoking the war, Rinuccini claimed that internal divisions had brought the Aretines to the verge of destruction before the Florentines had moved in and restored order. Having found their neighbor "despoiled of goods and almost consumed," the Florentines had "recomposed her, so that the good men of both the contending parties could rest in sweet tranquillity, affirming on both sides that they had never been in such repose."[49]

Aligning himself with Florence's patriotic tradition, Rinuccini viewed liberty and empire as the two complementary sides of his militant republican outlook. Having laid down that a popular form of government was superior to rule by a single man, Rinuccini brought up the example of the ancient Roman republic in connection with Florence: "Have you never read about how Rome under the kings grew only a little, but under the Senate in a short time acquired the empire over the world (*lo 'mperio del mondo*), and then was reduced to almost nothing under the emperors?" The general applicability of this ancient Sallustian theme, Rinuccini argued, had been confirmed by modern experience: "This you must also have observed in beautiful Italy, if you are not utterly blind: that the free cities are the greater,

[47] Ibid.

[48] Cino Rinuccini, "Risponsiva alla Invettiva di messer Antonio Lusco," text in Lanza, *Firenze contra Milano*, pp. 187–97. On Cino Rinuccini's *Risponsiva*, see Ronald Witt, "Cino Rinuccini's *Risponsiva all Invettiva di Messer Antonio Lusco*," *Renaissance Quarterly* 22 (1970): 133–49; Baron, *The Crisis*, pp. 94–99; Lanza, *Firenze contra Milano*, pp. 50–54. The question of the date is controversial, see ibid., p. 50. The text by Rinuccini referred to and quoted here is a contemporary Italian translation of the Latin original.

[49] Rinuccini, *Risponsiva*, p. 190.

that is, Florence, Venice and Genoa."[50] When Rinuccini later returned to the subject of Florence's Roman heritage, he articulated the imperialist perspective with even greater emphasis as he appropriated the Roman legacy for Florence:

So much intellect is there in us that in the same way as we in the past have been the defenders of beautiful liberty, we will in the future be its enlargers (*ampliatori*); it is very well known that we do not lack prudence, industry, eagerness and riches; these things will give our republic power, and when this has been acquired, we will, as the legitimate sons of the Romans, and as imitators of their virtue, maintain it.[51]

In Rinuccini's view, Florence's love of liberty and right to empire were therefore not to be called into question.

However, there can be no doubt that the fundamental text of the period when it comes to situating the modern Florentine republic within the tradition of Roman liberty and imperialism is Leonardo Bruni's *Laudatio Florentinae Urbis* of 1403–04.[52] Written in the same intellectual climate as Rinuccini's *Risponsiva* and Salutati's *Invectiva*, the tract contains many of the claims advanced in these two texts, but Bruni's more consistent and elaborate identification of modern Florence with the ancient Roman republic sets the *Laudatio* apart. According to Bruni, it was an indisputable fact of "utmost importance" that "the Florentine race arose from the Roman people,"[53] the most virtuous and glorious people ever to have existed. The right to lordship over the world, which God originally had bestowed upon the Romans, had now, Bruni proudly declared, been passed on to the Florentine people. This epochal event allowed him, the new, self-styled Cicero, to address his Florentine audience as a race of reborn and resurrected Romans, to whom belonged the right to exercise "dominion over the entire world." According to Bruni, all Florentine wars were thus by definition legitimate and just, since they were fought either in defense of Florentine liberty or in order to regain land that belonged to the free Florentine people by "a certain hereditary right."[54]

[50] Ibid., p. 192. [51] Ibid., p. 193.

[52] The original text of Leonardo Bruni's *Laudatio Florentinae Urbis* is in Hans Baron, *From Petrarch to Leonardo Bruni: Studies in Humanistic and Political Literature* (Chicago: University of Chicago Press, 1968), pp. 232–63; English trans., "Panegyric to the City of Florence," trans. B. G. Kohl, in *The Earthly Republic: Italian Humanists on Government and Society*, eds. B. G. Kohl and R. G. Witt (Philadelphia: University of Pennsylvania Press, 1978), pp. 135–75. References will be to these two editions.

[53] Bruni, *Laudatio*, p. 244 (English trans. p. 149).

[54] Ibid., p. 244: "Quamobrem ad vos quoque, viri Florentini, dominium orbis terrarum iure quodam hereditario ceu paternarum rerum possessio pertinet. Ex quo etiam illud fit, ut omnia bella que a populo Florentino geruntur iustissima sint, nec possit hic populus in gerendis bellis iustitia carere, cum omnia bella pro suarum rerum vel defensione vel recuperatione gerat necesse est, que duo bellorum genera omnes leges omniaque iura permittunt" (English trans. p. 150).

In order to explain how the rights and privileges which the Romans had originally received by divine decree or acquired through display of virtue had come to pass into the possession of the Florentines, Bruni offered a historical perspective on the Florentine people's Roman descent. In the Guelf tradition Florence's Roman origins had, as we have seen, been celebrated in a thoroughly eclectic manner. According to the thirteenth-century *Chronica*, the city had been founded under the aegis of Julius Caesar and rebuilt by the Romans in the sixth century. A republican readaptation of this foundation myth had been initiated in the fourteenth century when Giovanni Villani had linked the second founding of the city by Charlemagne to the granting of communal privileges to the republic of Florence. In the *Laudatio*, Bruni carried this republican reinterpretation of Florence's early history one step further.

After Florence's Roman descent had been called into question by Antonio Loschi, Salutati had researched the archives and classical sources in order to muster support for the city's Roman myth of origin. As a result of these investigations, he came to the conclusion that Florence had indeed been founded by the Romans – not under the auspices of Julius Caesar as had traditionally been assumed, but by a group of veterans from Sulla's army. This meant, in other words, that Florence had been born under the late republic and not during the early days of the empire.[55] While Salutati was content to have confirmed the city's Roman origins, in the *Laudatio* Bruni was to exploit this discovery further, by arguing that Florence had been born "at the very moment when the dominion of the Roman people flourished greatly (*populi Romani imperium maxime florebat*)" and "very powerful kings and warlike nations" were being brought under Roman sway. After centuries of warlike activities, the Roman people had finally put the world around them to rest: "Carthage, Spain, and Corinth were levelled to the ground; all lands and seas acknowledged the rule of these Romans, and these same Romans suffered no harm from any foreign state."[56]

Although Roman liberty and military virtue had been destroyed at the hands of the emperors, the republican spirit had not completely vanished. It had survived in the little Roman colony of Florence and in the heart of the Florentine people. This little Roman offshoot had now grown to maturity and revived the ancient virtues of her great forebear. By successfully emulating their Roman ancestors, the modern Florentines had come to gain

[55] For Salutati's contribution to the reinterpretation of Florence's origins, see Ronald Witt, *Hercules at the Crossroads: The Life, Works, and Thought of Coluccio Salutati* (Durham, NC: Duke University Press, 1983), pp. 246–52.

[56] Bruni, *Laudatio*, p. 245 (English trans. p. 151). On the implications of this passage, see Siegel, "'Civic Humanism' or Ciceronian Rhetoric?" p. 24.

might and glory, and through their achievements in all kinds of activities they had proved themselves to be without equals.[57] What remained for her to do now? Bruni asks. The answer he sets forth is as straightforward as it is revealing: "What greater thing, what more outstanding feat could this city accomplish, or in what way could it better prove that the virtue of its forebears was still alive than by liberating the whole of Italy, by its own efforts and resources, from the threat of servitude?"[58] Florence is thus set to repeat what her Roman ancestors had accomplished in the past: Italian liberty under the auspices of a strong, vigorous and hegemonic republic. Never before in the Florentine tradition had the connection between republican liberty and the move toward empire, growth and expansion, on the one hand, and between monarchy, the loss of liberty and the decline and demise of empire, on the other, been stated with such clarity and force.

THE CONQUEST OF PISA

At the time Bruni composed the *Laudatio*, the Florentine republic was recovering after her protracted war with Milan, which had ended with the opportune death of Giangaleazzo Visconti in the summer of 1402. The following years witnessed the collapse of the Milanese dominion and Florence's return to an aggressive expansionist policy in Tuscany. The republic's drive towards Tuscan hegemony was crowned with partial success when Pisa was conquered in 1406, Cortona acquired in 1411, and Livorno brought under its sway in 1421. Florence now emerged as an imperialist power in its own right, equipped not only with the economic resources of the wealthy merchant families and the banking houses, but also with a powerful ideological support in the form of the city's close, almost obsessive, identification with the triumphant Roman republic of antiquity.

The subjugation of Pisa was arguably the greatest military triumph in the history of the Florentine republic so far. Through this westward expansion Florence gained access to the sea and became one of the leading maritime powers on the peninsula. Michael Mallett has characterized the annexation as "one of the most significant territorial adjustments which took place in Italy during the period of the later Middle Ages."[59] The ninety years of Florentine domination that followed was characterized by an admixture of

57 Bruni, *Laudatio*, p. 251 (English trans. p. 159).

58 Ibid., p. 258: "Nam quid potuit maius, quid preclarius hec civitas edere, aut in qua magis re maiorum suorum virtutem in se conservatam ostendere, quam universa Italia suo labore suisque facultatibus a servitutis periculo liberata?" (English trans. p. 168).

59 Michael Mallett, "Pisa and Florence in the Fifteenth Century: Aspects of the Period of the First Florentine Domination," in *Florentine Studies: Politics and Society in Renaissance Florence*, ed. N. Rubinstein (London: Faber and Faber, 1968), p. 403.

mild repression and moderate benefices. Heavy taxation was imposed on the subject city soon after the conquest in order to finance its administration and the Florentine contingency garrisoned there. In times of external peril, leading Pisans were deported to Florence to prevent rebellion. But the Florentine authorities also devised a policy of benefits. Tax concessions and rent-free housing were introduced to attract foreign settlers to the city. During Lorenzo the Magnificent's reign, an attempt was also made to revive the city's university, the Studio Pisano.[60]

The momentous character of the conquest of Pisa was immediately apparent to the Florentines as attested to by the long series of contemporary patriotic chronicles narrating the events of the war and celebrating the acquisition. One of the first attempts in this genre was the wealthy silk merchant Goro Dati's *Istoria di Firenze*, probably written in 1407.[61] The *Istoria*, which Baron characterized as typical of the new civic humanist outlook, extols Florence's republican liberty and ambition to achieve Tuscan hegemony. Following the tradition from Matteo Villani's *Cronica*, Dati emphasizes the importance of Florence's past adherence to the Guelf cause, defining the Guelfs as defenders of liberty and the Church, and their opponents, the Ghibellines, as men of "an imperial and lordly spirit."[62] In Dati's view, the Florentines are a peace-loving people, who live by friendly trade and take up arms only as a last resort and in order to restore peace.[63] Consequently, they have throughout their history fought their wars in self-defense and in order to preserve their liberty in the face of external aggression. This benign mentality manifested itself after the death of Giangaleazzo in 1402, when the city without further ado could have acquired new territory on the other side of the Apennines, but refrained from doing so, being content to remain within her secure borders. The Florentines' devotion to the principles of justice and the rule of law is proved by the fact that they entered their recent campaign against Pisa, which Dati describes as a "just enterprise," after first having established the legitimacy and lawfulness of their purchase of the city.[64]

In Dati's *Istoria*, the other Tuscan cities offer a sharp contrast. Out of envy (*invidia*) of the prosperous Florentines, they had conspired with foreign powers, and even been prepared to forsake their own liberty, in order to destroy or to hurt their rival. A telling example occurred back in the

[60] Ibid., pp. 413 and 409.

[61] Dati's *Istoria* has recently been republished in Lanza, *Firenze contra Milan*, pp. 211–300. References will be to this edition.

[62] Dati, *Istoria*, p. 266. Cf. M. Villani, *Cronica* IV.77.

[63] Ibid., pp. 227 and 235.

[64] Ibid., pp. 271–72.

Trecento, when the Aretines "acted against themselves" by appointing the Duke of Anjou lord of their city in the hope that he would subjugate "the liberty of Florence and her Commune."[65] The Pisans are similarily said to have subjected themselves to the lordship of the Duke of Milan in order to bring down the Florentines. In Dati's view, this readiness to accept princely rule bespeaks a fundamental defect in the other Tuscans' commitment to republicanism. The shortcomings of Pisan liberty, he implies, were also evident from the way the city was ruled before falling under Florentine domination. Although the city claimed to be a free commune in which all magistracies were filled by Pisan citizens, her form of government was ambiguous, since it included a Captain of the People for life "who could almost be called a lord (*signore*)."[66] As long as this office was vested in the virtuous Pietro Gambacorta, who stood on friendly terms with Florence, this constitutional flaw had remained hidden, but when he withdrew from the political arena and his former chancellor, the ambitious Jacopo d'Appiano, seized control of the city, it had opened the way to tyranny. After Jacopo had placed himself under the protection of the Duke of Milan, the people of Pisa, compelled by fear, granted him unlimited power and appointed him *signore libero con vero e misto impero*.[67]

As a result of Dati's way of representing the internal developments in Pisa prior to Florence's purchase of the city, the conflict comes to stand, not between two free and independent city-states, but between Florentine liberty and Pisan servitude under Milanese tyranny. Only by ignoring a series of less than flattering circumstances can Dati claim that Florentine domination actually had come as a blessing to the Pisans. In his view, not only had it put an end to the horrendous sufferings inflicted on them by the war and the long siege, but it also meant that the Pisans from now on, since they no longer ran the risk of being sold or afflicted by war, would be free to participate in the growth and expansion of Florence, and become prosperous in their own right.[68] The fact that the peace-loving Florentines had been compelled to bestow these benefits on Pisa by force was, from

65 Ibid., p. 222: "E credendo gli Aretini che ei fusse nemico de' Fiorentini, per segni che si poteva così presumere, parve loro tempo da potere nuocere a' Fiorentini: facendo prima contro a loro medesimi con speranza di sottomettere la libertà di Firenze e suo Comune, sottomisono prima sé medesimi a colui che credevano fusse nimico de' Fiorentini e dierono la signoria della città d'Arezzo al sire di Cusì, maliscalco maggiore del Duca d'Angiò, in nome di detto Duca."

66 Ibid., p. 230: "La città di Pisa si diceva esser comune e tutti gli ufici d'essa erano amministrati per i cittadini pisani di quella parte che reggeva, ma aveva un capitano di popolo a vita che si poteva piuttosto dire signore."

67 Ibid., pp. 222, 230 and 236–37.

68 Ibid., pp. 258–59. Cf. Mikael Hörnqvist, "The Two Myths of Civic Humanism," in *Renaissance Civic Humanism Reconsidered*, ed. J. Hankins (Cambridge: Cambridge University Press, 2000), p. 119.

Dati's point of view, a regrettable, but inevitable, consequence of the Pisans' own obstinacy and failure to understand their own good.[69]

One of Dati's principal motives in writing the *Istoria*, there can be no doubt, was to justify Florence's acquistion of Pisa from both a commercial and a moral point of view. The wars had been costly for Florence, the military expenditures heavy and the debts contracted considerable. Would these economic sacrifices now prove fruitful when peace had been accomplished? If we are to believe Dati, the Florentines had pressed for the purchase of the city after recognizing "how much honor and exhaltation would accrue to [them] if they acquired Pisa and became her lord; how much convenience, balance and utility they would have on the commercial side; how eternally secure they would become by not risking being laid siege to anymore; how it would increase their revenues . . ."[70] In this passage, as we can see, Dati brings together three of the catchwords of classical imperialism – security, economic gain and prestige – to legitimate Florence's annexation of Pisa and the cancellation of the last vestige of Pisan liberty.

Within the context of the Florentine tradition into which we are inquiring, the akward coexistence of liberty and expansionism in Dati's *Istoria* needs little explaining. Dati's conventional outlook is also evident from his discussion of Roman liberty and imperialism, which interrupts the narrative of the Pisan–Florentine conflict at the sensitive point where the Pisan revolt against the plans to sell the city to Florence is about to be treated. In Dati's mind, there is no doubt that the world-wide empire the Romans acquired during the republic was just and divinely ordained.[71] By showing piety towards their gods, ruling according to the principle of justice, acting virtuously, and maintaining their ancient customs, the Romans had risen to the status of world rulers. The modern Florentines' love of liberty and hatred of tyranny, he claims, can be explained by the fact that "they are born as the descendants of those Romans who, by rule of liberty (*con reggimento di libertà*), acquired the lordship of the world and established Rome in a state of greater peace, tranquillity and honor than ever was; who, if they were to return to the world today would be the enemies of Caesar and of all

[69] In this regard, the willingness of the people of Montepulciano to accept Florentine rule contrasts sharply with Pisan resistence, see Dati, *Istoria*, pp. 220–21. The Montepulciani are said (ibid., p. 220) to be "tanto devoti de' Fiorentini che non pare abbiano altra anima e cuore."

[70] Ibid., p. 257: "conoscendo quanto onore ed esaltazione seguirebbe a' Fiorentini se acquistassono Pisa e fussono signori, quanto destro e acconcio e utilità n'arebbono nel lato delle mercatantìe, quanta sicurtà sarebbe in perpetuo di non potere essere mai più assediati, quanta utilità delle entrate e dell'uscite."

[71] Ibid., p. 261: "i Romani, per ispazio di tempo di settecento anni, per loro virtù ed eccellenzia di giuste operazioni e per grazia di Dio ebbono soggiogata la maggiore parte di tutta l'universa terra . . ."

those who destroyed that state and its popular government and reduced it to tyranny."[72] While distinguishing between empire understood as a state that successfully expands beyond its original borders, and as a state ruled by an emperor, Dati argues, like Salutati, Bruni, and Rinuccini before him, that the Roman republic's "rule of liberty" had been a direct cause of its acquisitiveness and its rise to world supremacy.

As the cases of Bruni's *Laudatio* and Dati's *Istoria* demonstrate, Florence had in the course of the Milanese and the Pisan wars, inspired by the Roman example, come to develop a new potent ideological identity. Like Roman liberty from which it derived its uniqueness, Florentine liberty was from now on not to be compared to other surrounding "liberties"; it was morally superior, purer, and more refined. Such an exclusive and utterly patriotic view of liberty can ill afford to respect the sovereignty of other cities, states, and peoples. On the contrary, it entails a commitment to empire understood as a defense and a militant extension of true liberty in a hostile world of threatening warlords and tyrants. In concrete terms, it translates into a pursuit of territorial security which justifies the intervention in the political life of neighboring states and the subjugation and annexation of foreign lands.

The Florentine conquest of Pisa also served as the chief source of inspiration for Leonardo Bruni's monumental history of the Florentine people, *Historiae Florentini Populi* (*c.* 1414–29), formally modeled on Livy's Roman history.[73] In his commentary of 1418 on the First Punic War, Bruni attempts to demonstrate that the *imperium populi Romani* had been created by the Roman republic and not by the emperors. Elaborating on this idea in the *Historiae*, he establishes the principle that the good of the republic consists in extending its empire (*imperium augere*), extolling its splendor and glory, and providing for its utility and security.[74] Already in the preface, Bruni unabashedly announces the imperialist program underlying the work, by

[72] Ibid., p. 266: "E questa natura ha quel populo per ragione che sono nati e discesi di que' Romani che, con reggimento di libertà, avevano acquistata la signoria del mondo e posta Roma in pace e riposo e onore più che mai fusse; i quali, se ora tornassono al mondo, sarebbono inimici di Cesare e d'ognuno che guastò quello stato e reggimento popolare e ridusselo a tirannia." For two examples of how Dati explicitly compares events in Florentine history and Florentine policies to Roman precedents, see ibid., pp. 225 and 232.

[73] Cf. Hankins, "The 'Baron Thesis,'" p. 323.

[74] See *The Humanism of Leonardo Bruni: Selected Texts*, eds. G. Griffiths, J. Hankins, and D. Thompson (Binghamton: Center for Medieval and Early Renaissance Studies, 1987), p. 36; Donald J. Wilcox, *The Development of Florentine Humanist Historiography in the Fifteenth Century* (Cambridge, MA: Harvard University Press, 1969), pp. 88–89.

comparing Florence's conquest of Pisa to Rome's ultimate victory over Carthage:

On the top of these events came the capture of Pisa which, whether because its spirit is so different, or because it was a rival power, or because of the outcome of the war, I think I could rightly call a second Carthage. The siege and final conquest, fought with equal obstinacy by victors and vanquished, includes deeds that are so worthy of memory that they appear in no way inferior to the greatest deeds of the ancients that we read about.[75]

This parallelism of Roman and Florentine history runs as a leitmotif through the *Historiae*. The historical trajectories of these two peoples, Bruni implies, teach that the development of free republican institutions at home and territorial expansion abroad are inextricably linked.[76] But while it is true that the domestic liberty of Florence cannot be isolated from the city's fortunes on the battlefield and vice versa, it is equally important to recognize that the conduct of internal and external, or foreign, affairs should be based on different sets of principles. For example, whereas frugality constitutes a virtue in private life and within the sphere of domestic policy, the contrasting virtue of magnificence is at home in the public domain and befits the conqueror. As so often, Bruni's model is the ancient Romans:

The Roman people, our forbears, never would have obtained world empire, if they had been content with the *status quo* and shunned new undertakings and responsibilities. A plan is completely different in its public and private aspects. For in public affairs magnificence is proper, which consists in riches and glory; for private life, modesty and frugality are more appropriate.[77]

Men ought to be expansive in respect to what lies outside the borders of the state, but moderate and contained in relation to what is their own. As we shall see, this was a lesson from Roman history that was to have a strong appeal for Machiavelli as well. Another central aspect of Bruni's work

[75] Quotation from *The Humanism of Leonardo Bruni*: p. 191.

[76] Leonardo Bruni, *History of the Florentine People*, vol. 1, ed. J. Hankins (Cambridge, MA: Harvard University Press, 2001). My presentation follows the general outline in Wilcox, *The Development*, pp. 32–98. For Donato Acciaiuoli's Italian translation of Bruni's *Historiae*, printed for the first time in 1476, see *Istoria Fiorentina di L. Aretino tradotta in volgare da D. Acciaiuoli* (Florence, 1861).

[77] "Populus romanus parens noster nunquam orbis imperium nactus esset, si suis rebus contentus nova coepta impensasque refugisset. Nec sane idem propositum est homini publice et privatim. Nam publice quidem magnificentia proposita est, quae in gloria amplitudineque consistit; privatim vero modestia et frugalitas." English translation in Nancy S. Struever, *The Language of History in the Renaissance: Rhetorical and Historical Consciousness in Florentine Humanism* (Princeton: Princeton University Press, 1970), pp. 137–38.

that draws inspiration from the Roman example, and anticipates Machiavelli's later elaboration, concerns Florence's policy vis-à-vis her neighbors. Like many other Florentines, Bruni viewed the endless conflicts pestering interstate relations in Tuscany as the principal reason for Florence's and the region's vulnerability in the face of foreign aggression. Florence's main objective in the field of foreign policy, Bruni argues, should therefore be the promotion of Tuscan unity.

For this purpose, Bruni adopts a differentiated view of Florence's Tuscan neighbors. As Donald Wilcox has argued, one can in the *Historiae* distinguish between three different categories of neighboring peoples.[78] The first consists of cities that, because of their relative weakness and favorable location, can easily be brought under direct Florentine control. To this group belong the neighboring cities of Prato and Pistoia, which the Florentines had subjugated in a brutal and unscrupulous manner after the ouster of the Duke of Athens in 1343.[79] The principal city of the second category is Pisa, which Bruni, in keeping with the established tradition, portrays as notoriously inimical to the Florentine people. A Ghibelline stronghold with close ties to Milan and a notable commercial rival, Pisa had for more than a century been a constant thorn in the side of Florence. The maritime city had rarely been strong enough to pose a threat on her own, but she had time and again called in outside help and sided with Florence's enemies in territorial conflicts. Consequently, the Florentines had been forced to adopt a rigid and uncompromising policy towards their neighbor.[80]

While Pisa's openly antagonistic stance towards Florence had left the republic with no choice other than total subjugation, the cities belonging to the third category offered greater scope for political maneuvering. These were either too strong or too remote to be easily brought in under the Florentine yoke, but sufficiently friendly to be open to proposals for leagues or alliances. On these grounds, Bruni implies that cities such as Arezzo, Lucca, and Siena should be fraternized and treated as potential allies. The virtue of this policy had been demonstrated most clearly in the case of Arezzo, Bruni's own native town. When the Aretines after the expulsion

78 Wilcox, *The Development*, pp. 84–85.

79 Ibid., p. 85. Whereas Florence had taken Prato by force, she had originally tried to win Pistoia by fraud. But when this attempt had failed as a result of the poor execution of the plan, the republic had gone on to lay siege to the neighbor and to conquer her by force. As Wilcox points out, Bruni in his account of the episode implies that the Florentines' attempt at annexing Pistoia was imprudent, but he nevertheless approves of the final decision to take the neighbor by force, since he believes that the Pistoiese by that time had come to view the Florentines with so much suspicion that they were unlikely to join with them in a league again.

80 Ibid., pp. 85–87.

of the Duke of Athens had proclaimed their independence from Florence, the Florentines had, instead of quenching the rebellion by force, sent an embassy to congratulate them on their regained liberty and to offer them their friendship. As a result, Bruni contends, the Aretines had become more dedicated and more loyal to Florence than they had been previously, when they had been treated like a subject people.[81] When later in chapter 4 we turn to consider Machiavelli's imperialist strategy and his analysis of Florentine imperialism, we will in the program of Bruni's *Historiae* recognize a clear precedent, and a possible source of inspiration.[82]

THE MEDICEAN GOLDEN AGE AND ITS CRITICS

The acquisition of Pisa brought wealth and prestige to Florence, but instead of appeasing her, the success whetted her appetite for territorial growth, power, and security further. The city's great aspirations are forcefully stated in an oration by Stefano Porcari, a citizen of humanist learning who served as Captain of the People in 1427: "And acting in this way [i.e. for the common good] you will see this your most fortunate rule (*imperio*) continually flourish: you will see this broad leadership (*amplissimo principato*) ever enlarge itself: you will see the triumphant name of Florence grow in the world in ever more honored fame, and earn the veneration of all peoples."[83] But the annexation of Pisa did not become the springboard to further expansion as many had hoped or expected. On the contrary, the unsuccessful wars of the 1410s and the 1420s came to have disastrous effects upon the Florentine economy and to contribute to the undermining of the city's republican institutions. Hostilities were renewed with Milan in 1424, but following a series of disappointing performances by their hired

[81] Ibid., p. 87.

[82] The fact that Bruni recommends the Florentines to pursue a policy of fraternization with respect to cities like Arezzo, Siena, and Lucca has induced Hans Baron to conclude that the ideal presented in the *Historiae* is a system of coexisting and independent city-states in Tuscany and Central Italy. See Baron, *In Search of Florentine Civic Humanism*, 1, pp. 46 and 81–82. Donald Wilcox, for his part, argues that the aim of the *Historiae* is to promote the idea of Florentine domination in Tuscany. In support of this reading, Wilcox adduces an oration from the second book of the work, where Florence's plans of purchasing the city of Lucca are discussed. According to Wilcox, Bruni in this speech offers his most explicit advice on the objectives of foreign policy, as he lets the speaker motivate his stance in favor of the purchase: "I confess that I am moved by what men think good: to extend one's border, to increase one's power (*imperium augere*), to extol the splendor and glory of the city, to look after its utility and security" (quoted from Wilcox, *The Development*, pp. 88–89).

[83] "E così facendo vedrete sempre questo vostro fortunatissimo imperio fiorire: vedrete questo amplissimo principato sempre magnificarsi: vedrete il trionfante nome di Firenze crescere nel mondo sempre in fama degnissima, e meritar venerazione di tutti i popoli" (quoted from Weinstein, *Savonarola and Florence*, pp. 58–59).

mercenaries, Florence's hope of success was thwarted.[84] In February 1430, the city embarked upon an expansionist war against the neighboring city of Lucca and its autocratic ruler, Paolo Guinigi. The war resulted in the overthrow of Guinigi and the restoration of the Lucchese republic, but after a decisive setback at San Pietro at the end of the year the Florentines were forced to settle for peace without having achieved their second war aim, the final subjugation of their neighbor.[85]

To the period immediately following these military failures and the instauration of the Medicean regime in 1433 belongs the humanist-statesman Matteo Palmieri's *Vita civile* (1435–40). This dialogue, which marks the final triumph of the new classicized culture over the eclecticism of the previous century, is set at a country estate outside Florence at the time of the plague.[86] Here Franco Sacchetto and Luigi Guicciardini, two young members of the *reggimento*, the unofficial ruling class of the republic, sit down to listen with deference to the collective humanist wisdom of the republic, handed down to them by one of the most renowned statesmen and diplomats of the day, Agnolo Pandolfini. The text invites us to participate in a free flow of classical republican wisdom and learning streaming down from Cicero, "the fountain of eloquence," to the rising generations of future statesmen. The time gap between the modern and the classical worlds does not pose a problem, nor does the breach within the tradition brought about by the advent of Christianity; instead, a next to perfect harmonization of past and present, classical and Christian, Rome and Florence, Latin and vernacular, secular and spiritual, stands before us.

When considering Palmieri's treatment of the subject of war in the third book of the *Vita civile*, it is important that we do not let the paradisiac background of the secluded rural setting and the detached tone of the conversation blind us to the fact that the treatise was written for a didactic and practical purpose, and that its aim was to offer remedies against the ills of the present time. The Roman nature of the teaching is established in a passage, closely modeled on *De Officiis*, in which Palmieri lets Pandolfini

[84] Bayley, *War and Society*, pp. 85–87.

[85] On the Luccan war, see ibid, pp. 100–04; Brucker, *The Civic World*, pp. 494–500. Cf. *The Humanism of Leonardo Bruni*, p. 113.

[86] For general introductions to Palmieri's work, see George M. Carpetto, *The Humanism of Matteo Palmieri* (Rome: Bulzoni, 1984); Claudio Finzi, *Matteo Palmieri dalla "Vita Civile" alla "Città di vita"* (Rome: Giuffrè, 1984). For a good concentrated account of the republicanism of *Vita civile*, see Viroli, *From Politics to Reason of State*, pp. 82–85. Hans Baron has argued (*In Search of Florentine Humanism*, I, p. 125) that the intention of the work was "to recreate the civic attitude of the *De Officiis* in its entirety."

reiterate Cicero's concept of the just war. Republics, we are told, should be equally scrupulous in conducting their wars according to the principles of justice as they are in administering justice for their own citizens. A just war can be waged for three different reasons: to recover lands unjustly occupied by the enemy, to defend oneself, and to avenge a received injury. Moreover, in order to be righteous, the war must be preceded by a formal declaration and fought for the purpose of restoring peace.[87] Leaving the sphere of theory behind, Palmieri goes on to commend the ceremonial and ritual aspects of ancient Roman warfare. Especially praiseworthy, he argues, was the Roman custom of framing the beginning of military enterprises and the conclusions of peace with rituals, oaths, and sacrifices, led by special priests and characterized by "great observance and religious solemnity."[88] Through these ceremonies, the Romans rendered their wars legitimate and inspired confidence in their soldiers. At a point where the question of the compatibility between Christian morality and the pagan art of framing war forces itself upon us, Palmieri breaks off his argument, leaving us guessing whether his praise of this ancient Roman practice should be seen as a recommendation for the present as well.

Palmieri is more explicit about the exemplary status of the Roman republic, when discussing their way of treating subject peoples. According to him, the Romans had preserved all people who surrendered to them or sought their protection. Not only had they defended them "like good fathers" when so needed, they had also welcomed them into their city and granted them citizenship, as in the case of the Volsci, the Tusculans, and the Sabines. The same policy, Palmieri argues, has in modern times been adopted by the Florentines, when they established their rule over the people of Figline in the upper Arno valley: "the people of the stronghold of Figline, being tightly besieged, threw themselves into the arms of the Florentines and sought freely their protection, whereupon they were kindly received by the Florentines and accepted as true citizens and allowed to participate in the government of the republic and in all its high magistrates."[89] This linkage

[87] Matteo Palmieri, *Vita civile* (Florence: Sansoni, 1982), p. 116: "s'elegga sempre la tranquilla pace inanzi alla tribolante guerra; et per ogni tempo si consigli et elegga quella pace che manca di fraude; et le guerre in tal modo si comincino che niuna altra cosa che pace paia cerco per quelle."

[88] Ibid., p. 116: "Grandissime observantie et religiose solennità erano apresso a' gloriosi Romani nel pigliare delle guerri et similemente nel fare le paci, in iustificatione delle quali cose degnissimi sacerdoti erano diputati, da loro nominati 'Fecial.'"

[89] Ibid., p. 130: "gli abitatori del castello di Feghine, essendo strectissimamente assediati, si dierono nelle braccia de' Fiorentini et alla loro fede liberamente ricorsono, onde benignamente ricevuti furono da' Fiorentini per veri cittadini acceptati et in e governi della republica facti partefici di qualunche honorato magistrato."

of ancient Rome and modern Florence is not an isolated instance in *Vita civile*, but pervades the work as a whole.[90] Shortly before the passage just quoted, the figure of Pandolfini comments on the great sacrifices the citizens of ancient republics made for the good of their *patria*. The Fabii, the Torquati, the Decii, the Marcelli, and many other ancient Romans had "no other thing on their mind than the health and the augmentation of the republic (*la salute et acrescimento della republica*) . . . and so ardently were they animated by the amplitude and health of the republic that they on their campaigns perseveringly overcame every difficulty and toil."[91] Their internal unity and virtuous customs allowed them to defeat all their enemies, extend their vast empire, and bring a great part of the world under their sway.[92]

On rare occasions in the past, when the Florentines had been united under the auspices of the Guelf party, they had been able successfully to imitate the ways of their Roman forebears. But as a rule, internal discord had hampered their imperial designs and prevented them from repeating their achievements. This observation prompts Palmieri to vent his frustration over the unfulfilled promises of Florentine territorial growth:

> It is not without tears I recall that the wits and the natural strength of the Florentines originally had been so disposed by God . . . that they, if dissensions and civil wars had not damaged the city from within, would have been more than fit to exercise their power not only in Italy, but also on foreign races outside its borders.[93]

Palmieri's analysis of Florentine history does not share the optimism of the triumphalist visions found in Bruni's *Laudatio* and *Historiae*, but the underlying formula remains the same: civic unity promotes republican liberty and increase of empire, while partisan strife gives rise to loss of

90 Palmieri draws another parallel between ancient Rome and modern Florence when he argues that a native militia serves the aim of territorial expansion better than hired mercenaries: "colle proprie persone feciono acquisti grandissimi, come si vede de' Romani, Cartaginesi, Ateniesi et molti altri. Et similemente nella nostra città, quasi tutto quello si possiede fu colle proprie mani de' nostri antichi padri conquistato," *Vita civile*, p. 186.

91 Ibid., p. 126: "le quali con animi generosi et tanto forti niuna altra cosa aveano nell'animo se non la salute et acrescimento della republica . . . et tanto caldamente erano inanimati alla amplitudine et salute della republica che negli exerciti ogni disagio et qualunche fatica perseverantemente superavano."

92 Ibid., p. 127: "che victoriosamente con armi et bataglie ogni altra potentia abbatterono, et infine il loro amplissimo imperio tanto gloriosamente dilatorono, che grandissima parte de' navicabili mari et quasi tutta l'abitata terra divenne loro sottoposta . . ."

93 Ibid., p. 134: "io non posso sanza lacrime ricordarmi che gl'ingegni et naturali forze de' Fiorentini sono da Dio tanto optimamente disposte a qualunche cosa excellente che, se le dissensioni et guerre civili non avessino drento dalla città quelle ne' proprii danni conferiti, certo non solo in Italia, ma fuori di quella, erano attissimi a dilatare loro signoria sopra le strane generationi."

liberty and a decline in territorial expansion.[94] The main themes of the Florentine tradition are remarkably constant.

The sixty years of Medicean rule that followed on Cosimo de' Medici's return from exile in 1434 did little to alter the traditional view that the republic should aspire to liberty at home and pursue empire abroad. On the whole, however, the Medici regime tended to conceive of the Roman imperialist legacy in cultural rather than in political terms, and to downplay the political and military aspects of the Roman exemplars they continued to quote. Cosimo il Vecchio, who during his life-time was celebrated for defending the liberty of Florence and hailed as *princeps* of the republic, received on his death the title of *Pater Patriae*, father of the country, which the ancient Romans had given to Cicero, Julius Caesar, and Augustus among others. But he was also, and perhaps more importantly with regard to the Florentine tradition we are exploring, celebrated as a Platonic philosopher-ruler, who promoted philosophy in the republic, and based his rule of Florence on the philosophical teaching of the ancients.[95] Cosimo's grandson, Lorenzo the Magnificent, developed this tendency further by supporting various forms of cultural manifestations, including Platonic studies, the staging of public festivals and poetry recitals, where references to Florence's Roman heritage were mixed with elements from the Tuscan vernacular poetic tradition and Neoplatonic lore in a truly eclectic fashion.[96]

The cultural emphasis of this propagandistic program notwithstanding, Medicean apologists were quick to exploit Florence's Roman connection, when justifying the regime's foreign and external policies. The political side of Medicean cultural politics emerges with particular clarity in connection the rebellion of Volterra in 1472.[97] The origin of this conflict can be traced back to 1470, when an alum deposit was discovered in the vicinity of the Florentine subject town of Volterra, and a local consortium was formed to

[94] While the subject of war is of secondary importance in *Vita civile*, which is mainly concerned with matters related to domestic politics and education, it plays a dominant role in Palmieri's *De Captivitate Pisarum*. On this latter work, see Hörnqvist, "Two Myths," pp. 132–41.

[95] On the celebrative writings on Cosimo il Vecchio, see Alison Brown, "The Humanist Portrait of Cosimo de' Medici, Pater Patriae," *Journal of the Warburg and Courtauld Institutes* 24 (1961): 186–222; reprinted in Alison Brown, *The Medici in Florence: The Exercise and Language of Power* (Florence: Olschki, 1992), pp. 3–40.

[96] On Lorenzo the Magnificent's cultural politics, see James Hankins, *Plato in the Italian Renaissance* (2 vols., Leiden: Brill, 1990); Hankins, "Lorenzo de' Medici as Patron of Philosophy," *Rinascimento* 34 (1994): 15–53; Charles Dempsey, *The Portrayal of Love: Botticelli's Primavera and Humanist Culture at the Time of Lorenzo the Magnificent* (Princeton: Princeton University Press, 1992).

[97] On empire as an ideal and an aspiration during the Medicean republic, see Welliver, *Impero fiorentino*, pp. 42–50; Brown, "The Language of Empire"; Emilio Santini, "La *protestatio de iustitia* nella Firenze Medicea del sec. XV," *Rinascimento* 10 (1959), pp. 64, 78 and 91.

exploit the mine. Realizing that his and his family's Italian alum monopoly was threatened, Lorenzo de' Medici succeeded in turning the affair into a political issue after two members of the town's pro-Medicean party had been murdered. The specter of Volterran rebellion was raised and Federigo of Montefeltro, Duke of Urbino, was hired to lead the Florentine intervention. Within a short time, the hilltop town was captured and put to the sack. In retaliation, the Florentines deprived Volterra of her countryside and reduced her to a subject city within their own *contado*.[98]

In a Latin poem, the *Volaterrais*, written shortly after the war, the humanist and Medici eulogist Naldo Naldi offered an epic and propagandistic representation of the revolt and its defeat. After giving a detailed account of the events leading up to the rebellion, Naldi called on the divinities of classical mythology to comment on the revolt and the growth of the Florentine empire under Medicean leadership. In a speech satiated with imperial mystery, Venus expresses her wonder over the audacity of Volterra, which has been daring enough to challenge her Florentine overlords, who, like their worthy ancestors, the ancient Romans, had made a habit of extending their borders. In his reply, Jupiter reassures Venus that Florence will remain the head of Tuscany and that "the empire of the Florentine people (*imperium populi Florentis*)" will continue to grow under its new hero, Lorenzo the Magnificent. As Alison Brown has argued, there can be no, or little, doubt that Naldi's principal aim in writing the *Volaterrais* was to justify "the harsh action taken against Volterra in terms of Florence's growing imperialism."[99]

However, Lorenzo's severe but successful handling of the Volterran revolt could by no means compensate for the fact that under his and his family's rule Florentine territorial expansion had been brought to a near standstill. As republican apologists later were to point out, the sixty years of Medicean power were a period of decline with regard not only to liberty, but to external growth as well. In Francesco Guicciardini's *Dialogue on the Government of Florence* (*c.* 1521–25), Piero Capponi, a leading representative of the new regime that had come into power after the expulsion of the Medici in 1494, is allowed to state the case against the city's former rulers. According to Capponi, the Medicean form of government and the loss of civic spirit resulting from it were directly responsible for Florence's failure to increase

[98] On the revolt of Volterra, see Enrico Fiumi, *L'impresa di Lorenzo de' Medici contro Volterra (1472)* (Florence: Olschki, 1948); Riccardo Fubini, *Quattrocento fiorentino: politica, diplomazia, cultura* (Pisa: Pacini, 1996), pp. 123–39. On Florence's rule of Volterra in general, see Lorenzo Fabbri, "Patronage and its Role in Government: The Florentine Patriciate and Volterra," in *Florentine Tuscany*, ed. Connell, pp. 225–41.

[99] Brown, "The Language of Empire," p. 44. For the *Volaterrais*, see Naldi Naldii Florentini, *Bucolica volaterrais hastiludium carmina varia*, ed. W. L. Grant (Florence: Olschki, 1974).

her dominion after the glorious conquest of Pisa in 1406. In what appears to be a direct application of the Sallustian interpretation of Roman history to the Florentine development, Capponi denounces the Medici for their inability to provide for one of the two fundamental ends of the republic, acquisition and territorial expansion:

> The explanation for this can only be that before the Medici, all the city's prowess, all its vigour in the field of foreign affairs, was devoted to its greatness. Thinking they were acting for themselves, the citizens were bolder in agreeing to help their native city with money and with everything they could. Thus they increased the dominion (*augumentorono el dominio*) and in times of crisis and serious danger were very successful in defending their freedom and honour; whereas afterwards we have scarcely increased it at all and we have lost reputation and standing in every little war.[100]

To Capponi, it would seem, internal liberty and external empire were two interrelated phenomena, on the basis of which the republic's health and vigor could be judged. In his view, Medicean Florence had failed this test. Rather than being a Golden Age, as Medicean eulogists claimed, it had been a dark era of decline, when liberty as well as the pursuit of empire had fallen into neglect.

THE RETURN OF EMPIRE

The invasion by Charles VIII of France in the fall of 1494 brought sixty years of Medici rule and almost ninety years of Florentine domination over Pisa to an end. The following years saw the meteoric rise and fall of Girolamo Savonarola, the apocalyptic preacher of San Marco. Dominating Florentine politics from the pulpit of the cathedral, the Dominican exhorted the Florentines to assume their divinely appointed role in the general purification and salvation of Italy and of the Church. For Savonarola, the reformation of Florence's republican constitution after the overthrow of the Medici was a divine work, which had to be performed by men purged of sin and pure in hearts and spirits. If the Florentines, whose devotion to republicanism had "become habitual and fixed in their minds," could bring about such a spiritual and constitutional reformation, he argued, immense riches and heavenly glory awaited them on the other side of the coming scourge.[101] While the Pope and the city of Rome would be castigated for their sinful

[100] Francesco Guicciardini, *Dialogo e discorsi del reggimento di Firenze* (Bari: Laterza, 1932), p. 89; English translation in *Dialogue on the Government of Florence*, trans. Alison Brown (Cambridge: Cambridge University Press, 1994), p. 87.

[101] On this aspect of Savonarola's thought, see Pocock, *The Machiavellian Moment*, pp. 109–12.

living, Florence was destined to be spared and to emerge as the future center of a spiritually renewed world.

In his proposal for a constitutional reform, *Treatise on the Constitution and Government of the City of Florence*, Savonarola identifies four virtues upon which good government should be based: fear of God, love of the common good, brotherly love, and justice. Commenting on the divine rewards bequeathed to those who pursue these noble ends, he repeatedly brings up the example of the ancient Roman empire. According to Savonarola, one of the reasons the Romans were so successful in expanding their empire was because they had cherished the common good of their city. As a consequence, God had "rewarded them with temporal goods corresponding to their virtue," and "caused the common good of their city to grow and extended their empire over the whole earth."[102] The second reason for the Romans' political accomplishments was their love for each other. From a divine point of view, this love constituted a "good and natural charity" which had induced God to bestow temporal rewards on them and to increase their power. A third explanation of the Roman world empire was their just rule. For God, we are told, rewards those who rule according to justice by increasing their empire. Having thus extolled the ancient Romans, Savonarola goes on to exhort the modern Florentines to follow their example. If the Florentines were to exercise the four virtues mentioned above, they would be "blessed with many spiritual and temporal blessings," among which would be growing power and imperial greatness. As we can see, also in Savonarola's millenarian script, republican liberty and territorial expansion came together in an imperialist fantasy inspired by the example of the ancient Roman republic.[103]

In the light of Savonarola's promises, it is easy to see how the new Savonarolan regime's failure to regain possession of Pisa contributed to tarnish the Dominican's reputation and hasten his downfall. The Pisan question, which we will consider in more detail in chapter 4, came to top the political agenda in Florence for well over a decade. When the maritime city was finally recovered in the summer of 1509, the enterprise was hailed by local commentators as an epochal event in the history of Florence. The contemporary historian Bartolomeo Cerretani reports a speech by Piero Soderini following the reconquest, in which the Gonfalonier for life

[102] Girolamo Savonarola, "Treatise on the Constitution and Government of Florence," text in English translation in *Humanism and Liberty: Writings on Freedom from Fifteenth-Century Florence*, ed. R. N. Watkins (Columbia: University of South Carolina Press, 1978), pp. 231–60.

[103] See Weinstein, *Savonarola and Florence*, pp. 114–17. Cf. Piero di Marco Parenti, *Storia fiorentina*, vol. I (Florence: Olschki, 1994), pp. 156–57.

rehearses the traditional themes of liberty and empire. Having expressed his and his compatriots' great joy over the recovery of the seaport, the Gonfalonier went on to address Florence's prospects for the future: "If ever there was an opportunity to make the city great, this is the one; because now in Italy there remains no republic or empire more potent than ours . . . Thus, it is in your hands to make this republic and this empire great, which can not be done without the observance of justice." If the city were to appoint good and just magistrates to handle her external affairs, that is, the administration of the dominion, her liberty would become great; if she acted otherwise, she would meet the same fate as the arrogant Venetians, who had recently lost more than a tenth of their mainland empire. The speech ends with an exhortation: "Regain hold of your spirits, revive your minds and your wills in order to make this precious liberty great."[104] The key terms of Soderini's speech – *imperio*, *grande*, *libertà*, and *iustitia* – had, as we have seen, a long and illustrious tradition of belonging together. Through the exercise of justice, or an appearance of justice, the Gonfalonier holds, Florence can make her empire and her liberty great, but without justice there will be no liberty and no empire. At the core of Soderini's speech, it would appear, is an expanisionist and imperialist notion of liberty inscribed in the catch phrase *fare grande questa libertà*.

When Machiavelli in his *Discourses on Livy* (*c.* 1514–18) lays down the basic tenet of Roman and Florentine republicanism, he draws on and summarizes this more than century-long tradition: "a city that lives free has two ends – one to acquire, the other to maintain itself free."[105] This dual purpose is grounded in human nature, he claims, because there are two kinds of men, or humors: those who desire not to be oppressed, and those who desire to command. The first of these two categories Machiavelli calls the people (*popolo*), the second, the great (*grandi*).[106] This distinction between the people and the great was later picked up and given a new twist by Guicciardini in his *Dialogue*. Here the figure of Pagolantonio Soderini, speaking in favor of a popular form of government, claims that all men have a "natural appetite" for liberty and a "horror" of servitude. For this reason, he argues, popular rule is the best and the most natural regime, since "one should prefer what satisfies one's nature better, to its opposite."[107] To this, the oligarchically inclined Bernardo del Nero objects that the word

104 Bartolomeo Cerretani, *Storia fiorentina* (Florence: Olschki, 1994), pp. 380–81.

105 *Discorsi* 1.29, p. 262: "Perché, avendo una città che vive libera duoi fini, l'uno lo acquistare, l'altro il mantenersi libera, conviene che nell'una cosa e nell'altra per troppo amore erri."

106 See *Il principe* 9.

107 Guicciardini, *Dialogo*, p. 34 (English trans., p. 33).

"liberty" is often used "more as a disguise and an excuse by those who want to conceal their cupidity and ambition than because men in fact have a natural desire for it." On the basis of this observation, Bernardo concludes that "men have a natural desire to dominate and be superior to others," and that "there are normally very few people who love liberty so much that if they had a chance to make themselves lords or superiors to others they would not do so willingly." This desire to dominate and to command causes problems in a republic, since men often "try to obtain lordship" not only "over neighboring lands and states," but also "among those who form part of the same body."[108] For Bernardo, imperialism and tyranny are thus intimately related, both phenomena deriving from the same natural desire for power.

What is Machiavelli's position on this crucial issue? Like the figure of Bernardo del Nero, he considers human nature to be acquisitive and prone to domination. On a closer scrutiny, his frequently made distinction between the great, who desire to command, and the people, who wish not to be oppressed, is also more apparent than real. In *Discourses* II.2, for example, he claims that the love of liberty permeating republics should be seen as the other, reverse side of free men's desire for territorial and economic expansion. Citizens love their republican liberty because the republic offers greater prospects of acquisition than the principality. Conversely, the republic's acquisitive character derives from its free form of government and free way of life. This is one of the fundamental lessons Roman history teaches:

> It is an easy matter to understand the origin of this love for a free way of life (*vivere libero*) among peoples, for experience shows that cities have never enlarged their dominion nor increased their wealth except while they have lived in liberty. It is truly a marvellous thing to consider to what greatness (*grandezza*) Athens arrived in the space of one hundred years after she freed herself from the tyranny of Pisistratus, but, above all, it is even more marvelous to consider the greatness (*grandezza*) Rome reached when she freed herself from her kings.[109]

To Machiavelli the early Roman republic's rapid growth and the love republican citizens experience for their free form of government testify to one and

108 Ibid., p. 37 (English trans., pp. 35–36).

109 *Discorsi* II.2, p. 331: "E facil cosa è conoscere donde nasca ne' popoli questa affezione del vivere libero: perché si vede per esperienza le cittadi non avere mai ampliato né di dominio né di ricchezza, se non mentre sono state in libertà. E veramente maravigliosa cosa è a considerare a quanta grandezza venne Atene per spazio di cento anni poiché la si liberò dalla tirannide di Pisistrato. Ma sopra tutto maravigliosissima è a considerare a quanta grandezza venne Roma, poiché la si liberò dai suoi re."

the same thing: human nature is, if allowed to develop in liberty, expansive, acquisitive, and imperialist.

Far from being two contrary or separate values, liberty and acquisition are thus inextricably connected; they lend each other mutual support, and they constitute together the nerve center of the healthy republic. When one of these categories is neglected, the other is bound to suffer as well. When men's desire to dominate is turned inward, tyranny results. But instead of quenching this natural drive to power, the task of the prudent statesman should be to direct it outward, towards the pursuit of empire, territorial growth, greatness, and glory.[110] What Machiavelli proposes in *The Prince* and the *Discourses* is an imperialist strategy and a constitutional arrangement in which the great and the people, the acquisitive and the security-seeking, can come together and collaborate for the common good of the *patria*. As we can see, this view of the republic as having a dual nature and a double end – desiring to maintain its liberty, on the one hand, and to acquire empire, on the other – situates Machiavelli firmly within a tradition of Florentine imperial republicanism dating back to the middle of the fourteenth century.

The prevailing orthodoxy within the historiography of Quattrocento humanism and Florentine republicanism bids us to view liberty and empire as two opposing, incompatible or theoretically unrelated ideals, or principles. This contraposition, or separation, of two concepts, which in the theoretical and diplomatic writings of the Florentine Renaissance were frequently combined, remains one of the most enduring fictions produced by Hans Baron and his many followers. Baron's categorical opposition of liberty and self-defense, on the one hand, and tyranny and imperialism, on the other, gives a good, if somewhat simplified, account of the position of a Florentine Guelf like Matteo Villani, but a false picture of the general outlook of Salutati, Bruni, Palmieri, Savonarola, and Machiavelli. In reality, the Florentine humanists of the early fifteenth century departed from the pieties of the Trecento commune in a more radical way than Baron wished to acknowledge. Inspired by the example of the ancient Roman republic and its notion *imperium populi Romani*, the civic humanists, spearheaded by Leonardo Bruni, appropriated on behalf of the Florentine republic the

[110] Although Machiavelli acknowledges that there exist two different modes of acquisition, trade and territorial expansion, he does not present commerce or peaceful exchange between independent states as a tenable alternative to the pursuit of territory and empire. In his zero-sum world, commerce is also a form of imperialism, based on the general assumption that "il fine della republica è enervare ed indebolire per accrescere il corpo suo tutti gli altri corpi," *Discorsi* II.2, p. 335.

title to *imperium*, understood not only as sovereignty and freedom from papal and imperial overlordship, but as the right to exercise dominion, or empire, over other peoples as well.

This chapter has allowed us to see that Machiavelli's Janus-faced republic, which aims at preserving liberty at home and pursuing empire abroad, belongs to a more than century-old tradition of Florentine imperial republicanism. Inspired by the Roman example, Machiavelli came, like Bruni and the other civic humanists before him, to view empire as an attribute of republican liberty, to be placed alongside justice, the common good and the equality of citizenship. But whereas the civic humanist ideology in general, and Bruni's *Laudatio* in particular, had rested on the claim that the Roman republican legacy was a Florentine birthright, Machiavelli nurtured no such idle beliefs. For him, the Roman model was just that – a model. As such, it could be picked up and used by anyone, by the French, by the Venetians, by Cesare Borgia, by the Swiss, or by the Florentines. Quick to exploit for rhetorical and strategical purposes his compatriots' deeply felt identification with the ancient Romans, Machiavelli made no secret of his view that the title of the "New Romans" could be earned only by hard toil and by great deeds. How he went about persuading his fellow citizens about the need to adopt a truly Roman outlook in politics and military affairs will be the subject of the next chapter.

CHAPTER 3

The natural desire of states

> È cosa veramente molto naturale e ordinaria desiderare di acquistare: e sempre, quando li uomini lo fanno, che possano, saranno laudati o non biasimati . . .
>
> Niccolò Machiavelli

In his essay, "Of the True Greatnesse of Kingdomes and Estates," Francis Bacon comments on the necessity of surrounding wars of conquest with a frame of legitimacy. Even though territorial expansion is a natural objective for states, he argues, military aggression needs to be justified, because "there is that Justice imprinted, in the Nature of Men, that they enter not upon Wars (whereof so many Calamities doe ensue) but upon some, at least Specious, Grounds and Quarrels." To overcome the human disposition to shun war and violence, states that desire to grow and make acquisitions should equip themselves with "those Lawes or Customes, which may reach forth unto them, just Occasions (as may be pretended) of Warre." They should, in other words, order themselves internally so that their statutes and conventions may provide the legitimating grounds that natural law refuses to supply. The ancient Romans, who well understood this necessity, never waged wars merely for the sake of extending their territory, or for the honor of their consuls, but took care to fashion themselves as the defenders of justice and liberty. They developed a great sensitivity to "Wrongs, either upon Borderers, Merchants, or Politique Ministers," and a remarkable swiftness in giving "Aids and Succours, to their Confederates." According to Bacon, the exceptional growth of ancient Rome could be explained by the fact that the Romans were always easy to provoke and quick to take up arms for the sake of high and incontestable principles.[1]

There is undoubtedly a great deal of truth in Bacon's cynical, but rather witty, account of the Romans' instrumental conception of the framing of war. Roman expansionism, it is widely acknowledged, progressed behind

[1] Sir Francis Bacon, *The Essayes of Counsels, Civill and Morall* (Oxford: Clarendon Press, 1985), p. 96.

an elaborate, highly regulated and meticulously attended façade of justice, divine command, search for peace, and defense of the liberty of the *patria*.[2] In contrast to the Greeks, who tended to conceive of warfare in ethical and philosophical terms, the Romans defined peace (*pax*) as a contractual relationship between two parties, and endeavored to contain war within a juridical framework.[3] In their view, a state might lawfully resort to armed force after having suffered an offense that violated the contract of peace, and when diplomacy and all other peaceful options for resolving the conflict had been exhausted. Having arrived at that point, the Romans traditionally sent out one of their *fetiales*, or fetial priests, who in an elaborate and prolonged ritual, invoking Jupiter and the borders of the Roman state, upon crossing the borders of the offending nation announced Rome's desire to recover her damage. If satisfaction was not rendered within thirty-three days, a formal declaration of war was made against the enemy through the Senate and the *fetiales*.[4] When all these legal, ritual, and religious rules, regulations, and constraints had been observed, the Romans felt free to take up arms under the pretext that the war they entered was just (*bellum justum*) and divinely sanctioned (*bellum pium*).

The most authoritative definition of the just war was set forth by Cicero in *De Republica* (lost during the Renaissance, but available through numerous references in Augustine) and *De Officiis*. According to the Roman statesman, three causes were required to make a war just. First, it had to be occasioned by a need to avenge an injury; second, it should result from a provocation by the adversary; and finally, it needed to be preceded by a formal declaration of war. In *De Officiis*, Cicero added that a war should be used as a last resort only, since the sole legitimate excuse for taking up arms is the desire to live in peace.[5]

The Roman strategy of framing war appears to have been based on two principal objectives. On the one hand, it served to make Roman

[2] On the imperialism of the Roman republic in general, see Ernst Badian, *Roman Imperialism in the Late Republic* (Ithaca: Cornell University Press, 1968); William V. Harris, *War and Imperialism in Republican Rome 327–70* BC (Oxford: Clarendon Press, 1979); Michael W. Doyle, *Empires* (Ithaca: Cornell University Press, 1986), pp. 82–103. For a brief and succinct account, see also Michael Crawford, *The Roman Republic* (London: Fontana, 1978), pp. 46–48.

[3] On the Roman conception of the just war, see Frederick H. Russell, *The Just War in the Middle Ages* (Cambridge: Cambridge University Press, 1975), pp. 16–39.

[4] On the *fetiales*, see Livy XXX.43.9 and XXXVI.3.7.

[5] Cicero, *De Officiis* I.11.36; English translation by W. Miller (1913; Cambridge, MA: Harvard University Press, 1990). It is worth noting that Cicero shortly afterwards, still in connection with the *bellum justum*, speaks of wars "fought out of supremacy (*imperio*) and glory (*gloria*)" as lacking these "righteous grounds" (ibid., I.12.38). Even so, his argument seems to imply that these types of wars can also be made just, or to appear just, if conducted in a just and upright manner.

expansionism appear legitimate in the eyes of the Roman populace, who were expected to provide the soldiers for the campaigns, and in those of their neighbors and their actual, or potential, allies, on whose support they depended. On the other hand, it provided the Roman state with a conceptual, legal, and ritual mean of containment, which enabled the city to protect the peaceful sphere of the *urbe* from the pollution associated with war.[6] Having been in force throughout the republic, the system lost much of its rationale with the coming of the principate. With Roman world hegemony firmly established, and with the emperors exercising full and unlimited authority in matters of war and peace in their capacity of *princeps*, Rome experienced no, or little, need to legitimize her policy of conquest, and the Roman art of framing war was reduced to its external and ceremonial aspects. After the fall of Rome, however, it came to serve as an important source of inspiration for the theory of just war developed by Christian theologians and Renaissance humanists. Cicero's principles were commented on by Augustine, revived and elaborated by Thomas Aquinas, and restated in unmodified form in the Florentine vernacular by Matteo Palmieri in the 1430s.[7]

But the continuity between the classical and the Christian conceptions of the just war should not be overemphasized. For in contrast to the ancient Romans, who made a habit of using the ideals of the legitimate war to disguise their imperialist ends, Christianity and its custodian, the Papacy, came from early on to regard the preservation and the restoration of peace as one of their principal moral and political concerns.[8] Christ himself is in Matthew 26:52 recorded to have exhorted his followers to embrace pacifism and to put up their swords, because "all they that take the sword shall perish with the sword." In Romans 12:17–18, Paul elaborates on this pacifist ideal by claiming that good Christians should "not repay anyone evil for evil" and should seek to "live at peace with everyone." The Christian believer, contrary to what Cicero had taught, should not avenge himself, but preserve his own peace and learn to forgive in order to conquer. In *City of God*, Augustine condemns the warlike Romans for their devotion to worldly glory, and their passion for dominion and empire.[9] In keeping with

[6] Cf. H. H. Scullard, *Festivals and Ceremonies of the Roman Republic* (London: Thames and Hudson, 1981), p. 213.

[7] On Augustine's influence on the Christian conception of the just war, see Russell, *The Just War*, pp. 16–39. Aquinas based his own definition of the just war on three criteria: legitimate authority, a just cause, and right intention. See Thomas Aquinas, *Summa Theologiae*, II.2, Qu. 40. For Palmieri's account of Cicero's theory, see Matteo Palmieri, *Vita civile*, (Florence: Sansoni, 1982), pp. 115–16.

[8] On this aspect of the Roman ideology, see especially Harris, *War and Imperialism*.

[9] See especially Augustine, *De Civitate Dei*, bk. v, ch. 12.

this tradition, medieval theorists continued to regard peaceful coexistence as the natural condition of man, and to view military conflicts within the *Respublica Christiana* as an anomaly and as a form of civil war. To dissuade states and rulers from resorting to arms, they invoked the traditional Christian virtues of charity, justice, and compassion, and kindled their belief in divine punishment and retribution.[10] As a rule, divine presence was required when Christian rulers should decide upon matters of war and peace. The promulgation of peace treatises was often staged at religious celebrations, when solemn oaths were taken on the Scripture or on a relic, and official documents signed, usually initiated by invocations of the Lord, the Virigin Mary, or some other holy person. Should such an oath be broken, it was considered a crime not only against men, but against God and the Church as well.[11]

However, this was a period of rapid and radical change in Italy in general and Florence in particular, when men began to question their inherited beliefs and cultural values. After the French invasion of 1494 and the start of the Italian wars, it was painfully clear to many Italians that there existed a specific logic of war, which had little to do with the idealist rhetoric of the preceding century. It now also became exceedingly difficult to invoke the military might of the ancient Romans without simultaneously openly, or indirectly, criticizing the present state of Italian political and military affairs. In light of the horrors of the wars even divine providence began to appear problematic. To many, it seemed as if God had either decided to vent his wrath on the Italians by letting the violence of the last days descend upon the country, or taken his hand from the peninsula completely. The times of the early Christians, when faith had been so ardent that the mere sign of the cross had been sufficient to cure diseases, seemed to have become very distant indeed. Signs of unbelief were abundant and spreading. The sacred things seemed to have gone cold, Machiavelli has the priest, Father Timoteo, say in *La mandragola*,[12] and the philosopher Pietro Pomponazzi similarly noticed that "everything today is cold in our religion and there are

10 Joycelyne G. Russell, *Peacemaking in the Renaissance* (London: Duckworth, 1986), pp. 3–4.

11 Russell, *Peacemaking*, p. 21. Cf. Richard C. Trexler, *Public Life in Renaissance Florence* (Ithaca: Cornell University Press, 1994), pp. 125–26. On the religious piety of the Italian *condottieri*, see Michael Mallett, "The Condottiere," in *Renaissance Characters*, ed. E. Garin (Chicago: University of Chicago Press, 1991), p. 42. On the conscience of Renaissance princes, see D. M. Bueno de Mesquita, "The Conscience of the Prince," in *Art and Politics in Renaissance Italy: British Academy Lectures*, ed. G. Holmes (Oxford: Oxford University Press, 1993), pp. 159–83.

12 Niccolò Machiavelli, *La mandragola*, p. 159: "lo mi ricordo esservi cinquecento imagine, e non ve ne sono oggi venti; questo nasce da noi, che non le abbiamo saputa mantenere la reputazione . . . Ora non si fa nulla di queste cose, e po' ci maravigliamo se le cose vanno fredde!"

no more miracles."[13] Attributing the unprecedented violence of the wars to the great sins committed by the Italians, the Florentine chronicler Piero Vaglienti bemoaned the fact that many of his compatriots had begun to deny the existence of a transcendent reality beyond the human intellect.[14]

It is against this background that the extraordinary development that political thought underwent in Florence during the first decades of the Cinquecento must be understood. For all the protagonists of the intellectual revolution we are inquiring into here – Niccolò Machiavelli, Francesco Guicciardini, and Francesco Vettori – the striking contrast between the realities of contemporary warfare and Chistian idealism serves as an important point of departure. The fact that war plays such an important role in their thought can in part be explained by their professional status, for besides being public servants, diplomats, political theorists, and historians, they were all military men as well.[15] Machiavelli was, of course, instrumental in setting up the Florentine militia in 1506, and experienced what could be described as the crowning moment of his chancery career in connection to Florence's recovery of Pisa in 1509; Vettori was appointed "commissario generale sopra la genti d'armi" on the eve of the Medici's return to the city in 1512;[16] and Guicciardini served in the 1520s as commissioner general for the papal army. Bearing in mind the military predicament of Florence and Italy at the time, and taking these writers' first-hand experience of military matters into account, we should not be surprised to find that they in their political thought came to give unprecedented scope to factors such as force, deceit, and deception, which had traditionally been associated more or less exclusively with military affairs.[17] In their eyes, war was not an anomaly external to politics, but an integral aspect of the political relations between, and within, states.

[13] As quoted in Eugenio Garin, *Astrology in the Renaissance: The Zodiac of Life* (London: Routledge and Kegan Paul, 1983), p. 103.

[14] Piero Vaglienti, *Storia dei suoi tempi 1492–1514* (Pisa: Nistri-Lischi e Pacini Editori, 1982), p. 3.

[15] On Francesco Vettori, see Rosemary Devonshire Jones, *Francesco Vettori: Florentine Citizen and Medici Servant* (London: Athlone Press, 1972); John M. Najemy, *Between Friends: Discourses of Power and Desire in the Machiavelli–Vettori Letters of 1513–1515* (Princeton: Princeton University Press, 1993), pp. 71–82.

[16] Ibid., pp. 86–87.

[17] In classical literature, war and politics were generally viewed as two distinct and separate spheres of activity. Plato and Aristotle treat military affairs in their political works, but only as a topic of secondary importance. Xenophon's *Cyropaedia* is a work on warfare, but only in a very limited sense a book on politics. The same can be said of most works on warfare by Roman writers. Vegetius, Frontinus, and Modestus all focus on the technical aspects of warfare, while leaving its political implications largely unattended. The exceptions to this general rule are the historians, both Greek and Roman, who tend to view domestic politics and foreign war as interrelated. Of ancient historians, Polybius is the one who probably comes closest to being defined as a political theorist.

This chapter examines how Machiavelli in his diplomatic writings and theoretical works addresses, challenges, and seeks to reshape the ideological conventions governing the view of expansionist warfare in contemporary Florence. While in the preceding chapter we were concerned with the ideological context of Machiavelli's political thought, we shall here explore his work in relation to the intermediary level of ideological manipulation, situated between the ideological and rhetorical levels of interpretation. To rephrase the problem in the terms of the methodological discussion of chapter 1, our present concern is with the applied, or rhetorical, aspect of Machiavelli's ideological intention. Our focus will be on the Florentine writer's engagement with two aspects of the ideological context, to which Skinner, Pocock, and their many followers have paid little attention: the classical and Christian theory of the just, or legitimate, war, on the one hand, and the doctrine of the middle way dominating contemporary Florentine foreign policy thinking, on the other.[18] These notions, and the ideological outlooks they represented, we shall argue, constituted two of the principal mental obstacles that Machiavelli would have to overcome, if he were to succeed in persuading the rulers of Florence, present or future, to adopt the imperialist program set forth in *The Prince* and the *Discourses*. As we in the course of this chapter shall see, this intellectual, rhetorical, and political project can be traced back to Machiavelli's chancery days and his diplomatic writings, attesting to the remarkable continuity of his thought.

In the preceding chapter, we considered how Florentine writers from the Dugento to the early Cinquecento used and developed a series of legitimatory devices to bolster the republic's claim to legitimacy, and to excuse military aggression and expansionism. In examining how Machiavelli's work relates to this tradition, we will concentrate on three of the most important elements of this justificatory rhetoric: divine sanction, the quest for peace, and the just war.

IN THE NAME OF GOD

Machiavelli's well-documented claim that Christian ethics cannot serve as a viable guideline for worldly rulers contrasts sharply with the views of predecessors such as Petrarch, Salutati, and Savonarola, but it was not without

[18] John Pocock, in *The Machiavellian Moment: Florentine Political Thought and the Atlantic Tradition* (Princeton: Princeton University Press, 1975), p. 163, holds that Machiavelli's originality "is that of a student of delegitimized politics," but takes the sting out of this claim by arguing that, in Machiavelli's view, longevity and custom can provide a ruler with legitimacy (see ibid., pp. 158–59 and 177).

precedent. A secular view of politics had begun to emerge in Florence already during the first period of Medici rule, when the saying that states cannot be ruled by pater nosters, attributed to Cosimo il Vecchio, gained wide currency.[19] This worldly outlook is also evident from the writings of Leonardo Bruni, who discusses politics and military affairs in a classicizing manner with few, if any, references to Christian beliefs and morality. But Machiavelli's and his contemporaries' open, or thinly veiled, attacks on Christian idealism and its detrimental effects on the political life, and their predilection for portraying themselves as skeptics, or unbelievers, set them apart from the preceding tradition.[20]

In a remarkable letter to Machiavelli of 27 June 1513, Francesco Vettori compares the relative merits of the Turkish and the contemporary Christian rulers. Distinguishing between a secular reason of state, here represented by the Turkish sultan, most certainly "a man of war and an excellent captain," who has "made government his end" (*ha posto il fine suo nel regnare*), and a Christian way of conducting politics, consisting of endless peace talks and the signing of accords, Vettori suggests that the political culture of the infidels is superior to that of Christianity.[21] Machiavelli elaborates on this idea in chapter 15 of *The Prince*, where he claims that a ruler who all the time tries to be a good Christian is bound to come to ruin in a world where the wicked outnumber the good. Therefore, Machiavelli maintains, "it is necessary for a prince, if he wants to maintain himself, to learn to be able not to be good, and to use and refrain from using this quality, according to necessity."[22] A similar view is expressed in Francesco Guicciardini's *Dialogue*, where the figure of Bernardo del Nero argues that the ruler at times must renounce piety and goodness (*usare la pietà e la*

[19] On numerous occasions, Savonarola explicitly challenges this outlook. Machiavelli's discussion of Savonarola's example in *Il principe* 6 should most probably be seen in connection to this debate.

[20] For a good example, see the correspondence between Machiavelli and Guicciardini in May 1521, in Niccolò Machiavelli, "Lettere," in *Opere*, ed. C. Vivanti (3 vols., Turin: Einaudi, 1997–), II, pp. 371–79 [hereinafter *Lettere*]. Cf. John Monfasani's characterization of the Quattrocento humanists: "If we understand a Renaissance neo-pagan to have been someone who no longer considered himself a Christian and who embraced instead what he believed to be a specifically pagan world view, then I know of no Italian humanist whom present-day scholarship would confidently label a neo-pagan," "Platonic Paganism in the Fifteenth Century," in *Reconsidering the Renaissance: Papers from the Twenty-First Annual Conference*, ed. M. A. di Cesare (Binghamton, NY: Center for Medieval and Early Renaissance Studies, 1992), p. 46.

[21] Vettori's letter can be found in Machiavelli, *Lettere*, p. 267.

[22] *Il principe* 15, p. 159: "perché uno uomo che voglia fare in tutte le parte professione di buono, conviene che ruini in fra tanti che non sono buoni. Onde è necessario, volendosi uno principe mantenere, imparare a potere essere non buono e usarlo e non usarlo secondo la necessità." The translation here is from Niccolò Machiavelli, *The Prince*, trans. H. Mansfield (Chicago: University of Chicago Press, 1985), p. 61.

bontà) and resort to cruelty and unscrupulousness (*usi la crudeltà e la poca conscienza*), since it is impossible to act politically and "live according to the practices of the world without offending God" (*male si può vivere secondo el mondo sanza offendere Dio*).[23]

This new political pragmatism is most evident in connection to military affairs. For Machiavelli and his contemporaries, victory in war does not depend on whether the struggle is just or unjust, divinely sanctioned or not, fought for the sake of peace or out of ambition. Instead, the determining factors in war, Guicciardini claims, are prudence, force, and good fortune (*la prudenza, le forze e la buona fortuna*). For Machiavelli, the key to military success is a healthy and competitive political culture, which gives priority to military discipline and organization, and holds individual valor and great deeds in esteem. When religious devotion and belief in the righteousness of the cause enter the early Cinquecento theorists' writings on war, they are generally assigned an instrumental or strategic role. If cleverly used, Guicciardini claims, "the idea that God gives victory to just campaigns" (*la opinione che Dio dia vittoria alle imprese giuste*) can dramatically affect the outcome of a battle by making the soldiers "ardent and obstinate" in a way that rational arguments and ordinary, human persuasion cannot.[24] Machiavelli repeatedly shows that, by surrounding the battle with good augury and by using various rhetorical devices to make the war *appear* divinely sanctioned, or legitimate, shrewd military captains have turned the blind and irrational force of religious faith into an effective source of motivation, heightening the soldiers' morale and inducing them to fight with greater determination.

Machiavelli's prime example in this regard is, of course, the ancient Romans. They interpreted their religion "according to virtue" and the principles of the active life, and contrived a number of superstitious beliefs based on portents and auspices, which could readily be invoked for political and military purposes. In the *Discourses*, Machiavelli pays special attention to the poultry-diviners (*pullarii*), who followed the Roman army on its

23 Francesco Guicciardini, *Dialogo e discorsi del Reggimento di Firenze* (Bari: Laterza, 1932), pp. 162–63; English trans., *Dialogue on the Government of Florence*, trans. Alison Brown (Cambridge: Cambridge University Press, 1994), pp. 158–59.

24 Guicciardini, *Ricordi*, 2nd series, n. 147 in Francesco Guicciardini, *Scritti politici e ricordi* (Bari: Laterza, 1933), p. 317: "Erra chi crede che la vittoria delle imprese consista nello essere giuste o ingiuste, perché tuttodí si vede el contrario, che non la ragione, ma la prudenzia, le forze e la buona fortuna danno vinte le imprese. É ben vero, che in chi ha ragione nasce una certa confidenzia, fondata in sulla opinione che Dio dia vittoria alle imprese giuste, la quale fa gli uomini arditi e ostinati, dalle quali due condizioni nascono talvolta le vittorie. Cosí l'avere la causa giusta può per indiretto giovare, ma è falso che lo faccia direttamente." On the use of divine will as an incentive in war, see also *Ricordi*, 2nd series, n. 1 in ibid., p. 281.

campaigns, vested with the ceremonial function of taking the auspices before battle. During this ceremony, the priests gave the sacred chickens food and observed their pecking behavior to ascertain whether the gods did, or did not, approve of the proposed course of action. Depending upon whether, and how, the chickens pecked, the auspices were interpreted as favorable or ill-omened. But if we are to believe Machiavelli, the ritual was a mere outward show. When a military captain wanted to give battle, the diviner, steeped in the *arcana imperii* and the art of framing of war, was expected to announce that the chickens had eaten. To the god-fearing Roman soldiers, this meant that the gods approved of the captain's decision to engage in combat.[25] Ostensibly staged as a ritual to explore the will of the gods, the pecking of the chickens came thus to serve as a means to ensure, in the eyes of the soldiers, complete harmony between the will of the gods and the will of their military commanders. Judiciously used, Machiavelli concludes, it contributed to instill confidence in the soldiers, which "almost always led to victory."[26]

A strong indication that Machiavelli viewed Christianity in analogy with Roman religion, and considered it capable of fulfilling the same political and military function, is given in *The Art of War*, where he comments on rulers and military captains who have professed to communicate with the divine.

> Sulla said that he spoke with an image he had taken out of the temple of Apollo. Many have said that God (*Iddio*) has appeared before them in dreams and commanded them to fight. In the days of our ancestors, when Charles VII of France was at war with the English, he said that he took counsel with a young girl sent by God (*diceva consigliarsi con una fanciulla mandata da Iddio*), commonly called the virgin of France, which was a reason for his victory.[27]

In this passage, Machiavelli's discussion of the fraudulent stratagems at the basis of official religion extends beyond paganism and comes to implicate Christianity as well. However, to say, as Benedetto Fontana does, that the former Secretary here, and in his comments on Moses and Savonarola, uncovers "the natural and human foundation of revealed religion," in order

[25] *Discorsi* I.14.

[26] Ibid., p. 238: "Né ad altro fine tendeva questo modo dello aruspicare, che di fare i soldati confidentemente ire alla zuffa, dalla quale confidenza quasi sempre nasce la vittoria."

[27] Niccolò Machiavelli, "Dell'arte della guerra," in *Opere*, ed. Vivanti, I, pp. 371–79 [hereinafter *Arte della guerra*], p. 626: "Silla diceva di parlare con una immagine ch'egli aveva tratta dal tempio di Apolline. Molti hanno detto essere loro apparso in sogno Iddio, che gli ha ammoniti al combattere. Ne' tempi de' padri nostri, Carlo VII re di Francia, nella guerra che fece contro agli inghilesi, diceva consigliarsi con una fanciulla mandata da Iddio, la quale si chiamò per tutto la Pulzella di Francia; il che gli fu cagione della vittoria."

to question "the sacred and divine character of Christianity," is only to spell out the negative, or demystifying, implications of his position.[28] We need also to acknowledge that Machiavelli, by drawing attention to Charles's instrumental use of Jeanne d'Arc, is giving positive advice on how Christianity, if "interpreted according to virtue," could be made to play the same role, and to serve the same purposes, as Roman religion had done in the past.[29] Modern examples like those of Charles VII, Alexander VI, and Ferdinand of Aragon show, if correctly understood, that this new approach to Christianity has already been adopted and put into practice with considerable success. Ferdinand is perhaps the best example in this regard. The Spanish king, who always "made use of religion,"[30] had first expelled the Jews from Spain, and then, "under this same cloak,"[31] gone on to wage a successful war of conquest in Africa.

In an attempt to counter the objection that modern men are too well informed and too sophisticated to be taken in by such machinations, Machiavelli points to the contemporary Florentines, who did not think of themselves as either ignorant or coarse, but "were persuaded by Friar Girolamo Savonarola that he spoke with God . . . without having seen anything extraordinary to make them believe him."[32] But while Savonarola's

[28] Benedetto Fontana, "Love of Country and Love of God: The Political Uses of Religion in Machiavelli," *Journal of the History of Ideas* 60 (1999): 639–58; quotations from p. 647.

[29] Cf. Harvey Mansfield and Nathan Tarcov, "Introduction," in Niccolò Machiavelli, *Discourses on Livy* (Chicago: University of Chicago Press, 1996), pp. xxxiv–xxxv; Fontana, "Love of Country and Love of God," pp. 647–48. On Machiavelli's view of religion in general, see also Anthony J. Parel, *The Machiavellian Cosmos* (New Haven: Yale University Press, 1992), pp. 27–31 and 45–62; Harvey C. Mansfield, *Machiavelli's Virtue* (Chicago: University of Chicago Press, 1996), pp. 109–22; Vickie B. Sullivan, *Machiavelli's Three Romes: Religion, Human Liberty, and Politics Reformed* (De Kalb, IL: Northern Illinois University Press, 1996); Ronald Beiner, "Machiavelli, Hobbes, and Rousseau on Civil Religion," *Review of Politics* 55 (1993): 617–38; Alison Brown, *The Medici in Florence: The Exercise and Language of Power* (Florence: Olschki, 1992), pp. 294–95; Emanuele Cutinelli-Réndina, *Chiesa e religione in Machiavelli* (Pisa and Rome: Istituti Editoriali e Poligrafici Internazionali, 1998); John Najemy, "Paperius and the Chickens, or Machiavelli on the Necessity of Interpreting Religion," *Journal of the History of Ideas* 60 (1999): 659–81; Marcia L. Colish: "Republicanism, Religion, and Machiavelli's Savonarolan Moment," *Journal of History of Ideas* 60 (1999): 597–616; Nathan Tarcov, "Machiavelli and the Foundations of Modernity: A Reading of Chapter 3 of *The Prince*," in *Educating the Prince: Essays in Honor of Harvey Mansfield*, eds. M. Blitz and W. Kristol (Lanham, MD: Rowman and Littlefield, 2000), pp. 30–44, esp. 41–42.

[30] *Il principe* 21, p. 179: "servendosi sempre della religione."

[31] Ibid., p. 180: "sotto questo medesimo mantello."

[32] *Discorsi* I.11, p. 231: "fu persuaso che parlava con Dio . . . sanza avere visto cosa nessuna straordinaria da farlo loro credere." In this chapter, Machiavelli inserts a precautionary remark concerning the reputation of Savonarola: "I do not wish to judge whether it is true or not, because one should speak with reverence of such a man (*Io non voglio giudicare s'egli era vero o no, perché d'uno tanto uomo se ne debbe parlare con riverenza*)." By leaving out discussion of whether the friar was a fraud or not, Machiavelli seems to suggest to his Florentine readers that the Savonarolan legacy should be treated with circumspection and respect, since it could be made to serve their purposes.

example shows that Christian beliefs can be exploited for political ends, it also teaches that religious manipulation, if not supported by more tangible and forceful means, is bound to prove ineffective in the long run. Savonarola and his "new orders" were ruined "as soon as the masses began to lose faith in him," Machiavelli explains, because the friar lacked the means that could have ensured "the support of those who had believed in him" and "made unbelievers believe."[33] Had he been able to protect his innovations and his divine inspiration, or "lies," by armed force, he would have remained "powerful, secure, honoured, and successful."[34] In other words, religion can furnish rulers with a host of legitimizing devices – be it pecking chickens, holy images, omens, ecstatic virgins, or preachers capable of speaking with God – but it cannot itself serve as a viable and lasting foundation for power.

THE MISERY OF PEACE

Considering the extreme cruelty of the Italian wars, attested to by contemporary chronicles and reflected in the unprecedented violence of the artistic language of the day (as seen for example in Signorelli's frescoes of the *Last Judgment* [1499–1504] in the cathedral in Orvieto, and Carpaccio's *St George and the Dragon* [1507]), there is surprisingly little yearning for peace in the writings of the early Cinquecento theorists.[35] Petrarch's passionate call for *pace* at the end of *Italia mia* finds no, or little, resonance among Machiavelli and his Florentine contemporaries. Instead, we encounter in their works frequent and fierce attacks on the pre-1494 generation's effeminate life-style and their neglect of the art of war. Francesco Guicciardini describes the wars waged during the period preceding the French invasions as pompous and richly decorated spectacles, bearing little resemblance to the bloody battles of real warfare.[36] When Charles VIII in the manner of a conqueror entered Florence at the head of his army, Guicciardini tells

[33] *Il principe* 6, pp. 132–33: "come ne' nostri tempi intervenne a fra Ieronimo Savonerola, il quale ruinò ne' sua ordini nuovi, come la moltitudine cominciò a non credergli, e lui non aveva modo a tenere fermi quelli che avevano creduto né a fare credere e' discredenti."

[34] *Il principe* 6, p. 133: "potenti, sicuri, onorati e felici." Machiavelli describes Savonarola as a liar in his letter to Becchi of 9 March 1498, in *Lettere*, p. 8: "e le sue bugie colorendo."

[35] For descriptions in contemporary historical chronicles of acts of violence committed during the Italian wars, see Eric W. Cochrane, *Historians and Historiography in the Italian Renaissance* (Chicago: University of Chicago Press, 1981), pp. 175 and 184–85.

[36] Francesco Guicciardini, *Storia d'Italia* (5 vols., Bari: Laterza, 1929), 1, p. 81: "Italia, giá lungo tempo assuefatta a vedere guerre piú presto belle di pompa e di apparati, e quasi simili a spettacoli, che pericolose e sanguinose." Priuli similarly condemned the Venetian aristocracy for neglecting the practice of military virtue for the sake of "delicate and soft things and lasciviousness and delicacies," which had made them grow "lazy, spineless and effeminate" (quoted from Cochrane, *Historians and Historiography*, p. 182).

us, the Florentines, "used to commerce and not to military practice," were so frightened by the sight of the powerful king and his ferocious soldiers that they were unable to take up arms to defend their beloved freedom.[37] Similarly, Lodovico Alamanni argued that the elder generation had caused Italy's present malaise by relying on mercenary soldiers, undermining the traditional political order, and reducing the country to "the governance of priests and merchants."[38] No less condemning of the peaceful pre-1494 period, Machiavelli claims in his *Istorie fiorentine* that the abjectness and the cowardice characterizing the wars fought in Italy from 1434 to 1494 (that is, during the first period of Medicean rule in Florence) had paved the way for the foreign invasions now tormenting the peninsula. In contrast to the ancient histories, which are full of great and virtuous deeds that excite admiration and incite the mind to imitation, he claims, recent times have witnessed princes, soldiers, and heads of republics employing every possible "deception, trick and scheme" to maintain "reputations that they do not deserve."[39]

Many critics have come to attach great importance to Machiavelli's attempt to find a military remedy for Italy's crisis. In Felix Gilbert's view, the Florentine was one of the first moderns to understand the role played by war in international relations. Being a military thinker long before he became a political theorist, Gilbert argues, Machiavelli based his political theory on his military thought, maintaining that the state must be ordered in such a way that it provides the preconditions for a strong and well-functioning military organization. In *The Prince* and the *Discourses*, where war emerges as "an inescapable, grandiose, and terrifying force," we find, according to Gilbert, "nothing about the desirability of peace."[40] A contrary view is taken by Maurizio Viroli, Sebastian de Grazia, and Quentin Skinner, who argue that Machiavelli's preoccupation with war and military affairs is conditioned by his desire for peace. In Viroli's view, Machiavelli's political objective is to live peacefully in a republic where the art of war is subordinated to the cultivation of "the arts of peace."[41] In keeping with the

37 Guicciardini, *Storia d'Italia*, I, p. 93. 38 See Trexler, *Public Life*, p. 520.

39 Niccolò Machiavelli, "Istorie fiorentine," in *Opere complete*, vol. VII, ed. F. Gaeta (Milan: Feltrinelli, 1962), [hereinafter *Istorie fiorentine*], V.1, pp. 326–27.

40 Felix Gilbert, "Machiavelli: The Renaissance of the Art of War," in *Makers of Modern Strategy from Machiavelli to the Nuclear Age*, eds. P. Paret, G. A. Craig, and F. Gilbert (Oxford: Clarendon Press, 1986), pp. 11–31; quotation from p. 24. For a related view see Neil Wood, "Introduction," in Niccolò Machiavelli, *The Art of War* (New York: Da Capo, 1990), pp. ix–lcxxix. On the importance of military affairs in *Il principe*, see also Robert Grundin, "Sequence and Counter-Sequence in *Il Principe*," *Machiavelli Studies* 3 (1990): 29–42.

41 Maurizio Viroli, *From Politics to Reason of State: The Acquisition and Transformation of the Language of Politics 1250–1600* (Cambridge: Cambridge University Press, 1992), p. 164.

established tradition, the Florentine holds that wars waged for the sake of peace – that is, wars fought out of necessity and in defense of the liberty of one's city, or for the protection of one's subjects – are legitimate, while he condemns military aggression and wars of conquest as unnecessary and unjust.[42]

To construe Machiavelli's position on war and peace, we should do well to turn to the *Discourses*, which contains his most extensive and probing discussions on the subject. In *Discourses* II.25, Machiavelli flatly states that "idleness and peace" (*l'ozio e la pace*) cause disunion and inner strife in a state, while "fear and war" (*la paura e la guerra*) bring about unity.[43] To prevent a republic from coming to ruin, he claims in *Discourses* III.16, one must choose between two diametrically opposed policies: the first is to keep the citizens poor and "without virtue" (*sanza virtù*) so that they can corrupt neither themselves nor others; the second, set forth with less sarcasm and based on the exemplary Roman republic, is to adopt military orders enabling the republic to wage war always and at all times (*ordinarsi in modo alla guerra che sempre si potesse fare guerra*).[44] In *Discourses* II.2, as we have seen, he explains people's love of liberty by attributing it to their desire for territorial acquisition and material gain. In a healthy republic, he claims, both the people and the nobility are animated by a passion for glorious military undertakings: the former because of their reverence for brave actions, and the latter because of their innate desire for military glory. These two humors, Machiavelli claims, must be contented if the republic is to remain strong and vigorous, and corruption and ruin avoided.[45]

Machiavelli's preference for war over peace needs to be seen in relation to his general conception of historical change and his zero-sum view of the world. In the introduction to book V of the *Istorie fiorentine*, which we have referred to above, he describes the history of states as a cyclical process. Since nature does not allow things of this world (*mondane cose*) to remain fixed, they must either rise or fall.[46] In so doing, they are bound to pass from order to disorder, from the utmost perfection (*ultima perfezione*) to the lowest depth (*ultima bassezza*), from good to evil. Virtue gives rise to moments of stability and tranquillity, but this peaceful state of affairs is not

[42] Sebastian de Grazia, *Machiavelli in Hell* (London: Picador, 1992), pp. 164–73; and Quentin Skinner, "The Vocabulary of Renaissance Republicanism: A Cultural Longue-durée?" in *Language and Images of Renaissance Italy*, ed. A. Brown (Oxford: Clarendon Press, 1995).

[43] *Discorsi* II.25, p. 397.

[44] Ibid., III.16, p. 466.

[45] On the role of the humors (*umori*) in Machiavelli's thought, see Parel, *The Machiavellian Cosmos*, pp. 101–12; and Mansfield, *Machiavelli's Virtue*, pp. 75–76 and 92–97.

[46] On Machiavelli's rejection of the status quo, see also *Discorsi* I.6, p. 216: "sendo tutte le cose degli uomini in moto, e non potendo stare salde conviene che le salghino o che le scendino"; and ibid., II, preface, p. 325: "essendo le cose umane sempre in moto, o le salgano o le scendano."

bliss, since it breeds indolence, corruption, disorder, and ruin.[47] Therefore, a peaceful existence, like the one enjoyed by Rome under her first emperors or by Italy during the pre-1494 era, is to be avoided at all costs. Having ruled out the possibility of maintaining the status quo, Machiavelli leaves us with no other alternative than to embrace the policy of acquisition, growth, and territorial expansion. Since these acquisitions take place within a zero-sum world, where the gains of one necessarily come at the expense of others, these claims come to have far-reaching consequences for Machiavelli's thinking on war and international relations in general. In *The Prince* 3, he draws out the implications of this position, by arguing that it is "a very natural and normal thing to desire to acquire" (*cosa veramente molto naturale et ordinaria desiderare di acquistare*), and that states that are successful in expanding and making acquisitions always will be "praised, or not condemned."[48] Having laid down this general rule, he goes on to claim that if Louis XII of France had been strong enough to attack the kingdom of Naples back in 1500, he should have done so. The question of whether his cause was just or legitimate, Machiavelli implies, does not, and should not, enter into the equation. On the basis of this survey, we may conclude that the idea of a just war pursued for the sake of peace is not only against the grain of Machiavelli's argument, but totally and utterly incompatible with the premises of his thought.

But peace can in Machiavelli's theory be invoked for other purposes than to warn against laziness and indolence. As he and his contemporaries were all too well aware, reassurances of peaceful intentions could be used to mask belligerent objectives and to mislead would-be adversaries. As Melissa Bullard has shown, Renaissance diplomats in general, and Florentine ambassadors in particular, had by the end of the Quattrocento developed a sophisticated understanding of rhetorical deception. Florentine envoys were expected to determine whether their counterparts were speaking in earnest, or were using *buone parole*, *parole fitte*, and *simulatione* to cover secret designs.[49] To describe political and military actions performed under cover of misleading verbal pretexts, they had at their disposal a

[47] *Istorie fiorentine* v.1, p. 325. Cf. *Discorsi* 1.2, p. 205.

[48] *Il principe* 3, p. 125: "È cosa veramente molto naturale e ordinaria desiderare di acquistare: e sempre, quando li uomini lo fanno, che possono, saranno laudati o non biasimati."

[49] Melissa Bullard, *Lorenzo il Magnifico: Image and Anxiety, Politics and Finance* (Florence: Olschki, 1994), pp. 81–108. A shorter version of this article has subsequently been published as "Lorenzo and Patterns of Diplomatic Discourse in the Late Fifteenth Century," in *Lorenzo the Magnificent: Culture and Politics*, eds. M. Mallett and N. Mann (London: The Warburg Institute, 1996), pp. 263–74. Bullard suggests that the sophisticated approach of Lorenzo the Magnificent's ambassadors to diplomatic discourse was an important legacy to the diplomats and political writers of the early Cinquecento, Machiavelli and Guicciardini included.

rich vocabulary, including numerous expressions based on the preposition *sotto*, or "under" – such as *sotto colore*, *sotto ombra*, *sotto nome*, and *sotto il mantello*.

In his theoretical works, Machiavelli frequently draws on this lexicon. For example, having in *Discourses* I.46 discussed the dangers caused in republics by ambitious citizens aspiring to the principality, he comes to the conclusion that a republic must be ordered in such a way that its citizens cannot do evil "under shadow of good" (*sotto ombra di bene*). In *Discourses* II.22, he argues that Pope Leo X back in 1514 had missed an opportunity to make himself lord of Lombardy. In the former Secretary's view, the Pope should, "under color (*sotto colore*) of wishing to guard his own affairs," have kept his army in the background waiting for the Swiss and the French to fight it out between them, before stepping in and despoiling the victor.[50] Machiavelli also touches upon the subject of territorial expansion under cover of innocent pretexts in his letter to Vettori of 10 August 1513: "The Swiss have entered Lombardy under the pretext (*sotto nome*) of reinstalling the duke in question [Massimiliano Sforza], and in reality they have become duke themselves."[51] The lesson to be drawn from such observations is unmistakable. In a world where sincerity is a rare commodity and the causal link between honesty and utility remains to be proved, political prudence demands that one develops an ability to see through the conceit of others.

But according to Machiavelli that is not enough. The political man must also master the art of deception himself, and be able to conceal his own, or his employers', true intentions behind deceptive appearances and pretexts. Undoubtedly, this double perspective, combining demystification and dissimulation, reflects Machiavelli's own diplomatic experience. During his mission in 1502 to the court of Cesare Borgia, where he had been dispatched with the task of temporizing (*temporeggiare*) with the duke, and finding out his true intentions, or investigating his soul (*d'intendere l'animo suo*) as the instructions went, Machiavelli reported home that everyone at the court was talking about, and negotiating, peace, while making preparations for war.[52] In *The Prince*, ten years later, he was to claim that many

[50] *Discorsi* II.22, p. 386: "sotto colore di volere guardare le cose sue." Cf. note 34 above and note 55 below.

[51] *Lettere*, p. 278: "sono entrati in Lombardia sotto nome di rimettervi questo duca, et in fatto son duca loro. Alla prima occasione e' se ne insignoriscono in tutto, spegnendo la stirpa ducale e tutta la nobiltà di quello stato." In his letter to Francesco Guicciardini of 17 May 1521 (*Lettere*, p. 372), Machiavelli comments on the misplaced trust people afford bad priests who hide their evil ways "under the cloak of religion" (*sotto il mantello della religione*).

[52] Niccolò Machiavelli, "Legazioni e commissarie," in *Opere*, ed. C. Vivanti (3 vols., Turin: Einaudi, 1997–), II [hereinafter *Legazioni e commissarie*], p. 689 (1 November 1502): "Et ad dire le cose di qua

princes in recent years had signed peace agreements only with the intention of breaking them at their first opportunity. As a rule, this lack of faith, or astuteness, had paid off, because experience shows that "those best able to imitate the fox have succeeded best."[53] Instead of deploring this fact, Machiavelli recommends his princely reader to join the game, and gives him advice on how to benefit from it. Thus, the prince should learn not only to cover his intentions and to be "a great feigner and dissembler,"[54] but also to build trust and establish credibility, by concealing, or "coloring," his foxy nature. If the ruler adopts this policy, Machiavelli promises, he will enjoy success, since he who wants to deceive and manipulate others never will run short of "legitimate reasons with which to color his lack of good faith."[55]

In the course of his discussion of political deception in *The Prince* 18, Machiavelli draws attention to an unnamed contemporary ruler, traditionally identified with Ferdinand of Aragon, who, he claims, is constantly preaching "peace and faith," while being "very hostile to both." Had the prince in question actually lived by these lofty principles, Machiavelli argues, he would not have been able to achieve what he had accomplished, but "would have lost either his reputation or his state several times over."[56] Antiquity teaches a similar lesson. The exemplary Roman republic rose to world domination, Machiavelli claims, in part because of her military power, in part because of her skill in using assertions of pacific intentions to conceal her preparations for war and to "put [her neighbors] to sleep."[57] In other words, Machiavelli in *The Prince* and the *Discourses* not only describes how declarations of peaceful intent have been employed as a façade for the pursuit of bellicose objectives, but also gives practical advice on how to use and to profit from such stratagems. Should a prince or a republic, by contrast, take peaceful coexistence between states as their guiding principle, he warns, they are not only doomed to fall prey to the vicious circle of laziness, discord, corruption, and destruction, but also destined to be

in dua parole: dall'un canto si ragiona di accordo, da l'altro si fanno le preparationi da guerra." Ibid., p. 692 (3 November 1502): "che se le parole et le pratiche mostrono accordo, li ordini et preparationi mostrono guerra." Ibid., p. 706 (13 November 1502): "Et prima, vostre Signorie ricercono se qui si pensa piú alla pace che alla guerra; rispondo avere detto che della pace si ragiona et fannosi provedimenti per la guerra."

[53] *Il principe* 18, p. 166: "quello che ha saputo meglio usare la golpe, è meglio capitato."

[54] Ibid., 18, p. 166: "gran simulatore e dissimulatore."

[55] Ibid., 18, p. 165: "né mai a uno principe mancorno cagioni legittime di colorire la inosservanzia."

[56] Ibid., 18, p. 167: "Alcuno principe de' presenti tempi, il quale non è bene nominare, non predica mai altro che pace e fede, e dell'una e dell'altra è inimicissimo: e l'una e l'altra, quando e' l'avessi osservata, gli arebbe piú volte tolto e la riputazione e lo stato."

[57] *Discorsi* II.1, p. 329: "parte ingannati da que' modi ch'egli terrà per adormentargli."

outmaneuvered and defeated by less scrupulous neighbors. The fundamental choice in Machiavelli's world is a simple one: it is between going up and going down, between deceiving or being deceived, between eating or being eaten.

ANTICIPATING NECESSITY

The third principal category adduced by Christian theorists and Quattrocento humanists to legitimate war was the principle of justice. Before we turn to consider how Machiavelli's conception differed from the just war tradition, originating with Cicero, Augustine, and Aquinas, it is important to point out that there existed within legal thought at the time a contrasting realist tradition based on pragmatic political considerations and the advocacy of reason of state. As John Bliese has shown, the battle speeches of the medieval chronicles are based on a very different conception of the just war than the one contained in the legal and theological treatises of the time. In these orations, designed to inspire confidence in the soldiers before battle, hatred of the enemy and the taking of spoils are frequently referred to as legitimate grounds for taking up arms.[58] As studies by Gaines Post, Lauro Martines, and Athanasios Moulakis show, medieval and early Renaissance legal theorists were also aware of the need to resort to extraordinary means and to suspend temporarily the ordinary legal authority in cases of emergency.[59] For example, Bartolus of Sassoferrato, the influential Trecento jurist, claimed that a government "without any admixture of tyranny" was inconceivable, since such a regime would have to be based on "a divine rather than a human condition of things."[60] Similar opinions were voiced in Florence during discussions on matters of state at the turn of the Cinquecento. In 1501, the lawyer Domenico Bonsi advocated during a *pratica* that the executive power of the *signoria* should be reinforced since "affairs must be conducted according to accident and circumstance." In the view of Bonsi, political prudence demanded that "one should not will the ruin of the city by remaining fixed in the observance of the laws."[61] So when

[58] John R. E. Bliese, "The Just War as Concept and Motive in the Central Middle Ages," *Medievalia et Humanistica* 17 (1988): 1–26.

[59] Gaines Post, *Studies in Medieval Legal Thought: Public Law and the State, 1100–1322* (Princeton: Princeton University Press, 1964), pp. 241–309 and 434–93; Lauro Martines, *Lawyers and Statecraft in Renaissance Florence* (Princeton: Princeton University Press, 1968), pp. 410–12; Athanasios Moulakis, *Republican Realism in Renaissance Florence: Francesco Guicciardini's* Discorso di Logrogno (Lanham, MD: Rowman and Littlefield, 1998); Moulakis, "Civic Humanism, Realist Constitutionalism, and Francesco Guicciardini's *Discorso di Logrogno*," in *Renaissance Civic Humanism Reconsidered*, ed. J. Hankins (Cambridge: Cambridge University Press, 2000), pp. 200–22.

[60] Bartolus of Sassoferrato, "Tractatus de tyrannia," in *Humanism and Tyranny: Studies in the Italian Trecento*, ed. E. Emerton (Gloucester, MA: P. Smith, 1964), p. 153.

[61] Quoted from Martines, *Lawyers and Statecraft*, p. 426.

Francesco Vettori two decades later claimed that all existing governments, past and present, monarchic and republican, for reason of political exigency must contain a degree of tyranny, he was merely reiterating an argument rooted in classical as well as medieval legal theory.[62]

But even if recourse to extraordinary and extralegal means in the face of crisis had become fairly commonplace by the time of the Italian wars, Machiavelli's and Guicciardini's radical denunciation of the politics of justice marked an important departure from the medieval and early Renaissance tradition. A jurist by training, Guicciardini exposes in a series of entries in his *Ricordi* the hollow claims to divine, natural, and human justice, by pointing to the inherent limitations of the human perspective, and by confronting human justice and the positivist view of the law with the absolute standards of divine justice.[63] Machiavelli aligns himself with the realist tradition by observing a strict silence on natural justice and natural law,[64] and by claiming that states and rulers at times must set aside the principle of justice for the pursuit of other, more fundamental interests.[65] In *Discourses* III.41, he comments on the Roman lieutenant Lucius Lentolus, who, after having been besieged by the Samnites, exhorted his men to use every means at their disposal, including the most ignominious, to defend the army and the *patria*. The lesson Machiavelli draws from this example is that, in matters concerning the preservation of one's country, one should, if deemed necessary, be prepared to act in a manner that is neither just, merciful, nor honorable.[66] This willingness to leave justice behind in military affairs is in keeping with Machiavelli's general position

[62] Francesco Vettori, *Scritti storici e politici* (Bari: Laterza, 1972), p. 145: "'È chiamato questo modo di vivere tirannide [i.e. the restored Medici regione of 1512]. Ma, parlando delle cose di questo mondo sanza rispetto e secondo il vero, dico che chi facesse una di quelle republiche scritte e imaginate da Platone, o come una che scrive Tomma Moro inghilese essere stata trovata in Utopia, forse quelle si potrebbono dire non essere governi tirannici; ma tutte quelle republiche o principi, de' quali io ho cognizione per istoria o che io ho veduti, mi pare che sentino di tirannide."

[63] See Guicciardini's *Ricordi*, 2nd series, n. 91, 92, 113, and 209 in Guicciardini, *Scritti politici e ricordi*, pp. 304, 309, and 333.

[64] Cf. Mansfield, *Machiavelli's Virtue*, p. 22.

[65] On Machiavelli's view of justice, see Quentin Skinner, "The Idea of Negative Liberty: Philosophical and Historical Perspectives," in *Philosophy in History: Essays on the Historiography of Philosophy*, eds. R. Rorty, J. B. Schneewind, and Q. Skinner (Cambridge: Cambridge University Press, 1984), pp. 215–17; Mansfield, *Machiavelli's Virtue*, pp. 17–19, 21–22, 180–81, 256–57, and 299–303; Anthony J. Parel, "Machiavelli's Notions of Justice. Text and Analysis," *Political Theory* 18 (1990): 530–36.

[66] *Discorsi* III.41, p. 515: "La quale cosa merita di essere notata ed osservata da qualunque cittadino si truova a consigliare la patria sua: perché dove si dilibera al tutto della salute della patria, non vi debbe cadere alcuna considerazione né di giusto né d'ingiusto, né di piatoso né di crudele, né di laudabile né d'ignominioso; anzi, posposto ogni altro rispetto, seguire al tutto quel partito che le salvi la vita e mantenghile la libertà." Read within the context of the chapter as a whole, it would seem that the policy that Lentolus proposed was designed primarily to save the face of the consuls, not the liberty of Rome. This would mean that the self-interest invoked in the chapter is of more limited nature than the notions of love of country or reason of state would suggest.

on war and foreign policy. In his view, the fact that interstate relations are based on a perennial antagonism between what lies inside and what lies outside the state, between us and them, which in the absence of an international court precludes arbitration and justice, comes to mean that moral concerns should have no, or little, direct bearing on the conduct of foreign policy. Against this background, we need not be surprised to find that in the many and lengthy discussions of armed conflict in *The Prince*, the *Discourses*, and *The Art of War* the issue of whether the war in question was just or unjust rarely, if ever, is raised.

Does Machiavelli's deep skepticism about the application of the concept of justice to war and foreign policy mean that he rejected the idea of the just war altogether, or is it still possible to attribute to him a notion of a legitimate war based not on justice, but on necessity and the defense of liberty? Anthony Parel, who considers force, prudence, and justice to be the mainstays of Machiavelli's political theory, argues this case. According to him, Machiavelli takes a deep interest in the notion of the just war, and holds that states are justified in resorting to arms when necessity, self-preservation, and liberty so require. But, as Parel acknowledges, this is a highly problematic position. The fact that there is no impartial authority who can determine what constitutes necessity means that "the application of the concept . . . always remains subjective."[67] In other words, necessity, being notoriously difficult to define, lends itself to abuse. Having demonstrated that Machiavelli was well aware of this risk, Parel lets us, by way of implication, understand that the former Secretary would have disapproved of necessity being manipulated for questionable ends, since for him the concept was associated with good government and justice.[68]

In the light of what has emerged above, there is reason to be skeptical about this reading. So far in this chapter, we have seen how Machiavelli endorsed the use of justification by faith and protestations of peaceful intentions to inspire courage in war and to cloak expansionist policies. To determine how far he was prepared to go in extending the use of necessity for similar ends, we need to take a closer look at the role this notion plays in his political thought at large. As has often been noted, Machiavelli frequently attributes a strong positive value to necessity, making it a procurer of good things in human affairs.[69] In *Discourses* I.I, for example, he claims that men

[67] Parel, "Machiavelli's Notions of Justice," p. 535. [68] See esp. ibid., p. 536.

[69] For Machiavelli's view on necessity, see Eugene Garver, "After *Virtù*: Rhetoric, Prudence and Moral Pluralism in Machiavelli," *History of Political Thought* 17 (1996): 195–222, esp. 205–10; John F. Trinkler, "Praise and Advice: Rhetorical Approaches in More's *Utopia* and Machiavalli's *The Prince*," *Sixteenth Century Journal* 19 (1988), pp. 199–200; Mansfield, *Machiavelli's Virtue*, pp. 14–15, 39–40 and 55–78; Pierre Manent, *Naissance de la politique moderne: Machiavel, Hobbes, Rousseau* (Paris: Payot, 1977), pp. 24 and 35–39.

living in fertile places can be saved from idleness and be made virtuous by the necessity imposed on them by a prudent lawgiver.[70] In *Discourses* I.3, he restates the point by arguing that "men never work any good unless through necessity."[71] This thesis is further supported by the example of the Roman republic, whose exemplary constitution, we are told in *Discourses* I.49, developed as a result of a succession of necessities (*nuove necessità*).[72] In *Discourses* II.12, Machiavelli reiterates the view that "necessity makes virtue" (*quella necessità fa virtù*),[73] and later in chapter III.6 he claims that men are slow to act when free from constraints, but swift to do so when prompted by necessity.[74]

But to state the problem of necessity in this way would be to give an incomplete and one-sided account of Machiavelli's position. In his view, necessity has a dual character. On the one hand, it is a procurer of good things and indispensable for human life; on the other, it is an uncontrollable, potentially devastating force that brings great dangers to the individual and to the state as a whole. Confronted with the two-faced, Janus-like nature of necessity, the task of the political theorist and the political actor is to separate these two aspects of necessity – the good from the danger.

The solution Machiavelli offers consists in the creation of an *apparent*, or fictitious, necessity; that is, a necessity which only appears as such from the viewpoint of the soldiers or the people, the ignorant, but in reality is a product of the ruler's manipulation, based on election, and perhaps, but not necessarily, on prudence.[75] Elaborating on this principle, Machiavelli teaches how the prudent and foresighted captain can anticipate necessity and exploit its ability to turn men into good and virtuous soldiers, while retaining control over the situation, and without exposing his troops to unnecessary danger.[76] But there is a dilemma involved here. For even though the strategy of *apparent* necessity often is to be preferred to waiting for *real* necessity to arrive, it is by no means free from political risk. If the ruler or the military captain were to fail to conceal the deception underlying their stratagem, and if the mere *apparentness* of the necessity they are invoking were to be revealed, this is likely not only to thwart their plans for the moment, but to damage their credibility, their *ethos*, and to impair their

70 *Discorsi* I.1, pp. 200–02.

71 Ibid., I.3, p. 208: "gli uomini non operono mai nulla bene, se non per necessità."

72 Ibid., I.49, p. 298. 73 Ibid., II.12, p. 356. 74 Ibid., III.6, pp. 443–44.

75 This double perspective is stressed in the heading of *Discorsi* I.14, p. 236, where Machiavelli discusses the function of the *pullarii*: "I Romani interpetravano gli auspizi secondo la necessità, e con la prudenza mostravano di osservare la religione . . ."

76 Conversely, Machiavelli demonstrates in *Discorsi* I.51 how prudent men can profit from making necessity appear as election, and in ibid., I.14, he shows how a prudent military captain can use the revelation of the arcana to his own benefit.

long-term credentials as well. Consequently, the choice between artificial necessity, with its risk of backfiring, and waiting for real necessity, and the dangers it entails, is a matter of expediency and should be judged on a case-by-case basis.

As we have come to see, there are two sides to Machiavelli's approach to the framing of war. Firstly, there is the skeptical and demystifying view of the rhetoric of justification, which challenged the claims to legitimacy inherent in traditional justificatory categories such as divine providence, the quest for peace, justice and necessity, and by extension, the very idea of the just and the divinely sanctioned war itself. In so far, his attitude can be said to reflect a general tendency in Western thought at the beginning of the sixteenth century. At the time Machiavelli formulated his revolutionizing theory on political legitimation and the justification of war, leading humanists like Thomas More, Erasmus of Rotterdam, Guillaume Budé, and Juan Luis Vives were beginning to dissociate themselves from the rhetoric of the just war and to develop a radical form of ideological pacifism.[77] But if it is true that Machiavelli shared Erasmus's and his companions' disenchantment with traditional political ethics, he responded to the frightening emptiness hiding behind the rhetorical screens by drawing conclusions of a very different kind. In keeping with them, he acknowledged that concealment and cloaking of intentions were essential to political and military success, but instead of condemning these practices, he took a pragmatic view, recommending his readers to use these strategies, and teaching them how to do so effectively and for their own benefit. Taking his inspiration from the Roman example, he set out in his theoretical works to reduce the legitimizing categories of the Western tradition to a set of rhetorical devices that could be used and manipulated for political ends. By emptying these concepts of their traditional contents and by dislodging them from their rootedness in natural and divine justice, transcendence and the natural order, he showed how they could serve as building bricks in the construction of pleasing and impressive façades for the pursuit of power and empire. Since empire-building, by definition, is a collective enterprise that depends on broad support and on participation of powerful groups both within and outside the expansionist state, Machiavelli implies, imperialist leaders must learn the art of framing war and to conceal from friends and

[77] See John R. Hale, *War and Society in Renaissance Europe 1450–1620* (London: Fontana, 1985), pp. 36–41. Writing in 1510, Erasmus denounced the bellicose rhetoric of his day (ibid., p. 36): "We will not attempt to discuss whether war is ever just; who does not think his own cause just? . . . Among so many treaties and agreements which are now entered into, now rescinded, who can lack a pretext of going to war?"

foes alike the naked and brutal facts of conquest and territorial acquisition. Empires, we may conclude with him, are built as much by persuasion and rhetorical manipulation as by force and military might.

THE FLORENTINE FOREIGN POLICY DOCTRINE

In the preceding sections, we have inquired into how Machiavelli's work engages, challenges, and seeks to redescribe the ideological and linguistic conventions governing contemporary discourse on war. By addressing issues, concepts, and rhetorical strategies that were of central importance at the time, this discussion has allowed us to see how Machiavelli in his treatment of the framing of war, and the question of justification in general, radically departed from the pieties of medieval political thought. When we now turn to consider Machiavelli's conception of war and expansionism in relation to the specific context of early Cinquecento Florence, we need to narrow, or readjust, our focus. For it could be argued that even though the notions of natural justice, divine legitimation, and the just war played an important role in the Florentine tradition, Florentine policy-making at the turn of the sixteenth century was dictated by factors and concerns of a different order.

Shortly after the Peace of Lodi in 1454, Florence had, together with the four other major powers on the peninsula – Venice, Milan, the kingdom of Naples, and the Papacy – signed a mutual non-aggression pact that temporarily froze the struggle for power in central Italy, and inaugurated four decades of peaceful coexistence in the region. This state of affairs had been upset by the French invasion in 1494, which triggered off the Italian wars, and placed the traditionally Francophile Florentines in an exceedingly delicate and awkward position. Although the city's pro-French line led to political isolation and accrued few rewards (the most bitter disappointment being France's failure to fulfill her promise to restore Pisa), her strong commercial links with the transalpine kingdom persuaded her to continue her traditional policy, while trying to avoid binding commitments to the changing alliance in the region. In 1509, however, the republic joined the league of Cambrai, which saw France and the other major Italian and foreign powers put a stop to Venice's mainland expansion. But when Pope Julius II and Ferdinand of Aragon shortly afterwards reconciled with the Venetians, forming the Holy League to counter French influence in northern Italy, Florence came under renewed pressure. After the Republic in 1511 had allowed the French to use Pisa as the site for the church council, Pope Julius II, who vehemently opposed the council, placed the city under interdict.

Florence's attempt to steer a middle course between openly siding with the French and breaking with them became increasingly untenable when open hostilities began in 1512 between the league on the one hand, and France and the emperor on the other. Unwilling to commit themselves, the Florentines first turned down the French demands for military support and refused to declare war on the league, then changed their minds and sent troops to assist the French in their defense of Lombardy. After a promising start, the French cause suffered a serious blow when the emperor later in the year decided to abandon the conflict, leaving the Florentines extremely exposed and vulnerable. But instead of seeking political reorientation, the Soderinian regime flatly rejected the Pope's invitation to join the league. This fatal decision provoked the attack of the papal army on the city in late August 1512, which led to the rout of the Florentine militia at Prato, sealed the end of the Soderinian regime, paved the way for the return of the Medici to Florence, and caused Machiavelli's dismissal from office later in the fall.[78]

During this turbulent and critical period, the Florentine republic came to develop a foreign policy doctrine which originally was designed to meet the specific needs of the moment, but soon gained the status of universal political wisdom. A central tenet of this doctrine was that Florence was militarily too weak to engage in armed conflicts and that the city's interests were best served by remaining neutral (*stare neutrale*) in the ongoing struggle for hegemony in Italy. In the diplomatic discourse and political debates of the day, a rich and intricate normative vocabulary emerged for defining and articulating the Florentine position. A key term in this lexicon was *temporeggiare*, to temporize. Together with a series of maxims and proverbial expressions involving time, such as to "enjoy" or to "use" the benefit of time (*godere el beneficio del tempo*, or *usare il beneficio del tempo*), "bide one's time" (*aspettare tempo*), and "gain time" (*acquistare tempo*), it summarized the self-consciously weak and dependent Florentine republic's cautious approach in matters of foreign policy.[79] Intimately linked to the

[78] On Florence's foreign policy during Machiavelli's time in office in general, see Sergio Bertelli, "Machiavelli e la politica estera fiorentina," in *Studies on Machiavelli*, ed. M. P. Gilmore (Florence: Sansoni, 1972), pp. 29–72; Felix Gilbert, "Florentine Political Assumptions in the Age of Savonarola and Soderini," *Journal of the Warburg and Courtauld Institutes* 20 (1957): 187–214. On the developments preceding the fall of the Soderinian regime in particular, see H. C. Butters, *Governors and Government in Early Sixteenth-Century Florence 1502–1519* (Oxford: Clarendon Press, 1985), pp. 145–63.

[79] In his letter to Pier Francesco Tosinghi of 6 July 1499, Machiavelli uses the term *temporeggiare* in connection with the expression *usare il beneficio del tempo*, see *Lettere*, p. 12. Guicciardini also refers to the proverb "el savio debbe godere el beneficio del tempo" and advocates that it should be used with discretion: *Scritti politici e ricordi*, p. 301. See also *Consulte e pratiche 1505–1512*, ed. D. Fachard (Geneva: Droz, 1988), pp. 32–34; *Legazioni e commissarie*, p. 791. Cf. Felix Gilbert, *Machiavelli and Guicciardini: Politics and History in Sixteenth Century Florence* (Princeton: Princeton University Press, 1965), p. 33.

strategy of temporization, or adaption, waiting, and delay was another concept, central to contemporary Florentine political thought, the principle of the middle way, or *via del mezzo*. Bolstered by its theoretical foundation in Aristotelian ethics and in the aesthetic theories of the day, the notion of the middle way was seen as the very epitome of conventional Florentine political wisdom. It was frequently referred to by the speakers in the *pratiche* when advocating a policy of moderate acquisition and cautious rule of the cities in the Florentine dominion.[80] Political writers of aristocratic persuasion, among them Francesco Guicciardini, also invoked it when extolling the aristocratic element in the classical theory of the mixed regime as a balancing mean, or *un mezzo*, between the two extremes, rule by one and rule by many.[81] Taken together, neutrality, noncommitment, temporization, and the middle way constituted what could be described as the foreign policy doctrine of the Florentine republic at the turn of the Cinquecento.

What did Machiavelli think of the foreign policy he on numerous diplomatic missions was requested to pursue, explain, and defend? His position can be inferred from the many direct, and indirect, comments he makes on the issue in his diplomatic correspondence, and from studying the way in which he treats the normative vocabulary underpinning contemporary Florentine foreign policy thought in his theoretical works. As is evident from his legation to the ambulant court of Cesare Borgia in late 1502 and early 1503, the Secretary of the Second Chancery and the Ten had already during his time in office begun to question the direction of the Florentine foreign policy. In the reports he sent home from Imola, Cesena, and Senigallia, a host of named and unnamed sources at the court are quoted as having expressed impatience and lack of comprehension about the Florentine policy. The Borgia courtiers are said to complain about the Florentines' "slowness (*tardità*) in coming to an agreement,"[82] their letting "a good occasion (*una bella occasione*)"[83] go by, and their failure to realize that the right time to secure themselves and the duke now had arrived.[84] In one of Machiavelli's two dispatches of 8 November, an anonymous friend of his at the court is said to have warned him that the republic must understand that as

80 On the *Pratiche*, see p. 108 below.

81 On Guicciardini's view of the aristocracy as *un mezzo* and a balancing element, see Gilbert, *Machiavelli and Guicciardini*, p. 87. Guicciardini also refers to *il mezzo* and *gli estremi* from an Aristotelian perspective in the *Ricordi*, see *Scritti politici e ricordi*, p. 327. Cf. Guicciardini, *Dialogo*, pp. 19–20, 22, 70, 80, 101, and 149.

82 *Legazioni e commissarie*, p. 656: "lui cominciò a biasimare questa tardità che si faceva tra le S. V. e sua Eccellenza circa l'intendersi."

83 Ibid., p. 645.

84 Ibid., p. 698: "non avete saputo conoscere el tempo ad assicurare el duca et voi."

long as things remain undecided between it and Cesare, the duke will have to look for companions elsewhere.[85] On 13 November, Machiavelli reports that his friend is besetting him all day long, complaining about the Florentine policy of waiting for a perfect opportunity (*l'occasione parata*) which might never come.[86] The mysterious *amico* reappears in Machiavelli's report of 9 December, where he is said to be wondering "why Your Lordships have not come to some conclusion with the duke, since this is a moment as good as any for doing so."[87] Machiavelli made no secret of the fact that he shared the Borgia courtiers' criticism of the policy of noncommitment and delay that he had been requested to conduct. Contrary to what was expected from a man in his subordinate position, he did not in his reports refrain from giving direct advice on matters concerning important policy decisions. Anxious to see the republic coming to an agreement with the duke, the Secretary exhorted, for example, in his dispatch of 16 October, the Ten to meet Cesare's request for military support, completely or in part, by sending troops to the Borgo Sansepolcro and Anghiari area, where their common enemies, the Vitelli, were soon expected.[88] However, as the letters of warning Machiavelli received from friends back in Florence make evident, his counsel and his unconventional way of reporting did not go down well with the leading circles in the palace, who were firmly committed to the policy of temporization.[89] Although Machiavelli heeded the warnings and avoided giving direct advice in his own name during the rest of the mission, the overall message of the *Legation*, forcefully conveyed through the Secretary's own direct and indirect counsel, as well as by the chorus of voices recorded by him at the court, is unequivocal: Florence should, by entering into an alliance with the duke, or by granting him a military contract (*condotta*), seize the opportunity to recover Pisa.[90]

[85] Ibid., p. 699: "perché il duca, vedendo rimanersi in aria con vostre Signorie, fermerà il piè con altri."

[86] Ibid., p. 706.

[87] Ibid., p. 750: "Quello amico, di chi io ho scripto per altre mia alle Signorie vostre, mi ha piú volte ad questi dí detto che si maravigliava che vostre Signorie non vengono con questo duca ad qualche conclusione, sendo ora un tempo tanto adcomodato ad farlo, che per adventura non si potrebbe desiderare più."

[88] Ibid., pp. 652–53. In the dispatch of 9 October, Machiavelli had asked the Ten for instructions on how to reply to the duke's request to have Florentine troops sent to Borgo Sansepolcro in case of troop movements by the Vitelli; see ibid., p. 637.

[89] That Machiavelli's reporting provoked strong negative reactions in the palace is particularly evident from the letter his friend in the Chancery, Biagio Buonaccorsi, sent to him on 28 October; see Machiavelli, *Lettere*, pp. 60–61. Cf. *Legazioni e commissarie*, p. 685.

[90] It is worth noting that Machiavelli's mysterious and nameless friend at the Borgia court begins to feature in his reports after he had received Biagio Buonaccorsi's letter of warning of 28 October. On Machiavelli's anonymous friend, see Najemy, *Between Friends*, p. 62. Cf. Giulio Ferroni, "La struttura epistolare come contraddizione (carteggio privato, carteggio diplomatico, carteggio concelleresco),"

When Machiavelli, after his dismissal from office in 1512, addressed the conventional Florentine political wisdom in *The Prince*, he could allow himself to speak with less reserve and greater openness about the policy of noncommitment and temporization. Comparing this cautious approach with the Roman mode of strong and efficient political action based on foresight, virtue, and force, the former Secretary pours scorn over his past employers and their foreign policy thinking:

The Romans, therefore, because they saw troubles from afar, were always able to find remedies for them. They never allowed them to develop in order to avoid fighting a war, for they knew that war is not to be avoided but is merely postponed to the advantage of others. This was why they wanted to wage war against Philip and Antiochus in Greece, so that they would not have to fight them in Italy; they could have avoided fighting both of them at the time, but this they did not wish. Moreover, the Romans never accepted a maxim heard every day on the lips of the wise men of our times (*de' savi de' nostri tempi*) – to enjoy the benefit of time (*di godere el benefizio del tempo*). They preferred to enjoy the benefits that derived from their own virtue and prudence; because time brings all things with it, and can produce good as well as evil, evil as well as good.[91]

Although Machiavelli's argument is couched in general terms, there can be little doubt that his chief targets are those Florentine *ottimati* who in recent years had shaped, directed, and defended a foreign policy of

in *Niccolò Machiavelli: Politico, storico, letterato*, ed. J. J. Marchand (Rome: Salerno, 1996), pp. 254–55. In a letter of advice of October 1522, adressed to Raffaello Girolami, a young diplomat about to embark on his first assignment as ambassador to the emperor in Spain, the aging Machiavelli argues that ambassadors should refrain from expressing judgment on the outcome of events in their own name, since such reporting is bound to cause offense. To maintan a reputation of prudence, and to avoid presumption, they should instead convey their own personal views indirectly, by attributing them to others: "E perché mettere il giudizio vostro nella bocca vostra sarebbe odioso, e si usa nelle lettere questo termine, che prima si discorre le pratiche che vanno attorno, gli uomini che le maneggiano, e gli umori che le muovono, e dipoi si dice queste parole: 'Considerato adunque tutto quello che vi si è scritto, gli uomini prudenti che si trovano qua, giudicano che ne abbia a seguire il tale effetto e il tale'. Questa parte fatta bene, ha fatto a' miei dí grande onore a molti ambasciatori, e cosí fatta male, gli ha disonorati," *Opere*, ed. Vivanti, I, p. 731. On this letter and its relation to Machiavelli's own diplomatic reporting, see Niccolò Machiavelli, *The Chief Works and Others*, trans. Allan Gilbert (3 vols., Durham, NC: Duke University Press, 1965), I, pp. 116–19.

91 *Il principe* 3, p. 124: "Però e' romani, veggendo discosto gl' inconvenienti, vi rimediorno sempre, e non gli lasciorno mai seguire per fuggire una guerra, perché sapevano che la guerra non si lieva, ma si differisce a vantaggio di altri: però vollono fare con Filippo e Antioco guerra in Grecia, per non la avere a fare con loro in Italia; e potevono per allora fuggire l'una e l'altra: il che non vollono. Né piacque mai loro quello che è tutto dí in bocca de' savi de' nostri tempi, di godere il benefizio del tempo, ma sí bene quello della virtú e prudenza loro: perché il tempo si caccia innanzi ogni cosa, e può condurre seco bene come male e male come bene." Machiavelli's criticism of the Florentine republic's temporizing can be contrasted with Bruni's celebration of the Florentine's brave and fearful mode of action in the *Laudatio* (p. 257): "Sed cetere quidem res publice tantas vires intuentes perterrite erant temporibusque cedebant. Florentina autem magnitudo animi terreri non potuit, neque remittendum aliquid censuit de pristina dignitate."

noncommitment and temporization. As we shall see later in this chapter, the epithet "the wise men of our times," *i savi*, signals the Florentine context, and points to influential citizens like Piero Guicciardini and Giovanbattista Ridolfi, who in the past had opposed Machiavelli's ideas and projects on numerous occasions. In contrast to these wise men of Florence, who seek to avoid wars and military expenditures at all costs, the Romans had not placed their trust in the changing times and the fluctuations of fortune, but made a virtue of actively anticipating necessity and remedying troubles in time.

In his theoretical works, Machiavelli also takes on another central principle of the Florentine foreign policy doctrine, neutrality, *la via neutrale* or *lo stare neutrale*. In chapter 21 of *The Prince*, where he explicitly comments on the Soderinian regime's position on the conflict between France and the Holy League in 1512, he argues that a state, pressed by necessity to join forces with another state more powerful than itself, as Florence was at the time, should "unhesitatingly support" one side against the other. This course of action, however, requires foresight and an ability to take calculated risks, which excessively cautious rulers – and here Machiavelli seems to have his former employer, Piero Soderini, in mind – are unlikely to display. In the hope of escaping present dangers, such rulers can instead be expected to follow the "neutral way" (*quella via neutrale*) which most of the time leads to ruin. Arguing in general terms, the former Secretary maintains that it is always more useful to act as "a true friend and a true enemy" than "to remain neutral," since no one desires "suspect friends" (*amici sospetti*) who do not help out in adversity, and since no one gives refuge to someone who is not prepared to "share his fate with arms in hand." Therefore, he concludes, neutrality is an option only for the notoriously weak, for whom every policy is wrought with great danger, whereas states aspiring to greater things should "without hesitation" ally themselves with other states in order to fight common enemies.[92]

[92] In *Il principe* 21, the Florentine context is suggested when Machiavelli introduces his argument on the dangers of neutrality (p. 180): "È ancora stimato uno principe, quando egli è vero amico e vero inimico: cioè quando sanza alcuno respetto e' si scuopre in favore di alcuno contro a uno altro. El quale partito fia sempre piú utile che stare neutrale." Further on he makes the connection explicit (p. 181): "quando e' non si può fuggirla [joining forces with someone else] – come intervenne a fiorentini, quando el papa e Spagna andorno con li eserciti ad assaltare la Lombardia, – allora si debbe el principe aderire per le ragioni sopraddette." Machiavelli rehearses and expands on this argument in *Discorsi* II.15, where he condemns Florence's slowness in allying herself with Louis XII of France against Ludovico Sforza of Milan in 1499, and implies that the Soderinian republic fell because it failed to take sides in the conflict between France and the Holy League. We should not here be confused by the fact that *lo stare neutrale* in this chapter is treated as a pro-French policy.

SPEAKING LIKE CAMILLUS

For Machiavelli the policy of neutrality, or the *via neutrale*, is intimately linked to another key element of the contemporary Florentine foreign policy outlook, the *via del mezzo*. His first explicit attack on the middle way occurs in a short, but momentous, text, known as *Del modo di trattare i popoli della Valdichiana ribellati*, "On the mode of treating the rebelling peoples of the Valdichiana."[93] Composed during the summer or the fall of 1503, with the Aretine rebellion of June 1502 a recent memory, the memorandum contains Machiavelli's first elaborate use of the Roman model. Quoting from Livy, the Florentine Secretary reproduces Lucius Furius Camillus's speech after his decisive victory over the Latin peoples in 338 BC, in which the Roman general offers the Senate a choice between two diametrically opposed ways of ensuring everlasting peace with the Latin peoples. This, Camillus argues, could be achieved either by adopting a cruel policy of destruction, or by showing mercy to the vanquished and incorporating them into the Roman state through the granting of privileges.[94] As Machiavelli informs us, the Senate responded to Camillus's exhortation by portioning out its graces and by treating the Latin peoples according to their individual merits. While some cities were either allowed to retain their former privileges, or assimilated into the Roman state by an extension of citizenship, others were secured through destruction or severe punishment. In dealing with the last category of cities, the Romans employed two different methods of elimination (*spegnere*): they either destroyed (*rovinare*) the cities and transferred their population to Rome to dwell there permanently, or they sent out colonizers to keep them in check.[95] Through this combined strategy, Machiavelli explains, loyal and obedient subjects are created, since well-treated and satisfied people do not rebel, and since

[93] "Del modo di trattare i popoli della Valdichiana ribellati," in Machiavelli, *Opere*, I, ed. Vivanti, pp. 22–26. The version of the text that has come down to us is incomplete. On the manuscript, see Jean-Jacques Marchand, *Niccolò Machiavelli: I primi scritti politici (1499–1512): Nascita di un pensiero e di uno stile* (Padua: Antenore, 1975), pp. 101–02. On the basis of internal and external evidence, it can be assumed that the oration was written on commission by a leading citizen to be delivered before one of the city's councils. Henceforth, the text will be referred to as *Del modo*.

[94] Livy VIII.13.14: "Di immortales ita vos potentes huius consilii fecerunt ut, sit Latium deinde an non sit, in vestra manu posuerint." Machiavelli's translation (*Del modo*, p. 23) reads: "Iddio vi ha facti al tutto potenti di potere deliberare se Latio debba mantenersi o no." Note that Machiavelli here transforms the Roman gods into the Christian God, by rendering "Di immortales" as "Iddio."

[95] As Jean-Jacques Marchand has pointed out, Machiavelli in *Del modo* refashions and simplifies Livy's account of the Senate's decision by giving added emphasis to the policy of the two extremes recommended by Camillus, see Marchand, *I primi scritti*, pp. 107–14.

former enemies who have been destroyed, or reduced to a state of utter and complete impotence, lack the means for doing so.[96]

Having laid down these Roman-inspired principles, Machiavelli goes on to establish a link between them and the pressing problem at hand, the recent rebellions of Arezzo and the Valdichiana region, by quoting the traditional humanist commonplace that history is "the teacher of our actions" (*la istoria è la maestra delle azioni nostre*). The world, he assures us, has "always been inhabited in the same way by men, who have always had the same passions." There have always been those who have served and those who have commanded, and among those who have served, some who have done so willingly, and others who have done so unwillingly. In this constant order of things, towns and peoples have rebelled and been reconquered according to the same basic pattern. Should someone doubt this, Machiavelli continues, he is welcome to reflect upon "Arezzo and all the towns in Valdichiana which last year did a thing very similar to what the Latin peoples did." For even if the ways in which the Aretines and the Latins revolted and were retaken differ considerably, the basic facts underlying the rebellion and the reconquest remain the same.[97]

At this point, Machiavelli turns on the Florentine policy-makers. For to the same extent as the judgment of the ancient Romans, who had been the "masters of the world" (*padroni del mondo*), merits to be recommended, that of the modern Florentines "deserves to be criticized."[98] It is true that the latter could be said to have followed the Roman example when benefiting the peoples of Castiglione, Borgo Sansepolcro, and Foiano della Chiana, but they had failed to do so in the important case of Arezzo. For although the Aretines had acted as treacherously as the Veliterni and the Antiates, whom the Romans had punished severely, the Florentines had tried to come to terms with them by adopting an ambiguous and ill-conceived middle way policy (*via del mezzo*) between destruction and benefiting. The punishment

[96] This is also implied by the words Livy attributes to Camillus in viii.13.16. See *Livy in Fourteen Volumes*, English translation by B. O. Foster (Cambridge, MA: Harvard University Press, 1919–59), pp. 56–57: "That government is certainly by far the strongest to which its subjects yield obedience gladly" (*Certe id firmissimum longe imperium est quo oboedientes gaudent*).

[97] *Del modo*, p. 24: "Io ho sentito dire che le istorie sono la maestra delle actioni nostre, et maxime de' principi, et il mondo fu sempre ad un modo abitato da uomini che hanno avute sempre le medexime passioni; et sempre fu chi serve et chi comanda, et chi serve malvolentieri et chi serve volentieri, et chi si ribella et è ripreso. Se alcuno non credesse questo, si spechi in Arezzo l'anno passato et in tutte le terre di Valdichiana, che fanno una cosa molto simile a quella de' popoli latini: quivi si vede la ribellione et dipoi il riacquisto come qui; ancora che nel modo del ribellarsi et del riacquistare vi sia differentia assai, pure è simile la ribellione et il riacquisto."

[98] Ibid., pp. 24–25: "Et se il giuditio de' romani merita di essere commendato, tanto il vostro merita di essere biasimato."

they had so far imposed on the Aretines had been half-hearted and ineffective. By depriving them of their honors, by selling their possessions, and by defaming them in public after quartering Florentine soldiers on their homes, they had merely kindled the Aretines' ancient hatred for Florence without removing their means for future rebellion. Nor could Florence be said to have benefited them, since not erasing their city walls and not sending out new settlers to keep them subjugated (*li tengano sotto*), as the Romans had done, could hardly be considered as rewards.[99] As a consequence, new rebellions were to be expected, which could turn Arezzo into a stepping-stone for foreign powers seeking to exploit Florence's current weakness. To give the speech a heightened sense of urgency, Machiavelli at this point invokes the danger posed by Pope Alexander VI, and his son Cesare Borgia, two "connoisseurs of the opportunity" (*conoscitori della occasione*), who at the time were known to nurture plans of unifying their scattered possessions by founding a Tuscan empire, presumably with Florence as their capital or power base.[100]

The importance of *Del modo* in Machiavelli's intellectual development can hardly be exaggerated. Here, we encounter his first open criticism of the traditional Florentine doctrine of the middle way, combined with an advocacy of the strong policy of the two extremes, which was to constitute one of the basic tenets of his political theory. His ardent call in *Del modo* for a direct and whole-hearted imitation of the methods of Roman imperialism and territorial rule was later to reverberate throughout his theoretical work, and to receive its most forceful and precise articulation in the preface to the first book of the *Discourses*, which denounces modern men's propensity to view imitation of the Romans in political and military affairs as "not only difficult, but impossible."[101] With this in mind, and considering that *Del modo* deals with a matter that was one of Machiavelli's chief occupations during his time in office, the reconsolidation of the Florentine dominion, it has come to receive surprisingly little attention from Machiavelli critics. Most interpreters have chosen to pass over the memorandum in silence, or to view it as a literary exercise of little political import. As a consequence,

99 Ibid., p. 25: "A me non pare che voi alli aretini abbiate fatto nessuna di queste cose, perché e' non si chiama benefitio, ogni dí farli venire a Firenze, avere tolto loro gli onori, vendere loro le possessioni, sparlarne pubblicamente, avere tenuti loro i soldati in casa. Non si chiama assicurarsene lasciare le mura in piedi, lasciarvene abitare e' cinque sesti di loro, non dare loro compagnia di abitatori che li tenghino sotto, et non si governare in modo con loro che nelli inpedimenti et guerre che vi fossero fatte, voi non avessi a tenere piú spesa in Arezzo che all'incontro di quello inimico che vi assaltasse."

100 Ibid., p. 26: "egli aspiri allo imperio di Toscana, come piú propinquo et atto a farne un regno con li altri stati che tiene."

101 *Discorsi* I, preface, p. 198: "iudicando la imitazione non solo difficile ma impossibile."

the political advice Machiavelli advances in *Del modo* – that Florence should treat the Aretines according to the Roman method of destruction, erasing their walls, moving their citizens, and sending out settlers "to keep them subjugated" – has either not been taken seriously, or been dismissed as politically naïve.[102]

The untenability of this interpretation is evident when we consider *Del modo* in connection to the *pratica* held on 28 January 1506 to debate the still unresolved Aretine question. From this advisory meeting, we learn that Machiavelli's radical call for a direct imitation of the Roman imperialist strategy of the two extremes had come to provoke strong opposition within the Florentine *reggimento*. On this particular occasion, the advice from *Del modo* of winning Arezzo either through benefits or through destruction was brought up and openly advocated by two seasoned statesmen, Francesco Pepi and Pierfrancesco Tosinghi. The proposal presented by Pepi at the beginning of the meeting strongly recalls the contents and the wording of *Del modo*: "There are two ways of getting rid of the trouble-makers. The first is to move, if not all, at least the most suspect among them from Arezzo to some other places in that territory. The inhumanity of such a proceeding would be outweighed by the security it provides. The alternative is to

[102] Gennaro Sasso established back in the 1950s what was to become the standard way of reading *Del modo*. According to Sasso, the memorandum is basically to be seen as a literary exercise with little connection to the contemporary political context. Its teaching is doctrinaire and the text contains an undeveloped version of Machiavelli's "myth of the Romans." In these pages, Sasso writes, "the motive of the necessity to imitate the Romans is still without that firm theoretical and polemical determination" which later was to characterize *Il principe* and the *Discorsi*. See Gennaro Sasso, *Niccolò Machiavelli: Storia del suo pensiero politico* (Naples: L'Istituto italiano per gli studi storici, 1958), pp. 65–67. A similar view is expressed by Sergio Bertelli, who argues that Machiavelli in *Del modo* overlooks the complexities of contemporary Florentine politics, and that the text, because of its literary character, is of little practical interest. See Sergio Bertelli, "Nota introduttiva," in Niccolò Machiavelli, *Arte della guerra e scrittici politici minori*, ed. S. Bertelli (Milan: Feltrinelli, 1961), p. 68. For a similar reading, see Roberto Ridolfi, *Vita di Niccolò Machiavelli* (2 vols., Florence: Sansoni, 1969), 1, p. 83. More recently, Elena Fasano Guarini has claimed that *Del modo* is the first text in which Machiavelli "comes under the spell of the Roman model." See Elena Fasano Guarini, "Machiavelli and the Crisis of the Italian Republics," in *Machiavelli and Republicanism*, eds. G. Bock, Q. Skinner, and M. Viroli (Cambridge: Cambridge University Press, 1990), p. 23. By contrast, Jean-Jacques Marchand claims that *Del modo* is invested with a "a pragmatic value," and that the memorandum is the only text from these years in which Machiavelli openly contests the official Florentine policy. See Marchand, *I primi scritti*, p. 324. Cf. ibid., pp. 105, 107, and 329. For other brief comments, see C. C. Bayley, *War and Society in Renaissance Florence: The* De Militia *of Leonardo Bruni* (Toronto: University of Toronto Press, 1961), p. 250; Mark Hulliung, *Citizen Machiavelli* (Princeton: Princeton University Press, 1983), pp. 64–65; Maurizio Viroli, *Il sorriso di Niccolò: Storia di Machiavelli* (Bari: Laterza, 1998), pp. 70–72. In his 500-page biography of Machiavelli, *Machiavelli in Hell* (London: Picador, 1992), Sebastian de Grazia does not devote a single word to *Del modo*. On Florence's rule of Arezzo in the Quattrocento and early Cinquecento, see Robert Black, "Arezzo, the Medici and the Florentine State," in *Florentine Tuscany*, ed. W. J. Connell and A. Zorzi (Cambridge: Cambridge University Press, 2000), pp. 293–311.

reinforce the town with sufficient forces."[103] Speaking towards the end of the meeting, Pierfrancesco Tosinghi, who had been a military commissioner during the Pisan campaign in 1499, a member of the Ten of War in 1502, and an envoy to the Pisan front together with Pepi in 1505,[104] supported the latter's proposal, explicitly rejecting the middle way (*el mezo*), and arguing that the only way of appeasing the discontented Aretines was either "by extinguishing or by favoring them."[105]

However, the *pratica* emphatically rejected this radical proposal, opting for a more moderate approach based on the traditional Florentine middle way. Piero Guicciardini, the father of Francesco, who had served together with Tosinghi on the Ten of War back in 1502,[106] summarized in the closing statement what appears to have been the general view of the meeting. Seconding Giovanbattista Ridolfi, he claimed that the Florentine authorities ought to furnish the fortress of Arezzo, keep her inhabitants under surveillance, and impose good government on the city. To gain the Aretines by means of favors and benefits, Guicciardini the elder judged to be impractical, if not outright impossible. The idea of sending new settlers to the town, a policy previously advocated by Machiavelli in *Del modo* and now restated by Pepi and Tosinghi, he opposed on the grounds that it "was a Roman thing" (*era cosa de' Romani*) that was not practiced anymore.[107] In other words, Piero Guicciardini, like Machiavelli in *Del modo*, associated the policy of the two extremes with the ancient Romans; but whereas the Secretary had brought up the Roman example in support of this strategy, Piero now used it to advise against it.[108]

103 *Consulte e pratiche 1505–1512*, p. 76: "Et ci sono duo modi di cavare li sospecti: et benché sieno tutti, almeno li più sospecti, commutandoli da Arezo a altri luoghi vostri. Et alla inhumanità suplisce la sicurtà, o mectervi tante forze che bastino." In preparation for his *Istorie fiorentine*, Machiavelli in the 1520s composed a biographical sketch on Francesco Pepi, in which he potrayed him – together with Piero Capponi, Antonio Giacomini, Cosimo de' Pazzi, and Francesco Valori – as an example of a virtuous and noble citizen who served the Florentine republic at the turn of the Cinquecento. See Mark Jurdjevic, "Machiavelli's Sketches of Francesco Valori and the Reconstruction of Florentine History," *Journal of the History of Ideas* 63 (2002): 185–206, esp. 190–91.

104 On the mission of 1505, see Bartolomeo Cerretani, *Storia fiorentina* (Florence: Olschki, 1994), p. 339. Francesco Guicciardini identifies Pierfrancesco Tosinghi as belonging to the inner circle of Piero Soderini's power group; see Francesco Guicciardini, *Storie fiorentine dal 1378 al 1509* (Bari: Laterza, 1931), p. 328.

105 *Consulte e pratiche 1505–1512*, pp. 76–77: "Et circha allo universale, della mala contenteza delli Aretini, che el mezo non serve, et bisogna o stirparli o benificarli."

106 See Guicciardini, *Storie fiorentine*, p. 227.

107 *Consulte e pratiche 1505–1512*, p. 77: "fornire la forteza, guardare bene la città et governarli bene. Che mandarvi nuovi habitatori era cosa de' Romani, et che non si usa al presente. Et vincerli con benefitii non si possano."

108 The possibility that *Del modo* exerted a certain influence in Florence at the time is also suggested by Bartolomeo Cerretani's account of the Aretine rebellion in his *Storia fiorentina*. Here Cerretani

Piero Guicciardini and Giovanbattista Ridolfi belonged to the conservative wing of the Florentine *reggimento*. They were two of the city's most reputed *savi*, or wise men, a category of respected citizens of high social standing, who traditionally convened in the *consulte* and *pratiche* to give their *parere,* or informed opinion, on matters of policy. Francesco Guicciardini describes his father as a "very wise man" (*uomo molto savio*), an advocate of moderation and the middle way, and a staunch opponent of the extreme policies, ranking him, together with Giovanbattista Ridolfi, as the best brain of the city.[109] Even though there is a considerable element of self-promotion involved in this portrait, it gives a fairly accurate account of the reputation Piero Guicciardini and Giovanbattista Ridolfi had come to enjoy in Florence during the Soderinian era. The fact that two of the republic's most influential citizens so emphatically rejected Machiavelli's proposal for a Roman-inspired policy of the two extremes gives us an indication of the kind of opposition the Secretary's imperialist project was up against.[110]

That Machiavelli was aware of this opposition is evident from his theoretical work, where he on repeated occasions attacks "the wise men of our city" (*i savi della nostra città*), an expression that seems to implicate Giovanbattista Ridolfi, Piero Guicciardini, and their power group. In *The Art of War*, he defends the militia ordinance, which he had been instrumental in introducing back in 1506, against the "many wise men (*molti savi uomini*) who have blamed it, and continue to blame it" for the fall of the Soderinian republic in 1512.[111] As we have already seen, the former Secretary condemns

speaks (p. 300) of Alexander IV's desire to make Cesare Borgia "signore di Toschana" and compares the rebellion of 1502 with an example drawn from Roman history: "come già si vidde insino al temppo della rebellione de' 12 popoli toschani contro a la romana republica . . ."

109 Francesco Guicciardini, *Scritti autobiografici e rari* (Bari: Laterza, 1936), p. 71: "Fu Piero uomo molto savio e di grande iudicio e vedere quanto alcuno altro che fussi a Firenze nel tempo suo . . . al tempo della morte era in grandissima riputazione, e si teneva che di cervello e gravitá, da Giovan Batista Ridolfi in fuora, non fussi in Firenze uomo che lo agguagliassi."

110 In Francesco Guicciardini's *Dialogo*, Piero is portrayed as holding a skeptical view of the imitation of the ancient Romans in political and military affairs. In *Discorsi* III.15, Machiavelli relates how Ridolfi, who "was a man of reputation" (*era uomo di riputazione*) (p. 464), in 1500 was sent as military commissioner to the Pisan front together with the considerably younger Antonio degli Albizzi. Machiavelli, who was present on the occasion, claims that Ridolfi during his stay in the camp hindered the younger man from showing "how much he was worth with spirit, with industry, and with counsel" (*quanto con l'animo, con la industria e col consiglio valeva*). After having contrasted this modern example with an ancient one, derived from Livy, Machiavelli draws the conclusion that it is better to place the administration of military affairs in the hands of one man, as the ancients did, than to appoint two or more commissioners, as modern republics tend to do. The criticism Machiavelli here passes on Ridolfi is subtle, but clearly discernible.

111 *Arte della guerra*, p. 547. On Piero Guicciardini's and Giovanbattista Ridolfi's opposition to Machiavelli's militia project, see Guicciardini, *Storie fiorentine*, p. 281.

in *The Prince* 3 "the wise of our times" (*savi de' nostri tempi*) for always advocating a policy of temporization, contrasting it with the confrontational approach of the foresighted Romans, who were truly wise. In this chapter, he also gets back, or so it seems, at Piero Guicciardini, who, as we recall, in the *pratica* of 28 January 1506, had recommended that Florence, instead of resorting to the extreme measure of sending out colonists, should take the moderate step of reinforcing the garrison in Arezzo. Such a strategy, Machiavelli now argues, is in reality not only more costly but also more oppressive than colonization:

> by maintaining armed men [in an annexed province] instead of sending colonists, one spends much more, because all the revenue of the region will be consumed on its garrison. The outcome is that the territory gained results in loss to [the conqueror]; and he commits far greater offenses, because it harms the whole of that region when his troops move round for lodgings. Everyone suffers this nuisance, and everyone becomes an enemy. And these are dangerous enemies because, although defeated, they remain in their own homes. From every point of view, then, such guards are as useless as colonists are useful.[112]

He returns to the issue later in chapter 20, where he criticizes "our ancients and those who were esteemed wise" (*li antichi nostri, e quelli che erano stimati savi*) for propagating the view that Pisa must be held by fortresses and Pistoia by factions, two policies which are here associated with the middle way and the maintenance of the status quo.[113] In *Discourses* II.24, he similarily castigates "these wise of our times" (*questi savi de' nostri tempi*) for insisting on using fortresses despite the fact that the Romans had decided against it.[114]

In *Discourses* II.23, Machiavelli continues to pursue his sustained campaign against the proverbial wisdom of the wise men of his time in connection to the Aretine question. Here, as in *Del modo*, he links Florence's reacquisition of Arezzo in 1502 with the Roman republic's conquest of Latium in 338 BC, quoting at length from Camillus's speech in Livy. Yet

[112] *Il principe* 3, pp. 122–23: "Ma tenendovi, in cambio di colonie, gente d'arme, spende piú assai, avendo a consumare nella guardia tutte le intrate di quello stato, in modo che l'acquisto gli torna perdita; e offende molto piú, perché nuoce a tutto quello stato, tramutando con li alloggiamenti il suo esercito; del quale disagio ognuno ne sente e ciascuno gli diventa nimico: e sono nimici che gli possono nuocere, rimandendo battuti in casa loro. Da ogni parte dunque questa guardia è inutile, come quella delle colonie è utile." Here in *Il principe* 3, as in *Del modo*, Machiavelli defines sending out colonists as part of the policy of the two extremes, destruction or benefits, reiterating the formula from Camillus's speech in Livy, while rehearsing the rationale behind the strategy (*Il principe* 3, p. 122): "Per ché si ha a notare che gli uomini si debbono o vezzeggiare o spegnere: perché si vendicano delle leggieri offese, delle gravi non possono; sí che la offesa che si fa all'uomo debbe essere in modo che la non tema la vendetta."

[113] *Il principe* 20, p. 176. [114] *Discorsi* II.24, p. 391.

again, he holds up the Roman mode of dealing with conquered peoples as the model for Florence to emulate. If the Florentines back in 1502 had followed the Roman example and bestowed "exemptions, privileges, and citizenship" (*donando loro la città*)[115] on some of the recovered cities, while securing the others through destruction, that is, by sending out colonists and by moving the population back to Florence, they would have "made their empire secure and the city of Florence most great (*grandissima*)."[116] But instead, they had, as was their habit, opted for the middle way, by banishing some of the Aretines, sentencing others to death, depriving everyone of their honors and ancient ranks, and leaving the city standing.[117] In a direct reference to the debates of the time, Machiavelli responds to the objections raised by the opponents of the policy of destruction: "If any citizen counseled in the deliberations that Arezzo should be destroyed, those who appeared to be wiser (*che pareva essere piú savi*) said that it would be of little honor to the republic to destroy her since it would seem that Florence lacked forces to hold her."[118] But that the destruction of Arezzo would have brought dishonor to Florence is a view that Machiavelli could not accept. What had given the city a bad reputation instead, he argues, was her ignorant and cowardly policy of neutrality and the middle way, the *stare neutrale* and the *via del mezzo*, advocated and defended by the "wise men" of the day. True honor, Machiavelli claims, does not consist in governing a state under a thousand dangers, but in providing for its security by punishing those individuals, or cities, who sin (*pecca*) against it.[119]

To sum up the preceding discussion, three general observations can be made. First, it should by now be clear that Machiavelli's repeated attacks on

[115] Ibid., II.23, p. 388: "faccendo ai beneficati esenzioni, privilegi, donando loro la città, e da ogni parte assicurandogli."

[116] Ibid, II.23, p. 389: "il che se avessono fatto, arebbero assicurato lo imperio loro e fatto grandissima la città di Firenze, e datogli quegli campi che per vivere gli mancono."

[117] Professor Harvey Mansfield notes that Machiavelli does not mention any benefits conferred by the Florentines upon the Aretines, and argues that the example is designed to show that it was the Romans, not the Florentines, who adopted a middle way between destroying and benefiting; see Harvey C. Mansfield Jr., *Machiavelli's New Modes and Orders: A Study of the Discourses on Livy* (Ithaca: Cornell University Press, 1979), p. 262. Perhaps it would be more correct to say that while the Florentines practiced the middle way by imposing modest and ineffectual punishments and by refraining from destroying the city, the Romans adopted a policy based on a combination of the two extremes. The benefit the Florentines bestowed on the Aretines could thus be said to consist in something they could have done, but refrained from doing, that is, destroying the city.

[118] *Discorsi* II.23, p. 389: "E se alcuno cittadino nelle diliberazioni consigliava che Arezzo si disfacesse, a quegli che pareva essere piú savi dicevano come e' sarebbe poco onore della republica disfarla, perché e' parebbe che Firenze mancasse di forze da tenerli."

[119] Ibid, II.23, p. 389: "E l'onore consiste nel potere e sapere gastigarla, non nel potere con mille pericoli tenerla: perché quel principe che non gastiga chi erra in modo che non possa piú errare, è tenuto o ignorante o vile."

the policy of the middle way and frequent invocations of the Roman model need to be understood in connection to the ideological context of contemporary Florentine political debate. As I have shown elsewhere, the ancient Romans had at the turn of the Cinquecento in Florence, following the Savonarolan religious revival and the spread of anti-Medicean sentiment, come to be invested with strong negative connotations.[120] In the eyes of most Savonarolans, the Romans were simply too pagan and too sinful to warrant imitation, and for the ruling *ottimati* the ancient Roman republic represented a political ideal that was at one and the same time too monarchic and too popular to serve their aristocratic aspirations. In addition to this, both groups had good reason to view the Roman example as ideologically tainted or suspect, because of the way in which in the recent past it had come to be used in Medicean propaganda. So when Machiavelli in 1503, in *Del modo*, quoted the imperial strategy of ancient Rome and exhorted his compatriots to emulate those who formerly had been the *padroni del mondo*, he was clearly going against the grain of current Florentine political opinion and challenging, purposely or inadvertently, contemporary religious, ethical, and moral sensibilities. Second, as we have begun to see, Machiavelli's forceful vindication of the Roman example in the *Discourses* and *The Art of War* should be seen in part as a return to the civic and patriotic outlook of Quattrocento humanism, in part as a new and radical departure. For although the policy Machiavelli recommends is animated by the same aims and the same aspirations as Florentine civic humanism, that is, liberty at home and empire abroad, the means he advocates for achieving these ends are of a radically different order. The Romans Machiavelli in *Del modo*, and later in his theoretical works, recommends his fellow citizens to follow are basically the same outrageously vicious and extremist Romans that the Savonarolans and the *ottimati* condemned or censured, not the decorous and good-natured Romans celebrated by Bruni, Palmieri, and the other civic humanists. Third, taken together, these observations give us reason to reconsider the genesis, the ideological contents and the rhetoric of *The Prince*. Situated in time between the explicit reference to the Roman model in *Del modo* and the detailed discussions on the civil and military orders of the ancient Roman republic in the *Discourses* and *The Art of War*, Machiavelli's comparatively low-key treatment of the Romans in *The Prince* poses something of a mystery that we shall have reason to return to in the chapters that follow.

[120] On the negative view of the ancient Romans in Florence at the turn of the sixteenth century, see Mikael Hörnqvist, "*Perché non si usa allegare i Romani*: Machiavelli and the Florentine Militia of 1506," *Renaissance Quarterly* 55 (2002): 148–91, esp. 164–66.

In this chapter, we have seen how Machiavelli undermines the theoretical foundation of the just war theory by arguing that states have a natural desire for conquest, and how he in his chancery writings and in his theoretical work addresses and challenges the normative vocabulary associated with the dominant foreign policy doctrine of early Cinquecento Florence, based on the notions of the middle way, neutrality, and temporization. To speak in terms of the three-tier interpretative model from chapter 1, our discussion has here been concerned with how Machiavelli's work on the intermediary level of ideological manipulation seeks to influence, to unsettle, and to refashion contemporary discourse on war and the established ways of defining and rationalizing Florentine foreign policy. If Florence were to rise to imperial greatness, his argument implies, the city's traditional way of thinking and conducting foreign and external policy would have to be abandoned. In his view, the policy of the middle way was not only ill-adapted to the unstable and fluctuating world of international politics, but contrary to human nature and to the general conditions of sublunar existence as well. The policy of temporization, while being congenial to weak states that lacked the force to act openly and aggressively, could if used routinely, as in Florence's case, become a sign of the very weakness it was meant to conceal. By remaining neutral and refusing to take sides in the ongoing battle for power, ancient and recent history teaches, one gains neither friends, nor peace and security, nor reputation, only a thousand dangers. In Machiavelli's conclusion, the Florentine wise men had by reifying these notions given an appearance of cautious realism to a policy that in reality was a short-sighted half-measure fraught with ambiguity and lack of resolve.

By confronting the political convictions and pieties of his day with the example of Roman imperialism and its strategic use of the two extremes, offensive alliances, and swift and decisive action, Machiavelli sought to open up a radically new way of conceiving and talking about war and foreign policy in contemporary Florence. The more specific aims of this rhetorical project will be the subject of the following chapter.

CHAPTER 4

To destroy them or to live there

The ruling nation seeks to transform other peoples into its own image.

Solomon Ibn Verga

When the Florentine colonist Piero Vaglienti, a few days before the entry of the French into Pisa in November 1494, approached the Florentine commissioner with a proposal for having one hundred fifty or two hundred leading Pisan citizens deported to Florence as a precautionary measure, he was received with a mixture of indifference and complacent arrogance. Since the commissioner found it inconceivable that the Pisans, who had been under Florentine rule for almost a century, would be able to recall the city's past liberty any more, he saw no reason to doubt their loyalty. Of course, he was spectacularly wrong. The night after the French had entered Pisa, the streets of the city resounded to the ancient cry "libertà! libertà!"[1] The marzocchi, the Florentine lions and the very emblem of Florentine rule, on the bridges over the Arno were destroyed and thrown into the river. Over night, lifelong friendships between Pisans and Florentines turned into animosity, as Florentine citizens were attacked and their houses sacked.[2] Around this time, a Pisan notary wrote in his *Ricordi*: "The Pisans have always been a free and generous people. The wars they have fought against the Ligurians and the Genoese since the commencement of the Pisan name

[1] Piero Vaglienti, *Storia dei suoi tempi 1492–1514*, eds. G. Berti, M. Luzzati, and E. Tongiorgi (Pisa: Nistri-Lischi e Pacini Editori, 1982), pp. 11, 17, and 224.

[2] Vaglienti, *Storia*, p. 19. On Florence's rule of Pisa 1406–94, see Michael Mallett, "Pisa and Florence in the Fifteenth Century: Aspects of the Period of the First Florentine Domination," in *Florentine Studies: Politics and Society in Renaissance Florence*, ed. N. Rubinstein (London: Faber and Faber, 1968), pp. 403–41. For the Pisan rebellion, see H. C. Butters, *Governors and Government in Early Sixteenth-Century Florence 1502–1519* (Oxford: Clarendon Press, 1985), pp. 26–31. Francesco Guicciardini relates (*Storie fiorentine dal 1378 al 1509* [Bari: Laterza, 1931], p. 99) how the Pisans, after it had become known that the French had taken possession of the fortress, assembled in order to go and "chiedere al re rendessi loro la libertá; la quale sendo conceduta, gridando 'libertá' andorono per fare villania agli uficiali fiorentini". The source for this account is most probably Piero Guicciardini, Francesco's father, who is mentioned among the Florentine officials who on the occasion were saved by the French king's troops from "la malignitá e perfidia de' pisani."

have demonstrated their worth . . . Liberty has always been dear to our people, because it was given to us by our ancestors and betters."[3] Later, after the French had left Pisa, leaving only a small garrison behind, the city rose in rebellion, reclaimed her ancient communal liberties, and expelled the remaining Florentines living in the city. To judge by contemporary Pisan sources, the inhabitants of the city would rather die than return under Florentine domination. As one chronicler puts it: "We defend and will go on to defend this city with firm and constant spirits, offering our blood unto death, supporting every hardship, difficulty and extreme condition for her health and our own; because every good citizen is obliged to act in this way. Miserable and mean is that republic which does not have citizens who are prepared to die for her dignity and conservation."[4]

For the Florentines, the loss of Pisa was a gruesome stain on the city's honor. As we recall, the conquest of the seaport back in 1406 had been celebrated as one of the greatest acquisitions in the history of Florentine territorial expansion. Goro Dati had extolled it as a victory of Good over Evil, while Leonardo Bruni compared it to the Roman republic's triumph over Carthage. At the turn of the Cinquecento, it was also universally acknowledged that the possession of the seaport, and the access to the sea it provided, was vital to Florentine interests. In the *pratiche*, Florentine statesmen like Bernardo of Diacceto and Giovanbattista Ridolfi referred to Pisa as "the heart" of Florence,[5] and her recovery as a priceless thing that would give "soul to the city."[6] While some felt that it would be preferable if the war could be waged in a just way, it was more often argued that principles like divine providence and justice should be left aside and Pisa retaken at all costs and "without hesitation" (*sanza respetto*).[7] Many claimed that the city's honor and reputation were at stake, but these concerns seem to have related to the outcome of the struggle rather than the means employed. As a rule, the justice of the Florentine cause was simply taken for granted, which helps to explain why the republic did not refrain from using questionable

[3] "Ricordi di Ser Perizolo da Pisa dall'anno 1422 sino al 1510," *Archivio storico italiano* 6.2 (1845), p. 391.

[4] "La guerra del millecinquecento," *Archivio storico italiano* 6.2 (1845), p. 379.

[5] *Consulte e pratiche 1505–1512*, ed. D. Fachard (Geneva: Droz, 1988), p. 49: "che Pisa era il core della città."

[6] Ibid., p. 48: "Et che non si poteva negare che il rihavere Pisa era uno rendere l'anima alla città; et però, quando si credessi che l'havessi ad riuscire, sarebbe da spendervi ogni cosa." In the *pratica* of 19 August 1505, four speakers referred to the reconquest of Pisa as "il desiderio dello universale della città," or in similar terms; see ibid., pp. 49–51. Cf. *Discorsi* 1.39 and 1.53. Cf. Guicciardini, *Storie fiorentine*, pp. 224–25.

[7] *Consulte e pratiche 1505–1512*, pp. 224–25.

methods such as raids on the Pisan countryside and attempts at draining the city by redirecting the flow of the river Arno.[8]

Despite enormous sums of money spent on hiring mercenaries and repeated French assurances about the restoration of Pisa, the Florentine war effort was met with failure for over a decade.[9] It was not until June 1509, when the Florentine army, in part consisting of the peasant militia recruited and organized by Machiavelli, finally managed to break down the Pisan resistance, that the seaport could be brought back under Florentine control. The official act of surrender, in which the Pisans "with humility and reverence" begged the Florentines to accept them and their descendants as their loyal subjects for all time to come, was signed in Florence on 4 June, and countersigned for the Florentines by the Secretaries of the First and Second Chanceries, Marcello Virgilio and Niccolò Machiavelli.[10] When Machiavelli during the summer, or the fall, of 1513 began to compose *The Prince*, Pisa had thus been back in Florentine possession for little over four years.

Machiavelli's treatment of the Pisan question, which will be the main topic of this chapter, must be seen within the broader context of his general criticism of the traditional ways of Florentine imperialism. Although considerable portions of *The Prince* and the *Discourses* are devoted to this issue, it has attracted surprisingly little scholarly interest.[11] This lack of attention is all the more surprising when we consider how intimately involved Machiavelli during his time in the Chancery was in the republic's rule of

8 Butters, *Governors and Government*, pp. 86–89. Bernardo Nasi, a former follower of Savonarola and a friend of Piero Soderini, argued that since Florence was waging a just war, she should place her trust in God and fight bravely until the enemy could be brought to Florence defeated and with a collar around his neck. See *Consulte e Pratiche 1505–1512*, p. 225. On the Arno project, see also Roger D. Masters, *Fortune is a River: Leonardo da Vinci and Niccolò Machiavelli's Magnificent Dream to Change the Course of Florentine History* (New York: Plume, 1999).

9 The Florentine failure can be ascribed in part to the support the Pisan rebels received from Venice, Milan, and Lucca, in part to the Florentines' own mismanagement of the war. See Jean-Jacques Marchand, *Niccolò Machiavelli: I primi scritti politici (1499–1512): Nascita di un pensiero e di uno stile* (Padua: Antenore, 1975), pp. 5–8; Butters, *Governors and Government*, pp. 27–31, and *passim.*

10 The official document is in Oreste Tommasini, *La vita e gli scritti di Niccolò Machiavelli nella loro relazione col Machiavellismo* (2 vols., Rome, 1883–1911), 1, pp. 685–701.

11 To the best of my knowledge there exists no comprehensive study on the subject. Harvey Mansfield discusses problems relating to this matter in the course of his running commentary to *Discorsi* in *Machiavelli's New Modes and Orders: A Study of the Discourses on Livy* (Ithaca: Cornell University Press, 1979). Sergio Bertelli and Jean-Jacques Marchand treat Machiavelli's involvement in the administration of the Florentine dominion during his time in the Chancery in their commentaries to Machiavelli's early writings; see Marchand, *I primi scritti*, and Niccolò Machiavelli, *Arte della guerra e scritti politici minori*, ed. S. Bertelli (Milan: Feltrinelli, 1961). See also William J. Connell, "Republican Territorial Government: Florence and Pistoia, Fifteenth and Early Sixteenth Centuries" Ph.D dissertation, University of California, Berkeley, 1989.

her subject cities, and the extent to which his preoccupation with external affairs and the maintenance and augmentation of the Florentine dominion is reflected in his writings from the period. The project of reconquering Pisa is the focus of interest in the *Discorso di Pisa* (1499), *Decennale primo* (1504), and in his treatises and memoranda on the militia; the question of how to subjugate and control Arezzo and the rebellious region of Valdichiana is addressed in *Del modo* (1503); and the problems associated with Florence's rule of Pistoia are the main concern of his *Ragguaglio delle cose fatte dalla repubblica fiorentina per quietare le parti di Pistoia* (1502). This general interest in conquest and the holding of annexed territories also informs the *Ghiribizzi* of 1506. As this brief survey suggests, the collapse and subsequent recovery of the Florentine dominion was one of Machiavelli's main concerns, if not his principal interest, during his time as Secretary for the Second Chancery, the Ten of War, and the Nine of the Militia.

Machiavelli's stand on the Pisan question in the Chancery writings did not depart considerably from that of his compatriots. In his *Discourse on Pisa* of June 1499, addressed to the Ten of Liberty, he claimed that it was universally agreed that "it is necessary to retake Pisa to maintain our liberty."[12] This could be accomplished in two different ways, he argued: either by force (*forza*) or by love (*amore*), that is, through siege or through voluntary surrender. But the Pisans' recent refusal to receive the Florentine ambassadors, and their general "perfidy" (*perfidia*), clearly indicated that they would "never enter under [Florence's] yoke by their own free will."[13] Therefore, Machiavelli concluded, the Florentines would have no choice other than to subdue them by force, either by siege and starvation, or by direct assault.

Florence's desire to recapture Pisa was also a constant theme during Machiavelli's mission to the court of Cesare Borgia in late 1502. In the reports he sent home to the Ten, he relates how the duke and various members of his court, by means of open suggestions and half-spoken promises and insinuations, sought to exploit the Florentines' hopes and desire of regaining the maritime city. On one occasion, an anonymous friend of Machiavelli's at the court hinted at the possibility that Cesare would be willing to put an end to the Pisan rebellion, if the republic were to hire him and grant him a *condotta*, or military contract.[14] During one of Machiavelli's audiences with Cesare, the duke praised Florence's brave attempts to

[12] "Discorso sopra Pisa," in Niccolò Machiavelli, *Opere*, ed. C. Vivanti (3 vols., Turin: Einaudi, 1997–), 1, p. 3: "Che riavere Pisa sia necessario ad volere mantenere la libertà, perché nessuno ne dubita." For the background and the date of this text, see Marchand, *I primi scritti*, pp. 5–16.

[13] "Discorso sopra Pisa," p. 3: "non si puote né debbe ad nessun modo credere che per se medesimi mai venghino voluntarij sotto el iugo vostro."

[14] *Legazioni e commissarie*, p. 700.

take the city and told the envoy that he regarded Pisa as "the most glorious conquest a captain could make."[15] Although the Ten in their instructions to Machiavelli claimed that the recovery of Pisa continued to be "the principal desire" (*il principal desiderio*) of the republic,[16] their suspicions concerning Cesare's intentions were too great to permit a rapprochement.

Later, when the threat of Cesare Borgia had subsided, Machiavelli returned to the question of Pisa in the *Decennale primo* (*c.* 1504), a chronicle in verse relating the political events in Italy during the ten-year period following the French invasion in 1494.[17] In his original dedication to Alamanno Salviati, Machiavelli celebrated this influential citizen for having "maintained the liberty of one of [Italy's] foremost members," and he went on to extol him in the poem for having remedied three of Florence's "four mortal wounds," that is, the rebellions of Pistoia, Arezzo, and the Valdichiana.[18] The fourth wound, the Pisan revolt, remained open though, and towards the end of the chronicle, Machiavelli argued that the Florentines' road to security and to a safe port (*porto*) would be "easier and shorter" if they decided to "reopen the temple to Mars."[19] By this time, it would seem, the repeated failures on the Pisan front had brought Machiavelli to the conclusion that, in order to reconquer the seaport, Florence needed to set up its own military force. Eventually, this conviction would lead to the arming of the Florentine *contado* and the institution of the new militia ordinance in 1506.[20]

THE FLORENTINE *HERE AND NOW*

Machiavelli returns to the question of Pisa in chapters 5 and 20 of *The Prince*, and in *Discourses* II.21 and II.24. In the following we shall explore Quentin Skinner's suggestion that there exists a close and intriguing connection between the argument of *The Prince* 5, and the political situation in and around Florence at the time.[21] But before we can begin to inquire into

[15] Ibid., p. 744: "la piú gloriosa expugnatione che potessi fare uno capitano."

[16] Ibid., p. 666. Cf. ibid., pp. 714, 722–23, 744, 760–62, and 765.

[17] On *Decennale primo*, see Gennaro Sasso, "Per alcuni versi del primo 'Decennale,'" *Cultura e scuola* 9 (1970): 216–28. See also Butters, *Governors and Government*, p. 72; Sergio Bertelli, "Machiavelli and Soderini," *Renaissance Quarterly* 28 (1975), pp. 10–13.

[18] "Decennale primo," vv. 355–69, in *Opere*, ed. Vivanti, I, p. 102.

[19] Ibid., vv. 549–50, p. 107: "ma sarebbe il cammin facile e corto / se voi il tempio riaprissi a Marte."

[20] On Machiavelli's contribution to the Florentine militia of 1506, see Mikael Hörnqvist, "*Perché non si usa allegare i Romani*: Machiavelli and the Florentine Militia of 1506," *Renaissance Quarterly* 55 (2002): 148–91.

[21] Quentin Skinner, *Machiavelli* (Oxford: Oxford University Press, 1981), p. 24. Cf. Skinner, "Introduction," in Machiavelli, *The Prince*, eds. Quentin Skinner and Russell Price (Cambridge: Cambridge University Press, 1988), p. xii.

how Machiavelli's discussion relates to contemporary Florentine politics, we need to take a closer look at some of the principal issues addressed in the local political debate of the day. Having provided this context, we will return to *The Prince* 5 to examine the role played in this chapter by the Pisan question.

The first issue of great topicality that Machiavelli addresses in the course of *The Prince* 5 concerns the difficulty of wiping out the memory of liberty among a conquered people used to living under a free, republican form of government. From 1494 to 1512 Florence had been ruled, at least in theory, as a broadly based republic with the Great Council (*Consiglio Grande*), a popular assembly of approximately 3,000 members, created in 1494 on the model of the Venetian *Consiglio Maggiore*, vesting considerable authority. But this republican experiment had been brought to an abrupt end when the Medici, within weeks of their return to the city in September 1512, decided to close the Great Council and to demolish its meeting hall, which for many Florentines had come to stand as the very symbol of the city's popular form of government.[22] However, to most political observers of the day, it was clear that Florence's more than two centuries' long tradition of republicanism, and seventeen years of popular participation in political life, could not be erased in a single stroke. Back in the 1490s, Savonarola had claimed that republicanism had become so "habitual and fixed" in the minds of the Florentines that it "would be difficult, if not impossible, to separate them from this form of government."[23] A similar opinion was later to be voiced in Francesco Guicciardini's *Dialogue*, where Pagolantonio Soderini, a leading representative of the Savonarolan regime, is allowed to break out in an inflammatory speech in defense of Florentine republicanism: "If free government is good elsewhere, in our city, where it is natural and based on what people universally want, it is the best, since in Florence liberty is no less engraved in men's hearts than it is written on our walls and banners."[24] Although the aristocratic Guicciardini himself did not sympathize with the radical views of the Savonarolans, he realized that the republican experience

[22] The last recorded meeting of the Great Council was held on 7 September 1512. On the proposals to reopen the Great Council, see Felix Gilbert, *Machiavelli and Guicciardini: Politics and History in Sixteenth Century Florence* (Princeton: Princeton University Press, 1965), p. 100. Cf. J. N. Stephens, *The Fall of the Florentine Republic 1512–1530* (Oxford: Clarendon Press, 1983), p. 59.

[23] Girolamo Savonarola, "Treatise on the Constitution and Government of the City of Florence," text in *Humanism and Liberty: Writings on Freedom from Fifteenth-Century Florence*, ed. R. N. Watkins (Columbia: University of South Carolina Press, 1978), pp. 231–59. For quotation, see p. 237.

[24] Francesco Guicciardini, *Dialogo e discorsi del Reggimento di Firenze* (Bari: Laterza, 1932), p. 18: "uno vivere libero, quale se negli altri luoghi è buono, è ottimo nella nostra cittá dove è naturale e secondo lo appetito universale; perché in Firenze non è manco scolpita ne' cuori degli uomini la libertá, che sia scritta nelle nostre mura e bandiere."

of the Great Council had made such a deep imprint on the hearts and minds of his compatriots that the Medici, no matter how benevolently and mildly they were to rule, never would be able to erase people's memory of the "sweet liberty" they had tasted during the days of the Council.[25]

There was disagreement on this point, however. In a small treatise of November 1516 addressed to the Medici, Lodovico Alamanni expressed a contrasting view.[26] Florence's unruly and violent history, Alamanni concedes, might suggest that no ruler will ever be able to possess the city with security, and there can be no denying that there are many who are discontented with the new regime and wish to see the Great Council reopened. Nevertheless, he goes on to claim, the Medici will, if they act with foresight and combine the ways of Lorenzo the Magnificent and a more openly princely style of government, succeed in establishing themselves even among this rebellious and tumultuous people.[27] Above all, they should seek the support of the young, whose behavior and habit of mind have not yet developed into a second nature. Once these *giovani* have been alienated from the old, civic ways of the republic, Alamanni claims, it will be possible to refashion them into loyal courtiers, soldiers, and Medici partisans.[28] In the light of these conflicting positions on the Florentine love of liberty, it is clear that when Machiavelli in *The Prince* 5 comments on the role of memory for the survival of republicanism under princely rule, he is addressing not only a central tenet of the republican tradition, but a hotly contested issue in contemporary Florentine debate as well.[29]

The second key issue in the contemporary debate discussed in *The Prince* 5 concerns what could be termed the Laurentian paradigm. As Alamanni's argument above suggests, many Medici partisans looked at the time to the indirect form of government exercised by Lorenzo the Magnificent towards the end of the Quattrocento as a model for how the city should be ruled in the future.[30] In Guicciardini's *Dialogue*, the figure of Piero Capponi sets forth the by now conventional view that the Medici during most of the Quattrocento had ruled the city as a principality, or an oligarchy, under a republican cloak. According to him, Lorenzo and his family had based

[25] Guicciardini, *Ricordi*, 2nd series, n. 38, in Francesco Guicciardini, *Scritti politici e ricordi* (Bari: Laterza, 1933), p. 293. Cf. Butters, *Governors and Government*, p. 209.

[26] Lodovico Alamanni, "Discorso sopra il fermare lo stato di Firenze nella devozione de' Medici," text in Rudolf von Albertini, *Firenze dalla republica al principato: Storia e coscienza politica* (Turin: Einaudi, 1970), pp. 376–84.

[27] Ibid., p. 379. [28] Ibid., p. 381.

[29] See also ibid. and Paolo Vettori's "Ricordi al cardinale de' Medici sopra le cose di Firenze," text in von Albertini, *Firenze dalla republica al principato*, pp. 357–59.

[30] On the importance of the Laurentian paradigm in Florence at the time, see Gilbert, *Machiavelli and Guicciardini*, pp. 105–42.

their control of the city on a group of friends, or partisans. Like all "narrow regimes" they had "elevated part of the city and debased the other in order to avoid suspicion and acquire partisans."[31] This strategy of friends and family alliances had also dictated the Medici's external and foreign policies, and in particular their dealings with the lesser powers in the region. In the *Istorie fiorentine*, Machiavelli thus claims that Lorenzo the Magnificent had "maintained his friends the Baglioni in Perugia, and the Vitelli in Città di Castello" by means of "subsidies and supplies," while personally exercising control over the government of Faenza. These puppet regimes along Florence's eastern borders had, the former Secretary maintains, served as "firm bastions for his city."[32]

The Laurentian paradigm had come to regain topicality in the summer of 1512, when the Spanish viceroy had openly declared his wish to see Florence returned to its old form of government through the reinstatement of Cardinal Giovanni de' Medici as her first citizen. Later, when the Medici had reentered the city with the aid of the Spanish troops of the papal army and reclaimed their ancient privileges, leading Florentine citizens counseled the cardinal to adopt a civil government after the example of his father. The first constitutional reforms imposed by the new regime also suggested that it intended to heed this advice: the Great Council was closed, the Gonfalonierate reduced to an annual office, and all the old ruling bodies – the Council of Seventy, the Council of Hundred, and the Councils of the People and the Commune – reinstituted.[33] How did Machiavelli view this

[31] Guicciardini, *Dialogo*, p. 87 (English trans., *Dialogue on the Government of Florence*, trans. Alison Brown (Cambridge: Cambridge University Press, 1994), p. 85).

[32] *Istorie fiorentine* VIII.36, p. 757: "Di poi con stipendi e provvisioni manteneva suoi amici i Baglioni in Perugia, i Vitelli in Città di Castello; e di Faenza il governo particulare aveva: le quali tutte cose erano come fermi propugnacoli alla sua città." Cf. *Discorsi* II.30. Generally speaking, Machiavelli describes Florence during Lorenzo's regime as a vulnerable city without a functioning government. The fact that Lorenzo and Florence survived these perils he generally ascribes to fortune, not to Lorenzo's virtue. On Lorenzo's policy vis-à-vis the Florentine dominion, see the essays by Robert Black ("Lorenzo and Arezzo," pp. 217–34), Michael Mallett ("Horse-Racing and Politics in Lorenzo's Florence," pp. 253–62), and Stephen J. Milner ("Lorenzo and Pistoia: Peacemaker or Partisan," pp. 235–52) in *Lorenzo the Magnificent: Culture and Politics*, eds. M. Mallett and N. Mann (London: The Warburg Institute, 1996). Riccardo Fubini has argued that Lorenzo's central system of government had a tendency to reproduce itself on the provincial level; see *Quattrocento fiorentino: politica, diplomazia, cultura* (Pisa: Pacini, 1996), p. 137. See also Patrizia Salvadori, "Florentines and the Communities of the Territorial State," in *Florentine Tuscany*, eds. W. J. Connell and A. Zorzi (Cambridge: Cambridge University Press, 2000), pp. 207–24, esp. 211–12 and 218–19; Black, "Arezzo, the Medici and the Florentine State," in *Florentine Tuscany*, pp. 302–03.

[33] Stephens, *The Fall of the Florentine Republic*, pp. 65–73. Around this time similar advice was forthcoming from Goro Gheri, Niccolò Guicciardini, and Lodovico Alamanni; see von Albertini, *Firenze dalla republica al principato*, pp. 362, 367–68, and 381–82. That Machiavelli was aware of this development at the time he wrote *Il principe* is evident from the letter he wrote to an anonymous gentlewoman sometime between 16 September and his dismissal from office on 7 November 1512. See *Lettere*, pp. 231–35.

development? Even if he does not mention Lorenzo by name in *The Prince*, he is far from silent on the type of rule and the policies he and his regime had come to represent.[34] In chapter 20, for example, Machiavelli acknowledges that the political situation in Italy during Lorenzo's time had been characterized by a certain balance of power. Under these exceptional circumstances, the Laurentian imperialist policy of the middle way – which had amounted to ruling Pistoia by means of internal divisions and Pisa by fortresses – had proved sufficient to maintain the Florentine dominion. But as soon as the precarious balance had been upset, as occurred with the coming of the French in 1494, this mode of holding subject peoples had revealed its inherent limitations with disastrous consequences for Florence.[35] As we shall see, a similar polemical thrust directed against the Laurentian legacy also underlies the argument of *The Prince* 5.

The third major theme in the contemporary political debate brought up in the course of *The Prince* 5 relates to the Medici's prolonged absence from Florence. With the election of Cardinal Giovanni de' Medici to the Papacy in March 1513, the conditions for Florentine politics and territorial government changed dramatically. However, this glorious achievement, without precedent in Florentine history, drew mixed reactions in the Arno city. On the one hand, the temporary unification of Rome and Florence under a single head was met with spontaneous jubilation and expressions of patriotic pride; on the other, it was viewed as a cause for apprehension and concern.[36] How were the Medici now to divide their interest and their time between the two cities? What role was Florence going to play in the new political landscape and in the Medici's plans for the future? Was the city, as the worst scenario would have it, to become merely another minor principality under papal jurisdiction, a tributary state to a politically and militarily revived Papacy, or to a Medici empire ruled from Rome, the legendary seat of the empire? Would Florence become another Urbino, Perugia, or Bologna?

34 Stephens, *The Fall of the Florentine Republic*, p. 55. The lack of references in *Il principe* to the history of the Medici family has also been noted by John Najemy; see his "Machiavelli and the Medici: The Lessons of Florentine History," *Renaissance Quarterly* 35 (1982), p. 556. As Najemy points out (ibid., p. 562), Machiavelli offers an implicit criticism of the effeminate life-style of Laurentian Florence in *Arte della guerra*. On Machiavelli's portrait of Lorenzo in *Istorie fiorentine*, see also J. N. Stephens, "Machiavelli's *Prince* and the Florentine Revolution of 1512," *Italian Studies* 41 (1986), pp. 56–57. The criticism Machiavelli levies against a government based on friends, or *amici*, in *Il principe* 9 should, in all likelihood, also be seen as directed against the Laurentian legacy.

35 See *Il principe* 20. In *Discorsi* II.24 Machiavelli explicitly describes the method of holding Pisa by means of fortresses as a policy of the middle way.

36 On the celebrations, see Stephens, *The Fall of the Florentine Republic*, p. 74. Cf. Luca Landucci, *Diario fiorentino dal 1450 al 1516* (Florence: Biblos, 1969), pp. 336–37.

The first signs were not reassuring. Already during the summer of 1513 prominent Medici servants in Florence began to voice complaints about the Medici neglecting their responsibilities in the city. The absence of Giuliano and Lorenzo had made it difficult to find officials for the *Monte*, the publicly sponsored debt and the most important financial institution of the city. Owing to Giulio de' Medici's apparent reluctance to return to Florence and take up his duties as archbishop, an office he had been appointed to after the recent death of Cosimo de' Pazzi, the city continued to be without a formally installed head of Church. Another indication that Florentine interests were not of the highest priority in the Medici camp was given in September the same year, when it became clear that Leo X, anxious to uphold an air of impartiality, was not going to intervene on Florence's behalf in the ongoing territorial dispute between the city and Lucca over the mountain of Gragno. Eventually, Lorenzo de' Medici arrived in Florence on 10 August to assume power after the departed Giuliano, but if Parenti's report is correct, the nephew of Lorenzo the Magnificent was not happy about his appointment and would rather have stayed on in Rome and exercised his authority over Florence from there.[37] In the light of these developments and given the interest with which they were followed in Florence at the time, a contemporary Florentine reader of Machiavelli's *Prince* could hardly have avoided placing his discussion in chapter 5 of where a conqueror should live, and from where he should exercise his power, in connection with the Medici's absence from the city.

ON THREE MODES OF HOLDING FORMER REPUBLICS

We now turn to *The Prince* 5 to see how Machiavelli in this chapter addresses the three issues we have discussed above: the freedom-loving nature of people used to living in republican liberty, the Laurentian paradigm, and the absenteeism of the Medici from Florence. At the outset of this short but momentous chapter, the former Secretary establishes that there exist three different modes of ruling conquered states "accustomed to living under their own laws and in liberty":[38] rule by destruction, rule by residing there personally, and indirect rule by local elites. After having set forth these alternatives, he goes on to elaborate on the third method, rule by a local oligarchy

[37] Butters, *Governors and Government*, pp. 219–23; Stephens, "Machiavelli's *Prince* and the Florentine Revolution of 1512," pp. 53–54 and 58–59. At a later date, Francesco Vettori was to claim that the reason the Medici at the time showed so little interest in Florentine affairs and were reluctant to go and stay in their native town was that they believed that greater benefits and greater honors lay in store for them in Rome. See Francesco Vettori, *Scritti storici e politici* (Bari: Laterza, 1972), p. 300.

[38] *Il principe* 5, p. 129: "consueti a vivere con le loro leggi e in libertà."

or a *stato di pochi*. Since such a proxy government has been installed by the conqueror and is completely dependent upon "his friendship and power," it will have to do "everything to maintain him." It can therefore be relied on and will contribute to render the new acquisition lasting, Machiavelli concludes: "If one wants to preserve a city that is accustomed to living in freedom, it is more easily held by the means of its own citizens than in any other way."[39] This seems to be a very strong and categorical statement in favor of this indirect and moderate form of imperial rule. What it appears to say is that a prince who intends to show mercy on the conquered state and refrain from destroying it should create partisans among its citizens and rule it through them according to its old laws.

Machiavelli has previously in chapter 3 commented on this delegated, or indirect, form of rule, when discussing how Rome made itself "head and defender" of the Greek city-states.[40] Entering Greece at the turn of the third century BC at the invitation of the weak Aetolians, currently under pressure from the powerful and expansionist kingdoms of Macedonia and Syria, the Romans had used the lesser powers in the region to subjugate the stronger ones. They had then gone on to consolidate their position by adopting a policy of containment, allowing the various Greek powers and rulers to exercise a limited authority, but preventing them from acquiring enough strength to threaten Roman hegemony. Through this strategy of containment and indirect rule, the Romans had been able to secure the friendship of the region as a whole without having to resort to open oppression. When we reencounter the Romans in chapter 5, however, we seem to be offered a somewhat different account of the conquest of Greece. As Machiavelli, after having in categorical terms endorsed the policy of ruling conquered republics by maintaining their laws and setting up friendly oligarchies, goes on to test this claim against the examples provided by history, the argument immediately begins to blur. The Spartans, we learn, employed this method after having subjugated Athens and Thebes, but failed to hold them. Rome, on the other hand, succeeded in maintaining possession of Capua, Carthage, and Numantia by using rule by destruction, the first of the three methods mentioned at the outset of the chapter. To show that this difference in outcome did not depend on varying circumstances, Machiavelli next confronts the Spartan with the Roman mode: "The Romans tried to hold Greece in a similar manner to the Spartans, by making it

[39] Ibid.: "perché, sendo quello stato creato da quello principe, sa che non può stare sanza l'amicizia e potenza sua e ha a fare tutto per mantenerlo; e piú facilmente si tiene una città usa a vivere libera con il mezzo de' sua cittadini che in alcuno altro modo, volendola perservare."

[40] Ibid., 3, p. 123: "capo e defensore."

free and leaving it under its own laws. This was unsuccessful, so they were then forced to destroy many cities in that province, in order to maintain their hold over it."[41] To underscore the general applicability of the Roman example, Machiavelli offers a categorical statement in support of the policy of destruction: "anyone who becomes master of a city accustomed to a free way of life, and does not destroy it, may expect to be destroyed by it himself, because in rebellion it will always have a refuge in the name of liberty and its ancient institutions, which are never forgotten, despite the passage of time and the bestowal of benefits."[42] As we can see, the argument about the liberty-loving and seditious nature of peoples used to living in freedom, which for more than two centuries had been used to defend and legitimize the communal government of the Italian city-states, is adduced here to counter and undermine the claims of the imperialist policy based on tributary oligarchies.

Since the third mode, rule by a local oligarchy, is dropped at this point, without being recalled later in the chapter's exhortatory closure, we may for a moment pause to consider the implications of its categorical rejection. Two important observations are warranted. First, there can be little doubt that this method conforms to the traditional Laurentian model of territorial government, based on a clientele of friends, or *amici*. Second, Machiavelli's description of this policy, which assumes that the conqueror will reside elsewhere and leave the rule of the conquered city to a puppet regime, seems in a not-so-oblique way to allude to the Medici's ill-disguised desire to control Florence from their new seat of power in Rome. If we accept this reading, Machiavelli's practical advice to the Medici at this stage of the argument would thus be to avoid the Laurentian form of government and to abandon any thought of governing Florence from Rome.

Although Florence is bound to be the first conquered republic to spring to the intended Medicean reader's mind here, the advice of *The Prince* 5 can of course be applied to other cities as well. Machiavelli presents his case in general terms and employs historical examples to stress the general applicability of his teaching, and even if we were to stay within the contemporary Medicean context, there are other former republics to be taken into account. Three years before the Medici returned to power in Florence, the Florentines had, as we recall, reestablished their rule over the

[41] Ibid., 5, p. 130: "vollono tenere la Grecia quasi come tennono gli spartani, faccendola libera e lasciandole le sua legge, e non successe loro: tale che furno constretti disfare di molte città di quella provincia per tenerla."

[42] Ibid.: "e chi diviene patrone di una città consueta a vivere libera, e non la disfaccia, aspetti di essere disfatto da quella: perché sempre ha per refugio nella rebellione el nome della libertà e gli ordini antiqui sua, e' quali né per lunghezza di tempo né per benifizi mai si dimenticano."

neighboring Pisans, another people "accustomed to living under their own laws and in liberty." Depending on what perspective one takes, the conquered city in *The Prince* 5 can thus be seen to refer to either Florence (lost by the Medici in 1494 and reconquered in 1512) or some other city under Medicean control, for example Pisa (lost by Florence in 1495 and regained in 1509). Since Machiavelli in this chapter explicitly mentions Florence's rule of Pisa, and returns to the subject later in chapter 20, the latter reading demands particular attention.

In *The Prince* 5, Machiavelli uses the Pisan example to illustrate the principles of divide and rule, which he previously has expounded in *Del modo* and in chapter 3 of *The Prince*. Former republics, he claims, are impossible to rule whatever one does, or provides for, unless the inhabitants are "disunited or dispersed." They are unlikely to forget the name of liberty and their old republican orders, and will therefore at every opportunity rally to them, "as Pisa did after one hundred years of being kept in servitude by the Florentines."[43] If Florence up to this point had seemed to figure foremost among the conquered cities "accustomed to living under their own laws and in liberty," the insertion of the Pisan example, and the adoption of the Florentine point of view vis-à-vis the neighbor, has the effect of reversing the perspective and of restoring Florence to her status as a conquering imperialist power. Indirectly, Florence's loss of Pisa in 1494 draws attention to the recovery of the seaport in 1509. Pisan republicanism and rebellion entail Florentine imperialism, and by comparing the unruly Pisans to the ancient Greek city-states, Machiavelli yet again, as in *Del modo* of 1503, casts Florence in the role of the ancient Roman republic.

Had the insertion of the Florentine point of view been an isolated instance in *The Prince*, it would not be admissible to interpret it as part of a conscious rhetorical strategy. But since Machiavelli at several other pivotal points in *The Prince* resorts to a Florentine, or Tuscan, perspective, the significance of this shift should not be easily dismissed. Another such reversal, rich in implications, occurs in *The Prince* 20 in a discussion of how a new prince should proceed when arming his subjects. Having laid down that such a ruler always should arm his own people, the former Secretary goes on to argue that it is necessary to disarm the subjects of a conquered state with the exception of those "who were your partisans in its acquisition." At a later stage, the conqueror will have to make these supporters "soft and effeminate," and to arrange "so that all the arms of his enlarged state are in the hands of his own soldiers, who served under him in his old

[43] Ibid.: "E per cosa che si faccia o si provegga, se non si disuniscono o dissipano gli abitatori non dimenticano quello nome né quegli ordini, e subito in ogni accidente vi ricorrono: come fe' Pisa dopo cento anni che la era suta posta in servitú da' fiorentini."

state."[44] If applied to the contemporary context, this advice could easily be interpreted as an exhortation to the Medici to follow the example of Lorenzo the Magnificent and disarm the Florentines, while continuing to rely on the mercenary troops who had assisted them in reentering Florence. But the fact that this is not Machiavelli's intended message becomes abundantly clear from the opening lines of the next paragraph: "Our ancestors (*li antiqui nostri*), and those who were thought to be wise, used to say that it was necessary to hold Pistoia by means of factions and Pisa by using fortresses . . ."[45] Here, as in *The Prince* 5, the Florentine point of view is introduced at a juncture in the argument where the Arno city is under threat of being mistaken for the conquered city or a subject city among others. Through this rhetorical move, Machiavelli restores his native city to her imperial rank and, as a consequence, promotes her as the main candidate for the seat of a Tuscan empire ruled by a new Medici prince.

Following his comment in chapter 5 on the Pisan rebellion and his not-so-oblique criticism of the Laurentian form of indirect rule, Machiavelli turns to consider the problems facing a conqueror of cities and provinces "accustomed to living under a prince" and used "to obeying." Since such peoples do not know "how to live free" and are "slow to take up arms," a conqueror can "easily win them over, and make sure that they will not harm him."[46] After having been confronted with the seditious and freedom-loving Pisans, this may come as comforting news to the princely reader. But on closer inspection, the new picture Machiavelli holds up for him is a rather gloomy and disheartening one. Subjects accustomed "to obeying" might be easy to command, but, servile by nature, they are hardly the stuff of which empires are made. If this is what the destruction of a once-free and spirited people eventually will result in, a princely reader with great ambitions might be inclined to look for alternative ways of dealing with the freedom-loving republics he conquers.[47]

[44] Ibid., 20, p. 176: "Ma quando uno principe acquista uno stato nuovo, che come membro si aggiunga al suo vecchio, allora è necessario disarmare quello stato, eccetto quegli che nello acquistarlo sono suti tua partigiani: e quegli ancora col tempo e con le occasioni è necessario renderli molli ed effeminati, e ordinarsi in modo che solo le arme di tutto il tuo stato sieno in quelli tuoi soldati propri che nello stato tuo antico vivèno appresso di te."

[45] Ibid.: "Solevano li antichi nostri, e quelli che erano stimati savi, dire come era necessario tenere Pistoia con le parte e Pisa con le fortezze . . ."

[46] Ibid., 5, p. 130: "Ma quando le città o le provincie sono use a vivere sotto uno principe e quello sangue sia spento, sendo da uno canto usi a ubbidire, da l'altro non avendo il principe vecchio, farne uno in fra loro non si accordano, vivere liberi non sanno: di modo che sono piú tardi a pigliare l'arme e con piú facilità se gli può uno principe guadagnare e assicurarsi di loro."

[47] This description recalls the fate of the ancient Greeks commented on in *Il principe* 4. In chapter 26, Machiavelli exhorts his princely reader to apply the new orders described in the treatise to a matter (*materia*), or a people, in which the ancient italic virtue is still alive.

When Machiavelli in the closure of chapter 5 returns to the republican discourse centered on the bellicosity of freedom-loving peoples used to a life in liberty, he also provides, or so it seems, an alternative solution to rule by destruction: "But in republics there is greater vitality (*vita*), greater hatred, and a stronger desire for revenge," since "the memory of ancient liberty does not and cannot permit them to rest." Therefore, he concludes, "the surest way is to destroy them (*spengerle*) or else go to live there (*abitarvi*)."[48] With this enigmatic piece of advice the chapter ends. After having discussed at length, and with several examples, the other modes of holding cities used to living under their own laws, Machiavelli now throws up before us, with spectacular suddenness, the second mode, rule by living there (*abitarvi*). He does not define the meaning of the expression or the policy it denotes, nor does he adduce any examples to support it. How, then, is this strange procedure to be explained?

Above, we have argued that a close analogy exists between the teaching of *The Prince* 5 and the problems that were facing the Medici regime at the time. First, we saw that there were strong contextual, as well as textual, reasons to assume that Machiavelli's third mode of holding conquered states used to a life under their own laws – rule by an oligarchy or a *stato di pochi* – is based on Lorenzo the Magnificent's way of governing Florence and her subject cities back in the Quattrocento. After dismissing this method, the former Secretary made an explicit reference to Florence's rule of Pisa, as he adduced the recovery of Pisan liberty in 1494 to illustrate the danger of not destroying a conquered city used to living in liberty. Since Machiavelli later in *The Prince* 20 makes the Laurentian imperialist policy directly responsible for the dissolution of the Florentine dominion after 1494, there is sound textual support for reading a chronological sequence of Florentine–Pisan relations into the initial stages of the chapter. Like the Spartans, who, as a result of their insistence on ruling by local oligarchies, had failed to hold Athens and Thebes, Machiavelli argues, Florence had, by opting for a similar policy, lost Pisa, when instead they should have imitated the Romans, who subjugated Greece by destroying "many cities in that province."

When Machiavelli now at the end of the chapter places before his princely reader an ultimatum – either you go and live in the republic you have annexed or you destroy it; otherwise it will destroy you – he invokes an

[48] Ibid., 5, p. 130: "Ma nelle republiche è maggiore vita, maggiore odio, piú desiderio di vendetta: né gli lascia, né può lasciare riposare la memoria della antiqua libertà; tale che la piú sicura via è spegnerle o abitarvi." On Machiavelli's use of the term *spengere*, see Quentin Skinner, "Notes on the Vocabulary of *The Prince*," in Machiavelli, *The Prince*, eds. Skinner and Price, pp. 111–12. Cf. Harvey C. Mansfield, *Machiavelli's Virtue* (Chicago: University of Chicago Press, 1996), pp. 299–305.

issue that was on everyone's mind at the time: the Medici's absenteeism from Florence. Within this contemporary context Machiavelli's final advice takes on a more precise meaning. If our interpretation is correct, the closing argument of the chapter should be read: go and live in Florence and destroy Pisa.

If Florence were to become a strong imperialist power, Machiavelli seems to imply, rebellious neighboring cities such as Pisa must cease to exist as independent political entities. Considering his uncompromising attitude in *Del modo* on the question of Arezzo, and his advocacy in *Discorso di Pisa* of 1499 of a strong policy based on force against the Pisan rebels, this proposition should not come as a surprise. But before we draw this far-reaching conclusion, we need to investigate further Machiavelli's view on the question of Pisa and Florentine imperialism. To do so, we will turn to the *Discourses*, where Florence's holding of Pisa is discussed at some length in chapters II.21 and II.24.

THE QUESTION OF PISA

When Machiavelli returns to the problems facing the Florentine territorial state in the opening of *Discourses* II.24, he explicitly compares the traditional Florentine policy of holding Pisa and other subject cities by means of fortresses with the ways of the ancient Romans:

> To the wise of our times (*questi savi de' nostri tempi*) it will perhaps seem a thing not well considered that when the Romans wished to secure themselves against the peoples of Latium and of the city of Privernum, they did not think of building some fortress, which would be a check to keep them faithful, especially since it is a saying in Florence, cited by our wise ones, that Pisa and other similar cities should be held with fortresses. And truly if the Romans had been made like them, they would have thought of building some; but because they were of another virtue, of another judgment, of another power, they did not build any.[49]

Here, as always, Machiavelli's condemnation of the traditional Florentine policy is based on his conviction that every attempt at striking a balance between destroying subject cities and winning them through favors is bound to fail. Methods such as impoverishing or disarming the subjects,

[49] *Discorsi* II.24, p. 391: "E' parrà forse a questi savi de' nostri tempi cosa non bene considerata che i romani, nel volere assicurarsi de' popoli di Lazio e della città di Priverno, non pensassono di edificarvi qualche fortezza, la quale fosse uno freno a tenergli in fede; sendo massime un detto in Firenze, allegato da' nostri savi, che Pisa e l'altre simili città si debbono tenere con le fortezze. E veramente se i romani fussono stati fatti come loro, egli arebbero pensato di edificarle; ma perché gli erano d'altra virtú, d'altro giudizio, d'altra potenza, e' non le edificarono."

the building of fortresses, mild and hesitant punishments, and half-hearted conferments of honors and rewards achieve little, and will in the long term prove counterproductive. While the manifest cruelty of these policies is bound to incur the hatred of the conquered, they are not sufficiently harsh and decisive to deprive them of their means for future rebellion. This circumstance is brought to explain why the Pisans in 1494–95, after almost a century of Florentine rule, took up arms to recover their liberty. According to Machiavelli, the Florentines had built fortresses in Pisa, not realizing that "if they wished to hold a city that had always been an enemy to the Florentine name, had lived free, and had in rebellion had freedom as its refuge, it was necessary to observe the Roman mode: either to make it a companion or to demolish it."[50] As the very wording of the passage indicates, the context of the argument is closely related to that of *The Prince* 5. In that chapter, Machiavelli claimed, as we recall, that a city "accustomed to a free way of life" (*consueta a vivere libera*), like Pisa, only could be ruled by destruction, since "in rebellion it will always have a refuge in the name of liberty" (*sempre ha per refugio, nella rebellione, el nome della libertà*). Here in *Discourses* II.24, Pisa is again referred to as having "lived free" (*vissuta libera*), and having had in rebellion "liberty as its refuge" (*ha alla rebellione per rifugio la libertà*).

These correspondences in vocabulary allow us not only to establish a connection between the two chapters, but also to distinguish between the different positions Machiavelli here assumes with regard to the Pisan issue. In *The Prince* 5, we have argued, he comments on the relationship between Florence and Pisa in an indirect and covert manner, when claiming that cities accustomed to freedom could be held in one of two contrasting ways: by eliminating them (*spengerle*) or by living in them (*abitarvi*). Since making Pisa into their seat of government must be considered a non-option for the Medici, this advice couched in general terms could, when applied to the *here and now*, be translated into a direct recommendation: reside in Florence and destroy Pisa. Also in *Discourses* II.24 Machiavelli proposes two alternative strategies on the Pisan issue. But here the options are different, since he now argues that Florence could have chosen to rule Pisa either by destroying her (*disfarla*) or by making her a companion (*farsela compagna*). As it appears, then, the less cruel *farsela compagna* emerges in the *Discourses* II.24 as an alternative to rule by destruction, recommended in *The Prince* 5.

[50] Ibid., p. 394: "e non conobbero che una città stata sempre inimica del nome fiorentino, vissuta libera, e che ha alla rebellione per rifugio la libertà, era necessario, volendola tenere, osservare il modo romano: o farsela compagna o disfarla."

What the expression *farsela compagna* actually stands for is not defined with any great precision in *Discourses* II.24. Machiavelli here only suggests that this policy, if adopted at the proper time, could have contributed to prevent the Pisan rebellion of 1495. A clearer idea of what is implied by this phrase is offered in *Discourses* II.21, where Florence's treatment of her Tuscan neighbors is the main focus of interest. From this discussion, we learn that the Florentines by tradition had demonstrated more friendliness towards the city of Pistoia than towards their other neighbors, Pisa, Lucca, and Siena included:

> Everyone knows how much time it has been since the city of Pistoia came voluntarily under Florentine rule (*imperio*). Everyone also knows how much enmity there has been between the Florentines and the Pisans, Lucchese, and Sienese. This difference of spirit has arisen not because the Pistoiese do not prize their freedom as do the others and do not judge themselves as highly as the others but because the Florentines have always comported themselves with them like brothers (*frategli*) but with the others like enemies (*inimici*). This has made the Pistoiese run willingly under their rule (*imperio*), while the others have exerted and exert all their force so as not to come under it. And without doubt if the Florentines by way either of leagues or of aids had tamed their neighbors and not made them more savage, they would without doubt at this hour be lords of Tuscany (*signori di Toscana*).[51]

These observations about Florence's successful fraternization with Pistoia induce Machiavelli to conclude that arms and force should be "reserved for the last place, where and when other modes are not enough."[52] Here we have, it would appear, a true alternative to the policy of destruction set forth in *The Prince* 5. The type of fraternization described in *Discourses* II.21 seems also to be related, if it is not identical, to the *farsela compagna* referred to later in *Discourses* II.24.

We now seem to have three different and conflicting accounts and recommendations on how to handle the subject city of Pisa. If we follow the order in which they appear in the work of Machiavelli, we first have the exhortation in *The Prince* 5, which, if our reading is correct, advises, or at least insinuates, the necessity of destroying Pisa. When Machiavelli returns

[51] Ibid., II.21, p. 384: "Ciascuno sa quanto tempo è che la città di Pistoia venne volontariamente sotto lo imperio fiorentino. Ciascuno ancora sa quanta inimicizia è stata intra i fiorentini, e' pisani, lucchesi e sanesi: e questa diversità di animo non è nata perché i pistolesi non prezzino la loro libertà come gli altri e non si giudichino da quanto gli altri, ma per essersi i fiorentini portati con loro sempre come frategli, e con gli altri come inimici. Questo ha fatto che i pistolesi sono corsi volontari sotto lo imperio loro: gli altri hanno fatto e fanno ogni forza per non vi pervenire. E sanza dubbio se i fiorentini o per vie di leghe o di aiuti avessero dimesticati e non insalvatichiti i suoi vicini, a questa ora sanza dubbio e' sarebbero signori di Toscana."

[52] Ibid.: "Non è per questo che io giudichi che non si abbia adoperare l'armi e le forze, ma si debbono riservare in ultimo luogo, dove e quando gli altri modi non bastino."

to the matter in *Discourses* II.21, he claims, quite to the contrary it would seem, that the Florentines would have become lords of Tuscany had they handled the Pisans and their other Tuscan neighbors in the same brotherly manner as they treated the people of Pistoia. These two conflicting recommendations, rule by destroying and by fraternization, then reappear in *Discourses* II.24, combined and contrasted in the by now familiar Roman formula of the two extremes, destruction or benefits.

How are these three seemingly incompatible positions to be accounted for? At a first glance it might seem hard, if not outright impossible, to reconcile them. But Machiavelli's conscious and consistent use of the Roman model to contrast, criticize, and correct the corrupt ways of modern republics warns us not to resort to explanations based on the author's confused state of mind or personal development, or the doings and undoings of textuality, before having tested the various positions against his Roman example. In the following sections, Machiavelli's views on Florence's policy towards the subject cities of Pisa, Arezzo, and Pistoia will therefore be discussed in relation to his more general, Roman-inspired teaching on the use of fraud and force for imperialist purposes.

THE ROMAN USE OF LEAGUES

On repeated occasions, Machiavelli compares the imperialist strategies of modern and ancient republics. His prime example is here, as always, the ancient Romans. In sharp contrast to modern republics, they had either destroyed the cities they conquered or allowed them to continue to live by their own laws under Roman supervision. This policy they had employed with great success, Machiavelli claims, up to the time they began to spread their empire outside Italy. A case in point is their treatment of the southern city of Capua. When the Capuans in 318 BC approached the Romans with a request for having a praetor sent to them to restore unity and internal order, it was, as Machiavelli points out in *Discourses* II.21, the first time in the history of Rome that a praetor was dispatched to a neighboring city. The reason the Capuans, who had continued to live by their own laws after coming under Roman protection in *c.* 343 BC, turned to the Romans for help, we are informed, was that they did not fear losing their liberty to a people who had always treated them in a "humane and familiar (*umano e dimestico*) way."[53] The Romans granted the appeal, Machiavelli continues, "not because of their ambition," but because the Capuans themselves asked

[53] Ibid.

for a praetor. The Capuans came thus, willingly and unsuspectingly, to hand over the rule of their city to the Romans, who could now strengthen their control over the province without having to disclose their more far-reaching aspirations.[54] The method the Romans used on the occasion, Machiavelli concludes, was exemplary because it was invisible to everyone but to themselves.[55]

But when we compare this account with Machiavelli's discussion of Rome's treatment of Capua in *The Prince* 5, we seem to be faced with inconsistencies and contradictions. On both occasions, it is true, Machiavelli compares Rome's handling of Capua with Florence's rule of Pisa. In *The Prince* 5, he initially claims that "a city that is accustomed to living in freedom" may be held more easily "by the means of its own citizens than in any other way." This view accords well with his position in the *Discourses*, where he praises the Romans for having ruled Capua in a humane, friendly, and "invisible" manner. But then, as we recall, he goes on to argue that the reason why the Romans had been able to hold Capua was that they had destroyed the city. To make matters even more confusing, in the *Discourses* he condemns Florence for having treated the Pisans as enemies and not as brothers, while in *The Prince* he seems to suggest that she should have destroyed the neighbor instead. Therefore, it is easy here to get the impression that Machiavelli is of two minds as to which Roman policy the Florentines should emulate in their dealings with Pisa.

To clarify Machiavelli's seemingly contradictory treatment of the Capuan example, two points need to be made. First, it should be clear that Rome's contrasting ways of treating Capua belong to two distinct phases in the history of Roman expansion. The rule based on a pretence of friendship, described in *Discourses* II.21, was successfully used in the fourth century BC, when the Romans still depended for their conquests on the voluntary cooperation of neighboring peoples like the Capuans. The destruction of

[54] When Machiavelli states that the Romans sent the praetor "non per loro ambizione, ma perché e' ne furono ricerchi dai capovani" (*Discorsi* II.21, p. 383), he is speaking from the point of view of the Capuans, not from that of the Romans. The Roman perspective remains concealed for most of the chapter. As Machiavelli points out in *Discorsi* II.20, the Romans in *c.* 342 BC left behind two legions in Capua to protect the city against the Samnites. When it became known in Rome that the captains of these legions conspired to oppress the defenseless Capuans, the new consul, Rutilius, was assigned the task of preventing this abuse of power, which he also succeeded in doing. See also *Discorsi* III.6, p. 443. Machiavelli's account of this episode is based on Livy VII.38–41.

[55] *Discorsi* II.21, p. 383: "Vedesi pertanto quanto questo modo facilitò lo augumento romano. Perché quelle città, massime, che sono use a vivere libere o consuete governarsi per sua provinciali, con altra quiete stanno contente sotto uno dominio che non veggono, ancora ch'egli avesse in sé qualche gravezza, che sotto quello che, veggendo ogni giorno, pare loro che ogni giorno sia rimproverata loro la servitú." On Machiavelli's theory of indirect government, see Mansfield, *Machiavelli's Virtue*, pp. 235–57 and 306–8. Cf. Mansfield, *Machiavelli's New Modes and Orders*, pp. 253–55.

Capua, referred to in *The Prince* 5, took place at a much later date, after the rebellion of the city during the Hannibalic War in 211 BC. At that time, Rome had gathered sufficient strength to subjugate her former companions and to adopt a rule by force. While the first of these policies could be seen as an example of fraud prudently employed by a still weak and dependent republic forced to adopt a façade of humanity and friendship to conceal her true ambitions, the latter policy, one could argue, was a demonstration of strength by the new lords of Italy in the face of external aggression.

This development prompts us to make a second observation. To judge from Machiavelli's description of the Roman way of ruling Capua, a sophisticated form of fraud was from the very outset an integral part of their policy. The Romans had treated the Capuans with humanity and familiarity not out of sheer goodness or compassion, but because they believed that this policy would enable them to expand their influence in the region. In Machiavelli's view, the Romans could thus be said to have acted in an exemplary manner both when they initially allowed the Capuans to live by their own laws and administer their own submission, and when they later destroyed them politically and brought them under their yoke. The common denominators of these two policies are Rome's desire to grow and the city's flexibile and sensitive imperialist approach, which enabled her to respond, and to adapt, to the demands of the changing circumstances. These features, as we shall see, are also at the center of Machiavelli's discussion of Roman expansionism in the controversial *Discourses* II.4.

Although most critics agree that Machiavelli in the *Discourses* sides with the republic against the principality, there is considerable disagreement as to the nature of his republicanism. Whereas many interpreters argue that the republic Machiavelli endorses is a predatory state of Roman inspiration,[56] other scholars, among them Hans Baron and Maurizio Viroli, have argued a contrary case. According to Baron, Machiavelli's political ideal is to be found in the ancient world at the time before the Roman conquests, when plenty of independent states and free republics still existed. Since the Florentine viewed the conflict between such freedom-loving city-states as a necessary prerequisite for the development and maintenance of political virtue, vitality, and health, he came to view the Roman subjugation of Italy and the rise of the empire as the principal cause of the decline of ancient virtue. On the basis of this observation, Baron claims that the ideal of the

[56] See especially Leo Strauss, *Thoughts on Machiavelli* (Chicago: University of Chicago Press, 1958), p. 89; Harvey C. Mansfield, "Introduction," in Machiavelli, *The Prince*, trans. Mansfield (Chicago: University of Chicago Press, 1985), pp. xii–xv; Mark Hulliung, *Citizen Machiavelli* (Princeton: Princeton University Press, 1983), pp. 5–6, 10, 26–27, and 96.

Discourses is a political pluralism based on "many independent, free small states."[57] From a theoretical position similar to Baron's, Viroli argues that Machiavelli in the *Discourses* in general, and chapter II.4 in particular, recommends his Florentine compatriots to follow the example of the ancient Tuscans and to "form leagues or federations on fair terms" with neighboring states. Machiavelli's purpose, we are told, is fundamentally defensive. For even though he considers the Roman mode of expansion to be the best policy absolutely speaking, he views, according to Viroli, the policy of leagues as a more realistic alternative for contemporary Florence, since the Roman way "appears to be too difficult" to imitate.[58]

Of paramount importance to Baron's and Viroli's interpretation is Machiavelli's comparison of the Roman and the Tuscan, or the Etruscan, modes of expansionism in *Discourses* II.4, where the former Secretary appears to privilege the ancient Tuscan league over the Roman example:

> And if the imitation of the Romans seems difficult, that of the ancient Tuscans should not seem so, especially to the present Tuscans. For if they could not . . . make an empire like that of Rome, they could acquire the power in Italy that their mode of proceeding conceded them. This was secure for a great time, with the highest glory of empire and of arms and special praise for custom and religion.[59]

In this passage, Machiavelli seems indeed to articulate what Baron and Viroli consider to be the true ideal of the *Discourses*, the cooperation between a multitude of free city-states, coexisting on fair and equal terms. If this reading holds good, it could be claimed that Machiavelli here expresses serious doubts about the practicability of the Roman ideal and seeks to formulate a more realistic alternative. But there is a major problem attached to this view. In the preface to the *Discourses*, where Machiavelli explains his reason for composing the work, he criticizes, in no uncertain terms, his contemporaries for considering the direct imitation of ancient modes and

57 Hans Baron, "The Principe and the Puzzle of the Date of Chapter 26," *Journal of Medieval and Renaissance Studies* 21 (1991), p. 102; Baron, *In Search of Florentine Civic Humanism: Essays on the Transition from Medieval to Modern Thought* (2 vols., Princeton: Princeton University Press, 1988), II, pp. 148–50. On these grounds, Baron dismisses Machiavelli's criticism of the Papacy in *Discorsi* I.12 for having prevented Italy from becoming united, as "a later insertion" resulting from the former Secretary's historical research in connection to his *Istorie fiorentine*.

58 Maurizio Viroli, *From Politics to Reason of State: The Acquisition and Transformation of the Language of Politics 1250–1600* (Cambridge: Cambridge University Press, 1992), p. 162.

59 *Discorsi* II.4, p. 341: "E quando la imitazione de' romani paresse difficile, non doverrebbe parere cosí quella degli antichi toscani, massime a' presenti toscani. Perché se quelli non poterono, per le cagioni dette, fare uno imperio simile a quel di Roma, poterono acquistare in Italia quella potenza che quel modo del procedere concesse loro. Il che fu per un gran tempo sicuro, con somma gloria d'imperio e d'arme, e massime laude di costumi e di religione."

orders in political and military affairs "not only difficult, but impossible."[60] To undeceive modern men, and to open their eyes to a new and better understanding of ancient history, he has judged it necessary, he claims, to expound the extant books of Livy. In the light of this declaration, the argument of *Discourses* II.4 sounds a rather curious note. How can Machiavelli here permit himself to complain about the difficulty involved in imitating the ways of the Romans, after at the outset of the work having sharply condemned this tendency among his contemporaries?

To make sense of this apparent contradiction, we need to consider the argument of *Discourses* II.4 in more detail. In this chapter, Machiavelli distinguishes between three different ways of expanding (*ampliare*) practiced by republics, ancient and modern: expansion by a league, by the making of friends, and by acquisition of subjects. Of these three modes, the method of acquiring subjects (*sudditi*) without first having made friends (*amici*), exemplified by Athens and Sparta, soon reveals itself to be "entirely useless."[61] Since the rule of an annexed province calls for strong action and the use of force, something only a conqueror who is "massive with arms"[62] can sustain, it can never be advisable to acquire dominion over subjects before first having made friends who can contribute to one's power.

Expansionism through a league (*una lega*) is a more effective and lasting form of acquisition. This method, Machiavelli claims, was in antiquity employed by the Tuscans, the Achaeans, and the Aetolians, and has in modern times been revived by the Swiss confederation. In the opening of the chapter, he defines the league as an association of "several republics together, in which none [is] before another in either authority or rank."[63] The league establishes its dominion and enlarges its territory, we are told, by incorporating other cities and giving them the status of companions (*compagne*). The ancient Tuscans created such an empire in central and northern Italy, but from Machiavelli's account we learn that this confederation, consisting of twelve independent cities, was unable to "go beyond Italy with [its] acquisitions,"[64] and that it eventually lost its dominion over Lombardy to the advancing Gauls. Having dealt with the overconfident Athenian and the triumphant Roman way of expanding, Machiavelli returns towards the end of the chapter to the Tuscan mode. He now claims that this is the second best way of making acquisitions after the Roman method, since it

[60] Ibid., I, preface, p. 198: "non solo difficile ma impossibile."

[61] Ibid., II.4, p. 338: "al tutto inutile." [62] Ibid.: "grosso d'armi."

[63] Ibid., p. 337: "una lega di piú republiche insieme, dove non sia alcuna che avanzi l'altra né di autorità né di grado."

[64] Ibid., p. 338: "né poterono uscire d'Italia con gli acquisti."

means that "you do not easily take a war on your back," and since it allows you to "easily keep as much as you take."[65] Without acknowledging the fact that the loss of Lombardy and the ultimate subjugation under Rome speak against this view, Machiavelli goes on to consider the disadvantages of this mode:

> The cause of its inability to expand is its being a republic that is disunited (*una republica disgiunta*) and placed in various seats, which enables them to consult and decide only with difficulty. It also makes them not desirous of dominating; for since there are many communities to participate in dominion, they do not esteem such acquisition as much as one republic alone (*una republica sola*) that hopes to enjoy it entirely. Besides this, they govern themselves through a council, and they must be slower in every decision than those who live within one and the same wall.[66]

Since these drawbacks impose limitations on how far such a league can expand, Machiavelli recommends its members to refrain from further acquisitions when they have reached a stage where "it appears to them that they can defend themselves from everyone."[67] This will have been accomplished, he argues, when twelve to fourteen cities have joined together.

However, before definitively closing the door on further acquisitions, Machiavelli intimates an opening by pointing out that a city within the confederation, which desires to proceed with its conquests must choose between two different strategies: it should begin either to make companions or to acquire subjects on its own. But such undertakings are wrought with difficulty, we are told. While the former policy is unattractive because it creates confusion, the latter strategy is likely to be judged impracticable by the members of the league, since most of them will neither discern the possibility, nor appreciate its usefulness.

65 Ibid., p. 339: "Il modo preallegato delle leghe, come viverono i toscani, gli achei e gli etoli, e come oggi vivono i svizzeri, è, dopo a quello de' romani, il migliore modo, perché non si potendo con quello ampliare assai, ne seguita due beni: l'uno, che facilmente non ti tiri guerra a dosso, l'altro, che quel tanto che tu pigli, lo tieni facilmente."

66 Ibid., pp. 339–40: "La cagione del non potere ampliare è lo essere una republica disgiunta e posta in varie sedie, il che fa che difficilmente possono consultare e diliberare. Fa ancora che non sono desiderosi di dominare: perché, essendo molte comunità a partecipare di quel dominio, non stimano tanto tale acquisto, quanto fa una republica sola che spera di godersela tutto. Governonsi, oltra di questo, per concilio, e conviene che sieno piú tardi ad ogni diliberazione che quelli che abitono drento a uno medesimo cerchio." Bondanella and Musa's translation glosses over the sharp contrast Machiavelli here establishes between the united republic with a single seat of power and the disjointed confederation, by inserting the term "republic" on three instances, where Machiavelli takes pain not to employ the word, see *The Portable Machiavelli*, eds. Peter Bondanella and Mark Musa (London: Viking Penguin, 1979), p. 304.

67 *Discorsi* II.4, p. 340: "perché, sendo giunti a grado che pare loro potersi difendere da ciascuno, non cercono maggiore dominio."

If we pause for a moment to summarize what we have learnt so far about Machiavelli's position on the policy of expansion through a league, it should be clear by now that this mode constitutes a middle way. The league is acquisitive, but only within certain preestablished limits; it is irresolute and slow in making its decisions; it is disjointed instead of united; it lacks a proper capital and a centralized form of government; its reluctance to make further acquisitions leads to contradictions and confusion.[68] From these observations, Machiavelli draws the conclusion that the Roman method is to be preferred. However, even though this is known to be "the true mode," it has never been attempted either before or after the Romans. Today, the "orders" that the Romans observed in their internal and foreign affairs "are not only not imitated but not held of any account," because "some are judged not true, some impossible, some not to the purpose and useless." For this reason, Machiavelli claims, "we are prey to whoever has wished to overrun this province."[69]

After having thus established that the modern Italians' inability to see the truth, the possibility, the appropriateness, and the usefulness of the Roman mode is one of the main causes of their current weakness, Machiavelli seems to resort to the more "realistic" example of the Tuscan league. To understand the real purpose of this advice, which we have quoted above, we need to inquire more thoroughly into the relationship between the Tuscan and the Roman ways of expanding. The Roman mode is discussed throughout the *Discourses*, of course, but if we confine ourselves to chapter II.4, we shall find that Machiavelli's representation of it interlocks remarkably well with his

[68] Machiavelli claims that the league's mode of acquisition leads to disorder, culminating when its members at the limit of its growth start taking neighboring provinces under their protection and exploiting them economically, and when they begin to wage war for others and to hire their soldiers to foreign princes for financial gain. To illustrate this point, Machiavelli adduces an episode from Livy, relating how Philip of Macedon complained before an Aetolian praetor about the Aetolians' "avarice and lack of faith," which he alleges had led them to "send their men in the service of his [Philip's] enemy," at the same time as they continued to honor an old agreement with him. As a result of this double-dealing, Philip grimly observed, it was now far from uncommon to see the banners of Aetolia flying in opposing camps. See *Discorsi* II.4, p. 340.

[69] Ibid., pp. 340–41: "Conoscesi pertanto essere vero modo quello che tennono i romani, il quale è tanto piú mirabile quanto e' non ce n'era innanzi a Roma esemplo, e dopo Roma non è stato alcuno che gli abbi imitati . . . E, come nel fine di questa materia si dirà, tanti ordini osservati da Roma, cosí pertinenti alle cose di dentro come a quelle di fuora, non sono ne' presenti nostri tempi non solamente imitati, ma non n'è tenuto alcuno conto: giudicandoli alcuni non veri, alcuni impossibili, alcuni non a proposito ed inutili; tanto che standoci con questa ignoranzia, siamo preda di qualunque ha voluto correre questa provincia." Mansfield and Tarcov translate *mirabile* as "wonderful." In *Il principe* 6 (p. 131) Cyrus and other legendary founders of states are also described as *mirabile*. From this we may conclude that *mirabile* is a designation Machiavelli reserves for those who are truly original and act without a model. Cf. Victoria Kahn, *Machiavellian Rhetoric: From the Counter-Reformation to Milton* (Princeton: Princeton University Press, 1994), p. 22.

description of the Tuscan league's way of acquiring. During the early stages of her growth, Machiavelli informs us, Rome had endeavored to acquire "many companions (*compagni*) in all of Italy."[70] While the Romans reserved the seat of the empire and the right to military command for themselves, their companions continued to live as their equals under the law. From a Roman point of view, this arrangement could not be defined as a league in the above-mentioned sense of the term, since the other members of the alliance were politically and militarily subordinated to them. But how did their companions conceive of the relationship? By assisting the Romans in their conquest of kingdoms bordering on Italy, transforming them into Roman provinces and their inhabitants into Roman subjects, they had, apparently without realizing it, come to surround themselves with peoples who were accustomed to monarchic rule, and who by now acknowledged no other authority than the city of Rome, to whose commanders they had surrendered. To judge by this account, it would appear as if the Romans, who were always looking beyond the confines of their alliances (or should we say leagues?), had managed to deceive their companions into believing that their relationship was based on equality and reciprocality, or, at least, that it did not pose a threat to their status as free cities. When the companions became aware of "the deception under which they had lived,"[71] they joined forces and marched on Rome, but the Romans had by now grown so powerful and acquired so much authority with their outer provinces that they were able to put down the rebellion. In a twist of irony, the former companions came henceforth to share the destiny of the peoples they had assisted Rome in conquering, as they themselves were reduced to Roman subjects and dispossessed of their ancient rights.

It should now be clear that Machiavelli in *Discourses* II.4 discusses expansion through leagues and through associating with companions from two radically different perspectives. On the one hand, he adopts the point of view of the Romans, who treated the alliance, or the "league," as a mere façade and as a stepping stone for further conquests and the future acquisition of subjects. On the other, he describes it from the standpoint of their gullible companions, who viewed it as a confederation, or a league, on fair terms, and as something of an end in itself. From the Roman persepective, which Machiavelli encourages us to develop, the two other modes of imperialism discussed in the chapter, expansion through a league and acquisition of subjects, reveal themselves to be contained within the Roman model as

[70] *Discorsi* II.4, p. 339: "perché, avendosi lei fatti di molti compagni per tutta Italia."
[71] Ibid.: "E quando ei s'avviddono dello inganno sotto il quale erano vissuti."

two successive stages in the city's expansion and growth. This fact also accounts for the hierarchical view Machiavelli takes of the three methods. While the Athenians and the Spartans acted in a topsy-turvy manner, by acquiring subjects before first furnishing themselves with reliable companions who could assist them in maintaining their acquisitions, the ancient Tuscans had proceeded in the right order, beginning by joining together in a league and making companions. Although no Tuscan city had attempted to exploit the possibilities offered by such a league, the Roman example shows that it can be shrewdly and deceptively used as a preparatory stage for further expansion and the acquisition of empire over subjects.

By recommending his Florentine readers to opt for the Tuscan model at the end of the chapter, while simultaneously holding up the Roman example as the ultimate, but difficult ideal, Machiavelli seems to insinuate that the best mode of action for Florence at the present time would be to create a Tuscan league, and to reserve for herself the traditional Roman prerogatives: to be the seat of the empire and to exercise military leadership within the league. But this alliance should only be seen as a temporary strategy, designed to enable the Florentines to exploit their companions as a means for acquiring subjects, military might, and empire in the same way as the Romans had done in the past. Therefore, the fact that Machiavelli describes the Tuscan model as more approachable than the Roman ideal should, contrary to what Baron and Viroli argue, not be seen as a rejection on his part of the basic principles of Roman expansionism. For as we have seen, we are in the *Discourses* II.4 encouraged to view the Tuscan league as the first step in a development which, if understood and practiced correctly, might eventually lead to the realization of the Roman ideal. By inviting his Florentine readers to participate in an inquiry into the different modes of expansionism set forth in the chapter, Machiavelli leads them to discover – behind his outspoken advice to revive the ancient Tuscan league – a half-concealed recommendation to imitate the cunning ways of the ancient Romans. It would appear, then, that the aim of Machiavelli's complex way of presenting his argument in *Discourses* II.4 is to initiate his readers into the strategic thinking of the Romans, and to convey a deeper, more dramatic understanding of the issues and the principles discussed in the chapter.

FRATERNIZE, SUBJUGATE, AND DESTROY

How well had the Florentines been able to live up to this Roman standard? Given Machiavelli's severe criticism of his compatriots' failure to imitate the ways of their ancestors, it might be tempting to claim, as Hulliung does, that he portrays Florence as "the republic of Rome turned upside down," and that his comparative study of the two cities serves as "an exercise in deflation."[72] But even though there can be no denying that there is such a side to Machiavelli's treatment of the subject, this black and white contrast between ancient Rome and modern Florence ignores the former Secretary's detailed and nuanced analysis of Florentine imperialism in the *Discourses*, and his surprisingly favorable view of the commune's first hesitant steps as an imperialist power. As we have seen, Machiavelli praises the city's former rulers for having employed a policy of fraternization vis-à-vis the neighboring city of Pistoia back in the Trecento, which, if they had persisted in it and expanded it, would have made them lords of Tuscany. In the *Istorie fiorentine*, he gives another early example of how Florence successfully used the strategy of fraternization for imperialist ends. The year was 1343, and the city was recovering from the short but traumatic tyranny of Walter of Brienne, the Duke of Athens. While the Florentines were busy sorting out their internal affairs, several cities in their dominion – Arezzo, Castiglione, Pistoia, Volterra, Colle Val d'Elsa, and San Gimignano included – seized the opportunity to "return to their liberty."[73] The ambiguity of the whole situation, which saw internal liberty and external empire pitted against each other, is beautifully captured in Machiavelli's condensed comment: "Thus Florence found herself at the same time deprived of her tyrant and her dominion, and in recovering her liberty, she taught her subjects how to recover theirs."[74]

With their newly acquired dominion breaking up around them, the Florentines appointed a special council, consisting of the bishop and fourteen prominent citizens, to deal with the situation. It soon came to the conclusion that Florentine interests would be best served if the city were to "placate the subjects through peace (*con la pace*) instead of making them into enemies through war (*con la guerra*)." Consequently, the council decided to inform the rebel cities that Florence had no territorial claims on them, and that they were "as content with their liberty as with their own."[75] For this purpose, they sent an embassy to Arezzo, arguably the most important of the rebel cities, to "renounce the empire (*imperio*) they had had over the city, and to sign an agreement," establishing that they no longer could avail

[72] Hulliung, *Citizen Machiavelli*, p. 61.

[73] *Istorie fiorentine* II.38, p. 204: "Questi accidenti seguiti nella città dettono animo a tutte le terre sottoposte a' Fiorentini di tornare nella loro libertà . . . e nel recuperare la sua libertà insegnò a' subietti suoi come potessero recuperare la loro."

[74] Ibid.: "talché Firenze, in un tratto, del tiranno e del suo dominio priva rimase; e nel recuperare la sua libertà insegnò a' subietti suoi come potessero recuperare loro."

[75] Ibid.: 8 "pensorono che fusse piuttosto da placare i sudditi loro con la pace che farsegli nimici con la guerra, e mostrare di essere contenti della libertà di quegli come della propria."

themselves of the Aretines as subjects (*sudditi*), but only as friends (*amici*), or as allies.[76] After the Aretines had accepted this token of friendship, similar conditions were offered to the other rebels. According to Machiavelli, the outcome of this "prudently employed" (*prudentemente preso*) policy of fraternization was that Arezzo shortly afterwards returned under Florentine rule, with the other towns following her example and allowing themselves to be "reduced to their pristine obedience."[77] On the basis of this episode, Machiavelli concludes: "this shows that things are many times obtained in a quicker and less dangerous way, and with less expense, by avoiding them, than by pursuing them with all your strength and with obstinacy."[78]

By adapting to the circumstances and to their own relative strength, the Florentines had on this particular occasion given proof of great pragmatism. They had granted the rebel cities a liberty which was not theirs to give (since the rebels were *de facto* already free, and Florence lacked the strength to recover them by force), and given a decision, which in reality had been forced upon them, an appearance of election.

But this must be considered an isolated instance, for on the whole the Florentines had failed to adopt the strategy of fraternization in a systematic way. In their treatment of subject cities like Arezzo, Pisa, and Pistoia they had instead resorted to partial destruction, the setting up of tributary oligarchies, rule by fortresses, and similar devices. This semi-tyrannical policy had among their neighbors earned them a reputation for being enemies, and not friends, and prevented them from securing their willing cooperation, or fearful obedience. If we examine more closely the passage in *Discourses* II.21 where Machiavelli speculates on Florence's possibility of becoming lord of Tuscany by adopting a policy of fraternization, we also find that it is couched in the past tense: "if the Florentines by way either of leagues or of aids had tamed (*avessero dimesticati*) their neighbors and not made them more savage, they would without doubt at this hour be lords of Tuscany." As the wording indicates, Machiavelli is here not giving advice for the present, but commenting on a lost opportunity. This observation is of paramount importance for understanding the former Secretary's call

[76] Ibid., pp. 204–05: "Mandorono pertanto oratori ad Arezzo, a renunziare allo imperio che sopra quella città avessero e a fermare con quelli accordo, acciò che, poi che come di sudditi non potevano, come amici della loro città si valessero."

[77] Ibid., p. 205: "Questo partito, prudentemente preso, ebbe felicissimo fine: perché Arezzo non dopo molti anni tornò sotto lo imperio de' Fiorentini, e l'altre terre in pochi mesi alla pristina ubbidienza si ridussono."

[78] Ibid.: "E cosí si ottiene molte volte piú presto e con minori pericoli e spesa le cose a fuggirle, che con ogni forza e ostinazione perseguitandole."

for harsh measure vis-à-vis the subject cities of Pisa, Arezzo, and Pistoia at the beginning of the Cinquecento.

Previously, we have seen how Machiavelli back in 1503, in *Del modo*, recommended the destruction of the rebellious city of Arezzo, a position which he later was to reiterate and defend with vigor in the *Discourses*.[79] In this work, and in *The Prince*, he takes a similar stand on the issue of the civil war in Pistoia. From Machiavelli's discussion here, we understand that Florence by this time had given up its policy of fraternization and begun to control her western neighbor by means of internal divisions instead.[80] In the summer of 1500, the domestic struggle between the Panciatichi and the Cancellieri factions, promoted by Florence, had deteriorated to the point of civil war. In *Discourses* III.27, Machiavelli relates how armed followers of the two groups clashed with bloodshed, the destruction of houses, and the plundering of property as a result.[81] The repercussions of the conflict were potentially devastating for Florence, since the Cancellieri enjoyed outside support from Giovanni Bentivoglio of Bologna, Cesare Borgia, and Piero de' Medici, who was plotting to return to Florence.

Initially, the Florentines had tried to resolve the crisis by making peace between the warring factions, but without punishing the ring-leaders. But this policy of half-measures, Machiavelli claims, had only led to "greater tumults and greater scandals."[82] It had from the very outset been doomed to fail, he argues, for it is unthinkable that "a peace made by force" will last, where "very much blood has run" among people who continue to meet face to face on a daily basis.[83] Under such conditions, the desire for revenge will cause a vicious circle of new disputes and new offenses. After a while, the Florentines had also been forced to change their tactics and had begun to punish the leaders by imprisonment or by exile. Even though Machiavelli could not deny that this strategy had proved successful so far, he viewed it as a weak policy and maintained that it could not provide a permanent

[79] *Discorsi* II.23 and III.27.

[80] Pistoia was incorporated into the Florentine dominion in 1328. On Florence's rule of Pistoia in the Quattrocento, see Stephen J. Milner, "Rubrics and Requests: Statutory Division and Supra-Communal Clientage in Fifteenth-Century Pistoia," in *Florentine Tuscany*, pp. 312–32. On the political situation in Pistoia at the turn of the Cinquecento, see also Marchand, *I primi scritti*, pp. 42–44. In chapter 17 of *Il principe*, we are told that Cesare Borgia, despite the manifest cruelty he employed when restoring unity, peace, and loyalty to Romagna, was much more merciful than the Florentine people, who "per fuggire il nome di crudele, lasciò distruggere Pistoia": *Il principe* 17, p. 162.

[81] This, it would seem, is the destruction of Pistoia that Machiavelli speaks of at the outset of *Il principe* 17.

[82] *Discorsi* III.27, p. 486: "maggiori tumulti e maggiori scandoli."

[83] Ibid.: "Perché gli è impossibile, dove sia corso assai sangue o altre simili ingiurie, che una pace, fatta per forza, duri, riveggendosi ogni dí insieme in viso."

solution to the problem. In order to reunite Pistoia and to bring the city under their control, he argues, the Florentines would have to execute the leaders of the two factions. But such measures, he claims, have in them "something of the great and of the generous" (*hanno il grande e il generoso*) which "a weak republic does not know how to perform" (*non le sa fare*). This observation prompts him to make a general reflection, which, at the same time as it recalls the preface of book one, serves to bring the whole project of the *Discourses* into focus. The rulers of the present day, he claims, ought to listen to "how those who have had to judge such cases in antiquity governed themselves," but their weak characters – which Machiavelli attributes to their lack of education and "slight knowledge of things" – make them "judge ancient judgments in part inhuman, in part impossible."[84]

From these recommendations on how Florence should stamp out the rebellions in Arezzo and Pistoia, it is clear that Machiavelli judged that the political situation in and around Florence had changed since the Trecento, when the policy of self-serving fraternization still had been a valid and attractive option. The violence unleashed by the revolts and their severe, but incomplete, suppression had brought the oppressive and cruel side of Florentine rule into the open, and closed the door to more subtle and complex forms of manipulation.

If we apply this line of reasoning to Machiavelli's conflicting positions on the question of Pisa, we shall begin to appreciate how consistent and how closely modeled on the Roman example his view of Florentine imperialism actually is. As we have seen, the recommendation in *Discourses* II.21 that the Pisans should be fraternized in the same manner as the Pistoiese referred to a period before the subjugation of Pisa in 1406. The two alternatives put forward in *Discourses* II.24, according to which Florentines should either offer Pisa their companionship or destroy her, related in all probability to the time before the Pisan rebellion in 1495. In chapter 5 of *The Prince*, these two alternative modes have collapsed into a simple imperative: eliminate Pisa. This was radical advice even by Machiavelli's standard, for as we recall, the former Secretary had in *Discourses* II.21 stated that arms and force should not be used other than in "the last place, where and when other modes are not enough."[85] This leads us to infer that Machiavelli when composing *The Prince* had come to the conclusion that Florentine–Pisan relations now

[84] Ibid., p. 487: "E questi sono di quegli errori che io dissi nel principio, che fanno i principi de' nostri tempi, che hanno a giudicare le cose grandi: perché doverrebbono volere udire come si sono governati coloro che hanno avuto a giudicare anticamente simili casi. Ma la debolezza de' presenti uomini, causata dalla debole educazione loro e dalla poca notizia delle cose, fa che si giudicano i giudicii antichi parte inumani, parte impossibili."

[85] Cf. note 52 above.

had reached this ultimate stage, and that the time when Florence could secure her neighbor's loyalty through a policy of friendship, humanity, and liberality had passed. After the recent rebellion, he seems to argue, the only form of imperialism remaining for Florence in relation to Arezzo, Pistoia, and Pisa is direct rule and undisguised repression.

Logical and consistent as this reading may appear, it is complicated by the fact that Machiavelli in *Discourses* II.4, as we have seen, in clear and unequivocal terms advocates a revival of the ancient Tuscan league. This proposal, which invokes the idea of a peaceful coexistence between independent states, does not refer to a past situation, but is presented as the most practicable policy for the Florentine republic *here and now*. It is evident that this advice stands in open conflict with the imperialist policy we have here come to attribute to Machiavelli. How is this inconsistency to be explained? Could it be that Machiavelli in the *Discourses* is arguing two different cases and advocating two different policies for Florence? Or could these policies somehow be brought together and reconciled?

THE TUSCAN LEAGUE

To appreciate the complexity of Machiavelli's imperialist theory, we should at this point recall the anatomy of the Florentine territorial state, or empire, which prompts us to distinguish between Florence's internal, external, and foreign affairs. In keeping with contemporary political and diplomatic discourse, we may define as *external* those policies that concerned the Florentine dominion, distinguishing them from the republic's *internal* affairs related to the city proper, and from her *foreign* policy pursued in relation to foreign powers and independent neighboring states. The territory belonging to the sphere falling under the designation *external* consisted, according to the legal definitions of the day, of the countryside (*contado*) and the outlaying district (*distretto*). In 1503, when Machiavelli drafted *Del modo*, Arezzo and Pistoia were thus part of the Florentine *distretto*, whereas Pisa was still defending her independence and republican self-rule. Later, when he composed *The Prince* and the *Discourses*, Pisa had been reconquered and incorporated in the Florentine dominion anew. But we also need to keep in mind that Florence during Machiavelli's life-time never was able to extend her jurisdiction to encompass all of Tuscany. City-states like Lucca and Siena continued to assert their independence, wherefore Tuscan hegemony remained the distant goal of Florentine aspirations.[86]

[86] While Siena was conquered by Florence in 1555, Lucca remained free until 1799, when the city fell to Napoleon.

Given the complexity of the political landscape of the day, we should, when assessing Machiavelli's position on Florence's external and foreign affairs, differentiate between her Tuscan neighbors. When Machiavelli back in 1503 recommended that Arezzo should be destroyed politically, he was addressing a problem relating to Florence's external affairs. Similarly, when in the *Discourses* he calls for coercive and disciplinary action against the instigators of the civil war in Pistoia, he is giving advice on external, not on foreign, policy. It is also in this context we should perceive his oblique advice in *The Prince* 5 to destroy Pisa, since the question of Pisa at this time had ceased to be an issue of foreign policy – a definition few Florentines would have accepted anyway – and instead become a matter of Florentine external affairs. All Machiavelli's recommendations to use strong and uncompromising action and force of arms are, in other words, aimed at restoring obedience in a territory that Florence already considered her own.

The logic underlying this policy is most clearly spelled out in Machiavelli's proposal for a new militia ordinance, the so-called *Cagione dell'ordinanza*, of 1506. Here Machiavelli claims that the enrollment of a militia in the Florentine dominion, for reasons of security, should begin in the *contado*, and not in the *distretto*. The loyalty of the inhabitants of the *contado* can be trusted, he argues, for the simple reason that they have nowhere else to turn than to Florence for protection, and therefore "recognize no other patron." Since the cities in the *distretto* – Arezzo, Borgo Sansepolcro, Cortona, Volterra, Pistoia, Colle Val d'Elsa, and San Gimignano in particular – desire to become independent from Florence, they cannot be trusted in the same way. On the contrary, these cities could easily become stepping stones for a foreign power wanting to impinge upon the Florentine territory. Recent experience also gives one reason to believe that, if Florence were to furnish them with arms, they would use them to rebel against the city, rather than to defend her. Therefore, Machiavelli concludes, one should either abandon every thought of arming the *distretto*, or postpone this decision until the *contado* had been properly organized militarily. As it would seem, then, the militia project of 1506 and the pacification of the cities in the *distretto*, advocated in *Del modo* and insisted on in Machiavelli's theoretical works, are part and parcel of one and the same imperial strategy.

As we have seen in this chapter, the other half of Machiavelli's imperial thinking is made up of a foreign policy based on a deceptive use of leagues, directed at independent and sovereign neighboring states. Since there could be no question of cooperation and fraternization on equal, or quasi-equal, terms between Florence and the subject cities of Pisa, Arezzo, and Pistoia, Machiavelli's Tuscan league would have to be made up of independent republics like Lucca and Siena, and cities belonging to an extended Tuscany, such as Bologna and Perugia.[87]

If this was the kind of alliance Machiavelli had in mind when he advocated a revival of the Tuscan league in *Discourses* II.4, the idea was not far removed from the political realities of the day. The idea of a Tuscan league had been a recurrent theme in Florentine and Tuscan diplomacy ever since the Trecento. After the war between Florence and Lucca in the late 1430s, the two cities, which by tradition had been on opposing sides in the conflict between Guelfs and Ghibellines, had joined in a fifty-year league. Despite periods of tension and Florentine attempts to reinforce her control over the ally, the league had remained in force.[88] At the beginning of the Cinquecento, the idea of a Tuscan league was brought up by Pandolfo Petrucci, the ruler of Siena, in discussions with Florentine representatives. Concerned with the threat posed by Cesare Borgia, Pandolfo is reported to have proposed an alliance between all Tuscan states during a meeting with a Florentine ambassador in late 1502. The negotiations proved fruitless, however, and when Cesare Borgia shortly afterwards attacked Siena, Pandolfo was forced to seek refuge in Lucca. He was later restored to power with Florentine support after having promised to cede the territory of Montepulciano to the Arno city.[89] Early in 1509, Florence entered a new alliance with Lucca for a term of three years. In the treaty, it was laid down that the pact could be prolonged for another twelve years if Florence failed to recover Pisa during the stipulated period.[90] On this occasion the policy of a league proved useful, for the Luccan alliance came in a substantial way to contribute to Florence's final victory over Pisa later in the summer.[91] Given

[87] During his mission to Cesare Borgia in 1502, Machiavelli appears to have been favorably inclined to the duke's idea of a league consisting of Ferrara, Bologna, Florence, and Cesare's newly created duchy in Romagna; see *Legazioni e commissarie*, pp. 629–805, esp. 699–702.

[88] See M. E. Bratchel, *Lucca 1430–1494: The Reconstruction of an Italian City-Republic* (Oxford: Clarendon Press, 1995), pp. 74–83. If Bratchel is correct (pp. 81–82), the Medici used this league in part as a cover for their project of making themselves rulers of the whole of Tuscany.

[89] Guicciardini, *Storie fiorentine*, p. 229: "Pandolfo, conoscendo che e' successi del Valentino ed ogni acquisto che egli facessi in Toscana sarebbe in fine la ruina sua come degli altri, desiderava posare questo fuoco e reconciliare Vitellozzo colla città e fare una intelligenzia di tutti questi stati di Toscana." Pandolfo is referred to in highly positive terms in *Il principe* 20 and 22. In chapter 22, Machiavelli comments on Pandolfo's minister, Antonio Giordani, in a way suggesting that the two were close friends. Machiavelli was sent on missions to Siena on at least four occasions during the period 1502–07; see Roberto Ridolfi, *Vita di Niccolò Machiavelli* (2 vols., Florence: Sansoni, 1969), I, pp. 74, 104, 135, and 158. He was dispatched there on 18 August 1502, that is, at the time Cesare Borgia was threatening Tuscany, and Pandolfo's idea of a Tuscan league was being discussed. Unfortunately, we seem to have no further information about this legation.

[90] On the league between Florence and Lucca of 1509, see Butters, *Governors and Government*, pp. 134–35. Previously during the war, Lucca had given direct as well as indirect support to the Pisan rebels.

[91] See Stephens, *The Fall of the Florentine Republic*, pp. 97 and 107.

the close, if yet complex, relations between Florence, Lucca, and Siena during the first decade of the Cinquecento, it does not seem far-fetched to assume that Machiavelli conceived of these three cities as the mainstay of the Tuscan league he advocated in *Discourses* II.4.

Emerging from this long and intricate discussion of Machiavelli's view on Florentine expansionism is an imperialist theory based on the ancient Romans' combined use of fraternization and force of arms. When this general principle has been uncovered, we can see that no real contradiction exists between Machiavelli's advice on the destruction of the once-free communities within the Florentine dominion, and his call for a revival of the ancient Tuscan league. While the destruction and the pacification by force should be understood as an external policy reserved for cities already effectively under Florentine control, the fraudulent use of leagues and fraternization was meant to serve as the basis for the republic's foreign policy vis-à-vis independent states and self-governing cities on her frontiers. The methods differ thus according to time and circumstance, but the underlying aim remains the same: the security, power, and expansion of Florence.

CHAPTER 5

The triumphator

> But in Ancient Times; The *Thropies* erected upon the Place of the Victory; The Funerall Laudatives and Monuments for those that died in the Wars; The Crowns and the Garlands Personal; The Stile of Emperor, which the Great Kings of the World after borrowed; The Triumphes of the Generalls upon their Returne; The great Donatives and Largesses upon the Disbanding of the Armies; were Things able to enflame all Mens Courages. But above all, That of the Triumph, amongst the *Romans*, was not Pageants or Gauderie, but one of the Wisest and Noblest Institutions, that ever was.
>
> Sir Francis Bacon

Dedicating his *Istorie Pisane* to the Grand Duke Ferdinand de' Medici at the turn of the Seicento, Raffaello Roncioni deplored the fact that the glorious history of Pisa, his "most sweet and most loved fatherland (*patria*)," had fallen into oblivion. To remedy this sorry state of affairs, he promised the grand duke an epic account of the great deeds (*gran fatti*) of his most illustrious subject city, which would bring back to memory the power, the riches, the glory, the triumphs, the victories, and the greatness she once had enjoyed.[1] From Roncioni we learn that the Pisans for centuries had fought the Saracens and defended and advanced the cause of Christianity throughout the Mediterranean, from the Balearic Islands in the West to the Holy Land in the East. Like other great cities, she had not remained quiet for long but pursued her conquests with relentless appetite.[2] Her thirst for glory and new dominions had brought her fleets to exotic places such as Arabatalgidith and Elmodenia, and her daring campaigns had been crowned by the conquests of Majorca, Sardinia, and Palermo.

Thus far Roncioni's history reads much like a replica of his literary models, Livy and Bruni, but there is one important element missing from his account: the traditional connection between imperial greatness and

[1] Raffaelo Roncioni, "Istorie Pisane," *Archivio storico italiano*, 6.1 (1844), pp. 2–3.
[2] Ibid., p. 275.

republican liberty permeating the Roman republican tradition. The legacy of Pisan liberty, which we have seen being invoked with patriotic pathos at the turn of the Cinquecento, has in *Istorie Pisane* disappeared without leaving a trace. Instead, Roncioni depicts the Pisans as a valiant and warlike people with a great capacity for cruelty, but who are also deferential and eternally obedient. Underlying the narrative is the implied message that a ruler who understands how to honor and to draw benefit from such valorous subjects is himself destined for imperial greatness.

A recurrent motif in the *Istorie Pisane* is the Pisans' public celebrations of their territorial acquisitions and victories in war. We are told, for example, that the Pisan fleet, after its glorious conquest of Sardinia in 1052, entered the mouth of the river Arno with the banners of the enemy trailing in the water behind as a sign of victory. Fires were made in the towers on both sides of the river to signal the news to the city. Instantly, a great multitude gathered along the shore to listen to an account of the successful campaign being read to the city magistrates. Cheered by the crowd, the victorous admiral, Jacopo Ciurini, who had not only conquered the island of Sardinia and defeated its king, Musetto, but also brought back the queen and her son as prisoners of war, demanded to enter the city in triumph. After the consuls and the senators, convening in the church of Santa Reparata, had granted the request, Ciurini and his army set camp outside the city walls, and began preparing for "entering the city in triumph like the ancient and famous Romans had done after defeating the enemy."[3]

On the following day, the triumphal procession entered Pisa by the Porta d'Oro, the Golden Gate. Wagons loaded with spoils and booty came first; then captives, ten thousand in number, bound in chains and with their arms pinioned; a display of the enemy banners and the conquered royal insignia preceded the victorious army, full of joy and exultation, and it was followed by the Sardinian queen and her son on a cart drawn by two horses. The victory parade was concluded by the triumphator, Ciurini, himself, seated on a triumphal chariot drawn by four white horses. After having been received by the city magistrates in front of the public palace, where the prisoners and the booty were handed over to the commune, the general requested permission to return to his former life as a private citizen. When the Senate, as a sign of gratitude, offered him many gifts "of great value," he rejected them with the explanation that "the glory conferred on him by the Senate was no small gift, and that it alone was enough for him."[4]

[3] Ibid., p. 97. [4] Ibid., p. 99.

This imaginary account of the medieval Pisan entry ceremony, which if historically accurate, would be the first documented classicized triumph after the fall of Rome in 476, was written at a time when the revival of the ancient Roman triumph was reaching its peak in Europe. The moving spectacles of the French monarchs' *joyeux entrées* and the Habsburg emperors' victory parades had in the course of the Cinquecento begun to assume proportions equaling those of the ancient Roman triumphator. Triumphal motifs of ancient Roman inspiration figured prominently in poetry, the visual arts, festival pageants, civic parades, and ceremonial decorations for royal and papal entries; they permeated the iconography of astrological and religious broadsheets, and the decorations of wedding chests. Scores of titles describing real or imagined triumphs poured over Europe: "La trymphante Entree de Charles Prince des Espagnes en Bruges" (1515), "Grand Triomphe et Entrée . . ." (1531), "Triomphes d'Honneur" (1539), "La magnificque et triumphante Entrée du trés illustre et sacré Empereur Charles César toujours Auguste" (1540), "Descrizione dell'entrata della sereniss. Reina Giovanna d'Austria et dell'apparato, fatto in Firenze . . ." (1566), etc.[5] Protocols codifying the ceremonial order for triumphal entries were evolving into a new thriving genre. The discovery in 1546 of the Capitoline tablets, recording all the triumphs ordained by the ancient Romans, did nothing to dampen the enthusiasm. By the mid-century, this development, which can be traced back to Petrarch's and Cola di Rienzo's almost boyish experimentations in the Trecento, had grown into one of the distinguishing features of the age. When Francis Bacon in his *Essays* claimed that the ancient Roman triumph had been "one of the Wisest and Noblest Institutions, that ever was,"[6] he was merely repeating the prevailing wisdom of the age.

But the fact that the revival of Roman triumphalism was given strong caesarian and royal overtones must not make us forget that the ancient Roman triumph had reached its accomplished stage during the republican period. Included in the list of great Roman triumphators were not only imperial figures like Julius Caesar, Augustus, and Trajan, but also republican heroes such as Furius Camillus, Manlius Torquatus, and Scipio Africanus. Against this background, it should not come as a surprise that the classical Roman triumph, and the idea of the triumphator, played an important part in the history of medieval and Renaissance republicanism as well. This chapter sets itself the task of exploring the impact of the Roman triumph upon the political culture of the Italian Renaissance and its role

[5] René Schneider, "Le thème du triomphe dans les entrées solennelles en France," *Gazette des beaux-arts* 55 (1913), p. 92.

[6] Sir Francis Bacon, *The Essayes of Counsels, Civill and Morall* (Oxford: Clarendon Press, 1985), p. 99.

in the political thought of Niccolò Machiavelli. However, before entering into this inquiry, a few words need to be said about the classical Roman triumph.

THE ROMAN TRIUMPH

The highest honor attainable for a Roman general was to be granted the right to return to Rome in triumph.[7] To enjoy this prestigious reward the victorious general – who was normally a consul, a *praetor*, or an *imperatore* – should have conclusively defeated a foreign army, slain a minimum of five thousand enemy soldiers in battle, and provided for the safe return of his soldiers.[8] In republican times, the triumph was decreed by the Senate, often after weeks of negotiations, intensive debates, and defamation campaigns orchestrated by opponents of the candidate in question.[9] When the triumph had been awarded, the people of Rome prepared themselves to greet their hero and benefactor. On the day of the celebration, the triumphal procession entered Rome from the Campus Martius by a triumphal gate specially chosen for the occasion, or alternately by a symbolic breach made in the city walls. It moved along a circuitous route past the Circus Flaminius, the Circus Maximus, round the Palatine, along the Via Sacra, before finally reaching its destination, the Capitolium. At the head of the parade went magistrates and senators, followed by musicians, white bulls crowned for sacrifice, carts laden with the spoils of war, and captives in chains dressed according to rank. In the middle of the procession rode the triumphator himself, standing in a chariot drawn by four white horses and festooned with laurel. He was dressed in royal purple and gold, and his face was painted with red lead in resemblance of the terracotta statue of Jupiter, the supreme god. In his right hand, he held a laurel branch, and in the left, the eagle-crowned scepter, the insignia of Jupiter. Behind the triumphator in

[7] On the Roman triumph, see H. S. Versnel, *Triumphus: An Inquiry into the Origin, Development and Meaning of the Roman Triumph* (Leiden: Brill, 1970); H. H. Scullard, *Festivals and Ceremonies of the Roman Republic* (London: Thames and Hudson, 1981), pp. 213–18; Ernst Künzl, *Der römische Triumph: Siegesfeiern im antiken Rom* (Munich: Beck, 1988); Randolph Starn and Loren Partridge, *Arts of Power: Three Halls of State in Italy, 1300–1600* (Berkeley, CA: University of California Press, 1992), pp. 157–58. For a comprehensive general bibliography of the literature on triumphalism, see *"All the World's a Stage . . .": Art and Pageantry in the Renaissance and Baroque*, eds. B. Wisch and S. S. Munshower (2 vols., University Park: Pennsylvania State University Press, 1990), vol. I: *Triumphal Celebrations and the Rituals of Statecraft*, pp. 359–85.

[8] It is possible that these formal regulations were introduced in an attempt to come to terms with the accelerating number of triumphs being staged at the beginning of the second century BC; see Scullard, *Festivals and Ceremonies*, pp. 214–15.

[9] According to Livy, Aemilius Paulus was subject to such calumny; see Livy XLV.35.5.

the chariot rode traditionally a slave, holding a laurel wreath or a golden crown over his head, while whispering in his ear words reminding him that all glory is transitory. At the end of the parade the soldiers of the victorious army marched, crowned with laurel, singing obscene songs, hailing or uttering insults against their commanders, and shouting "Io triumphe!", invoking the spirit of Triumph. Upon the procession's arrival at the temple of the Capitoline Jupiter, the triumphator laid down the laurel branch and the scepter, along with other votive offerings. The prisoners were usually slain, the bulls sacrificed, and the ritual normally brought to an end by a sumptuous feast held in honor of the senators under whose auspices it was celebrated. The booty, at least the major part of it, was handed over to the state treasury for public consumption, and the triumph was commemorated by an engraving on the Capitoline tablets, on which all the triumphs decreed by the Senate and the Roman people were recorded. With the fall of the republic, the triumph became an exclusive right of the emperor, and following the reign of Diocletian the tradition appears to have fallen into disuse.

Interpreting the meaning of the classical triumph is a hazardous task. But a few general remarks can be ventured. During the republican period, it appears, the triumphal procession was conceived of as a sacramental rite, a tribute to the ancestral gods, and a celebration of Roman justice, virtue, fame, and glory.[10] It concluded a cycle of war and peace, which had been initiated when the general, upon his departure from Rome, had sworn his sacred oath on the Capitolium. After having brought the campaign to a victorious completion, he now returned to the same site, to the same temple, and appeared before the same gods with the gifts and the trophies he had promised them in his vow. The triumph offered containment by confronting and separating opposite categories as well. As they welcomed home their victorious army, the Romans brought the war into the city in a highly spectacular, but rigorously controlled manner, purging the protected and sanctified area of the *urbe* from its pollution. By enacting the principle of difference in a dynamic and all-encompassing spectacle, the triumph reestablished the boundary between war and peace, military and civil authority, foreign and Roman, charismatic power and the routine order, or

[10] Cf. Livy XLV.38.5–7: "A triumph will make Lucius Paulus neither greater nor less a general; rather it is the reputation of the soldiers and that of the Roman People as a whole which is at stake in this matter, in the first place that Rome may not gain a reputation for a jealous and ungrateful spirit toward her most distinguished citizens, and seem in this respect to be imitating the people of Athens who in their envy buffet their leading men" (English translation by A. C. Schlesinger, *Livy in fourteen volumes* [Cambridge, MA: Harvard University Press, 1919–59], XIII, p. 381).

to speak with Machiavelli, between what was conceived of as *estraordinario* and *ordinario*. In so doing, it restored distinction to the Roman state, and renewed the link between the city's temporal inhabitants and the eternal realms of the gods above and the holy soil of the *patria* below. It demonstrated that the glorious exploits, the conquests, and all the novelty that war brings had done nothing to change the Romans' traditional commitment to the republic, the common good of their city, and their ancestral gods. After the enhancement of the victorious general followed his dethronement. Through the reversal of signs at the end of the ceremony, the divine, or semi-divine, triumphator was returned to human proportions before the temple of Jupiter, and his charismatic power brought under the control of the routine order, represented by the Senate.[11] The territory and the booty he had conquered not for himself personally, but for the city of Rome and for its gods. His feat did not give him precedence over his compatriots, and after having participated in the enormous glory conferred on him, he was expected to step down from his office and to return to live as an ordinary citizen. A cycle of war had been concluded, but there was no doubt in the minds of the Romans that new cycles were to follow, and that Rome would grow richer, greater, and more glorious in the process.

THE REVIVAL OF TRIUMPHALISM

Transmitted through the works of Livy, Plutarch, and Appian, and various archeological remains, the ancient Roman triumph exerted an immense, almost spell-binding fascination on the Renaissance mind.[12] The first documented attempt to revive this classical ritual after the collapse of Roman imperial authority occurred in 1237, when Emperor Frederick II entered Rome in triumph following his victory over the Milanese at Cortenuova. The Luccan warlord Castruccio Castracani, to whom Machiavelli later was to dedicate a short biography, entered his home town in 1326 on a triumphal chariot in Roman imperial style, preceded by captured prisoners.[13] In his unfinished national epos *Africa*, and in his immensely influential *Trionfi*, a series of poems celebrating the victories of Chastity over Love, Fame over Death, and Divinity over Time, Petrarch gave vivid descriptions of Scipio

[11] Cf. Versnel, *Triumphus*, pp. 58–93; Künzl, *Der römische Triumph*, pp. 85–108.

[12] On Renaissance triumphalism in general, see Starn and Partridge, *Arts of Power*; Bonner Mitchell, *The Majesty of the State: Triumphal Progresses of Foreign Sovereigns in Renaissance Italy (1494–1600)* (Florence: Olschki, 1986), p. 7; Sergio Bertelli, *Il corpo del re: Sacralità del potere nell'Europa medievale e moderna* (Florence: Ponte alle Grazie, 1990), esp. ch. 3.

[13] For Machiavelli's biography on Castruccio Castracani, see "La vita di Castruccio Castracani da Lucca," in *Opere complete*, vol VII, ed. F. Gaeta (Milan: Feltrinelli, 1962), pp. 9–41.

Africanus's triumph after his victory over Hannibal, conjuring up triumphal elements in a dreamlike atmosphere with strong religious, philosophical, and political connotations.[14] The ceremony in which Petrarch received the laurel crown as Roman poet on the Capitol in 1341 was also staged as a triumph *all'antica*,[15] and the poet's close friend, the zealous republican Cola di Rienzo, arranged several processions of triumphal character during his turbulent and short-lived attempt at reviving the Roman republic in 1347.[16]

In the course of the Quattrocento humanist scholarship and archeological inquiries triggered a vogue for triumphal motifs in visual art, poetry, and ritual. As the boundaries between the aesthetic, the religious, and the political realms began to intersect and blur, borrowings and exchanges between artistic fantasy and political aspirations became increasingly frequent and complex. Appearing within short intervals around the middle of the century were Francesco Laurana's relief on the gate of the Castel Nuovo in Naples, depicting Alfonso of Aragon's triumphal entry into the city in 1443,[17] Flavio Biondo's *Roma Triumphans* (1457–59), which included a lengthy description of a Roman triumph, Roberto Valturio's *De re militari* (1460), and Mantegna's classicizing and epoch-making canvases of the *Triumph of Caesar* (1478–92). To this period belong also two painted triumphs by Piero della Francesca (1472) and Francesco del Cossa's frescoes of the *Triumphs of the Months* (1470s) in Palazzo Schifanoia in Ferrara. Italian and transalpine rulers began now to cast themselves in the role of reborn Romans, and to seek ways of imposing their imperial fantasies on the material world of human beings and concrete things. Alfonso of Aragon had in the mid-fifteenth century set the tone by styling himself as the new Ceasar and by assuming titles such as "divus" and "rex triumphator et pacificus."[18] The trend gained momentum during the papacy of Alexander VI, which saw the rebels of Ostia being taken to Rome in chains in the manner of ancient Roman triumphal processions after their defeat to Gonzalvo in 1497. In the

14 Francesco Petrarca, *Trionfi* (Milan: Rizzoli, 1984). On Petrarch's influence on Renaissance triumphalism, see Prince D'Essling and Eugène Müntz, *Pétrarque: ses études d'art, son influence sur les artistes, ses portraits et ceux de laure, l'illustration de ses écrits* (Paris, 1902).

15 See Ernest Hatch Wilkins, *The Making of the Canzoniere and Other Petrarchan Studies* (Rome: Edizioni di Storia e Letteratura, 1951), pp. 9–69; J. B. Trapp, "The Poet Laureate: Rome, *Renovatio* and *Translatio Imperii*," in *Rome in the Renaissance: The City and the Myth*, ed. P. A. Ramsey (Binghamton: Center for Medieval and Early Renaissance Studies, 1982), pp. 100–05.

16 Mitchell, *The Majesty of the State*, p. 7.

17 Already in 1434, Pope Eugenius IV is reported to have celebrated a triumph *all'antica* after his victory over the Colonna party; see D'Essling and Müntz, *Pétrarque*, p. 131.

18 On Alfonso's entry and his ideological claims, see Joanna Woods-Marsden, "Art and Political Identity in Fifteenth-Century Naples: Pisanello, Cristoforo di Geremia, and King Alfonso's Imperial Fantasies," in *Art and Politics in Late Medieval and Early Renaissance Italy: 1250–1500*, ed. C. M. Rosenberg (Notre Dame: University of Notre Dame Press, 1990), pp. 11–37, esp. 17.

year 1500, a triumph of Julius Caesar with eleven *carri* was performed in Rome in honor of the ancient Roman dictator's modern namesake, Cesare Borgia. Two years later, pageants representing the triumphs of Hercules, Scipio, Aemilius Paulus, and Caesar were staged in the city on the occasion of the marriage of the duke's sister, Lucrezia.[19] The banners under which Cesare Borgia was pursuing his relentless quest for power and a new state in central Italy made no secret of his ambitions: *Aut Caesar aut nihil*, "Caesar or Nothing."[20]

But the Borgias were far from alone in their thirst for ancient glory. The Italian wars, with their frequent taking and retaking of cities, gave ample opportunity for triumphal entries. On 11 November 1506, Alexander's sucessor, Pope Julius II, entered Bologna in a ceremony, designed by the Papal Master of Ceremonies, Paris de Grassis, which one modern historian has characterized as "a deliberate echo of ancient triumphs."[21] When the French king Louis XII entered Milan the year after, he was preceded by a triumphal chariot of Mars, the Roman god of war.[22] The ceremony was repeated in 1509, when Louis entered the Lombard metropole following his victory over the Venetians at Agnadello, in a procession featuring five triumphal chariots with miniature castles representing as many of the conquered cities.[23] North of the Alps, meanwhile, the Swiss were continuing to develop the concept of the citizen militia, inspired by the ancient Roman military system. In 1508, the newly elected Emperor Maximilian entered the ancient imperial city of Trent for his coronation in a ceremony staged as a classical triumph. Present on the occasion was the Florentine envoy, Niccolò Machiavelli, who, in his and Francesco Vettori's joint report home, gave a brief description of the event: "The other day they made a solemn procession here, in which [the emperor] went in person with his imperial heralds in front of him, and with his sword unsheathed; having arrived at the church, [the bishop of Gurk] Lang von Wellenburg spoke to the people, mentioning the Italian enterprise."[24] To judge from this comment, the emperor's ceremonial entry

19 D'Essling and Müntz, *Pétrarque*, p. 131.

20 Roberto Ridolfi, *Vita di Niccolò Machiavelli* (2 vols., Florence: Sansoni, 1969), I, p. 91.

21 Bonner Mitchell, *Italian Civic Pageantry in the High Renaissance: A Descriptive Bibliography of Triumphal Entries and Selected Other Festivals for State Occasions* (Florence: Olschki, 1979), p. 15. On Julius's Bolognese entry, see also Ludwig von Pastor, *Geschichte der Päpste seit dem Ausgang des Mittelalters* (21 vols., Freiburg im Breisgau: Herder, 1891–1933), III, pp. 739–40.

22 Schneider, "Le thème du triomphe," pp. 86 and 91.

23 Luisa Giordano, "Les entrées de Louis XII en milanais," in *Passer les monts: Français en Italie – l'Italie en France (1494–1525)*, ed. J. Balsamo (Paris: Honoré Champion, 1998), pp. 142–43.

24 *Legazioni e commissarie*, p. 1096: "L'altro dí poi si fece qui una processione solenne, dove andò la persona sua con li araldi imperiali innanzi, e con la spada nuda, e giunto in chiesa, el Lango parlò al popolo, dove significò questa impresa d'Italia."

was here envisaged as a form of preparation for future triumphs. Although little came out of Maximilian's plans for an Italian campaign, his imperial dreams remained alive, and around 1515 the artists at his court produced, under the supervision of Albert Dürer, a series of 172 different woodcuts depicting an imaginary triumphal arch and a triumphal procession of classical inspiration, bringing the ideology of victory and empire to new and unprecedented heights.[25]

TRIUMPHALISM IN FLORENCE

In Florence, paintings of triumphal motifs on *cassone* panels, inspired by Petrarch's *Trionfi*, had become common by the middle of the Quattrocento.[26] Around that time, Medicean eulogists began to employ Roman triumphal themes, symbols, and exemplars on a grand scale for propagandistic purposes. In private letters, public orations, and other panegyrical writings, Cosimo il Vecchio was compared to Cato, Furius Camillus, Scipio Africanus, Cicero, and other prominent Roman statesmen.[27] Roman history continued to serve as a store-house for propagandistic art, literature and ritual during the ascendancy of Lorenzo the Magnificent. The poet Luigi Pulci was not abashed to compare Lorenzo's victory in the joust of 1468 to the triumphs of Aemilius Paulus, Marcellus, and Scipio, who, according to him, had all been celebrated in Rome after their great conquests "without envy" (*sanza invidia*). The fact that the joust in question had been arranged to celebrate an inconclusive, and not very glorious, peace settlement between Venice and a papal coalition, of which Florence was a member, did not temper Pulci's literary enthusiasm.[28]

Lorenzo's own personal interest in Roman triumphalism is evident from his *Comento sopra alcuni de' suoi sonetti*, where he praises the Roman triumphs and the Greek Olympic Games for the way they inspired military and cultural feats by bestowing honors and fame on worthy individuals. For

[25] On Maximilian's triumphalism, see Larry Silver, "Paper Pageants: The Triumphs of Emperor Maximilian I," in *"All the World's a Stage . . ."*, 1, pp. 293–331.

[26] For a sumptuous depiction of the triumph of Aemilius Paulus on a Florentine wedding chest from the mid-Quattrocento, see *Le temps revient, 'l tempo si rinuova: Feste e spettacoli nella Firenze di Lorenzo il Magnifico*, ed. P. Ventrone (Florence: Silvana, 1992), p. 249. At about this time, Piero de' Medici, the son of Cosimo il Vecchio, is known to have commissioned painted panels from Matteo de' Pasti inspired by Petrarch's *Trionfi*; see D'Essling and Müntz, *Pétrarque*, p. 136.

[27] See Alison Brown, "The Humanist Portrait of Cosimo de' Medici, Pater Patriae," *Journal of the Warburg and Courtauld Institutes* 24 (1961): 186–222; reprinted in Alison Brown, *The Medici in Florence: The Exercise and Language of Power* (Florence: Olschki, 1992), pp. 3–40.

[28] Charles Dempsey, *The Portrayal of Love: Botticelli's Primavera and Humanist Culture at the Time of Lorenzo the Magnificent* (Princeton: Princeton University Press, 1992), p. 81.

the sake of glory, which "enflames the mortal souls" more than anything else, he writes, "the triumphal chariot and arch, the marble trophies, the richly decorated theatres, the statues, the palms, the crowns, the funerary orations, for it alone, infinite other wonderful ornaments were commissioned."[29] Lorenzo later sought to reenact such a triumphal scenery when, on St. John's Day of 1491, he staged an extravagant pageant consisting of fifteen *trionfi*, featuring the triumph of Aemilius Paulus, the conqueror of Macedonia in 168 BC. According to a contemporary witness, the triumph was an allegory of Lorenzo as Aemilius Paulus, and had been set up to broadcast the message that Florence owed its prosperity to the Medici, and to him, Lorenzo, personally.[30]

The expulsion of the Medici from Florence in 1494 was followed by the meteoric rise of Girolamo Savonarola, who for the next four years dominated the city's religious and political life. As the Dominican's influence grew, he began to take an increasing interest in the ritual culture of the city, and his campaign against the alleged paganism of the Florentines soon took to the streets.[31] During the carnivals of 1497 and 1498, Savonarola and his followers staged what could best be described as a series of anti-triumphs targeting the hedonistic classicism of the Laurentian era. On both occasions, the traditional bonfire, or *capannuccio*, was transformed into a powerful instrument of Savonarolan propaganda, as processions of young boys devoted to the friar's cause marched down to the Piazza della Signoria, the traditional site of the celebration, where they exhorted the bystanders to throw their objects of vanity into the fire. These famous Burnings of the Vanities saw the destruction of decks of cards, carnival masks, wigs, perfumes, paintings with equivocal, or overtly pagan, motifs, literary works of well-known heretics and, most notably, in the context of the present study, Livy's Roman history and a magnificent volume of Petrarch's poetry, two of the most important sources for Roman triumphalism.[32]

[29] *Prosatori volgari del Quattrocento*, ed. C. Varese (Milan and Naples, n.d.), p. 985. Cf. Warman Welliver, *L'impero fiorentino* (Florence: La Nuova Italia, 1957), p. 225; Dempsey, *The Portrayal of Love*, p. 117.

[30] Richard C. Trexler, *Public Life in Renaissance Florence* (Ithaca: Cornell University Press, 1994), pp. 451–52 and 486. According to Trexler this was the first time in Florentine history that a truly classicized motif processed through the streets of the city on this profoundly Christian festival. On the Florentine triumph of Aemilius Paulus, see also Paola Ventrone, *Gli araldi della commedia: Teatro a Firenze nel Rinascimento* (Pisa: Pacini Editore, 1993), pp. 44–46. On Lorenzo the Magnificent's ritual culture, see also Brown, *The Medici in Florence*, pp. 233–34.

[31] On Savonarola's ritual politics, see Trexler, *Public Life*, pp. 462–90.

[32] Pierre Antonetti, *Savonarole: le prophète désarmé* (Paris: Perrin, 1999), pp. 197–200 and 222–23. The burning of Livy's history was commented on in Savonarola's sermon of 9 February 1497, see ibid., p. 200.

In Savonarola's vision, Florence was destined to become the New Rome and the center of a spiritual renewal, but to become truly triumphant she would have to purge herself of her Laurentian past, abandon her pagan emphasis on worldly glory and material riches, and recover her Christian innocence. Spiritual reformation should precede and prepare the way for political renewal, Jerusalem must triumph over Rome, and Christ over the temporal rulers of the world. Savonarola's language could be quite evocative: "Oh emperor of Rome . . . oppressor of the whole world . . . bend down your head towards earth, kiss the feet of a fisherman, give him your crown, crave for his words, obey his laws, submit the whole world to this youth."[33] The new conquerors, who would fly the Florentine banners and spread the city's future empire, were to be cast not in the form of Roman consuls reborn, but as ardent followers of Christ, whom the Dominican now had begun to exhort the Florentines to elect as their king.[34]

In his religious treatise, *The Triumph of the Cross*, Savonarola draws on classical triumphal imagery and the tradition of Florentine pageantry, as he allegorically depicts the triumph of Christianity in the form of a triumphal procession. Since it is difficult for the human mind to imagine the supernatural and invisible works of Christ, the friar argues, they need to be presented and visualized in metaphorical form. The image of the triumphal chariot serves this purpose well.

Let us first place before our eyes a chariot with four wheels, and on that chariot Christ in triumph, crowned with thorns and wounded all over, through which his whole passion and death is shown, and by which he overcame the whole world . . . On the left side of Christ is a cross together with all the other instruments of his passion, and on the right side, the Scripture of the New and the Old Testaments . . . Under this first level, on which Christ is, one sees the most pious mother of God, Virgin Mary; arranged around her on that level are vases of gold, of silver and of precious stones, filled with ashes and the bones of the dead. In front of the chariot are the Apostles and the Preachers, who appear to be pulling the chariot, and on whom are following the Patriarchs and the Prophets together with an immense multitude of men and women from the Old Testament. Standing around the chariot, like a crown, is a great multitude of Martyrs among whom are the Holy Doctors with sacred books open in their hands, and an immense multitude of virgins with crowns decorated with lilies. Behind the chariot follow an infinite number of men and women of all conditions of life, Jews, Greeks, Latins, barbars,

[33] Girolamo Savonarola, *Scritti vari* (Rome: Belardetti, 1992), p. 61: "O imperatore di Roma . . . oppressore di tucto el mundo . . . Poni el capo in terra, basa e' piedi a uno pescatore, donagli la corona, desidera le sue parole, obedisci alle sue leggie, sottoponi tucto el mondo a questo fanciullino."

[34] On Florence's double mission, and Christ's role in Savonarola's thought, see Donald Weinstein, *Savonarola and Florence: Prophecy and Patriotism in the Renaissance* (Princeton: Princeton University Press, 1970), pp. 146–47 and 294–96.

rich as well as poor, wise, educated, uneducated, small, great, old and young, who by all their hearts are praising Christ. And around this multitude drawn from the Old as well as the New Testaments, we place innumerable hordes of enemies and opponents of the Church of Christ, emperors, kings, princes, powerful men, wise men, philosophers, heretics, slaves, free men, males, females, and people of every language and nation . . .

This chariot, thus described and arranged before our eyes, will be almost like a new world from which we can derive a new philosophy . . .[35]

By appropriating the modes of representation and the cultural forms of his paganizing opponents and by filling them with Christian contents, Savonarola here turns the classical Roman triumph and its Florentine festival version on its head.[36] In so doing, it could be argued, he is falling back on a long Christian tradition, and on Christ's own appropriation and reversal of the Roman triumph when entering Jerusalem on the back of an ass, holding an olive-branch as a symbol of eternal peace, instead of the scepter of the traditional emblem of the triumphal Roman warlord.

After more than a decade of strong anti-Roman sentiments, the reinstallment of the Medici in Florence in 1512 triggered a massive resurgence of carnivalesque festivities of classical Roman inspiration. Shortly after their return to the city, Lorenzo and Giuliano de' Medici formed in imitation of their namesakes, Lorenzo the Magnificent and his brother Giuliano, two rival carnival companies, the *broncone* and the *diamante*, for the organization of the 1513 carnival. On 6 February the *broncone* staged a pageant with an elaborate allegorical program representing Medicean rule in the guise of ancient Roman models. The program included seven *carri* featuring: (1) The Age of Saturn and Janus (understood as the Golden Age); (2) Numa Pompilius; (3) Titus Manlius Torquatus; (4) Julius Caesar; (5) Caesar Augustus; (6) Trajan; and (7) The return of Golden Age. The classicizing elements displayed in connection to these *trionfi* included imitations of ancient footwear, priests in ancient dress, torches resembling ancient candelabra, six pairs of mounted senators in togas, fasces, and axes, and soldiers in ancient armor.[37]

[35] Girolamo Savonarola, *Triumphus Crucis*, ed. M. Ferrara (Rome: Belardetti, 1961), pp. 8–9. For an Italian translation, see ibid., pp. 296–97.

[36] A similar mechanism is at work in Savonarola's sermons on the victory of the Christian religion, which he often depicts in terms of combat, siege, the forcing of gates, conquest, and other battle metaphors associated with Roman militarism. See for example Savonarola, *Scritti vari*, p. 65: "Eccho ch'egli ha inclinato e' celi, rotte le porte, aperti e' fonti, radiata la terra et schacciate le tenebre. Hora sarà sconfitto el re di Babilonia."

[37] Anthony M. Cummings, *The Politicized Muse: Music for Medici Festivals, 1512–1537* (Princeton: Princeton University Press, 1992), pp. 16–21.

The performance was repeated in connection with St. John's Day later in the year, when four Medici-sponsored triumphs *all'antica* with Roman imperial motives paraded through the streets of Florence. First, there was the triumph of Julius Caesar, symbolizing forgiveness and clemency; then followed the triumph of Pompey, embodying liberal donations; next came Augustus's triumph bringing peace in its train; and the procession was concluded by the triumph of Emperor Trajan, the epitome of justice. All triumphs contained the appropriate display of spoils and were accompanied by scrolls and tablets imprinting the propagandistic message on the public mind.[38] The fact that these triumphs featured two emperors, one perpetual dictator, and an aspiring general from the time of the late Republic instead of traditional republican heroes such as Scipio Africanus, Camillus, and Aemilius Paulus, announced that a fundamental change in the city's style of government was now under way.

The main attraction of the next year's feast of St. John was the exuberant Triumph of Camillus, staged to celebrate the return of Lorenzo de' Medici the younger to Florence from exile.[39] The pageant was held in the Piazza della Signoria before a huge crowd, including Giuliano de' Medici and seven prominent cardinals, who had come all the way from Rome to assist at the event. The triumph consisted of seventeen *carri*, on which the great deeds of Camillus were represented, accompanied by battle trophies, spoils of war, captives, and countless other objects associated with his conquests. The carnival songs written for the occasion left people in no doubt about the parallels they were expected to draw between the ancient hero and his modern counterpart. Thus, Lorenzo the younger was allegorically portrayed as a modern Camillus returning from exile, liberating his despoiled native city from the barbarians, and reviving it after a time of devastation.

It soon became clear that these carnival triumphs were mere dress rehearsals for things to come. On 15 August 1515, the Florentine authorities decreed, under pressure from Pope Leo X, that Lorenzo should be created Captain General of the Florentine militia, the first Florentine citizen to be so honored within living memory. In the prologue to the official document proclaiming Lorenzo's appointment, this constitutional innovation was motivated and justified with an explicit reference to the ancient

[38] Heidi L. Chretien, *The Festival of San Giovanni: Imagery and Political Power in Renaissance Florence* (New York: Peter Lang, 1994), p. 63.

[39] On the 1514 St. John's Day, see Cummings, *The Politicized Muse*, pp. 87–92; Trexler, *Public Life*, p. 508. Cf. Luca Landucci, *Diario fiorentino dal 1450 al 1516* (Florence: Biblos, 1969), p. 345; Giorgio Vasari, *Le vite dei piú eccellenti pittori, scultori e architetti*, ed. C. L. Ragglianti (3 vols., Milan: Rizzoli, 1942–45), II, p. 492.

Roman republic. Unable to find any foreign, or non-Florentine, captain fit for the assignment, the Eight had decided to nominate Lorenzo de' Medici after having been

> moved by the example of past, foreign and Italian republics and especially of the Roman republic, which with its own captains ruled its armies and wars in such a way that it made itself most glorious and almost Lady of the whole world. They have thought that it might easily be that a similar thing (if not completely at least in some part) might happen to the Florentine Republic when they would begin to use some man of their own as captain of their army.[40]

Since the appointment lacked precedents in modern Florentine history, it was met with resentment, and the Venetian ambassador to Florence could report home that Lorenzo now had been created captain of the Florentine army against the city's own laws and against the will of the people. In the ambassador's view, Lorenzo had now begun to act like a tyrant (although the Venetian avoids using the actual word) by giving orders and by having his wishes carried out in a way that did not appeal to the other citizens.[41]

The year 1515 was a particularly good one for triumphal entries in Europe. Early in the year, the young Prince Charles of Habsburg, the future Emperor Charles V, had entered Bruges to assume the title of viscount of Flanders in a triumph modeled on Christ's entry into Jerusalem. On 12 July Francis I of France, Charles's future contender for the imperial title, made a triumphal entry into Lyons, based on a program established by Charles VIII thirty years earlier, which vividly emphasized the sacrality of the French crown. Since there were strong Florentine colonies in Bruges as well as Lyons, information about these spectacular events is bound to have reached Florence with no, or little, delay.[42] The details of these reports were probably digested and worked into the program for the staging of Pope Leo X's long-awaited *entrata* into the city on 30 November, which wrapped up this memorable year in the history of European triumphalism.[43] During

[40] Quoted from J. N. Stephens, *The Fall of the Florentine Republic 1512–1530* (Oxford: Clarendon Press, 1983), p. 154.

[41] See John R. Hale, *Florence and the Medici* (London: Thames and Hudson, 1977), p. 99. On the ceremonial consignment of the baton of command to Lorenzo, see Trexler, *Public Life*, pp. 502–03. St. John's Day in 1516 was celebrated in honor of Lorenzo de' Medici's reconquest of Urbino.

[42] John Shearman, "The Florentine *Entrata* of Leo X, 1515," *Journal of the Warburg and Courtauld Institutes* 38 (1975): 136–54, esp. p. 142.

[43] On Leo's 1515 entry, see Felix Gilbert, *Machiavelli and Guicciardini: Politics and History in Sixteenth Century Florence* (Princeton: Princeton University Press, 1965), pp. 142–43; Shearman, "The Florentine *Entrata* of Leo X, 1515"; Janet Cox-Rearick, *Dynasty and Destiny in Medici Art: Pontormo, Leo X, and the Two Cosimos* (Princeton: Princeton University Press; 1984), pp. 35–36; Anna Maria Testaverde

his entry, Leo was celebrated as the new Romulus and as the founder, or refounder, of the city of Florence, with frequent references being made to his second given name, Romolo. To create the impression of Florence's temporary transformation into ancient Rome, eight classicizing triumphal arches were erected along the processional route, together with replicas of other famous Roman monuments such as the obelisk, the Column of Trajan (or possibly that of Marcus Aurelius Antoninus), and the equestrian statue of Marcus Aurelius. The impressive list of artists involved in the production of ephemera for the occasion included Andrea del Sarto, Jacopo Sansovino, Francesco Granacci, Baccio da Montelupo, Jacopo Pontormo, Baccio Bandinelli, and Rosso Fiorentino.

MACHIAVELLI ON TRIUMPHS

How did Machiavelli react to these ceremonial and ideological maneuverings? His writings from the period before and after the Medici's return to power give us reason to assume that he followed the developments with keen interest. When Machiavelli in chapter 21 of *The Prince*, for example, recommends his princely reader to keep his people "occupied with festivals and spectacles" during appropriate times of the year, he manifests a sharp awareness of the propagandistic value of this type of public display.[44] Also the Medici's highly conscious and elaborate use of Roman exemplars should have caught his attention. In *Del modo* of 1503, Machiavelli had argued that the basic conditions of the world were constant, and that therefore a direct imitation of the Romans, the former rulers of the world, was still possible. Now, similar claims were being made in connection to the Medici-sponsored pageants and to Lorenzo's appointment as Captain General of the Florentine militia. While composing *The Prince*, where he advises his princely reader to take great men of classical antiquity as his examples and model his behavior after them,[45] Machiavelli could with his own eyes witness how the Medici were playing out their political ambitions in the ritual arena of the city by associating themselves with ancient Roman exemplars. In exhorting the Medici in the final chapter of *The Prince* (commonly dated to around 1515) to liberate Italy from the barbarians, he could recall how they themselves on St. John's Day of 1514 had staged a triumph

Matteini, "Le Decorazione festiva el'itinerario di 'rifondazione' della città negli ingressi trionfali a Firenze tra XV e XVI secolo," *Mitteilungen des Kunsthistorischen Instituts in Florenz* 32 (1988), p. 339; Ilaria Ciseri, *L'ingresso trionfale di Leone X in Firenze nel 1515* (Florence, 1990); Cummings, *The Politicized Muse*, pp. 67–82.

44 *Il principe* 21, p. 182: "tenere occupati e' populi con feste e spettaculi."

45 See especially *Il principe* 14.

of Camillus, in which Lorenzo the younger, the addressee of *The Prince*, had been celebrated as a new Camillus, who had saved Florence, his *patria*, by freeing her from foreign domination.[46]

In the light of these and many other intriguing connections between Machiavelli's work and the ritual culture of contemporary Florence, it is surprising how little attention has been paid to this aspect of his thought. To the best of my knowledge, no attempt has been made at studying the Florentine's political theory in relation to the tradition of classical and Renaissance triumphalism, outlined above, or at assessing how his writings contributed to the development leading up to the modern ruler's self-fashioning as classicized conqueror and triumphator.[47] This is all the more remarkable, since there are many direct and probing observations in Machiavelli's work concerning the classical Roman triumph. In the following I shall attempt an investigation into this overlooked subject; first, by considering what Machiavelli explicitly says on the matter of the Roman triumph in the *Discourses* and *The Art of War*; then, by arguing that chapter 16 of *The Prince* is structured around the idea of the Roman triumphator – here appearing in the guise of the big giver (*gran donatore*). This discussion will lead to a detailed treatment of the use of the term greatness, or *grandezza*, in *The Prince* and the *Discourses*, before we return to the role played by the republican triumph in Machiavelli's political theory at large.

In giving an outline of Machiavelli's view on the Roman triumph, we shall here concentrate on three of the principal values he attributes to this institution; first, its ability to inspire love of virtue and glory in the Roman people; second, the way in which it contributed to keeping private interest subordinated to the common good of the city; and third, its fostering of a commitment to the city's free and republican way of life.

The most obvious reason why Machiavelli attaches such importance to the institutionalized Roman triumph is because it celebrated an active

46 Cummings, *The Politicized Muse*, pp. 88–90. In *Discorsi* I.33 and III.1, Machiavelli compares Medicean and Roman examples in a way that might have been inspired by the family's own use of Roman garb in self-glorifying purposes during these festivals.

47 For discussions of the related theme of glory, see Russell Price, "The Theme of *Gloria* in Machiavelli," *Renaissance Quarterly* 30 (1977): 588–631; Dan Eldar, "Glory and the Boundaries of Public Morality in Machiavelli's Thought," *History of Political Thought* 7 (1986): 419–38. Both Price and Eldar fail to recognize the important role played by the idea of the triumph and the triumphator in Machiavelli's thought. Instead, they treat glory as a purely theoretical concept. See also Claude Lefort, *Le travail de l'œuvre Machiavel* (Paris: Gallimard, 1972), pp. 380–81; Victoria Kahn, *Machiavellian Rhetoric From the Counter-Reformation to Milton* (Princeton: Princeton University Press, 1994), pp. 29–30; Harvey C. Mansfield, *Machiavelli's Virtue* (Chicago: University of Chicago Press, 1996), p. 52; and Robert A. Kocis, *Machiavelli Redeemed: Retrieving His Humanist Perspectives on Equality, Power and Glory* (Cranbury, NJ: Associated University Presses, 1998). Gerald Sfez comes closest to addressing the historical figure of the triumphator in connection to Machiavelli in "The Enigma of the Political Stage Director," *SubStance* 25 (1996): 30–45.

and vigorous form of virtue (*virtù*), and contributed to reinforce and to enhance the warlike qualities of the Roman people. Since the *imperium*-holding magistrates from the middle of the fourth century BC, at least in theory, were open to Romans regardless of age and social rank, the prospect of being awarded a triumph was shared by a large portion of the Roman society. The fact that many Romans aspired to this honor, and many also actually achieved it, induces Machiavelli to conclude that the institution created a competitive atmosphere in the city, making the Romans into "great lovers of glory" (*amatori grandi della gloria*),[48] and filling the city with virtuous men "adorned with various victories" (*ornati di varie vittorie*).[49] This general thirst for glory had a more practical and short-term effect as well. Since the consuls served only for one year, they were, in order to obtain their triumphs, eager to conclude their campaigns within their brief time in office.[50] This contributed to make the Roman wars short and relatively inexpensive up until the time the republic began to pay her soldiers and to wage wars ouside the Italian peninsula. Another effect of the triumph on the Roman mentality was that it contributed to make shame (*ignomia*), the reverse of glory, into a powerful factor in the political life of the city. The shame suffered by a supreme commander who failed to return to Rome in triumph, Machiavelli argues, was of such magnitude that the republic did not need to impose any further punishment for the errors he might commit in the course of his service. As a consequence of this strong emphasis on glory and shame, he goes on to claim, the Roman captains were free to concentrate on winning the war and on achieving glory, without having to worry about being punished in the process.[51] All these factors contributed, in Machiavelli's view, to make the Roman republic into the most acquisitive power in world history.

The second point concerns the way the triumph and the procedure regulating the distribution of the spoils of war influenced Rome's way of enriching herself. In *The Art of War*, Machiavelli relates with approval how the Romans, following their victories, sent out questors authorized to supervise the collection of booty and to prevent undisciplined plundering

[48] *Discorsi* I.36, p. 275.

[49] *Discorsi* I.30, p. 265 and I.60, pp. 322–23. The young triumphators Machiavelli mentions here are Valerius Corvinus, Scipio Africanus, and Pompey. Although Machiavellli in these chapters does not explicitly mention the triumph, he discusses the Roman system of incorporating territorial acquisitions and distributing glory to its virtuous generals. On the relationship between territory, booty, and glory in the institution of the Roman triumph, see pp. 152–53 above.

[50] *Discorsi* II.6, p. 344: "Perché nel primo ordine gli tenne, circa il fare le guerre brevi, oltra a il loro naturale uso, l'ambizione de' consoli; i quali avendo a stare uno anno e di quello anno sei mesi alle stanze, volevano finire la guerra per trionfare."

[51] Ibid., I.31.

by the soldiers. As a consequence, the Romans, keener on winning their battles than on pursuing and despoiling defeated and fleeing enemies, came to wage war for the glory and the well-being of the *patria*, and not for private economic gain. Since "every consul in his triumphs brought with him great riches to the treasury, which was made up completely of spoils of war," it came about that "the public was enriched," while the private citizens remained poor.[52] The Romans' dedication to the common good, their pursuit of glory, and the little importance they attached to the acquisition of private wealth, Machiavelli maintains, enabled Rome to expand and enrich herself through her wars, whereas most other peoples, less judicious and well-ordered than Rome, have been impoverished by theirs.[53] Despite all the wealth that was pouring into the city, Rome managed to maintain her traditional life-style and her simple and austere mores, because it was sufficent for her citizens to "get honor from war," and leave all material goods (*l'utile*) to the public.[54]

The third value Machiavelli attaches to the Roman triumph was that it served to uphold and to reinforce Rome's free way of life and the civic ideals invested in her republican institutions. In this regard, it functioned as a form of exchange. Through the active involvement of the ancestral gods and their intermediaries, the Senate and the officiating priests, the material goods and the territorial possessions the victorious generals brought back to the city were transformed into a spiritual quality called glory. In this exceptional, almost mysterious, but firmly institutionalized way, the city demonstrated its gratitude towards its most virtuous members, while ensuring their loyalty. Since the triumphator's short, but intense, moment as charismatic hero and semi-god left his thirst for glory satisfied, he experienced no need to seek further gratification through extraordinary or private means. Remaining attached to the civic ways of the city, the generals were content to return to their civil life and to their normal occupations, or to go on to serve in the army with a lesser rank.[55] The importance of the triumph within the republican context consisted thus largely in the fact that it provided a constitutional framework, within which ambitious and

[52] *Arte della guerra*, p. 636: "Di qui nasceva pertanto che il publico arricchiva, e ogni consolo portava con gli suoi trionfi nello erario assai tesoro, il quale era tutto di taglie e di prede."

[53] Ibid., pp. 636–37. See also *Discorsi* II.6, p. 345: "feciono che Roma arricchiva della guerra; dove gli altri principi e republiche non savie ne impoveriscono."

[54] *Discorsi* III.25, p. 484: "la poverta, e come vi stavano dentro contenti, e come e' bastava a quelli cittadini trarre della guerra onore, e l'utile tutto lasciavano al publico."

[55] *Arte della guerra*, p. 540: "Ma quegli che erano capitani, contenti del trionfo, con disiderio tornavono alla vita privata; e quelli che erano membri, con maggior voglia deponevano le armi che non le pigliavano; a ciascuno tornava all'arte sua mediante la quale si aveva ordinata la vita; né vi fu mai alcuno che sperasse con le prede e con questa arte potersi nutrire." See also *Discorsi* I.28–31 and I.36.

virtuous Romans could pursue personal glory, not to the detriment, but to the common benefit of the republic.

To sum up this argument, in Machiavelli's eyes, the institution of the triumph proved beneficial to the Roman republic because it inspired a desire for glory and because it promoted the virtue of her citizens and military captains; this in turn forced the pace of the Roman conquests and the enrichment of the city. Since the spoils of war were left to the treasury to be disposed of as the Senate saw fit, the private citizens remained poor, while Rome as a whole grew immensely rich. Content with the glory bestowed upon them through their triumphs, the victorious generals remained faithful to the civic tradition of the city and refrained from seeking ascendancy outside the orders of the republic. As we shall see when we return to Machiavelli's view on the Roman triumph towards the end of this chapter, the gradual breakdown of the institution after the Second Punic War contributed in his eyes in a substantial way to the fall of the republic. But before readdressing this issue, an attempt will be made to situate Machiavelli's discussion of the enigmatic figure of the "big giver" in *The Prince* 16 within the context outlined above.

LIBERALITY AND MISERLINESS

In comparison with *The Prince* 15, which traditionally has been viewed as one of the climaxes of the work, chapter 16 has attracted relatively little scholarly interest. It has frequently been regarded as an appendix to, or as a mere illustration of, the principles laid down in the preceding chapter. Even if this view is understandable in the light of the striking novelty of *The Prince* 15, it does not give this ingenious and carefully worked out chapter the attention and the recognition that it deserves. Reading *The Prince* in part as a traditional mirror-for-princes, in part as an innovation within the genre, Quentin Skinner has argued that Machiavelli in chapter 16 advises his princely reader to cultivate a reputation for generosity, while refraining from actually exercising this virtue. On the basis of Machiavelli's own conclusion, which explicitly states that a ruler who tries to maintain an appearance of liberality by necessity will come to ruin, Skinner infers that the message the Florentine wants to convey is that "the alleged princely virtues of liberality and magnificence" should not be seen as virtues at all, but be included instead "amongst the most dangerous of the princely vices."[56] Virginia Cox

[56] Quentin Skinner, *The Foundations of Modern Political Thought* (2 vols., Cambridge: Cambridge University Press, 1978), I, p. 135.

similarly claims that Machiavelli in *The Prince* 16 seeks to demonstrate that "the cause of liberality is better served by parsimony than munificence."[57] A major problem with Skinner's and Cox's readings is that they fail to take into account the distinction Machiavelli makes in the chapter between liberality and magnificence. For while Machiavelli here condemns the traditional use of liberality, he speaks warmly of the magnificent man, to whom he refers as the "big giver," and of magnificence, which in the course of the chapter emerges as the other, brighter, and more spectacular side of the recommended policy of miserliness.[58]

The apparent strangeness of the argument of chapter 16 has induced Mary Dietz to claim that its advocacy of miserliness "is more a matter of republican sympathies than helpful advice." According to Dietz, Machiavelli's counsel that the Medici should depart from their traditional policy of liberality constitutes, together with his recommendations to come and reside in Florence (ch. 5) and to arm their subjects (chs. 12–14), a subversive strategy designed to mislead the Medici and to hasten their downfall in Florence.[59] The main weakness with this argument is that it is based upon the dubious assumption that a restrictive fiscal policy would have been harmful to Medicean interest at the time. As recent research by Stephens and Butters has shown, the Medici had upon their return to Florence many reasons to be concerned about the financial situation in the city. Not only were they faced with the imminent need of raising money to pay off the imperial troops employed in its retaking, but they had also inherited from the Soderinian regime a series of financial problems of a more structural and long-term nature. One of the main tasks of the *balìa* created in September 1512 was to find a way of settling these matters in order to ensure the financial stability of the new regime.[60] Even though in subsequent years

[57] Virginia Cox, "Machiavelli and the *Rhetorica ad Herennium*: Deliberative Rhetoric in *The Prince*," *Sixteenth Century Journal* 28 (1997), p. 1131.

[58] In their translation of *Il principe*, Bondanella and Musa render *misero* as "miserly," while both Mansfield and Price translate it as "mean." Cf. Machiavelli's distinction between *misero* and *avaro* in *Il principe* 15, p. 159.

[59] Mary G. Dietz, "Trapping the Prince: Machiavelli and the Politics of Deception," in *American Political Science Review* 80 (1986): 777–99, esp. 785; Dietz, "Machiavelli in Dispute: A Reply to My Critics," *Machiavelli Studies* 4 (1991): 77–93. Dietz's argument has been refuted by John Langton (with a reply by Dietz) in "Machiavelli's Paradox: Trapping or Teaching the Prince," *American Political Science* 81 (1987): 1277–83. For further reactions, see Edmund Jacobitti, "Trapping the Prince with *The Prince*"; Anthony Parel, "Why did Machiavelli Write *The Prince*?"; David Boucher, "The Duplicitous Machiavelli," all published in *Machiavelli Studies* 3 (1990): 139–71. Cf. Roger Boesche, *Theories of Tyranny from Plato to Arendt* (University Park, PA: Pennsylvania State University Press, 1996), pp. 111–65, esp. p. 114.

[60] H. C. Butters, *Governors and Government in Early Sixteenth-Century Florence 1502–1519* (Oxford: Clarendon Press, 1985), pp. 189–90 and 194.

they took pains to preserve a high degree of economic continuity, the Medici came to rely less on tax revenues in comparison with their predecessors, and more on loans from wealthy citizens.[61] Still, with the threat of war hanging over the city in January 1517, heavy taxation is reported to have given rise to widespread discontent.[62] If there is a general lesson to be drawn from these scattered facts and observations, it is that a regime should avoid overstretching its limited resources, since financial disorder makes it vulnerable, externally as well as internally, in case of war. Against this background, Machiavelli's counsel in chapter 16 that the prince should be economic with his resources, and accept a reputation for miserliness in order to be able to wage war, reads like a piece of sound political advice, rather than as a conspiratorial strategy designed to overthrow the Medici. Dietz's argument, moreover, is damaged by the fact that similar views were at the time forthcoming from Medici supporters, whose partisanship and loyalty to the regime cannot be doubted.[63]

A more classically oriented reading of *The Prince* 16 is offered by Clifford Orwin, who places Machiavelli's argument in relation to Aristotle's discussion on liberality in the *Ethics*. In Orwin's view, Machiavelli's point here is not primarily to recommend miserliness, but to teach the necessity of the prince being expansive and acquisitive. While Aristotle had paid little attention to the political aspects of liberality, Orwin argues, Machiavelli redefines this virtue, and virtue in general, in political terms. Viewed instrumentally, as a "means to political success," in a world where war is inescapable and "preemptive expansion" necessary, the practice of liberality "implies or presupposes" for Machiavelli "a policy of perpetual expansion." According to Orwin, Machiavelli insinuates therefore that the prince should "place himself at the head of his people, as general of an army of takers," and that he should satisfy their real or imagined needs, by "unleashing [their] acquisitiveness."[64] The analysis of *The Prince* 16 we are about to present here follows the basic outline of Orwin's reading, but expands on it in two important respects: first, by paying closer attention to the rhetorical aspects of the chapter, which includes several inconsistencies, contradictions, and unintended, or intended, lapses of memory, left uncommented on by Orwin; and second, by situating its argument within the contemporary ideological

[61] Stephens, *The Fall of the Florentine Republic*, pp. 132–35.

[62] Ibid., p. 104. [63] Ibid., p. 153.

[64] Clifford Orwin, "Machiavelli's Unchristian Charity," *American Political Science Review* 72 (1978): 1217–28; quotations from pp. 1222 and 1226. For a similar reading, see Grant B. Mindle, "Machiavelli's Realism," *Review of Politics* 47 (1985): 212–30, esp. 225.

and ritual context of Medicean politics, which Orwin's abstract and conceptual discussion completely ignores.

But before we can turn to consider *The Prince* 16 from a rhetorical and contextual point of view, we must give some thought to the theoretical framework Machiavelli erects in chapter 15. Here, the former Secretary denounces, in his characteristic, forceful, and uncompromising way, all political philosophers who have written about imaginary republics and princes, and about how one ought to do (*quello che si doverrebbe fare*), and how one ought to live (*come si doverrebbe vivere*), instead of treating real states and life as it is actually lived.[65] In this connection, he itemizes a number of qualities that might render a prince either praise or blame. Arranged in eleven binary pairs – the same number as the virtues discussed in Aristotle's *Ethics* – the list reads:[66]

liberal	miserly
giver	rapacious
cruel	merciful
treacherous	faithful
effeminate and pusillanimous	fierce and spirited
humane	haughty
lascivious	chaste
honest	cunning
hard	agreeable
grave	light
religious	unbelieving

This catalogue comes in chapters 16 through 19 to serve as the basis for Machiavelli's discussion of the princely virtues and vices. But before the former Secretary goes on to address these binary pairs one by one, he concludes chapter 15 by establishing a distinction between the conventional definition of virtue based on a philosophical speculation on how things ought to be, and his own redefinition of the concept founded on a close consideration of what he earlier in the chapter has called "the effectual truth of the thing" (*la verità effettuale della cosa*): "because if one considers

[65] *Il principe* 15, p. 159.

[66] *Il principe* 15, pp. 159–60: "E questo è che alcuno è tenuto liberale, alcuno misero (usando uno termine toscano, perché avaro in nostra lingua è ancora colui che per rapina desidera di avere: misero chiamiamo noi quello che si astiene troppo di usare il suo); alcuno è tenuto donatore, alcuno rapace; alcuno crudele, alcuno piatoso; l'uno fedifrago, l'altro fedele; l'uno effeminato e pusillanime, l'altro feroce et animoso; l'uno umano, l'altro superbo; l'uno lascivo, l'altro casto; l'uno intero, l'altro astuto; l'uno duro, l'altro facile; l'uno grave, l'altro leggieri; l'uno religioso, l'altro incredulo, e simili."

everything carefully, one will find that doing some things that seem virtuous may result in one's ruin, whereas doing other things that seem vicious results in one's security and well-being."[67] Since no direct causal link between what is conventionally held to be virtue and political success can be found, a ruler must on occasion be prepared to disregard the imperatives of traditional ethics, and accept the reputation that goes with the vices, for only by acting in this way will he be able to rule effectively and to maintain himself. A prince who proceeds otherwise is destined for destruction.

Having laid down these fundamental principles, Machiavelli goes on to discuss when, and to what extent, a ruler should use, or avoid using, the various qualities quoted in the list above. Apart from the fact that the titles of *The Prince* 16 and 17 inform us that these chapters deal with liberality and miserliness, and cruelty and mercifulness respectively, the systematic procedure announces itself by the way Machiavelli introduces his discussions. The argument on liberality and miserliness in chapter 16 opens thus with the words: "Beginning then, with the first of the above-mentioned qualities . . ."[68] Chapter 17, dedicated to cruelty and mercifulness, is initiated in a similar manner: "Descending next to the other qualities set forth before . . ."[69] The question of the relative utility of being faithful or treacherous is addressed in the introduction to chapter 18, and so on.[70]

What is somewhat puzzling, however, in this otherwise highly systematic treatment of the virtues and vices, which seems to imitate, or to rival, Aristotle's presentation in the *Ethics*,[71] is the treatment of the second binary couple on the list: "giver" (*donatore*)/"rapacious" (*rapace*). While the first and the third pairs, liberal/miserly and cruel/merciful, are explicitly treated in chapters 16 and 17, which have also been named after them, "giver" and "rapacious" are mentioned in chapter 16, but only in passing, and without the qualities being properly defined, or explicitly compared with each other. Furthermore, the term "giver," or *donatore*, is the sole item on the list not to appear in adjective form. This means that regardless of how we choose to interpret this portion of the work, there can be no denying that the term

[67] Ibid., p. 160: "perché, se si considera bene tutto, si troverrà qualche cosa che parrà virtú, e seguendola sarebbe la ruina sua: e qualcuna altra che parrà vizio, e seguendola ne nasce la sicurtà e il bene essere suo."

[68] Ibid., 16, p. 160: "Cominciandomi adunque alle prime soprascritte qualità, dico come . . ."

[69] Ibid., 17, p. 162: "Scendendo appresso alle altre qualità preallegate . . ."

[70] Ibid., 18, p. 165.

[71] Cf. Aristotle, *The Nicomachean Ethics*, trans. J. A. K. Thomson (London: Penguin, 1976), 1114b15, p. 126: "Let us now resume our discussion of the virtues, taking them one by one, and explaining what each is, and with what sort of object it is concerned, and in what way."

donatore stands out conspicuously from the rest of the virtues and vices included on Machiavelli's list.

As Orwin has made clear, the argument of *The Prince* 16 needs to be understood in relation to Aristotle's ethical teaching. The Greek philosopher had in the *Ethics*, in keeping with his general geometrical view of the virtues and the vices, defined the virtue of liberality as the mean between the vices of prodigality and illiberality.[72] The liberal man, according to his definition, should practice the art of giving in the right manner, in relation to the right people, at appropriate times, according to his means, and for a good end. He should also be of the right disposition and base his giving on a just and appropriate form of acquisition. A man who went too far in spending and not far enough in getting was in Aristotle's view to be defined as prodigal. Being a private citizen with limited means, such a man would soon run the risk of exhausting his resources and, in order to maintain his immoderate spending, would have to become excessively acquisitive, or rapacious. The illiberal man, on the other hand, was someone who committed the contrary vice of giving too little in relation to his property and his income.[73]

Our presentation of Aristotle's treatment of liberality would not be complete, though, if we did not take into account the related virtue of magnificence (*megaloprepeia*). In contrast to liberality proper, which Aristotle seems to regard mainly as a private virtue, magnificence is directed towards the public sphere. It involves great and ostentatious expenditures, which befit religious ceremonies and public festivals, but tend to become vulgar and tasteless when practiced in private. Therefore, the magnificent man must, apart from considerable material riches, possess good taste and a well-developed sense for the socially and politically appropriate.[74] From Aristotle's discussion it is not altogether clear, however, how the virtues of magnificence and liberality relate to each other. According to him, magnificence is the more limited in scope of the two, since it only applies to "actions dealing with the spending of wealth" and not to financial transactions in general. On the other hand, magnificence exceeds liberality when it comes to the consumption of wealth since it consists in "befitting expenditure on a large scale." For this reason, Aristotle argues, it is possible to be liberal without being magnificent, but not the other way around.[75] As it seems, then, magnificence can be viewed both as a form of liberality and as an independent virtue subject to its own rules and principles. The bearing

[72] Ibid., 1119b22–30. [73] Ibid., 1119b22–1122a17.
[74] Ibid., 1122a18–1123a33. [75] Ibid., 1122a18–29; English trans., p. 149.

of Aristotle's presentation in the *Ethics* on Machiavelli's treatment of the virtues and the vices will become immediately clear when we now turn to consider *The Prince* 16.

THE GORDIAN KNOT

In *The Prince* 16, Machiavelli discusses four different definitions of, or ways of using, liberality, which we with his assistance may call the virtuous, the liberal, the miserly, and the donative mode. These four approaches to liberality are, as we shall see, analogous to the Aristotelian qualities liberality, prodigality, illiberality, and magnificence, and they are in chapter 16 presented in the same order as they appear in the *Ethics*.

Machiavelli begins by discussing the virtuous way of practicing liberality. If liberality is used "as it ought to be used" (*come le si debbe usare*), there is a risk, he claims, that "it will not become known." But since the virtuously liberal man will not strive to gain a reputation for being liberal, he will also avoid the infamy that goes with displaying the opposite quality, that is, illiberality or miserliness.[76] This form of liberality is thus harmless but at the same time politically ineffective, since it does nothing either to aid, or to hurt, the liberal man's political standing. Irrespective of whether we choose to view this virtuous way as a private and nonpolitical form of liberality, or as an ideal that belongs to the imaginary sphere of *come si doverrebbe vivere* (which the closely related phrase *come le si debbe usare* seems to indicate), we have good reasons to assume that Machiavelli associates this use of liberality with the traditional Aristotelian definition of the virtue.

Having set aside the virtuous mode of using liberality, Machiavelli goes on to discuss the liberal (*liberale*) way. A ruler who has acquired a reputation for being liberal, and wants to maintain it, he argues, must continue to display liberality in a costly and ostentatious manner. Since one can assume that his personal means and the resources of his state are limited, he will eventually, in order to be able to sustain his sumptuous way of living, be forced to oppress his subjects with taxes or invent other ways of obtaining their money. As a result, he will become rapacious and hateful in the eyes of

[76] *Il principe* 16, p. 160: "Nondimanco la liberalità, usata in modo che tu sia tenuto, ti offende: perché, se la si usa virtuosamente e come la si debbe usare, la non fia conosciuta e non ti cascherà la 'nfamia del suo contrario." Harvey Mansfield renders the end of this passage: "and you will not escape the infamy of its contrary," see Niccolò Machiavelli, *The Prince*, trans. H. Mansfield, p. 63. Several other English translators, including Bondanella and Musa, as well as Price, translate the sentence in a similar way. However, since this rendition reverses the original meaning of "non ti cascherà la 'nfamia del suo contrario," it cannot be correct. I am greatful to John Najemy for pointing this out to me.

his subjects, who at this point can be expected to turn against him in anger and seal the end of his regime. If the prince at this stage were to renounce his liberal ways and to adopt a more moderate course, this change of policy would do him no good, since his new and more confined ways would appear miserly and contemptible in the eyes of his people who are accustomed to a more generous level of display. The conclusion Machiavelli prompts us to draw is that liberality used in the liberal way cannot be considered a political virtue, but should instead be counted among the vices, since it leads to rapacity and ruin.[77] As we can see, this liberal use of liberality bears a close resemblance to Aristotle's descriptions of prodigality.

Next, Machiavelli turns to consider the other extreme use of liberality, the miserly (*misero*) way, closely modeled on the Aristotelian vice of illiberality. On the basis of the preceding discussion, Machiavelli claims, it should be clear that princes who want to maintain themselves must not fear the reputation of being miserly.[78] For even if a prince who uses his resources sparingly will run the risk of being called a miser, his reputation will soon improve when the people see that his revenues are sufficient to allow him to "defend himself against any enemies that make war on him," and enable him to "undertake campaigns without imposing special taxes on the people."[79] However, since such a ruler in the course of time will begin to seem increasingly liberal in the eyes of his people, it is important that he maintains a reputation for being miserly to avoid falling into the vicious circle of prodigality, described above.

Machiavelli sums up the miserly use of liberality in the following way: "So [the prince] comes to use liberality with all those from whom he does not take, who are countless, and miserliness with all those to whom he does not give, who are few."[80] These purely negative definitions of liberality and miserliness have the effect of making both qualities invisible. Liberality is here thus understood as something one "shows" by not taking from others, while miserliness is stowed away as a quality that manifests itself in the act of not giving. This line of reasoning seems to go back to Aristotle, who in the *Ethics* had claimed that a man who does not give, but abstains from taking, is to be regarded as righteous, or just, rather than liberal.[81] It

[77] *Il principe* 16, pp. 160–61. [78] Ibid., p. 161: "non si curare del nome del misero."

[79] Ibid.: "può difendersi da chi gli fa guerra, può fare imprese sanza gravare e' populi."

[80] Ibid.: "Talmente che viene a usare liberalità a tutti quelli a chi e' non toglie, che sono infiniti, e miseria a tutti coloro a chi e' non dà, che sono pochi." The translation is here based on Machiavelli, *The Prince*, trans. H. Mansfield, p. 63.

[81] Aristotle, *The Nicomachean Ethics*, 1120a10: "Again, those who give are called liberal, but those who do not take are praised not for liberality but quite as much for justice; and those who do take are not praised at all" (English trans., p. 143).

would seem that Machiavelli is here playing with the Aristotelian repertoire of virtues and vices, defining liberality first as Aristotelian liberality, then as prodigality, then as illiberality, and now finally as righteousness. But as we might begin to suspect, this logical sophistry, which seems to have been designed to confuse rather than to assist the princely reader, does not contain Machiavelli's last word on the subject of liberality.

Up to this point, Machiavelli's argument has been based on a closed economic system in which no real possibility for growth or expansion exists. While the liberal prince, who failed to understand this, turned his acquisitiveness inward and became rapacious as a result, the virtue of the miserly prince appears to consist in his acceptance and his adaption to the narrow conditions of this zero-sum world. But when Machiavelli now sets out to demonstrate wherein the usefulness of miserliness really consists, he breaks out of this temporary confinement to domestic affairs and returns to the vast expanses of foreign policy, which has dominated the discourse of *The Prince* so far. Leaving the paradoxes and entanglements of scholastic dispute behind, he begins to introduce his princely reader to a more attractive, more vigorous, and less confusing solution to the dilemma surrounding the virtue of liberality. In modern times, he contends, great things (*gran cose*) have been achieved only by those who have had a reputation for being miserly. Pope Julius II, Louis XII of France, and Ferdinand of Aragon, we are told, all used miserliness to lay strong foundations for waging war and for pursuing greatness.

The choice of the three rulers is not fortuitous. Together they represent the three most expansive powers on the Italian peninsula during the first decades of the sixteenth century: France, Spain, and the Papacy. All three of them figure prominently in *The Prince* as successful, or partially successful, warlords and acquisitive rulers. Julius II is described in chapter 11 as continuing the expansionist policy of his predecessor, Alexander VI, by striving to increase the territorial dominion and temporal greatness of the Church. Louis XII's partially successful imperialist policy is the topic of a detailed analysis in chapter 3; and Ferdinand of Aragon is the principal character of chapter 21, where he epitomizes the formerly weak prince who, by cleverly cloaking his various designs, has grown strong enough to wage wars of conquest not only in Italy, but in Africa as well. Miserliness, Machiavelli's choice of examples seems to imply, should not be understood as an end in itself, but as a means to achieve great things and to make great acquisitions.

Having thus discreetly, but decisively, moved from the sphere of domestic politics to foreign affairs, Machiavelli now pauses for a moment to comment on the importance of miserliness for the foundation of a strong state: "Therefore, in order not to have to rob his subjects, to be able to defend himself, not to become poor and contemptible, and not to be forced to become rapacious, a prince should worry little about incurring a reputation of miserliness, because this is one of those vices which enable him to rule."[82] This sounds much like a final statement and it could even be argued that Machiavelli here makes a show of wanting to bring his argument to an end. But closure is denied as a dissenting voice from the outside attracts the author's attention: "And if someone (*alcuno*) were to say: Caesar obtained empire with liberality . . ."[83] The argument on liberality, it would appear, has not been exhausted. Instead of closure and a return to a discourse based on the self-contained world of domestic affairs, a debate now follows between Machiavelli and this imaginary interlocutor on what could best be described as the donative use of liberality.

Confronted with the objection from this fictitious *alcuno*, Machiavelli is forced to concede that it is necessary for someone who aspires to power, or to high office, to gain a reputation for being liberal, as the example of Julius Caesar shows. But as soon as a ruler has established himself, Machiavelli continues to insist, he must begin to keep his expenditures in check. Thus, Machiavelli is here, while continuing to privilege miserliness over liberality, conceding a limited and conditional value to liberality. The hypothetical *alcuno* presses on though, arguing that "many have been princes and have accomplished great things (*gran cose*) with their armies, who have been considered very liberal (*liberalissimi*)." In the face of this argument, Machiavelli yields the point:

> I would reply: a prince spends either what belongs to him or his subjects, or what belongs to others. In the first case, he should be sparing; in the second, he should not leave behind anything that belongs to liberality (*non debbe lasciare indretro alcuna parte di liberalità*). And for that prince who accompanies his army and lives by looting, sacking, and extortions, who disposes of what belongs to others, such liberality is necessary; otherwise he would not be followed by his soldiers. And with what does not belong to you or to your subjects you can be a bigger giver (*largo donatore*), as were Cyrus, Caesar, and Alexander; for spending what belongs to others in no way damages your reputation; but adds to it; it is only spending your own that harms you.[84]

[82] *Il principe* 16, p. 161: "Pertanto uno principe debbe estimare poco – per non avere a rubare e' sudditi, per potere difendersi, per non diventare povero e contennendo, per non essere forzato di diventare rapace – di incorrere nel nome del misero: perché questo è uno di quelli vizi che lo fanno regnare."

[83] Ibid.: "E se alcuno dicessi: Cesare con la liberalità pervenne allo imperio . . ."

[84] Ibid., pp. 161–62: "E se alcuno replicassi: molti sono stati principi e con li eserciti hanno fatto gran cose, che sono stati tenuti liberalissimi; ti respondo: o el principe spende del suo e de' sua sudditi, o di quello d'altri. Nel primo caso debbe essere parco. Nell'altro, non debbe lasciare indretro alcuna parte di liberalità. E quel principe che va con li eserciti, che si pasce di prede, di sacchi e di taglie,

Previously, Machiavelli had corroborated his thesis that miserliness is conducive to "great things" (*gran cosa*) by setting forth three modern examples. Now he adduces three ancient rulers famous for their conquests and for having performed "great things" (*gran cose*) – Cyrus, Caesar, and Alexander – in order to establish a distinction between a form of liberality based on taking from one's own, and one based on conquest and on taking from others. Of the three rulers cited here, Cyrus also figures in chapters 6, 14, and 26 as a legendary founder and a military captain, always with strong positive connotations; Alexander has previously been referred to as an epitome of military virtue in chapters 4 and 14; and Caesar has in chapter 14 been mentioned as a virtuous imitator of Alexander.

As a concession, Machiavelli's response is excessive. If he had wanted to shield himself behind a mask of moderation and to make pretense of having been led to this conclusion only reluctantly, as his little staged dispute with the anonymous *alcuno* seemed to suggest, he would most certainly have opted for a different strategy. Instead of merely insinuating the possibility of being liberal without having to suffer the negative effects associated with this quality, he makes his point with a lavishness similar to the one expected from ancient military commanders on their triumphal returns to Rome. Highly self-consciously, it would seem, Machiavelli chooses a spectacular mode of writing that reflects the kind of imagery the passage is designed to conjure up. As he exhorts the conqueror not to spare *alcuna parte di liberalità* in his triumph, Machiavelli himself leads the way by not showing any restraint in his mode of expression. The contrast between this spectacular passage and the constrained, entangled, and often ambiguous argument offered previously in the chapter is, to say the least, striking, and seems itself to constitute a part of Machiavelli's argument. As one of the ancient worthies adduced in the chapter, Alexander the Great, once demonstrated, Gordian knots should be not untangled, but cut.

THE BIG GIVER

The introduction of the possibility of territorial expansion and acquisition beyond the borders of the state has in a radical and decisive way changed the context for Machiavelli's discussion. Since we are no longer confined within the zero-sum game and the closed and self-contained economic

maneggia quello di altri, gli è necessaria questa liberalità: altrimenti non sarebbe seguito da' soldati. E di quello che non è tuo o de' sudditi tuoi si può essere piú largo donatore, come fu Ciro, Cesare e Alessandro: perché lo spendere quel d'altri non ti toglie reputazione ma te ne aggiugne; solamente lo spendere el tuo è quello che ti nuoce."

system characterizing the first part of the chapter, Machiavelli can now imply that the use of liberality will hurt only the weak prince, who makes liberal use of what belongs to himself or to his subjects, and not the strong acquisitive ruler, who uses what he acquires from others to increase his own reputation and to enrich his country. Such a ruler and conqueror will eventually gain the name of being a "big giver," or *largo donatore*, whereas his weak counterpart, who must exploit his own subjects in order to uphold his display of liberality, soon will be regarded as rapacious, or *rapace*. But having established these connections between liberality and rapacity, on the one hand, and between miserliness and big giver, on the other, Machiavelli seems to fall into a sudden lapse of memory. Forgetful of the fact that shortly before he had informed his princely reader that "spending what belongs to others in no way damages your reputation; but adds to it," he goes on to claim that there is "nothing that is so self-consuming as liberality: the more you practice it, the less you will be able to continue to practice it; and either you will become poor and contemptible or your efforts to avoid poverty will make you rapacious and hateful."[85] This respectable comment sets the tone for the conclusion of the chapter, which marks a return to the closed economic system we thought we had left behind after the introduction of the big giver and the possibility of foreign acquisition:

> Among all the things that a prince should guard against is being contemptible and hated; and liberality will lead you to both. So it is wiser to cultivate a reputation for miserliness, which will lead to infamy without hatred, than to be forced, through wanting to be considered liberal, to incur a reputation for rapacity, which will lead to infamy with hatred.[86]

Liberality, we are yet again informed, is destructive because it leads to rapacity and hatred. Miserliness should be cultivated instead, since it procures only infamy, not hatred. This is once again a purely negative definition. Miserliness is good because of something it does not lead to (hatred), not for what it actually brings. This conclusion may follow naturally from the premises existing at the outset of the chapter, but it is hard, not to say impossible, to see how it applies to the expansionist policies of Cyrus, Caesar, and Alexander. None of these warlords can be said to have used rapacity against their own people to "avoid poverty," or to have engaged in the

[85] Ibid., p. 162: "E non ci è cosa che consumi sé stessa quanto la liberalità, la quale mentre che tu usi perdi la facultà di usarla e diventi o povero e cotennendo o, per fuggire la povertà, rapace e odioso."

[86] Ibid.: "E in tra tutte le cose di che uno principe si debbe guardare è lo essere contennendo e odioso: e la liberalità all'una e l'altra cosa ti conduce. Pertanto è piú sapienza tenersi el nome del misero, che partorisce una infamia sanza odio, che, per volere el nome del liberale, essere necessitato incorrere nel nome del rapace, che partorisce una infamia con odio."

self-consuming form of liberality associated with this confined and limited state of affairs. Therefore, we may infer that the expansive and acquisitive context to which the Persian, the Greek, and the Roman conquerors belong, and the donative use of liberality they epitomize, is contained neither within the chapter's explicitly stated premises, nor in its conclusion. It is, to use one of Machiavelli's favorite terms, excessive. In the light of this argument, Machiavelli's true advice in *The Prince* 16 appears instead to be that a ruler should seek a reputation of miserliness, enabling him to make foreign acquisitions and act as a "big giver," or *largo donatore*, towards his own people. By adopting this policy, he will appear not merely as a miser in the eyes of his subjects, but also, and above all, as a great and exceedingly generous triumphator.

Much of the confusion surrounding Machiavelli's treatment of liberality and *donatore* in *The Prince* 16 can be resolved if we read the chapter in the context to Aristotle's treatment of liberality and magnificence in the *Ethics*. For as we have come to see, Machiavelli in *The Prince* 16 employs the term liberality in two different and contrasting meanings. On the one hand, he uses it within the self-contained world of domestic affairs, where it is seen to lead to rapacity and a loss of power. On the other hand, he refers to it in the expansive and acquisitive context of foreign conquest where it is associated with excessive display, enhancement of reputation, and the enigmatic term *donatore*. This latter use of liberality, which we have defined as the donative mode, bears a close resemblance to the Aristotelian virtue of magnificence.

As the Greek term *megaloprepeia* and its Latin equivalent *magnificentia* indicate,[87] magnificence is concerned with great things. The word's etymological meaning squares well with Aristotle's definition of magnificence as a grandiose form of giving which exceeds ordinary liberality in scale and in level of expenditure. The magnificent man, Aristotle teaches, should spend "gladly and generously" without giving too much thought to the costs involved.[88] In chapter 16 of *The Prince*, Machiavelli similarily associates the term *donatore* with princes and conquerors who, after performing, or achieving, great things (*gran cose*), engage in lavish spending. In his view, the private virtue of liberality, which, if used politically within the zero-sum world of domestic affairs, will inevitably lead to rapacity and ruin, should not be confused with the expansive and grandiose virtue of magnificence, pertaining to the conqueror who can spend what he has acquired outside his state without burdening his own people.

[87] Both the Greek word *mega* and the Latin word *magnus* mean "great."
[88] Aristotle, *The Nicomachean Ethics*, 1122b8; English trans., p. 150.

But here it is not enough to say that Aristotle's distinction between liberality and magnificence plays a crucial role in *The Prince* 16. For in borrowing Aristotle's distinctions, Machiavelli makes two important innovations with regard to his predecessor, which together have the effect of exposing the inherent limitations of the Greek philosopher's *polis*-centered theory. First, he argues that the resources of princes and tyrants are limited, and that they therefore, just like private men, run the risk of falling prey to the vicious circle of prodigality. In Aristotle's view, tyrants rarely arrive at this point since their resources are next to inexhaustible.[89] Second, Machiavelli implies that the practice of magnificence, understood as giving on a grand scale, is dependent on foreign acquisitions, since the expenditures involved in such display are so great that they cannot be sustained within the zero-sum world of domestic affairs.[90] On this point, Aristotle is less than precise when he claims that the magnificent man should acquire his means in appropriate ways, either by his own effort or by inheritance.[91]

The Prince 16, which on a superficial level seemed to reiterate a conventional theme from the mirror-for-princes genre, has on closer examination proved to contain a direct assault on the very foundation of this traditional moralist genre, the ethical teaching of Aristotle. Through this radical move, Machiavelli opens up a new form of political discourse based on Roman imperialism and the idea of the Roman triumph, here associated with the Aristotelian virtue of magnificence, and defined in terms of the "big giver," or *largo donatore*. As we have previously established, the term *donatore* has a curious ring to it when it appears in chapters 15 and 16. Why does Machiavelli insert a noun among the more than twenty adjectives making up his list of qualities that might render a prince praise or blame? From where did he derive the term? To the best of my knowledge, *donatore* was not a commonly used word in political discourse of the time, and it does not appear elsewhere in Machiavelli's work. From where then does it derive?

Without hoping to arrive at a conclusive answer to this question, I believe that a reasonable hypothesis can be made. In the detailed account of the celebration of St. John's Day in 1513, found among the *Carte Strozziane* and published by Cesare Guasti back in 1884, there is a series of short descriptions of the four Roman triumphs staged by the Medici in the course

89 Ibid., 1122a7. Cf. ibid., 1120b25 and 1121a17.

90 Cf. Mansfield, *Machiavelli's Virtue*, pp. 13–16; Hanna F. Pitkin, *Fortune is a Woman: Gender and Politics in the Thought of Niccolò Machiavelli* (Berkeley, CA: University of California Press, 1984), p. 261.

91 Aristotle, *The Nicomachean Ethics*, 1122b30–33.

of the celebration. The second triumph, that of Pompey, is presented in the following way:

Triumph of Pompey, with his spoils, imitating liberality, since he was a very liberal man towards friends as well as towards enemies, and a great giver.

(*Trionfo di Pompeo, con sua spoglie, imitando la liberalità; perchè lui fu uomo molto liberale con li amici et etiam co' nimici, e gran donatore.*)[92]

It cannot escape anyone how remarkably well this short description interlocks with the argument of *The Prince* 16. Pompey is in the pamphlet described as liberal, or more exactly, as imitating liberality, which is also the principal subject matter of chapter 16. The ancient warlords Machiavelli comments on there are portrayed not as liberal, but as acting in the role of the "big giver" (*largo donatore*). Similarly, in the description of the carnival pageant Pompey is portrayed as a "great giver" (*gran donatore*). While the carnival text states that the Roman general was liberal towards friends and enemies alike, Machiavelli uses the same categories, but turns the message of the pamphlet on its head, by making a sharp and explicit distinction between what is one's own and what belongs to others, arguing that one should take from the enemy in order to give to one's own. Considering how closely related the two texts are contextually – the triumph of Pompey was set up on 26 June 1513, that is, about the time Machiavelli is generally believed to have begun composing *The Prince*, and both texts are addressed to, or produced by, the Medici – it seems reasonable to assume that Machiavelli expected his Medicean readers to recognize these connections, and to read *The Prince* 16 as a comment, in part approving, in part critical, on the new triumphalist ideology they were introducing in Florence at the time. Read from this point of view, Machiavelli's argument constitutes not only an attempt at transforming a carnival display into a model for serious policy-making, but also subtle advice designed to redirect Medicean aspirations away from the inward-looking princely context to an outward-looking imperialist one.[93]

To summarize our reading of *The Prince* 16, Machiavelli initially identifies three different types of weak policies and methods of using liberality – the

92 Quoted in Cesare Guasti, *Le feste di S. Giovanni Batista in Firenze* (Florence, 1884), p. 26.

93 Since Machiavelli's general interest in the carnival culture of Florence is well documented, and the celebration of St. John was, and still is, Florence's most important civic and religious festival, it cannot be excluded that he was present on the occasion, even though at the time he was exiled to his farm at Sant'Andrea in Percussina. However, whether or not Machiavelli personally attended the manifestation should not be an issue here, since there were innumerable other ways in which he could have acquired information about the contents of the pamphlets distributed during the celebration.

virtuous middle way, the over-confident and prodigious mode, and the confined and miserly way – which he for various reasons dismisses, partly or completely, in favor of a strong policy of acquisition and conquest. This policy is here presented as a process in several stages. In order to lay a sound foundation for his state, the ruler should free himself from the unrealistic ideal of the middle way, give up his desire to have a name for being liberal, and gain independence by pursuing a restrictive financial policy without paying any respect to the infamy associated with miserliness. This prudent use of miserliness will eventually pay off as it will enable him to accomplish "great things," that is, to make conquests and to enrich his state by new acquisitions abroad. At this point, the prince can make liberal use of the riches he has acquired during his foreign conquests and win himself the name of "big giver," or *largo donatore*, among his subjects. But at this point a new problem arises: how does the princely quest for greatness and glory, uncovered here, relate to the republican teaching of the *Discourses*? To arrive at a better understanding of this crucial issue, we shall have to inquire more deeply into the meaning the term greatness assumes within Machiavelli's ideological vocabulary in general.

GREATNESS – PRINCELY AND REPUBLICAN

There can be little doubt that greatness, or *grandezza*, is one of the central themes of *The Prince*. At the end of the dedicatory letter accompanying the final version of *The Prince*, Machiavelli promises Lorenzo de' Medici, the future ruler of Florence, that the book he is offering him contains the proof of his own "extreme desire" to see Lorenzo "arrive at the greatness that fortune and [his] other qualities" promise him (*quella grandezza che la fortuna e l'altre sua qualità le promettano*).[94] Supported by good fortune and a dedicated and well-read counselor, Lorenzo is expected to achieve greatness by exercising his various "qualities." Given that greatness, or *grandezza*, is the stated aim of the dedicatory letter, it can be argued that one of the keys to understanding Machiavelli's intention in writing *The Prince* consists in giving meaning to this elusive term. In other words, what kind of greatness is it that fortune has in store for Lorenzo, and that his "other qualities," to which Machiavelli now attaches his own "extreme desire," promise him?

As we have seen, achieving greatness is in *The Prince* associated with modern conquerors such as Ferdinand of Aragon, Louis XII, and Julius II,

[94] *Il principe*, dedication, p. 118. The translation is from Machiavelli, *The Prince*, trans. H. Mansfield, p. 4.

and with ancient warlords like Cyrus, Caesar, and Alexander. Greatness and great acts are attributed to Ferdinand also in *The Prince* 21, where Machiavelli refers to him as a formerly weak prince, who, through a combined use of force and deceit, has acquired the strength necessary for pursuing a strong expansionist policy. Before embarking on a war of conquest in Africa and Italy, he had laid a strong foundation for his state by liberating Granada, and by uniting the whole of Spain under his jurisdiction. Through these "great enterprises" (*grande imprese*), and by giving "fine examples of himself," he has, in the Florentine's eyes, acquired the status of "an almost new prince" and become "by fame and by glory" the foremost king in Christendom. If we examine his actions more closely, Machiavelli argues, we will find them "all very great (*tutte grandissime*) and some of them extraordinary,"[95] and that the Spaniard has always "done and ordered great things (*cose grandi*), which have kept the minds of the subjects in suspense and admiration."[96] Ferdinand's exploits, which are here described in almost triumphant terms, have earned him all the rewards and honors that lie in store for a strong and successful ruler: fame (*fama*), glory (*gloria*), reputation (*reputazione*), empire (*imperio*), honor (*onore*), admiration (*admirazione*), and greatness (*grandezza*).[97]

Greatness is also a major theme in Machiavelli's account of France's failure to establish a firm foothold in Italy under Louis XII. In *The Prince* 3, the former Secretary claims that if the French had understood the art of state "they would not have allowed the Church to reach such greatness (*grandezza*)." For recent experience shows that the Church's and Spain's "greatness (*grandezza*) in Italy" has been "brought about by France," and that they in turn have "brought about France's ruin."[98] Later in chapter 11, Machiavelli takes upon himself to answer the question of how it has come about that "the Church has reached such greatness (*grandezza*) in temporal

[95] Ibid., 21, p. 179: "Nessuna cosa fa tanto stimare uno principe, quanto fanno le grande imprese e dare di sé rari esempli. Noi abbiamo ne' nostri tempi Ferrando di Aragonia, presente re di Spagna: costui si può chiamare quasi principe nuovo, perché d'uno re debole è diventato per fama e per gloria el primo re de' cristiani; e se considerrete le azioni sua, le troverrete tutte grandissime e qualcuna estraordinaria."

[96] Ibid., p. 180: "sempre ha fatte e ordite cose grandi, le quali hanno sempre tenuti sospesi e ammirati gli animi de' sudditi."

[97] On Machiavelli's view of Ferdinand, see Edward Andrew, "The Foxy Prophet: Machiavelli Versus Machiavelli on Ferdinand the Catholic," *History of Political Thought* 11 (1990): 409–422; John M. Najemy, *Between Friends: Discourses of Power and Desire in the Machiavelli–Vettori Letters of 1513–1515* (Princeton: Princeton University Press, 1993), pp. 127–35.

[98] *Il principe* 3, p. 126: "non lascerebbono venire in tanta grandezza la Chiesa. E per esperienza si è visto che la grandezza in Italia di quella e di Spagna è stata causata da Francia, e la ruina sua è suta causata da loro."

power."[99] During the reigns of Alexander VI and Julius II, he argues, the Church had by adopting a combined policy of economic extortion and force managed to expel the French from Italy and to reduce the power of the Venetians. A crucial role in its rise to greatness was played by Pope Alexander VI, the father of Cesare Borgia, who demonstrated "how much a pope could achieve through money and military means." Although, Machiavelli continues, his intention was to make the duke great, rather than the Church, everything he did "contributed to the greatness (*grandezza*) of the Church."[100]

The approving tone of this account of how Alexander exploited the power and the influence of the Church to promote the temporal ambitions of his son may give us an indication of what kind of role Machiavelli expected Pope Leo X to play with regard to Giuliano or Lorenzo de' Medici, the two secular arms of the Church. But the failure of the Borgias may also be taken as a note of caution addressed to the Medici. As their example shows, the Church has a tendency to swallow up the personal aspirations of individual popes and to use them to her own benefit and to increase her own greatness.

The connection Machiavelli in *The Prince* establishes between greatness and military might is also suggested by the way in which he portrays the relationship between virtue and fortune. Curiously inserted in a lengthy discussion on the pros and cons of fortresses, Machiavelli describes how fortune often assists a new prince in attaining greatness by providing him with enemies and military opportunities:

> Without doubt princes become great (*grandi*) when they overcome the difficulties and the opposition they encounter. Therefore fortune, especially when she wants to make a new prince great (*grande*) (who has more need to gain a reputation than a hereditary one) causes enemies to arise, and makes them fight against him, so that he may have the opportunity of overcoming them, and thus rise higher, as if by a ladder that his enemies have provided him with. Accordingly, many judge that a wise prince should, whenever he has the occasion, foster with cunning some hostility, so that when he crushes them his greatness (*grandezza*) will increase as a result.[101]

[99] Ibid., 11, p. 148: "donde viene che la Chiesa nel temporale sia venuta a tanta grandezza."

[100] Ibid., p. 149: "Surse di poi Alessandro VI, il quale, di tutti e' pontefici che sono mai stati, mostrò quanto uno papa e col danaio e con le forze si poteva prevalere; e fece, con lo instrumento del duca Valentino e con la occasione della passata de' franzesi, tutte quelle cose che io discorro di sopra nell'azioni del duca. E benché la 'ntenzione sua non fussi fare grande la Chiesa, ma il duca, nondimeno ciò che fece tornò a grandezza della Chiesa: la quale dopo la sua morte, spento il duca, fu erede delle sua fatiche."

[101] Ibid., 20, p. 177: "Sanza dubio e' principi diventano grandi quando superano le difficultà e le opposizioni che sono fatte loro; e però la fortuna, massime quando vuole fare grande uno principe

The princely reader is here asked to recall the imagery of the dedicatory letter. Fortune, acting as an agent on a superhuman level, elects new princes to carry out her design. To make them great, she sets up obstacles for them, which she expects them to overcome with her assistance. As they proceed with their conquests, their greatness will gradually increase and they will begin to climb the ladder of fame. The greatness that Machiavelli promises Lorenzo in the dedicatory letter seems in this passage to take on connotations pointing in the direction of aggressive expansionism and imperialist conquest.

This interpretation is largely confirmed by Machiavelli's use of the term *grandezza* in the final chapter of *The Prince*. Here he contends that Lorenzo will arrive at his promised greatness only if he first acquires and displays *virtù*. Even though everything now has "converged for [his] greatness (*grandezza*)," Lorenzo will have to act his part, since "God does not want to do everything, in order not to deprive us of our free will and that share of glory which belongs to us."[102] Given the political realities of contemporary Italy, the virtuous exploit Machiavelli here is referring to – the seizure and the liberation of Italy – could hardly be accomplished in any way other than through a war of liberation and conquest. In the light of this textual evidence, we may conclude that there exists in *The Prince* a general pattern governing the meaning of the term *grandezza*. Greatness is conceived as resulting from an introduction of novel, but classically inspired, civil laws and military orders, enabling a new prince to embark upon a war of conquest that will eventually lead to the seizure and the liberation of Italy.

But is this greatness identical to the *greatness* Machiavelli attributes to the Roman republic in the *Discourses*, or is republican greatness somehow different from princely greatness? As Quentin Skinner has shown, the notion of *grandezza* entered the vocabulary of medieval republicanism at an early stage. Together with concepts such as the common good, liberty, and justice, it served as the foundation for the republican ideology the *dictatores* in the course of the Dugento began to articulate to meet the legitimatory needs of the Italian city-states. In their vocabulary, greatness came to signify the attainment of a series of ends at which every city-state should aim:

nuovo, il quale ha maggiore necessità di acquistare reputazione che uno ereditario, gli fa nascere de' nimici e fagli fare delle imprese contro, acciò che quello abbi cagione di superarle e, su per quella scala che gli hanno porta li inimici suoi, salire piú alto. Però molti iudicano che uno principe savio debbe, quando e' ne abbia la occasione, nutrirsi con astuzia qualche inimicizia, acciò che, oppressa quella, ne seguiti maggior sua grandezza."

102 Ibid., 26, p. 190: "Oltre a di questo, qui si veggono estraordinari sanza esemplo, condotti da Dio . . . Ogni cosa è concorsa nella vostra grandezza. El rimanente dovete fare voi: Dio non vuole fare ogni cosa, per non ci tòrre el libero arbitrio e parte di quella gloria che tocca a noi."

magnitude, standing, power, and prosperity. Implicit in their argument, Skinner contends, was the more far-reaching assumption that *grandezza* could flourish and be preserved only under a republican form of government, based on the principles of civic liberty, peace, and tranquillity. In the course of the fourteenth century, a heightened awareness of the necessity of defending the republic's freedom by military means gave rise to the idea that war sometimes must take precedence over the maintenance of peace. But in spite of this shift in emphasis, republican theorists continued, if we are to believe Skinner, to view wars of conquest and expansionism as illegitimate and foreign to republics.

How, then, does Machiavelli's use of the term *grandezza* in the *Discourses* relate to this vernacular tradition? In Skinner's view, Machiavelli remains here "content to fit his ideas into a traditional framework, a framework based on linking together the concepts of liberty, the common good and civic greatness in a largely familiar way." Like the Trecento *dictatores*, he posits in the *Discourses* "civic glory and greatness" as "the highest end to which any city can aspire." According to him, Skinner argues, it is only in republics with a free and elective system of government that "the goal of civic greatness can ever be achieved." In Machiavelli's view, we are told, *grandezza* presupposes a way of life based upon republican liberty, and it is, in a sense, identical with the realization of this form of government and the civic ideals it entails.[103]

Before anything else is said, it must be conceded that Skinner is absolutely right in claiming that in the *Discourses* there exists an intimate relationship between greatness and the Roman republic's elective constitution. The greatness that Rome arrived at shortly after the expulsion of her kings, Machiavelli argues, following the republican tradition from Sallust to Bruni, was as a direct consequence of the city's newly adopted republican form of government and free way of life (*vivere libero*). In the Florentine's view, the freedom experienced under the early republic, and its development into what he calls "a perfect republic" (*una republica perfetta*), constituted the fundamental conditions under which Rome could achieve her "ultimate greatness" (*ultima grandezza*).[104] However, this is not to say that greatness should be equated with liberty, or with a republican way of life, as Skinner

[103] Quentin Skinner, "Machiavelli's *Discorsi* and the Pre-humanist Origins of Republican Ideas," in *Machiavelli and Republicanism*, eds. G. Bock, Q. Skinner, and M. Viroli (Cambridge: Cambridge University Press, 1990), pp. 137 and 140. For Skinner's attempt at situating Machiavelli's *Discorsi* in the republican tradition, see *The Foundations*, I, pp. 156–80. Cf. Sebastian de Grazia, *Machiavelli in Hell* (London: Picador, 1992), p. 172

[104] *Discorsi* I.2, I.20, and I.58.

asks us to do. For it is one thing to claim that greatness depends on, or is promoted by, liberty, and quite another to argue that the two concepts are identical or interchangeable.

In reality, there is ample evidence to show that Machiavelli's use of *grandezza* in the *Discourses* is closely related to that in *The Prince*. In both works, the term connotes growth, expansion, acquisition, territorial gain, honor, reputation, fame, and glory. That is to say that the term belongs to the vocabulary of empire, and not to that of liberty, as Skinner claims. If we were to hold on to Skinner's liberty-oriented view of the republican tradition, this contextual relocation of *grandezza* would place the concept, and the type of policies it connotes, in open conflict with the republican outlook. But from what has emerged in this study, we can see that this need not be the case. Since Machiavelli, like many other contemporary republicans, conceived of the republic as having two ends – to maintain its liberty and to expand its empire – it could be argued that *grandezza* for him belonged to the other, the external, or imperialist, side of classical republicanism. Consequently, there is no contradiction involved when Machiavelli describes the greatness that the Roman republic arrived at shortly after the expulsion of the Tarquins in terms of expansion and territorial acquisition:

> It is an easy thing to understand whence arises among peoples this affection for the free way of life (*vivere libero*), for it is seen through experience that cities have never expanded either in dominion or in riches if they have not been in liberty. And truly it is a marvelous thing to consider how much greatness (*grandezza*) Athens arrived at in the space of a hundred years after she freed herself from the tyranny of Pisistratus. But above all it is very marvelous to consider how much greatness (*grandezza*) Rome arrived at after she freed herself from her kings.[105]

To the former Secretary, the rapid growth of the early Roman republic, and the Roman people's love of their new, free form of government, were two intimately connected phenomena. Rome became great and expansive because she was free, and she remained free because she continued to pursue greatness and to grow. Therefore, the greatness of the Roman republic cannot, as Skinner falsely implies, be equated with her "civicness" or her "elective government." Instead it must be seen in relation to, and as a

[105] Ibid., II.2, p. 331: "E facil cosa è conoscere donde nasca ne' popoli questa affezione del vivere libero: perché si vede per esperienza le cittadi non avere mai ampliato né di dominio né di ricchezza, se non mentre sono state in libertà. E veramente maravigliosa cosa è a considerare a quanta grandezza venne Atene per spazio di cento anni poiché la si liberò dalla tirannide di Pisistrato. Ma sopra tutto maravigliosissima è a considerare a quanta grandezza venne Roma, poiché la si liberò dai suoi re."

consequence of, her glorious conquests, which in their turn were made possible by her free form of government.[106]

Viewed from this perspective, there appears to be no, or little, difference between the *grandezza* of conquerors like Cyrus or Ferdinand of Aragon, and the *grandezza* of an acquisitive republic of the Roman type. But if greatness cannot be equated with civicness or republican institutions, how should it then be defined? In open polemic with Baron and Skinner, Mark Hulliung has argued that in Machiavelli's lexicon the term simply means territorial extension and dominion resulting from conquest and acquisition. According to Hulliung, the end of Machiavelli's thought is neither the restoration of republican government in Florence, nor the liberation of Italy, but greatness, "the glorious, violent, and aggrandizing deeds that are better performed by republican citizens than monarchical subjects."[107] This can be seen, for example, he implies, in the way in which Machiavelli in the *Istorie fiorentine* uses the concept to denote "the list of cities once free and now subject to the yoke of Florence."[108] Although Hulliung's interpretation has the merit of drawing our attention to the concrete, territorial, and action-centered aspects of greatness, it offers too crude and too restrictive a definition of Machiavelli's understanding of the term. If Skinner could be accused of overemphasizing the internal, or liberty-oriented, side of Machiavelli's republicanism by subsuming greatness under liberty, Hulliung

[106] The connection between republican greatness and imperialism, evident from *Discorsi* II.2, cannot be dismissed as an isolated instance in the work. On the contrary, a conceptual pattern, equally consistent and pervasive as the one we have detected in *The Prince*, underlies the use of the term *grandezza* in the *Discorsi*. Throughout the latter work, Roman greatness is celebrated as the result of Roman acquisitions and territorial growth. For example, in *Discorsi* I.6, where the internal conflict between the plebs and the Senate is described as "uno inconveniente necessario a pervenire alla romana grandezza" (p. 217), the greatness of the Roman republic is understood in explicitly imperialist terms: "Ma venendo lo stato romano a essere piú quieto, ne seguiva questo inconveniente, ch'egli era anche piú debile, perché e' gli si troncava la via di potere venire a quella grandezza dove ei pervenne: in modo che, volendo Roma levare le cagioni de' tumulti, levava ancora le cagioni dello ampliare" (p. 215). Machiavelli's message here is unequivocal. Faced with the choice between two different constitutional ideals – one conducive to concord and internal stability, the other promoting conquest, growth, and *grandezza* – the exemplary Romans opted for the latter alternative.

[107] Mark Hulliung, *Citizen Machiavelli* (Princeton: Princeton University Press, 1983), p. 220. On Machiavelli's view of greatness and liberty, see also Patrick J. Coby, *Machiavelli's Romans: Liberty and Greatness in the Discourses on Livy* (Lanham, MA: Lexington, 1999). Coby argues that liberty and greatness (p. 265) are not opposites and that the two concepts differ "by degree rather than by kind." According to him, they should be seen as "separate stages in the history of that human excellence called virtù." By contrast, we here argue that liberty and greatness in Machiavelli's thought are related, not as a means to an end (Hulliung), or as two different stages (Coby), but as the two sides of the healthy republic, constituting its internal and external end or aspiration. In *Discorsi* I.29, Machiavelli says that a republic, which, "per troppo amore," overemphasizes either the maintenance of its liberty or the pursuit of acquisitions, makes a grave error. See chapter 2, note 105.

[108] Hulliung, *Citizen Machiavelli*, p. 14.

can conversely be criticized for overstating its external and imperialist side by making liberty into a mere means for achieving greatness. The manifest limitations of these two conflicting interpretations oblige us to inquire more deeply into Machiavelli's general understanding of Roman history and the inner workings of the Roman republic. What we need to clarify, above all, is how princely and republican greatness relate to each other.

TRIUMPHS – REPUBLICAN, IMPERIAL, AND CHRISTIAN

In *Discourses* II.2, Machiavelli explicitly compares the types of greatness attainable for republics and princes respectively. We here learn that the conquests of the Roman republic promoted the common good of the city, and that this is "what makes cities" (*che fa grandi le città*).[109] The acquisitions of a prince, by contrast, are usually harmful to his people as a whole, since "what suits him usually harms the city and what suits the city harms him."[110] For this reason, Machiavelli argues, it is better for a city that has come under princely, or tyrannical, rule to cease to increase in power and wealth than to continue to expand, since a strong and virtuous ruler who is successful in extending his dominion will bring good only to himself. But this is a truth with modification, since a policy of conquest is bound to undermine the position of the prince as well. While his power and his personal greatness may increase with his acquisitions, he will end up being unable to "honor any of his citizens" who displays goodness or valor, since such rewards are likely to create dangerous rivals.[111] To avoid having to compete with others for the glory that military triumphs bring, the prince will eventually be left with no other choice than to act as a Roman consul and personally lead his armies in the field.[112]

Machiavelli's fierce criticism of such long-term concentration of power in a single ruler is closely linked to his understanding of the negative effects of the republican triumph's transformation into an imperial monopoly. In *Discourses* I.30, which we have commented on above, he contrasts the gratitude shown by the Roman republic with the ungratefulness common among princes. During the republican era, he argues, virtuous Romans of all ages and of all social orders were allowed to participate in the city's drive to empire and to compete for glory under the auspices of the Senate.

[109] *Discorsi* II.2, p. 331: "perché non il bene particulare, ma il bene comune è quello che fa grandi le città."

[110] Ibid.: "dove il piú delle volte quello che fa per lui offende la città, e quello che fa per la città offende lui."

[111] Ibid., p. 332.

[112] Ibid., I.30.

This general quest for glory had the salubrious effect of turning the collective energies of the Romans outwards, and of engendering a multitude of ambitious young men whose pursuit of personal greatness contributed to keeping the tyrannical ambitions of the others in check.[113] Since attaining glory *within* the republic required displays of military skill and acquisitions *outside* the republic, Rome's political ambitions and territorial expansion came to increase as a result of this institutionalized rivalry. While the great heroes of the republican period understood that without Rome there would be no way to glory open to them, the Roman people acknowledged that without these glorious triumphators there would be no Rome. All this was brought to an end, however, with the advent of the principate, when all the glory, honor, and fame invested in the Roman state were appropriated by the emperors. As they started to view these divine gifts as their hereditary right, the quest for glory, the love of virtue, and the commitment to the common good, which had been the hallmarks of republican Rome, began to wane.

The decline of liberty and empire resulting from the disintegration and the transformation of the republican triumph into an imperial monopoly, and its subsequent appropriation by Christianity, is the implict issue at the heart of *Discourses* II.2. While the republican triumphators after their brief moment of divine status had stepped down and left the road to temporary deification open to others, the emperors had deprived their fellow citizens of the possibility of triumphing and of achieving worldly glory, by claiming for themselves the status of permanent gods.[114] This development, Machiavelli implies, continued and reached its climax with the coming of Christianity, which, through the permanent and eternal deification of one human being, Jesus Christ, brought about the complete usurpation of all worldly glory under a single head. The emperors had quenched the republican spirit, but they had been able to do so only temporarily, and for as long as they remained alive and continued to vest their imperial authority. Not depending upon any living ruler for its power, Christianity could, by contrast, lay claims to have killed the freedom-loving and acquisitive republican spirit once and for all.

[113] Ibid., p. 265: "Perché adoperandosi tutta la città, e gli nobili e gli ignobili, nella guerra, surgeva sempre in Roma in ogni età tanti uomini virtuosi ed ornati di varie vittorie che il popolo non aveva cagione di dubitare d'alcuno di loro, sendo assai e guardando l'uno l'altro. E in tanto si mantenevano interi e respettivi di non dare ombra di alcuna ambizione, né cagione al popolo come ambiziosi d'offendergli che, venendo alla dittatura, quello maggiore gloria ne riportava che piú tosto la diponeva."

[114] The Roman triumphators' status as gods is commented on in *Arte della guerra*, p. 539: "io non so donde si nasca la gloria di Cesare, di Pompeo, di Scipione, di Marcello, e di tanti capitani romani che sono per fama celebrati come dii."

Nowhere is the complete reversal of the order of things caused by the Christian religion more evident than in relation to the ancient Roman triumphs. Whereas these had included bloody sacrifices and the slaying of captured enemies, the Christian triumphator had achieved glory by sacrificing himself.[115] While the former constituted a rite of passage in an ever-returning cycle of peace and war, attuning men and society to the changing times of sublunar reality, Christ had brought eternal peace, the end of all wars, and a promise of a transcendental dimension beyond all change. Instead of carrying the scepter of war, the insignia of Jupiter, which the Roman generals displayed during their triumphal processions, the eternal human god of Christianity had entered Jerusalem holding an olive branch, the symbol of peace. As a consequence of this religious, ideological, and political revolution, Machiavelli argues, the "world had become effeminate" and "the heaven disarmed."[116]

The former Secretary's aim with regard to Christianity can be compared with Savonarola's strategy in *The Triumph of the Cross.* Although Machiavelli does not refer to him by name, it is tempting to read his attack in *Discourses* II.2 on the modern mores as a rebuttal of the friar's celebration of the triumph of Christ. While the Romans, Machiavelli claims, had "beatified" (*beatificava*) men who were "full of worldly glory (*mondana gloria*), as were captains of armies and princes of republics," and placed their highest good "in greatness of spirit (*grandezza dello animo*), strength of body, and all other things capable of making men very strong," the Christians had come to glorify "humble and contemplative" men, and to conceive of "humility, abjectness, and contempt of things human" as their highest good.[117] To counteract this topsy-turvy state of affairs, Machiavelli operates a double negation. Whereas Savonarola had turned the Roman military triumph on its head and filled it with Christian contents, the former Secretary negates this negative Christian ethics, turning Roman republicanism, with its love

115 Machiavelli appears to have the Roman triumph in mind when he contrasts the humility of the Christian sacrifices to the ferocity of the Roman. Among the ancient Romans, he writes (*Discorsi* II.2, p. 333), "non mancava la pompa né la magnificenza delle cerimonie, ma vi si aggiungneva l'azione del sacrificio pieno di sangue e di ferocità, ammazzandovisi moltitudine d'animali; il quale aspetto, sendo terribile, rendeva gli uomini simili a lui." After this comes the passage in which Machiavelli remarks that the ancient Romans raised to the heavens, or beatified, only men who had achieved worldly glory, such as military captains and republican consuls; see below note 117.

116 *Discorsi* II.2, p. 334: "paia che si sia effeminato il mondo e disarmato il cielo."

117 *Discorsi* II.2, p. 333: "La religione antica, oltre a di questo, non beatificava se non uomini pieni di mondana gloria, come erano capitani di eserciti e principi di republiche. La nostra religione ha glorificato piú gli uomini umili e contemplativi che gli attivi. Ha dipoi posto il sommo bene nella umiltà, abiezione e nel dispregio delle cose umane: quell'altra lo poneva nella grandezza dello animo, nella fortezza del corpo ed in tutte le altre cose atte a fare gli uomini fortissimi."

of liberty and pursuit of empire, back on its feet. While the inverted triumph of Christianity, in the eyes of Savonarola, had appeared as almost "a new world" and the basis for a "new philosophy," the original, republican triumph seems to play a similar role in Machiavelli's thought. His new world and his new philosophy, it would appear, aspire to nothing less than a revival of Roman triumphalism and the substitution of the glorious triumphators of the ancient Roman republic for Jesus Christ, the Christian triumphator.

In this connection, the expression "greatness of spirit" (*grandezza dello animo*), which in *Discourses* II.2 we have seen being attributed to the Roman triumphators, takes on added importance.[118] The phrase suggests that the true meaning of the term *grandezza* in Machiavelli's theory differs from those proposed by Skinner and Hulliung. For it is clear that this spirited, mental, or gutsy form of greatness can be reduced neither to territory or deed, as Hulliung claims, nor to the republic's civic institutions, as Skinner argues. Although the greatness of spirit demonstrated by the Roman triumphators depended on republican institutions as well as on territorial expansion, it cannot be equated with either. Instead, it must be understood within the context of Machiavelli's conception of the Roman triumph, and the love of virtue and glory it nurtured. In the general scheme he uncovers, glory and deification are the qualities or the attributes the Senate and the religious authorities confer on the triumphator, and greatness of spirit the inner quality the Roman captains, in rivalry with other ambitious and virtuous citizens, develop and display in their quest for glory. The Roman republic's greatness consisted in part in its civic institutions, in part in its territorial expansion, but above all in its ability to engender and to foster this type of character.

In a famous passage, Livy argues that the Roman republic was greater than Alexander the Great's Macedonian empire, not because the Roman generals were more virtuous than the Macedonian world conqueror, but because Rome had been able to produce many captains who could equal Alexander's military skill and other virtues.[119] In Livy's view, greatness of spirit is thus not to be seen as an exclusively republican quality. Although most at home in the well-ordered and acquisitive republic, it can be developed by rare men of outstanding natural talent, like Alexander the Great,

[118] *Animo*, or spirit, should here be understood as heart, courage, or guts, not as soul. On Machiavelli's use of *animo*, see Russell Price, "The Senses of *Virtú* in Machiavelli," *European Studies Review* 3 (1973), pp. 328–31.

[119] Livy IX.17–19. Livy also uses the Latin equivalent to greatness of spirit, *magnitudo animo*, when discussing Alexander the Great. See ibid., IX.18: "Quantalibet magnitudo hominis concipiatur animo; unius tamen ea magnitudo hominis erit collecta pauolo plus decem annorum felicitate."

operating outside the institutional framework of the republic as well. In the final chapter of *The Prince*, Machiavelli similarly attributes *grandezza dello animo* to the greatest hero of the work, the Persian founder and conqueror Cyrus: "the Persians had to be oppressed by the Medes so as to discover Cyrus's greatness of the spirit (*grandezza dello animo*)."[120] Cyrus the Great, the founder of *The Prince* 6, the conqueror and the great giver of *The Prince* 16, and the triumphator of *The Prince* 26, embodies in *The Prince*, more than any other ancient hero, the foundational quality that Machiavelli denotes with the term greatness of spirit. To understand the true nature of Machiavelli's republicanism, it is necessary to acknowledge the role he attributes to men like Cyrus in relation to the republic. In his view, the republic is more vigorous and more acquisitive than the kingdom and the principality, because it gives men greater scope to develop their greatness of spirit. But republics do not fall down from the skies, nor are they maintained by divine will. They must be founded, and according to Machiavelli, they must founded on the greatness of spirit of one man, capable of establishing difference and distinction among men. Having laid the foundation for future consolidation and growth, the founder leaves his example and his principles behind as a memento for future generations. If the body politic is to remain healthy and vigorous, this legacy needs to be kept alive, commemorated, and reenacted at regular intervals. The Roman triumph, during which the victorious general temporarily entered the realm of the divine to restore absolute distinction and difference among men, was such an occasion.

In this chapter we have argued that Machiavelli's republican and imperialist theory is built around the figure of the ancient Roman triumphator. This idea is most explicitly developed in the *Discourses*, but plays an important role in *The Prince* as well, particularly in chapter 16. In that chapter, Machiavelli encourages his princely reader to perceive the possibility of breaking out of the constraints imposed by the closed and self-contained political context that characterizes the small hereditary principality and the parochial city-state. As we have seen, this rhetorical strategy closely resembles the argument on the Tuscan league and the Roman way of expanding presented in *Discourses* II.4. On both occasions, the former Secretary associates a successful imperialist approach with an ability to secure the willing

[120] *Il principe* 26, p. 189: "e a conoscere la grandezza dello animo di Ciro, ch'e' persi fussino oppressati da' medi."

participation of others through a mobilization of their inidividual and collective interests, desires, and energies. In the next chapter we will see how Machiavelli in *The Prince* 19 follows up the covert imperialist argument of chapter 16, by manipulating his princely reader into a position where he is left with no other option than to concede power to the people and to found an embryonic version of the mixed regime.

CHAPTER 6

Rhetoric of hope and despair

> Dangerous conceits are in their natures poisons,
> Which at the first are scarce found to distaste,
> But with a little act upon the blood,
> Burn like the mines of sulphur.
>
> Shakespeare, *Othello*

Set at that crucial moment in history, when Rome began to break out of the confines of the *polis* and to emerge as an expansionist power in the pursuit of *imperium*, Shakespeare's *Coriolanus* offers one of the most penetrating and disturbing analyses of republican politics in the Western tradition. The play opens and ends with two triumphal processions, one fairly traditional and the other highly unconventional. Having almost singlehandedly fought and defeated the city of Corioles, the Roman patrician Caius Marcius returns to Rome in triumph, carrying with him the title Coriolanus that Cominius, his fellow commander, has given him.[1] The conqueror's moment of glory is short-lived, however. In his disastrous campaign to be elected to the consulship, Coriolanus displays contempt for the people, makes himself hated by the majority, and is banished from Rome as a result. The exiled triumphator makes his way to Antium, where he takes hire with the Volsces, long-time enemies of Rome. Soon, the arrogant and self-complacent Romans will have reason to regret their rash decision, as Coriolanus leads the Volscian army in an assault on the city, spreading panic among his internally divided and defenseless compatriots. When the city seems certain to fall, the Romans, in a last desperate attempt to quell the general's wrath, send out an improvised delegation, headed by the general's mother, Volumnia, and his wife, Virgilia, to plead for mercy. In an emotionally charged and skillfully crafted speech, Volumnia eventually succeeds in persuading her son to lift the siege. Upon their return to Rome,

[1] William Shakespeare, *Coriolanus* act 1, scene 9, vv. 53–65, and act 2, scene 1. The text quoted is in William Shakespeare, *Tragedies*, ed. S. Barnet (2 vols., New York: Knopf, 1993), II, pp. 619–770.

the women are carried through the city gate in triumph, and Volumnia is hailed for having achieved a peace that, in Coriolanus's own words, "All the swords / In Italy, and her confederate arms" (act 5, scene 3, 207–08) could not have accomplished. Praising Volumnia's feat, Menenius, an old patrician, recognizes that she has proved herself to be the "worth of consuls, senators, patricians,/ A city full; of tribunes . . . / A sea and land full" (5.4.55–57).

The Rome of *Coriolanus* is an archaic state which still has a long way to go before becoming the perfect republic Machiavelli speaks of in the *Discourses*. Personal, political, and constitutional shortcomings permeate the play, and account for its tragic end. Its princely element, the strong and courageous Coriolanus, is brave in war, but demonstrates time and again a notorious lack of political sense and a stubborn inability to adapt to peacetime politics. His inflexibility and his open disdain for the tribunes is a main cause of the social conflict that threatens to tear the Roman state apart. By contrast, the people are fickle, unstable, and devoid of virtue. They are timid in war and arrogant in peace. They despise the truly virtuous and are quick to let themselves be swayed by demagogues. Their representatives, the tribunes, are no less ambitious than Coriolanus; but their abilities are described as "infantlike" in comparison to his.[2] Instead, they derive their power from their ability to manipulate the people emotionally, by appealing to their basest instincts and their most irrational fears. However, the main responsibility for Rome's failure in *Coriolanus* rests with the middle element of the constitution, the senatorial class, represented by Menenius and Cominius. These men support Coriolanus, and recognize the needs of the people, but they are unable to control or to influence either of them. Their failing is foremost a rhetorical one. They are full of words of wisdom: they plead, they call out for moderation, and they admonish. It could plausibly be argued that they are the only characters in the play who have Rome's best interest at heart, but their arguments lack persuasive force and their good intentions remain ineffective, because of their manifest failure to address the political *here and now*.

Since *Coriolanus* tackles the problem of defining the extraordinary individual's place within the well-ordered republic, exposes the senatorial class's need for basing its power on a prudent and effective use of rhetoric, and gives ample represention to popular perceptions, aspirations, and needs, it can be read as a play on the mixed constitution. This constitutional ideal,

[2] Shakespeare, *Corolianus* 2.1.35–38 [MENENIUS:] "I know you can do little alone; for your helps are many: or else your actions would grow wondrous single: your abilities are too infantlike for doing much alone."

which had appeared in a somewhat cryptic form in Plato's *Laws*, before figuring prominently in the writings of Aristotle, Polybius, and Cicero,[3] was based on the contention that a more stable and lasting form of government would result if elements from two or three of the good regimes – i.e. monarchy, aristocracy, and democracy – were combined. The theory held that power should be shared between the single ruler, the few, and the many in such a way that the different orders of the regime could check and counterbalance each other, thus hindering the constitution from growing corrupt and lapsing into one of the three bad or unjust forms – tyranny, oligarchy, and anarchy. The translation and the assimilation of Aristotle's *Politics* into Latin around 1260 made the notion available to medieval political thought and gave rise to a broad range of theories of divided government and power-sharing – the most common division being that between the king and the body of the citizens.[4] In the late Middle Ages and the Renaissance, ancient Rome, ancient Sparta, and modern Venice were often invoked as examples of harmonious and well-balanced constitutions embodying the classical ideals. At the turn of the Quattrocento, Leonardo Bruni advanced in the *Laudatio* the same claims on behalf of Florence by arguing that the Florentine *signoria*, the captains of the Guelf Party, and the other magistrates and social classes performed constitutional functions equivalent to these of the Roman emperor, the senatorial censors, and the tribunes of the Plebeians respectively.[5] Shakespeare's *Coriolanus* has a place in this

[3] The most important classical sources on the mixed constitution are Plato, *Laws* 681d, 693b-e, 712d-e; Aristotle, *Politics* 1267b, 1269a-73b, 1278b-80a, 1289a, 1293a-96b, 1298a-b, 1302a, 1318b-19a, 1320b; Polybius, 6.11.11–13; Cicero, *De Re Publica*, I.35.54–55; I.45.69; II.23.41; III.13.23. On the classical notion of the mixed constitution in general, see Kurt von Fritz, *The Theory of the Mixed Constitution in Antiquity: A Critical Analysis of Polybius' Political Ideas* (New York: Columbia University Press, 1954); Neal Wood, *Cicero's Social and Political Thought* (Berkeley, CA: University of California Press, 1991), pp. 159–75; Carl J. Richard, *The Founders and the Classics: Greece, Rome, and the American Enlightenment* (Cambridge, MA: Harvard University Press, 1994), esp. p. 126; F. W. Walbank, *Polybius* (Berkeley, CA: University of California Press, 1990).

[4] James M. Blythe, *Ideal Government and the Mixed Constitution in the Middle Ages* (Princeton: Princeton University Press, 1992), pp. 5, 13, 112–13, and *passim*.

[5] Leonardo Bruni, *Laudatio Florentinae Urbis* is in Hans Baron, *From Petrarch to Leonardo Bruni: Studies in Humanistic and Political Literature* (Chicago: University of Chicago Press, 1968); English trans. "Panegyric to the City of Florence," trans. B. G. Kohl, in *The Earthly Republic: Italian Humanists on Government and Society*, eds. B. G. Kohl and R. G. Witt (Philadephia: University of Pennsylvania Press, 1978), pp. 168–69: "As Florence is admirable in foreign affairs, so it has outstanding civil institutions and laws. Nowhere else do you find such internal order, such neatness, and such harmonious cooperation. There is proportion in strings of a harp so that when they are tightened, a harmony results from the different tones; nothing could be sweeter or more pleasing to the ear than this. In the same way, this very prudent city is harmonized in all its parts so there results a single great, harmonious constitution whose harmony pleases both the eyes and minds of men. There is nothing here that is ill proportioned, nothing improper, nothing incongruous, nothing vague; everything occupies its proper place, which is not only clearly defined but also in right relation to all the other elements.

tradition not because it sings the praises of the mixed regime, but because it contributes to a critical understanding of its underlying dynamics. By breaking up the mixed constitution in to its constituent parts – in this case, the virtuous individual (Coriolanus), the Senate and the people – and by examining how the three orders of Roman society on this particular occasion failed to perform their proper and designated roles within the whole, the play leaves constitutional abstractions behind, and immerses itself in the formative process Machiavelli previously so probingly had analyzed in the *Discourses*.

It is also from this open and unresolved state of affairs that the playwright's intriguing portrait of Coriolanus draws its force. Who is he? Is he a devoted republican triumphator and the glory of Rome, or a would-be tyrant, threatening the pristine liberty of the Roman republic? The people, who are haunted by memories of royal and patrician oppression and care little for empire and glory, suspect him of wanting to restore their ancient slavery, because he opposes the authority of the tribunes. These fears are undoubtedly justified. But even though the play construes Coriolanus's desire to dominate as a virtue in war, but a vice in time of peace, there is little, or nothing, in the play to suggest that he is seeking personal power within the republic.[6] If we are to believe the general himself, it is in his nature to serve, and to do so valiantly, but on his own terms.[7] Although Coriolanus shows remarkably little respect for them, the senators seem to share this view. For them, he is a man of deeds rather than of words, who does not bother about the material gains his conquests bring, and seeks no rewards other than the glory that goes with his deeds. His military virtue and his services to the republic on the battlefield, they acknowledge, are

Here are outstanding officials, outstanding magistrates, an outstanding judiciary, and outstanding social classes. These parts are so distinguished so as to serve the supreme power of Florence, just as the Roman tribunes used to serve the emperor." Later in *On the Florentine Constitution*, Bruni describes the Florentine constitution as an admixture of aristocractic and democratic elements, and in the *Oration for the Funeral of Nanni Strozzi*, he defines it as democratic. See *The Humanism of Leonardo Bruni: Selected Texts*, eds. G. Griffiths, J. Hankins and D. Thompson (Binghamton: Center for Medieval and Early Renaissance Studies, 1987), pp. 171–74 and 124–25. On Bruni's conception of the mixed regime, see Russell Dees, "Bruni, Aristotle, and the Mixed Regime in 'On the Constitution of the Florentines,'" *Medievalia et Humanistica* 15 (1987): 1–23.

6 Plutarch, who was one of the principal sources for Shakespeare's *Coriolanus*, claims that the people initially wanted to prosecute Coriolanus for attempting tyranny. But when this could not be proved, they charged him with abasing the price of corn instead. See Plutarch, *Life of Caius Marcius Coriolanus* 20.2–3. Shakespeare towards the end has Coriolanus asking Virgilia, his wife, for forgiveness: "Forgive my tyranny; but do not say, / For that 'Forgive our Romans'" (5.3.30–31).

7 Coriolanus's ideal appears to be to serve politically and to command militarily. Speaking of his fellow patricians, he says: "I do owe them still / My life and services" (2.2.133–34). Before the meeting with the people on the Capitol, he states: "I had rather be their servant in my way / Than sway with them in theirs" (2.1.208–09). Cf. Coriolanus: "My affairs / Are servanted to others" (5.2.83–84).

essential to the growth, the glory, and the honor of the Roman state. In the final analysis, Coriolanus is thus a highly ambiguous figure, at one and the same time a potential tyrant and a crude and unpolished version of the glory-seeking military leader who, in the course of the subsequent centuries, was to extend the borders of the Roman republic and make the city great and triumphant.[8]

The dilemma at the heart of *Coriolanus* – how to deal with the princely, and potentially tyrannical, element within a mixed republic – was also a controversial issue in the Florentine tradition and one of the central concerns of Machiavelli's work.[9] In terms of practical politics, the Florentines had from early on developed a habit of coping with the problem by purging the city of its more ambitious citizens and giving military command to foreigners, thus perpetuating a climate of suspicion and factionalism. The civic humanists, despite their insistence on empire and liberty as the twin goals of the republic, had largely ignored the question, praising the mixed constitution as a source of unity and internal stability rather than external growth. But for Machiavelli, who was fiercely critical of this policy of exile as well as the self-congratulatory rhetoric of the humanists, it was paramount to find ways of securing the services of the city's most commanding, valorous, and warlike individuals, necessary for its greatness and growth, without jeopardizing the liberty of the republic. In this chapter we will explore how the former Secretary's own particular notion of the mixed constitution serves as a formula for combining tyranny and bellicose republicanism. By focusing on how Machiavelli's new prince, or *principe nuovo*, relates to the classical idea of the tyrant, and on the role he assigns to the princely element within his dynamic conception of the mixed constitution, we will also begin to address more directly the fundamental and still-disputed question of the relationship between *The Prince* and the *Discourses*.

PRINCE OR TYRANT?

According to most classical political philosophers and Renaissance humanists, a cruel and deceitful ruler, who governs for his own advantage, instead of for the common good of the state, is to be defined as a tyrant. Unanimously

[8] The ambiguous nature of Coriolanus's character is well captured in the following exchange between the two tribunes, Brutus and Sicinius: BRUTUS: "Caius Marcius was / A worthy officer i' th' war, but insolent,/ O'ercome with pride, ambitious past all thinking, / Self-loving." SICINIUS: "And affecting one sole throne, / Without assistance" (4.4.29–33).

[9] On Machiavelli's work as a source of inspiration for *Coriolanus*, see Anne Barton, *Essays, Mainly Shakespearean* (Cambridge: Cambridge University Press, 1994), pp. 148–52.

condemned by princely ideologues and republican apologists alike, the tyrant is vicious, unjust, and selfish. He is driven by an insatiable thirst for power, and detests anyone who expresses a desire for freedom. Since his principal aim is to maintain power, he is constantly stirring up wars and spying on those around him. He is cunning and faithless, and operates his evil schemes in secret under the cover of deceptive pretexts. To conceal the true nature of his rule, he feigns religiosity and surrounds himself with great pomp and circumstance. Tyrannized by his own passions and sinful lusts, he is seen to exist outside the human and the civil orders, and is often likened to a beast, a madman, and in the Christian tradition, even to the devil himself.[10]

This stock figure, who has continued to haunt Western political philosophy well into the modern age, appears fully developed already in Plato's *Republic*, where he occupies the lowest place in the five-fold scheme of constitutions, embodying the principles of pure injustice and utmost unhappiness.[11] Aristotle situated tyranny at the bottom of his six-fold categorization of good and bad constitutions, defining it as a deviated form of kingship, in which one man rules for his own personal benefit instead of according to justice and the common good.[12] The same fundamental principles continued to be endorsed by Roman theorists, medieval Aristotelians, and Renaissance humanists. In his influential commentary, Thomas Aquinas defines tyranny as the rule of "one man who seeks his own benefit and not the good of those subject to him [and] uses force to oppress the people instead of justice to rule."[13] According to Petrarch, the king is a ruler who governs with justice, displays moderation and mercy, and acts as a servant of his people, while the tyrant, who uses his royal office for private ends and devastates his kingdom with harshness, is "hateful and terrifying

10 On the historical conception of tyranny, see *The Great Ideas: A Synopticon of Great Books of the Western World*, eds. M. J. Adler and W. Gorman (2 vols., Chicago: Encyclopaedia Britannica, 1982), II, pp. 939–56; and Roger Boesche, *Theories of Tyranny from Plato Arendt* (University Park, PA: Pennsylvania State University Press, 1996).

11 Plato, *The Republic* 562a–580c.

12 Aristotle, *Politics*, 1285a30–1285b19. Adopting a historical perspective, however, Aristotle concedes that in the past there existed elective tyrants and a heroic and ancestral form of kingship, in which virtuous autocrats ruled lawfully over willing subjects. These rulers reserved for themselves only the power to command the army in war, and to perform sacrifices not specially assigned to the priests. As this autocratic rule gradually developed into a more civil and developed form of government, the kings renounced their privileges either by their own free will, or after having been divested of them by the people. As men became more equal with regard to virtue and their other capacities, these despotic rulers, whom Aristotle in a related passage refers to as gods among men and as the living law, lost their legitimacy and became obsolete. Cf. ibid., 1284a3–16.

13 Thomas Aquinas, "On Kingship," ch. 1; quoted from *St. Thomas Aquinas on Politics and Ethics*, trans. P. E. Sigmund (New York: Norton, 1988), p. 16.

to everybody."[14] Contrasting the tyrant with the lawful prince, Coluccio Salutati characterizes the former as someone who either "usurps a government, having no legal title for his rule, or one who governs *superbe* or rules unjustly or does not observe law or equity."[15] For Leon Battista Alberti, a ruler who loves his private good more than the public, and governs without regard for justice, moderation, and honesty, is to be called a tyrant, not a king.[16] In his view, Rome acquired her worldwide dominion by just means, but lost it, because "the desire to tyrannize" (*la libidine del tiranneggiare*), the love of private things, and "unjust wishes" began to count for more than the laws and the sacred customs.[17] In his *Treatise on the Constitution and Government of the City of Florence*, Savonarola draws extensively on this tradition, as he denounces tyranny for promoting "the private good of its members," while neglecting the common good and disregarding "the character of the people and the way they live."[18] The tyrant, the friar argues, seeks domination through force, sometimes by "cunning and hidden means," and sometimes by "obvious ones." His mind is always set on "plotting fraud and treachery," and he tries to keep his rule secret, by creating an impression of "not . . . governing at all."[19]

The question of how Machiavelli's *Prince* relates to this time-honored tradition was formerly one of the most hotly disputed among Machiavelli critics. One of the great mysteries in the history of mankind, Ernst Cassirer wrote, is how "a great and noble mind," like Machiavelli, could become the champion of "splendid wickedness." Cassirer had little patience for those who failed to acknowledge that Machiavelli in *The Prince* recommended his princely reader without any reservation whatsoever to use "all sorts of deception, of perfidy, and cruelty," or for those who argued that these immoral means were meant only to promote the common good.[20] The alleged contradiction between the tyrannical teaching of *The Prince* and the republican idealism of the *Discourses* later induced Garrett Mattingly

[14] *Petrarch's Remedies for Fortune Fair and Foul: A Modern English Translation of* De remediis utriusque Fortune, trans. C. H. Rawski (5 vols., Bloomington: Indiana University Press, 1991), I, pp. 245–64; quotation from p. 254.

[15] Coluccio Salutati, "De tyranno," in *Humanism and Tyranny: Studies in the Italian Trecento*, ed. E. Emerton (Gloucester, MA: P. Smith, 1964), p. 78.

[16] Leon Battista Alberti, *De iciarchia* in *Opere volgari*, ed. C. Grayson (3 vols., Bari: Laterza, 1960–73), II, p. 194.

[17] Leon Battista Alberti, *I primi tre libri della famiglia* (Firenze: Sansoni, 1946), pp. 10–11.

[18] Savonarola, "Treatise on the Constitution and Government of the City of Florence," text in *Humanism and Liberty: Writings on Freedom from Fifteenth-Century Florence*, ed. R. N. Watkins (Columbia: University of South Carolina Press, 1978), p. 233.

[19] Ibid., pp. 241–43.

[20] Ernst Cassirer, *The Myth of the State* (London: Oxford University Press, 1946), pp. 145 and 142.

to claim that the former work in reality was intended to be seen as a satire. As Mattingly notes, Machiavelli in *The Prince* never uses the word "tyrant," but seems to take great pleasure in "dancing all around it until even the dullest of his readers could not mistake his meaning."[21] Others have claimed that the radical discrepancy between the two works marks a turning point in Machiavelli's intellectual development. In Hans Baron's view, *The Prince* and the *Discourses* are based upon two completely different political outlooks and value systems. While Machiavelli in the latter work favors republican reform and condemns tyranny and autocratic rule in general, he offers in the former a "tyrannical solution" to the political crisis of his day centered around the idea of a "usurper prince."[22]

Some critics have questioned the validity of the perceived contrast between *The Prince* and the *Discourses*. According to Leo Strauss and Harvey Mansfield, Machiavelli's advice on tyranny is not limited to *The Prince*, but prevades the *Discourses* as well. In Machiavelli's view, they contend, tyranny is to be seen as an integral aspect of all forms of rule, good government included. Strauss claims that in Machiavelli's work the "distinction between public-spirited virtue and selfish ambition is irrelevant since selfish ambition on the broadest scale can be satisfied only by actions from which very many people profit." The appeal to patriotism and the common good in the final chapter of *The Prince*, Strauss dismisses as an attempt on Machiavelli's part at creating "the impression that all the terrible rules and counsels given throughout the work were given exclusively for the sake of the common good." In reality, Strauss goes on to argue, Machiavelli justifies these means "exclusively on grounds of the self-interest of the prince, of his selfish concern with his own well-being, security and glory."[23]

A radically different view is taken by J. H. Whitfield, who claims that Machiavelli's portrait of the new prince was intended as a contrast to Savonarola's description of the tyrant. According to Whitfield, Machiavelli imitates Savonarola when advising the new prince "to avoid tyranny," using the writings of the Dominican friar as "the prototypes of the anti-tyrannical maxims of *The Prince*." Since Machiavelli "envisaged his prince as legislator, not as tyrant," and "never dreamt of giving other counsel to a tyrant,

[21] Garrett Mattingly, "Machiavelli's *Prince*: Political Science or Political Satire?" *The American Scholar* 27 (1958): 482–91; quotation from p. 486.

[22] Hans Baron, "Machiavelli the Republican Citizen and Author of *The Prince*," in Baron, *In Search of Florentine Civic Humanism: Essays on the Transition from Medieval to Modern Thought* (2 vols., Princeton: Princeton University Press, 1988), II, p. 122.

[23] Leo Strauss, *Thoughts on Machiavelli* (Chicago: University of Chicago Press, 1958), pp. 44, 48–49 and 79–80. Cf. Harvey C. Mansfield, *Machiavelli's Virtue* (Chicago: University of Chicago Press, 1996), p. 7.

than the wise one, to lay down his tyranny," Whitfield concludes that no fundamental difference exists between the anti-tyrannical advice of *The Prince* and the republican teaching of the *Discourses*.[24] A similar opinion is expressed by Gennaro Sasso, who argues that the true ideal of *The Prince* is the civil principality discussed in chapter 9 of the work. This consensual form of principality, in which the ruler has achieved his position through the support of either the great or the people, contrasts sharply with the deplorable and tyrannical principalities of Agathocles and Oliverotto, analyzed in the preceding chapters. While celebrating the civil prince, Sasso argues, Machiavelli condemns the tyrant and defines him as a ruler who, in opposition to both the great and the people, builds his power without "social foundation."[25]

How are we to find our way in this forest of conflicting interpretations? One way to approach the issue is to explore how tyrannical means and good ends converge, or seem to converge, in the example of Cesare Borgia, held up by Machiavelli in *The Prince* as worthy of imitation by all new princes.[26] To judge from Machiavelli's account in chapters 7, 8, and 17,

[24] J. H. Whitfield, *Discourses on Machiavelli* (Cambridge: W. Heffer, 1969), pp. 33, 35, and 87.

[25] Gennaro Sasso, *Machiavelli e gli antichi e altri saggi* (3 vols., Milan: Ricciardi, 1987–88), II, pp. 351–490; quotation from p. 386. As a rule, scholars who argue that the cruel and fraudulent methods advocated in *Il principe* aim at the restoration of the republican form of government analyzed in the *Discorsi* refrain from defining Machiavelli's new prince as a tyrant. Mark Hulliung, for example, claims that Machiavelli, in spite of his many tyrannical recommendations in *Il principe*, condemns the violence of "a tyrant who seizes power for purely personal reasons and crushes all men of *virtù* so that he may rule alone," *Citizen Machiavelli* (Princeton: Princeton University Press, 1983), pp. 220–21. Victoria Kahn argues that *Il principe* contains "an immanent critique of tyranny" and thereby "anticipates the argument for republicanism in the *Discourses*," *Machiavellian Rhetoric From the Counter-Reformation to Milton* (Princeton: Princeton University Press, 1994), pp. 36–37. Roger Boesche deviates from this general pattern by claiming that Machiavelli in *Il principe* lays the foundation for "popular government" by establishing "a mobilizing tyranny." See Boesche, *Theories of Tyranny*, p. 133. Robert Kocis argues that Machiavelli's ideal in *Il principe* is the "good prince . . . whose motivation has shifted from ambition to *gloria* and who seeks to establish good laws that will empower him during his lifetime and work to his glorious reputation after his death," *Machiavelli Redeemed: Retrieving His Humanist Perspectives on Equality, Power and Glory* (Cranbury, NJ: Associated University Presses, 1998, p. 155). In his view, Machiavelli's new prince is not a tyrant, since he is motivated not by ambition, but by a thirst for glory.

[26] Scholars disagree about how to interpret Cesare Borgia's role in *Il principe*. For Cassirer and Baron, the duke is simply an epitome of tyranny. See Cassirer, *The Myth of the State*, pp. 145–46; Baron, "Machiavelli the Republican Citizen," pp. 114–15. Cf. George H. Sabine, *A History of Political Thought* (London: Harrap, 1937), p. 348. Mattingly in "Machiavelli's *Prince*," pp. 487–89, invokes Machiavelli's choice of Cesare Borgia as his primary model in *Il principe* as the conclusive proof of the satirical intent of the work. Vickie B. Sullivan in *Machiavelli's Three Romes: Religion, Human Liberty, and Politics Reformed* (De Kalb, IL: Northern Illinois University Press, 1996), pp. 19–24, claims that Machiavelli's potrayal of Cesare Borgia was meant to serve as a warning to the Medici and not as an example worthy of imitation. By contrast, Whitfield in *Discourses on Machiavelli*, p. 87 views the duke as the modern counterpart to Romulus, the legendary founder of the Roman state, who, in Machiavelli's words, by founding Rome as a *vivere civile e libero* paved the way for the republic.

the duke rose to power through a spectacular and well-timed use of cruelty and fraud. Through a series of theatrically and cunningly staged killings of former allies, like Remirro de Orco, Vitellozzo, Oliverotto of Fermo, and Paolo Orsini, he managed to establish his authority over Romagna and to bring the unruly province back to order. He gave it good government, the inhabitants a taste of well-being, and introduced a rudimentary legal system in the form of a civic court presided over by "a most distinguished president," and where "each city had its own advocate."[27] The fact that Machiavelli so emphatically stresses the good effects of Cesare's actions may tempt us into believing that he meant to convey that the duke's use of evil means could be justified, or legitimized, by the good ends for which they were employed.

However, Machiavelli's carefully couched account of Cesare Borgia's meteoric career resists this inference. To understand the point the Florentine is trying to make here, we need to distinguish between ends and effects. Nowhere in Machiavelli's text is it said, or even implied, that the duke introduced the civil court, or adopted the principles of good government, for the sake of justice or the common good, or because he judged these measures, or orders, to be good in themselves. Instead, Machiavelli states that Cesare found it necessary to give Romagna "good government, in order to make it peaceful and obedient to the kingly arm,"[28] and that he instituted the civil court because he did not want to appear hateful (*odiosa*) in the eyes of his subjects.[29] Thus, good government is here not defined as an end in itself, but as a mean to peace and obedience. The fact that the duke on this particular occasion chose to adopt good means, instead of tyrannical, should not be misread as a moral choice on his part, but merely be seen as a strategic move, motivated by the view that such measures under the present circumstances would be more effective and serve his interests better. In short, Machiavelli's exemplary duke always acted on the basis of

For the view of Cesare Borgia as a potential founder, or lawgiver, see Federico Chabod, *Scritti su Machiavelli* (Turin: Einaudi, 1964), p. 62; August Buck, *Machiavelli* (Darmstadt: Wissenschaftliche Buchgesellschaft, 1985), p. 65–66; Sydney Anglo, *Machiavelli: A Dissection* (London: Gollancz, 1969), pp. 225 and 229–30; Jack D'Amico, "Machiavelli's Borgia: Founder and Failure," *Rivista di studi italiani* 5 (1987): 18–30; Anthony J. Parel, *The Machiavellian Cosmos* (New Haven: Yale University Press, 1992), pp. 86, 88, 92, 117 and 158; Mansfield, *Machiavelli's Virtue*, pp. 38–39 and 186–87. For J. G. A. Pocock, in *The Machiavellian Moment: Florentine Political Thought and the Atlantic Tradition* (Princeton: Princeton University Press, 1975), p. 175, who has surprisingly little to say about tyranny, the fact that Machiavelli in *Il principe* holds up Cesare Borgia as a model suggests that his intent was to fashion his new prince not as a founder, but as a political innovator.

27 *Il principe* 7, p. 136: "con uno presidente eccellentissimo, dove ogni città vi aveva lo avvocato suo."

28 Ibid.: "a volerla ridurre pacifica ubbidiente al braccio regio, dargli buono governo."

29 Ibid.: "Di poi iudicò il duca non essere necessaria sí eccessiva autorità perché dubitava non divenissi odiosa, e preposevi uno iudizio civile nel mezzo della provincia."

his own self-interest. His good, or apparently good, actions, which brought order, unity, and peace to Romagna, he performed for the sake of his own personal security, his thirst for power and reputation, and his desire to continue with his conquests. In this regard, Cesare Borgia was no different from the other modern rulers and the ancient warlords portrayed in *The Prince*.[30]

How do these observations bear on the question of whether Machiavelli's prince should be considered as a tyrant or not? If tyranny is to be defined as government by a single ruler for his own personal good and without respect for the principles of justice and the common good, as Aristotle had claimed, there can be no doubt that Machiavelli in *The Prince* has fashioned Cesare Borgia, his prime example of a new prince, as a tyrant. Rule by force and deceit for the personal benefit of the ruler, and the view of good government as a mean by which to secure oneself, enhance one's reputation, and augment one's power, rather than as an end in itself, are all main characteristics of a tyrannical exercise of power.

But this conclusion immediately gives rise to a new problem: why and for what purpose did Machiavelli fashion his new prince (and by extension, his intended princely reader) as a tyrant? To attend to this question, we should do well to begin by comparing the rhetorical strategy of *The Prince* with the most authoritative advice to a tyrant the tradition had to offer – that of Aristotle's *Politics*. In other words, we need to resume our inquiry into the complex and intricate relationship between Machiavelli's and Aristotle's political teachings.[31]

[30] This general view is consonant with Machiavelli's observation back in 1502, when from the court of Cesare Borgia in Imola he reported that everyone there was living according to their own personal interests (*utilità propria*). See *Legazioni e commissarie*, p. 727. It is also in keeping with his claim in chapter 17 about the selfish nature of men in general, see *Il principe* 17, p. 163.

[31] In the light of the fact that many Renaissance writers found it natural to situate Machiavelli's work in connection to that of Aristotle, it is surprising how little attention the relationship between *Il principe* and Aristotle's moral and political philosophy has attracted within recent Machiavelli scholarship. Back in 1950 Leslie Walker provided a lengthy list of passages from Machiavelli's *Discorsi* that in his view echoed, or made use of material from, Aristotle's work. On the basis of this observation, Walker drew the conclusion that Machiavelli must have been familiar with the *Politics*, especially book V, which he on one occasion also quotes from in the *Discorsi*. But Walker did not make much use of this catalogue, and his only comment on *Il principe* consisted in the claim that Machiavelli in chapter 18 offered a restatement of Aristotle's theory on how tyranny could be preserved through the feigning of the princely virtues. See Leslie J. Walker, *The Discourses of Niccolò Machiavelli* (2 vols., London: Penguin, 1950), 1, pp. 86–89 and 273–77. More recent attempts at reading *Il Principe* in relation to Aristotle have as a rule been vague and general in character. A notable exception is Clifford Orwin, "Machiavelli's Unchristian Charity," *American Political Science Review* 72 (1978): 1217–28, commented on in chapter 5. For a penetrating analysis of the general differences between Machiavellian and Aristotelian ethics, see Mansfield, *Machiavelli's Virtue*, pp. 11–22. Among the sixteenth-century commentators who read Machiavelli's *Prince* in relation to Aristotle's *Politics* were Louis Le Roy, Bernardo Segni, and Giovanni Botero. See Kahn, *Machiavellian Rhetoric*, esp. pp. 63–65.

MACHIAVELLI VS. ARISTOTLE

In book v of the *Politics*, Aristotle claims that there exist two different and completely opposed ways of maintaining tyranny: it can be done either through a reign of open terror and oppression, or through the cloaking of tyranny as a virtuous form of kingship, understood as one-man rule exercised according to the principles of justice and the common good. If the tyrant adopts the first strategy, which Aristotle calls "the traditional method," he should, among other things, make sure to elevate base men and to lower those of outstanding virtue and free spirit. He should also make his subjects poor, keep them constantly occupied with their daily affairs, and use informants to spy on them. All these measures, Aristotle claims, should aim at preventing the subjects from establishing mutual confidence, depriving them of all power, and humbling them. This method, based on rule by force, Aristotle condemns as "utterly depraved."[32]

The second policy, rule by fraud, which Aristotle – without explicitly stating so – appears to prefer to the first method, can best be understood as a reversal of the lapse of kingship into tyranny. Just like monarchy will be destroyed, if it is taken in the direction of tyranny, he argues, tyranny can be preserved by becoming, or appearing to become, more monarchic. Should the tyrant in all his proceedings perform the role of the monarch, while continuing to exercise only one tyrannical prerogative, the right to rule over unwilling subjects, his regime would become more stable and long lived.[33] As has been noted, this section of the *Politics* could be read in a dual sense: both as advice to tyrants on how they should conduct themselves in order to preserve their regimes, and as an oblique counsel aimed at converting tyranny into a more moderate, just, and virtuous form of kingship.[34] Since the ruler who opts for the second method, rule by fraud, is expected not only to assume the appearance of a good, or semi-good, prince, but also to act as such, one may wonder what sense it makes to go on calling him a tyrant.

In chapters 17 and 18 of *The Prince*, where Machiavelli discusses the role of cruelty and deception in politics, he appears to align himself with Aristotle, acting as an instructor in tyranny. Paraphrasing Cicero's *De Officiis*, the former Secretary contends that there are two complementary ways of combat that a prince must learn to use – he should be able to fight "with

[32] Aristotle, *Politics*, 1313a34–1314a29; English trans., *The Politics*, trans. T. A. Sinclair (London: Penguin, 1992), pp. 346–47.

[33] Ibid., 1314a30–40 and 1315a41–1315b11.

[34] Cf. Rebecca W. Bushnell, *Tragedies of Tyrants: Political Thought and Theater in the English Renaissance* (Ithaca, NY: Cornell University Press, 1990), pp. 27–28.

laws" as well as "with force." While the first method is characteristic for man, the second is proper to beasts.[35] The brutish mode can be subdivided into two categories, metaphorically represented by the lion and the fox. In Machiavelli's view, these two animals, which Cicero and Dante had associated with tyrannical and unlawful government,[36] should be employed in combination, because the fox is needed to "recognize traps," and the lion to "frighten away wolves."[37] Having treated the lion, or force proper, in chapter 17 when discussing Cesare Borgia's prudent use of cruelty, he devotes chapter 18 to the political use of fraud and deception. Here, he recommends his princely reader to use the traditional virtues and vices according to expediency and to cover his use of evil means under a display of the commonly recognized virtues. Above all, the prince should maintain a constant appearance of faithfulness in order to conceal his foxy nature and the double-play upon which his power rests.[38] The close similarities between Machiavelli's teaching in these chapters and Aristotle's advice on how to maintain tyranny should be immediately apparent. As many early commentators on *The Prince* also noted, the Florentine's rule by cruelty (ch. 17) corresponds to Aristotle's first method (rule by force), and his rule by deception (ch. 18) to the Greek philosopher's second method (rule by feigning kingship).[39]

However, it would be a serious mistake to regard Machiavelli's advocacy of rule of force and fraud in *The Prince* 17 and 18 as a mere restatement of Aristotle's advice in the *Politics*. For upon closer inspection, we find that the former Secretary's counsel on several vital points not only differs from, but openly, or implicitly, undermines and challenges Aristotle's position. The first and most obvious difference between the two texts, of course, is that while Aristotle explicitly addresses his advice to a tyrant, that is, to an unjust and evil ruler, Machiavelli, as Mattingly and others have observed, never uses the word tyrant or tyranny in *The Prince*, preferring instead to speak in terms of *principe* and *principe nuovo*. A second point of departure, exemplifying the contrast between the moralizing tendency of Aristotle's teaching and Machiavelli's more instrumental approach, concerns the reasons the two thinkers give for feigning the princely virtues. While Aristotle

[35] *Il principe* 18, p. 165: "Dovete adunque sapere come e' sono dua generazioni di combattere: l'uno con le leggi, l'altro con la forza. Quel primo è proprio dello uomo; quel secondo, delle bestie."

[36] Cicero, *De Officiis* 1.13.41; Dante Alighieri, *Inferno* 27, esp. v. 75. Cf. Albert Russell Ascoli, "Machiavelli's Gift of Counsel," in *Machiavelli and the Discourse of Literature*, eds. A. R. Ascoli and V. Kahn (Ithaca, NY: Cornell University Press, 1993), pp. 242–45.

[37] *Il principe* 18, p. 165: "bisogna adunque essere golpe a conoscere e' lacci, e lione a sbigottire e' lupi."

[38] Ibid., pp. 166–67.

[39] See note 31 above.

recommends the tyrant to cover his tyrannical *nature* behind a virtuous façade of kingly behavior, Machiavelli advises his princely reader to conceal his tyrannical *actions* – his entries into evil – behind an appearance of conventional virtue. If Aristotle's counsel can be said to initiate an upward movement away from tyranny towards kingship, Machiavelli, by contrast, seems to incite his prince to enter the contrary, downward, spiral, from princely to tyrannical conduct. Whereas Aristotle's advice has the effect of transforming vice into a passive and ineffective quality (the tyrant is vicious, but does not act viciously in the fear of giving himself away), vice becomes in Machiavelli's teaching an active and indispensable faculty of princely government.

Third, while Aristotle presents the two strategies – rule by force and fraud – as opposite and mutually exclusive ways of preserving tyranny, Machiavelli in *The Prince* 17 and 18 treats them as complementary and sets out to show how they can be effectively combined. This general difference in approach contributes to explain the two authors' conflicting stands on the important issue of whether or not a ruler should inspire fear in his subjects. Here Aristotle advises the tyrant who wishes to masquerade as king to display dignity in his dealing with men, and to refrain from harshness in order to avoid appearing as "the kind of person who inspires not fear but respect in those who meet him."[40] For the Greek philosopher, this point is crucial, since rule of fear is characteristic of an open and undisguised form of tyranny, that is, the type of regime from which the tyrant cloaked in a monarchic façade should dissociate himself. Machiavelli challenges Aristotle's view that rule of fear automatically provokes hatred, by claiming that it is possible to make a moderate use of fear that strikes a balance between the noxious extremes of being too indulgent and too harsh, between having to rely on the love of the subjects and incurring their hatred. According to the Florentine, the prince should therefore "make himself feared in such a way that, even if he does not acquire love, he avoids hatred, since to be feared and not to be hated can go very well together."[41] With a subtle twist of irony, it would seem, Machiavelli, the advocate of the two extremes, here turns the tables on his Greek predecessor by using the middle-way argument against him.

Through the discussion on fear in chapter 17 a pivotal theme is being introduced in *The Prince*. As Machiavelli notes time and again, fear is a powerful motivator that can be used to make soldiers fight more valiantly,

[40] Aristotle, *Politics*, 1314b18; English trans., p. 348.

[41] *Il principe* 17, p. 163: "Debbe nondimanco el principe farsi temere in modo che, se non acquista lo amore, che fugga l'odio: perché e' può molto bene stare insieme essere temuto e non odiato."

to keep subjects in check, and to prevent citizens from overstepping the limits of the civil life. But with regard to princely or tyrannical government, it is important to recognize that fear, and the rhetorical use of it, can cut both ways. Preparing his advice on the necessity of being feared in *The Prince* 17, the former Secretary warns his princely reader not to create "fear for himself" ([*non*] *si fare paura da sé stesso*).[42] Through this brief, and admittedly cryptic remark, which in English translations often is taken to mean that the prince should not be "afraid of his own shadow," Machiavelli seems to gesture towards an anti-tyrannical tradition with roots in classical political philosophy, centered around the time-honored image of the fear-stricken tyrant. This observation gives us reason to take a closer look at the complex relationship between tyranny and fear in the classical and humanist tradition underpinning Machiavelli's rhetorical discourse.

THE FEAR OF THE TYRANT

In his *Rhetoric*, which together with Cicero's rhetorical works, the pseudo-Ciceronian *Ad Herennium*, and Quintilian's *Institutio Oratoria* provided the later Middle Ages and the Renaissance with the basic principles and techniques for rhetorical composition, Aristotle addresses the subject of tyranny briefly in the course of discussing how the rhetorical performance should be adapted to the political context.[43] In deliberative oratory, he argues, the most effective and the most persuasive arguments are those that address the specific purpose of the political constitution in question. While democracy is said to have liberty as its aim, oligarchy wealth, and aristocracy virtue, Aristotle identifies security as being the purpose of tyranny. Although it must be admitted that the discussion in this section of the *Rhetoric* is vague and sketchy, Aristotle's general point seems to be that the most effective form of persuasion before a tyrant consists in arguments promoting the safety of the ruler and the stability of his regime.[44]

This emphasis on security in connection to tyranny follows naturally from the teaching of classical political philosophy, in which tyrannical rule generally is associated not only with injustice, cruelty, and deception, but also with fear and instability. Being the most unhappy of men, Plato's

[42] Ibid., 19, p. 163: "Nondimanco debbe essere grave al credere e al muoversi, né si fare paura da sé stesso: e procedere in modo, temperato con prudenza e umanità, che la troppa confidenzia non lo facci incauto e la troppa diffidenzia non lo renda intollerabile."

[43] On the influence of Aristotle's *Rhetoric* during the Renaissance, see Lawrence D. Green, "Aristotle's *Rhetoric* and Renaissance Views of the Emotions," in *Renaissance Rhetoric*, ed. P. Mack (New York: St. Martin's Press, 1994), pp. 1–26.

[44] Aristotle, *Rhetoric*, 1365b–1366a.

tyrant lives a life of nightmarish terror, surrounded by enemies, unable to trust his own subjects, and protected against assassination only by a personal bodyguard consisting exclusively of foreigners.[45] The ruler Hiero, in Xenophon's dialogue of the same name, complains that princes cannot derive pleasure from their power, because they live in constant fear of their subjects, who hate them and who want to see them destroyed.[46] Aristotle similarly claims that tyranny, combining the worst aspects of oligarchy and democracy, is likely to provoke the hatred of both the nobles and the people. Consequently, it is the least stable and the most short-lived of the constitutions, and the one that needs most watching. Rebellions against tyrants, we are informed, tend to be particularly vicious and violent, since the many who have suffered under him seek not only his overthrow, but personal vengeance as well.[47]

This anti-tyrannical tradition was revived during the late Middle Ages and the Renaissance. In his dialogue *Remedies for Fortune*, Petrarch reiterates the view that the despotic ruler is both unhappy and insecure, by letting the figure of Reason admonish Joy, who boasts of having seized tyrannical power over his people: "You had a safe and quiet life, but now, unless you bolster your madness with crime, no day, no night shall be without fear and panic in your mind, no meal without suspicion, no sleep without nightmare, while you imagine everywhere the sword hanging over your head."[48] Similar observations can be found in the Florentine chronicles and in the writings of the Italian humanists.[49] Giving advice in his *Ten Books on Architecture* on how to design a palace for a tyrant, Leon Battista Alberti recommends the architect to install secret pipes within the palace walls to enable the tyrant to spy on the people around him, and to create a hidden passage through which he may escape in the event of rebellion.[50] Savonarola describes the conditions under which the tyrant lives along similar lines: "He lives beset with fantasies of grandeur and with melancholy and with fears that always gnaw at his heart . . . He maintains friendships with lords and masters

45 Plato, *Republic*, 566b and 579e. 46 Xenophon, *Hiero* III–V.

47 Aristotle, *Politics*, 1311a8–22, 1315b12, and 1320b40.

48 Quoted from *Petrarch's Remedies for Fortune Fair and Foul: A Modern English Translation of* De Remediis Utriusque Fortune, I, p. 253.

49 See for example Matteo Villani, *Cronica* VI.I and IX.56; Donato Acciaiuoli, "Protesto," in Emilio Santini, "La *Protestatio de iustitia* nella Firenze medicea del sec. XV," *Rinascimento* 10 (1959), p. 52. Similiar views were also expressed in the middle of the Quattrocento by Poggio Bracciolini: see Iiro Kajanto, "Poggio Braciolini's *De Infelicitate Principum* and its Classical Sources," *International Journal of the Classical Tradition* 1 (1994): 23–35.

50 Leon Battista Alberti, *The Ten Books of Architecture*, English trans. J. Leoni (New York: Dover, 1986), pp. 86 and 88.

of foreign peoples, for he views his citizens as rivals and is always afraid of them."[51] The conventional understanding is summarized by Erasmus, when in his *Education of a Christian Prince* he claims that the tyrannical ruler is tormented by all the fears he has instilled in others: "He who is feared by all must himself be in fear of many, and he whom the majority of people want dead cannot be safe."[52]

Before exploring the implications of this context for Machiavelli's princely advice, we need to return for a moment to Aristotle's *Rhetoric* to see what the Greek philosopher has to say about the two emotions most closely related to the tyrant's quest for security, fear, and confidence.[53] Aristotle opens the section in book II devoted to the rhetorical manipulation of fear by defining this emotion as "a kind of pain or disturbance resulting from the imagination of impending danger."[54] An orator who wants to inspire fear in his hearers should consequently strive to put them into a state of thinking that danger is imminent. This he can achieve by drawing their attention to the fact that others greater than them, or of equal standing, are suffering, or have suffered, for similar reasons. Fear tends to make men deliberative, but since no one deliberates about lost causes, the orator must also offer his audience some remedy, or some hope of escaping the danger that awaits them. Having laid down this principle, Aristotle next turns to consider the contrary emotion, confidence. This feeling, we are told, is caused by "the hope of safety . . . accompanied by the imagination of its proximity and of the non-existence or remoteness of fearsome things."[55] To inspire confidence in his audience, the orator can draw attention to the means and the arrangements that offer them protection, or remind them of the fact that they on previous occasions have escaped unhurt from similar circumstances. He might also choose to bring up the various assets that contribute to make the listeners fearsome in the eyes of others, such as "abundance of money, bodily strength, the strength of one's friends and land and equipments for war."[56]

On the basis of these observations, we may conclude that fear and confidence in Aristotle's system represent two opposite poles on an emotive scale based on the proximity and the remoteness of fearsome and salutary things.

[51] Savonarola, "Treatise," pp. 242–43.

[52] Erasmus, "The Education of a Christian Prince," English trans. in *Collected Works of Erasmus*, vol. XXVII: *Literary and Educational Writings 5*, ed. A. H. T. Levi (Toronto: University of Toronto Press, 1986), p. 231.

[53] Aristotle, *Rhetoric* 1382a–1383b.

[54] Ibid., 1382a; English trans., *The Art of Rhetoric*, trans. H. C. Lawson-Tancred (London: Penguin, 1991), p. 153.

[55] Ibid., 1383a; English trans., p. 155.

[56] Ibid.; English trans., p. 156.

From Aristotle's premises follows also, it would seem, that an increase in fear automatically will cause a decrease in confidence, and vice versa. Accepting this line of reasoning, it is difficult to see how these two emotions can be combined, or made simultaneously present, other than in reversed proportion to each other. Yet, as we shall see, this is exactly what Machiavelli seeks to accomplish in *The Prince* 19, the longest chapter of the work, to which we now turn.[57]

THE CONSPIRATORIAL TEXT

In *The Prince* 19, Machiavelli addresses the problem of how a princely ruler should avoid hatred and contempt, an issue that Aristotle had discussed at length in relation to tyranny in book v of the *Politics*. At the outset of the chapter, Machiavelli's princely reader is reassured that he will be free to exercise his other vices or "infamies" (*infamie*) without danger, provided that he avoids those things that make him "hateful and contemptible."[58] To escape hatred, the prince is advised to recall the counsel given in chapter 17, where Machiavelli exhorted him not to be rapacious, and to refrain from usurping his subjects' property and women. If he adheres to this advice, he will have nothing to fear from the majority of men, and will only have to deal with "the ambition of the few, which can easily be restrained in various ways."[59] There follows a list of qualities the prince should steer clear of in order not to incur contempt. He should not be variable, light, effeminate, pusillanimous, or irresolute, but should in all his actions take care to display greatness, spirit, gravity, and strength. If he acts in this way and maintains his reputation, he will be safe and secure, since no one will try to deceive him.

Up to this point, Machiavelli's argument is confusingly similar to Aristotle's in book v of the *Politics*, where the Greek philosopher also identifies hatred and contempt as the two principal causes of rebellions against

[57] On the role of security in *Il principe* in general, see Ezio Raimondi, *Politica e commedia: Dal Beroaldo al Machiavelli* (Bologna: Il Mulino, 1972), pp. 153–54; Quentin Skinner, *The Foundations of Modern Political Thought* (2 vols., Cambridge: Cambridge University Press, 1978), I, p. 138; Kahn, *Machiavellian Rhetoric*, p. 35; John M. Najemy, *Between Friends: Discourses of Power and Desire in the Machiavelli–Vettori Letters of 1513–1515* (Princeton: Princeton University Press, 1993), pp. 197–201; Maurizio Viroli, *Machiavelli* (Oxford: Oxford University Press, 1998), pp. 85–104. Machiavelli explicitly comments on the rhetorical manipulation of fear in *Il principe* 10, p. 147, and in *Arte della guerra*, pp. 625–26. On this aspect of Machiavelli's rhetoric, see Ezio Raimondi, "Machiavelli and the Rhetoric of the Warrior," *Modern Language Notes* 92 (1977): 1–16.

[58] *Il principe* 19, p. 167: "di fuggire quelle cose che lo faccino odioso o contennendo; e qualunque volta e' fuggirà questo, arà adempiuto le parti sua e non troverrà nelle altre infamie periculo alcuno."

[59] Ibid.: "la ambizione de' pochi, la quale in molti modi e con facilità si raffrena."

tyrants.[60] But whereas Aristotle's advice appears in an anti-tyrannical context, shaped by the notion that rule by violence and fraud inevitably leads to a condition of constant peril and chronic instability, Machiavelli's reassuring counsel gives the impression of wanting to control and allay the fears of his princely reader. In claiming that there exists a form of rule by fear that does not automatically produce hatred, and by promising the princely reader that he will be able to use freely all those infamies which do not make him hated or despised – a broad spectrum which appear to include a prudent use of both cruelty and deception – Machiavelli's aim seems to be to counter and disarm the traditional anti-tyrannical argument.

However, Machiavelli's comforting assertions sound a strange tone for a series of reasons. First of all, it is difficult to see how they can be reconciled with his constant warnings about the great dangers and the uncertainties facing the political innovator. The exposed and vulnerable position of the new prince, Machiavelli stresses time and again, is a natural consequence of the violent means he is forced to employ in order to acquire and consolidate his position. Are we now to believe that all these problems will simply dissolve if the prince avoids incurring the hatred and the contempt of his subjects? Second, the argument stands in open conflict with the position Machiavelli assumes in his long and famous essay on conspiracy in *Discourses* III.6, where he claims that conspiracies are so dangerous that "many more princes are seen to have lost their lives and states through these than by open war."[61] More damaging yet, Machiavelli's attempt to play down the dangers of conspiracies will, as we shall see, be called into question by the historical examples and the factual circumstances he later in the chapter adduces to support this view. How, then, are we to understand the surprisingly confident tone in the opening of chapter 19? To answer this question, we

[60] Aristotle, *Politics*, 1312b17–37. As usual, Aristotle is more generous with definitions than Machiavelli. According to the Greek philosopher, contempt is an attribute which attaches itself primarily to rulers who have inherited their positions, not to those who have acquired them by their own virtue. Hatred, on the other hand, is a natural product of tyranny and is always present under a despotic regime. It remains harmless to the ruler, however, until it is transformed into anger, which Aristotle defines as a more active and irrational feeling than hatred proper. Since anger has a tendency to make men daring and "unsparing of themselves," it has in the past, we are informed, caused the downfall of many tyrants. In order not to incur hatred, a tyrant, ruling under the guise of a good monarch, should abstain from seizing the wives and the children of his subjects and refrain from all other forms of unnecessary ill-treatment; to escape contempt he should display military virtue and strive to gain a reputation for being a good soldier. Aristotle also warns the tyrant to guard especially against "the ambitious," who are unlikely to be appeased by a mere display of moderation and chastity. As we can see, this is basically the same advice that Machiavelli offers in the opening of *Il principe* 19.

[61] *Discorsi* III.6, p. 426: "essendo cosa tanto pericolosa ai principi ed ai privati; perché si vede per quelle molti piú principi avere perduta la vita e lo stato che per guerra aperta."

need, as we proceed with our analysis, to continue to pay close attention to the pathos, or the emotional aspect, of Machiavelli's rhetoric.

Returning now to *The Prince* 19, we find that Machiavelli continues to address his princely reader in a reassuring mode, as he sums up the opening of the chapter: "The prince who succeeds in creating such an image of himself [i.e. displays greatness, spirit, gravity, and strength] is highly esteemed; and against someone who is esteemed it is difficult to conspire, and difficult to launch an attack, provided that he is known to be very able and revered by his subjects."[62] Apart from introducing the risk of conspiracies, this passage adds little to the previous argument. The strong emphasis on the ruler's reputation as a source of his security is also to be found in Aristotle's advice to the tyrant who wants to disguise himself as a monarch. Book v of the *Politics* continues to serve as model, as Machiavelli goes on to claim that a prince should have "two fears" (*dua paure*), one external, concerning foreign powers, and one internal, concerning threats posed by his own subjects.[63] Yet again, where Aristotle has nothing but uncertainty and despair to offer, Machiavelli provides comfort and security for his princely reader. Against threats from outside

> he is defended by good troops and good friends; and if one has good troops, one will always have good friends; and affairs inside will always be stable when affairs outside are stable, unless they have already been disturbed by a conspiracy; and even if affairs outside should be stirred up, provided he lives and arranges his affairs as I have said, and does not despair, he will always be able to repel every attack, just as I said that Nabis the Spartan did.[64]

If we leave the repeated reference to the possibility of conspiracy aside, the passage seems to give a reassuring and serene picture of princely security. But things might be more complicated than they seem. Nabis the Spartan, who here is portrayed as a prince capable of repelling "every attack," has previously in *The Prince* 9 been held up as a model for a ruler of a civil principality and praised for his heroic defense of the *patria* against a combined Greek and Roman army.[65] What Machiavelli fails to disclose here, though,

[62] *Il principe* 19, pp. 167–68: "Quel principe che dà di sé questa opinione è reputato assai, e contro a chi è reputato con difficultà si congiura, con difficultà è assaltato, purché s'intenda che sia eccellente e che sia reverito da' sua."

[63] Cf. Aristotle, *Politics*, 1312a39–1312b18.

[64] *Il principe* 19, p. 168: "Da questa [paura di fuora] si difende con le buone arme e con e' buoni amici: e sempre, se arà buone arme, arà buoni amici. E sempre staranno ferme le cose di dentro, quando stieno ferme quelle di fuora, se già le non fussino perturbate da una congiura: e quando pure quelle di fuora movessino, s'egli è ordinato e vissuto come ho detto, quando e' non si abbandoni, sosterrà sempre ogni impeto, come io dissi che fece Nabide spartano."

[65] Ibid., 9, p. 145.

but takes care to mention later in the course of discussing conspiracy in the *Discourses* III.6, is that the Spartan ruler actually was murdered in a conspiracy. While Nabis in *The Prince* 9 is referred to as a prince (*principe*), he is in the *Discourses* called a tyrant (*tiranno*).[66] Whatever Machiavelli's intention may have been for bringing up the unfortunate Nabis in this context, the example suggests that something out of the ordinary may be going on here.

When there are no external threats to preoccupy the prince's mind, Machiavelli goes on to contend, he "has to fear" (*si ha temere*) that his subjects "may be conspiring secretly." Against this he will best protect himself by heeding the advice set forth earlier in *The Prince* 19, that is, by not making himself hated or despised, and by keeping "the people satisfied with him."[67] For the second time in the chapter, Machiavelli introduces, in a seemingly inadvertent way, a new element into the argument while repeating an already established and reassuring conclusion. On the previous occasion, he had insinuated the subject of conspiracy within an assertion about the inviolability of the revered and reputed prince. This time he brings up the prince's need to win the support of his people as an appendix to a restatement of the advice given at the beginning of the chapter. These two potential sources of peril, the risk of aristocratic conspiracy and the need of popular benevolence, are now brought together for the first time in the chapter:

> One of the most powerful remedies that a prince has against conspiracies is not being hated by the people; for he who conspires always believes that killing the prince will satisfy the people, but if he believes that it will offend them, he will not have the courage to undertake such a deed, for the difficulties on the side of the conspirators are infinite.[68]

Instead of undermining the position of the prince, the injection of the people as a potential political power seems here only to further reinforce his position. By winning the people, the prince will be able to isolate the ambitious few who, unable to acquire popular support for their cause, can be expected to refrain from conspiring against him. This is evident, Machiavelli claims, because "one sees from experience that there have been many conspiracies, but few have had a good end."[69] This observation

66 *Discorsi* III.6, p. 433. 67 *Il principe* 19, p. 168: "tenendosi el populo satisfatto di lui."

68 Ibid.: "E uno de' piú potenti remedi che abbi uno principe contro alle congiure, è non essere odiato da lo universale: perché sempre chi coniura crede con la morte del principe satisfare al populo, ma quando creda offenderlo non piglia animo a prendere simile partito. Perché le difficultà che sono da la parte de' congiuranti sono infinite."

69 Ibid.: "e per esperienza si vede molte essere state le congiure e poche avere avuto buono fine."

induces him to draw a categorical and far-reaching conclusion about the general futility of conspiracies:

> And to treat the matter briefly, I say that on the part of the conspirator there is nothing but fear, jealousy, and the prospect of punishment; but on the part of the prince there is the majesty of the principality, the laws, the protection of friends and the state to defend him; so that, if popular goodwill (*la benivolenzia populare*) is added to all these things, it is impossible that anyone should be so rash as to conspire.[70]

This passage carries a strong and unmistakable echo of Aristotle's *Rhetoric*. As we recall, the Greek philosopher had there recommended the orator to bring up, in order to enhance the confidence of his hearers, all the things that may contribute to make them seem frightful to others, such as, for example, "abundance of money, bodily strength, the strength of one's friends and land and equipments for war."[71] Machiavelli now follows suit by adducing "the majesty of the principality, the laws, the protection of friends and the state" as factors that give the prince a fearful and formidable appearance in the eyes of those who are thinking of plotting against him. But among these awe-inspiring assets, as will become apparent as we proceed, Machiavelli has inserted an element which is also a potential source of weakness: the need of popular support. The claim that the prince will be truly safe only when "popular goodwill" (*la benivolenzia populare*) is added to "all these things" has the effect of keeping the door for conspiracy ajar, despite Machiavelli's great display of wanting to close it.

To substantiate the claim that experience shows that conspiracies rarely have a "good end" (*buon fine*), Machiavelli now brings up the plot of June 1445 against Annibale Bentivoglio, the prince of Bologna, orchestrated by the Canneschi family. As we learn, Annibale was murdered in the conspiracy, but since the Bentivogli enjoyed the goodwill of the people, the rebellion was immediately crushed and the Canneschi killed. Backed by the devoted support of the people, the Bentivogli were then reinstalled under rather curious circumstances. Since the Bolognese branch of the family could produce no heir old enough to govern the city, and since a rumor had it that there existed in neighboring Florence a Bentivoglio who until then had been considered the son of a blacksmith, the Bolognese went there to find him and offered him the government of their city. Later in 1463,

[70] Ibid.: "E per ridurre la cosa in brevi termini, dico che da la parte del coniurante non è se non paura, gelosia e sospetto di pena che lo sbigottisce: ma da la parte del principe è la maestà del principato, le leggi, le difese delli amici e dello stato che lo difendono. Talmente che, aggiunto a tutte queste cose la benivolenzia populare, è impossibile che alcuno sia sí temerario che congiuri."

[71] Aristotle, *Rhetoric*, 1383b; English trans., p. 156.

when Giovanni II Bentivoglio, the only legitimate heir of Annibale, reached mature age, he was, Machiavelli informs us, reinstated as the city's rightful ruler. From this example, Machiavelli concludes that "a prince should take little account of conspiracies if the people are benevolent (*benivolo*) towards him."[72]

Given the fact that Machiavelli, on his own statement, has "countless examples" of failed conspiracies at his disposal, the Bentivogli example must be considered a curious choice.[73] First, it is odd that Machivelli shortly after having argued that it is impossible that someone who lacks the backing of the people "should be so rash as to conspire," offers an example where the conspirators actually went ahead and executed their plans without first having acquired popular support. Second, it must remain an open question which aspect of the example counts for more: the Canneschi's failure to seize power in Bologna, or their successful murder of Annibale Bentivoglio, the head of the ruling family. In any case, the fact that the Bolognese afterwards went to great lengths to reinstall the Bentivogli must, from the point of view of the murdered Annibale, be considered a poor consolation, and can hardly vouch for the categorical inference Machiavelli draws from the example. No prince acting on the basis of his own self-interest, as Machiavelli's princely reader is assumed to do, could possibly accept the conclusion that princes need to "take little account of conspiracies if the people are benevolent (*benivolo*) towards him" on the basis of this episode. And third, the premises underlying the example conflict with Machiavelli's general teaching on the relationship between the prince and his people. It contradicts, for example, the argument in chapter 9, where Machiavelli, immediately after having set forth the example of Nabis the Spartan, argues that a prince in a civil principality who "allows himself to believe that the people will come to his rescue if he is oppressed by enemies" is seriously mistaken and will come to grief.[74] Similarily, it is at odds with his claim in *The Prince* 17 that a ruler should not base his power on the love of the people, since they can be expected to abandon him in adversity. As it now stands, the Bentivogli example not only demonstrates that conspiracies are risky undertakings for those who engage in them, but also that they pose a great danger to princes, even to those who enjoy the goodwill of the people and listen to the auspicious name of *Ben-ti-voglio*, I love you.[75]

[72] *Il principe* 19, p. 169: "uno principe debbe tenere delle congiure poco conto, quando il populo gli sia benivolo."

[73] Ibid.: "infiniti esempli."

[74] *Il principe* 9, p. 145: "dassi a intendere che il populo lo liberi quando fussi oppresso da' nimici."

[75] It seems likely that Machiavelli chose the Bentivogli example with a special view to the intended readers of the work, the Medici. In the *Rhetoric*, Aristotle argues that one way of boosting the

As a direct consequence of the Bentivogli example, the importance of the people in Machiavelli's argument has increased immeasurably. In the reassuring picture of the well-fortified ruler set forth previously in the chapter, the benevolence of the people had appeared only as an item on a list of protective measures available to the prince. In the Bentivogli example, on the other hand, the restoration of the princely family had come about exclusively because of the Bolognese people's support for their ruling dynasty. At this point in the argument, the security of the prince has thus come to depend more or less entirely on the goodwill of the people. This is also the conclusion Machiavelli now draws, as he finally allows his subtext to break through the well-tended surface of the text.

> I conclude, therefore, that a prince should take little account of conspiracies if the people are benevolent towards him; but if they are hostile and hate him, he should fear everything and everyone. And well-ordered states (*li stati bene ordinati*) and wise princes have taken every care not to exasperate the nobles, and to satisfy the people and keep them contented; for this is one of the most important concerns that a prince can have.[76]

Up to this moment, Machiavelli has in secret been building up a threat scenario centered around two principal dangers – the risk of conspiracy associated with the ambitious few, and the discontent of the many – which the prince must temper and bring in under his control. Previously in the chapter, these two menaces had been kept apart, or brought together only to strenghten the position of the prince. Now, as the reassuring discourse on princely self-sufficiency, which has dominated the chapter from the outset, gives way to a discourse of anxiety, they join forces in an open assault on the

confidence of an audience is to show that those who are their equals are not frightened by the threat under discussion. Since the Bentivogli of Bologna and the Medici of Florence could be considered as "equals" within the present context, the Canneschi conspiracy must be seen as having a direct bearing on the situation of the Medici at the time. There are also reasons to believe that the example was designed to call up Medicean memories of the Pazzi conspiracy of 1478, when members of the Pazzi family, backed by Pope Sixtus IV, plotted to assassinate Lorenzo and Giuliano de' Medici in the Florentine cathedral. Although Lorenzo, the head of the family, survived the attack on his life and later was able to quench the revolt, the event marked one of the darkest days in the family's history, since Giuliano, Lorenzo's beloved brother, lost his life in the conspiracy. The Pazzi conspiracy is referred to on several occasions in *Discorsi* III.6, see pp. 427, 431, 436, and 438. On the Pazzi conspiracy, see Lauro Martines, *April Blood: Florence and the Plot Against the Medici* (Oxford: Oxford University Press, 2003).

76 *Il principe* 19, p. 169: "Concludo, pertanto che uno principe debbe tenere delle congiure poco conto, quando il populo gli sia benivolo: ma quando gli sia nimico et abbilo in odio, debbe temere d'ogni cosa e di ognuno. E gli stati bene ordinati ed e' principi savi hanno con ogni diligenzia pensato di non disperare e' grandi e satisfare al populo e tenerlo contento: perché questa è una delle piú importanti materie che abbi uno principe."

princely reader, confronting him with the discomforting vision of political life traditionally connected with tyranny.

How are we to understand this about-face? It is as if in the course of the chapter, Machiavelli has been drawn, inadvertently and against his own will, to the conclusion that conspiracies are indeed a matter of great danger to princes. Gradually, his confidence-inspiring discourse seems to have collapsed under pressure from factual circumstances and historical examples with the appearance of being, not textual or subject to rhetorical manipulation, but "real." However, such a reading would most certainly be mistaken. For as we have seen, Machiavelli has in reality simultaneously been developing two distinct forms of rhetoric on two different levels of discourse. On the one hand, he has been leading an overt discussion on the measures a prince should employ to protect himself against conspiracies. This discourse has been carried out in a reassuring tone with repeated references to Aristotle. Beneath this comforting surface, however, Machiavelli has slowly but surely been unfolding a subtext of more disturbing implications, evoking the terror traditionally associated with the conditions of the tyrant. Time and again, he assures his princely reader that he need not fear conspiracies, but each and every time the threat of conspiracy resurfaces and returns with increased strength, like the heads of the mythological Hydra.[77] In the approximately two pages we have been discussing here, the word *congiura* and the related terms *coniurare* and *coniurante* appear no fewer than thirteen times. This density of vocabulary should be weighed against the minimal risk Machiavelli on the manifest level of discourse ascribes to conspiracies.

To rephrase our argument in terms of Aristotle's discussion in the *Rhetoric*, it would seem as if Machiavelli here is exploiting the implicit potential of Aristotle's theory by making a combined use of the rhetorics of fear and confidence – which in the Greek philosopher's presentation were seen as mutually exclusive – to create a double-layered text, in which the manifest discursive level predicated on the rhetoric of confidence is contradicted and undermined by an underlying subtext based on the rhetoric of fear.

After having seen how we got from Machiavelli's original observation about the futility of conspiracies to the threatening scenario, in which the ruler who lacks popular support must "fear everything and everyone," we now arrive at the salient point of the chapter, and perhaps of *The Prince*

77 The image of the Hydra is explicitly referred to by Machiavelli in a related context in *Discorsi* II.24, p. 392.

as a whole. For the first time in the argument, the question of rule by law and constitutional means is brought up. Prudent princes and "well-ordered states," we learn, have found ways to cope with the ambitions of the great and the needs of the people. As an example of a well-ordered and well-governed modern kingdom, Machiavelli singles out the French monarchy, in which, according to him, countless good institutions guarantee the liberty and the security of the king. Foremost among these is the Parlement of Paris, which Machiavelli also describes as a third judicial body, *uno iudice terzo*. Since this is the counsel that Machiavelli with such meticulous care has prepared us for, it is worth quoting at length:

> of these [institutions] the first is the Parlement and its authority. For he who founded that kingdom, being aware of the ambition and arrogance of the powerful, judged that they needed a bit in their mouths to restrain them; and, on the other side, being aware of the hatred of the populace, founded in fear, against the great, he wished to protect them. But since he wanted to take away the blame that could be placed on him by the great for favoring the people, and by the people for favoring the great, he did not wish this to be the particular care of the king. Consequently, he set up a third judicial body (*uno iudice terzo*), who could beat down the great and favor the lesser, without blame being placed on the king. This institution could neither be better nor more prudent, nor could there be a greater source of security to the king and the kingdom.[78]

The essence of the French model Machiavelli here holds up as worthy of imitation, it would seem, is a form of mixed government based on a certain, if yet limited, division of power. By allowing conflicts between the two classes making up society – the great and the people – to be settled by independent judicial bodies, this constitutional arrangement has the virtue of diverting the resentment of the few and the hatred of the many away from the prince. Being able to withdraw from the ignominious bickerings of internal affairs, Machiavelli implies, the prince will be free to devote himself to more glorious enterprises. Indications of wherein these activities would consist, we have already been given in chapters 14 and 16, where the prince was exhorted to dedicate all his time to the art of war and its

[78] *Il principe* 19, pp. 169–70: "In tra e' regni bene ordinati e governati a' tempi nostri è quello di Francia, e in esso si truovono infinite constituzione buone donde depende la libertà e la sicurtà del re: delle quali la prima è il parlamento e la sua autorità. Perché quello che ordinò quello regno, conoscendo l'ambizione de' potenti e la insolenzia loro, e iudicando essere loro necessario uno freno in bocca che li correggessi, – e da l'altra parte conoscendo l'odio dello universale contro a' grandi fondato in su la paura, e volendo assicurargli, – non volle che questa fussi particulare cura del re, per torgli quello carico che potessi avere co' grandi favorendo e' populari, e co' populari favorendo e' grandi. E però constituí uno iudice terzo, che fussi quello che, sanza carico, del re battessi e' grandi e favorissi e' minori: né poté essere questo ordine migliore né piú prudente, né che sia maggiore cagione della sicurtà del re e del regno."

orders and discipline, and was encouraged to enrich his state and to enhance his own reputation by waging wars of conquest. On the latter occasion, Louis XII of France was cited among the modern rulers who have achieved *gran cose* and expanded their territory by conquering foreign lands.

The rest of chapter 19 consists of a brief – or in the context of *The Prince*, not so brief – account of Roman imperial history from Marcus Aurelius to Maximinus, that is, from AD 161 to 238. Of the ten emperors who held power during this 77-year-period, we learn that only Marcus and Septimus Severus died natural deaths. All the rest were killed . . . in conspiracies! At the end of this digression, Machiavelli recommends his princely reader to imitate the two successful emperors, Marcus and Severus. According to this advice, which can be read as a summary of Machiavelli's teaching in chapters 17 through 19, the prince "should take from Severus those qualities (*parti*) which are necessary to found his state and from Marcus those which are appropriate and glorious to conserve a state that is already established and stable."[79] While to imitate Severus means to use the lion and the fox, cruelty and fraud, along the lines already established in chapters 17 and 18, the counsel to imitate Marcus brings us back to the constitutional solution put forward earlier in the chapter, based on a rudimentary mixed regime. Marcus, who had neither the people nor the soldiers (who by this time, according to Machiavelli, had taken over the role of the senatorial class in Roman politics) to thank for his title, kept, "while he lived, both the one order and the other within their bounds, and was neither hated nor despised."[80] Hence, imitating Marcus here means to balance the orders of society in such a way that everyone involved remains satisfied.[81]

Now that we have come to the end of our discussion of *The Prince* 19, let us pause for a moment to consider the general rhetorical structure of the chapter. In the opening, Machiavelli presents his princely reader with a reassuring discourse, promising him that he will have no, or little, need to fear conspiracies. But as the argument unfolds, the danger of conspiracy increases and mounts to a point where Machiavelli can claim that the only way for the prince to evade the conspiratorial ambitions of the great and the discontent of the people is to institute some form of mixed government

[79] Ibid., p. 175: "debbe pigliare da Severo quelle parti che per fondare el suo stato sono necessarie, e da Marco quelle che sono conveniente e gloriose a conservare uno stato che sia di già stabilito e fermo."

[80] Ibid., p. 171: "tenne sempre, mentre che visse, l'uno e l'altro ordine in tra e' termini suoi, e non fu mai né odiato né disprezzato." Cf. Giorgio Cadoni, *Crisi della mediazione politica e conflitti sociali: Niccolò Machiavelli, Francesco Guicciardini e Donato Giannotti di fronte al tramonto della* Florentina Libertas (Rome: Jouvence, 1994), p. 118.

[81] For a related example, see the discussion of Philip V of Macedon in *Il principe* 24. According to Machiavelli, Philip (p. 186) "sapeva intrattenere il populo e assicurarsi de' grandi."

on the model of the French monarchy. Then follows a discussion on the role of conspiracy in Roman history, which confirms the impression from the first half of the chapter that conspiracies do indeed pose a great threat to princes. The gruesome fate of the Roman emperors leads to a new recommendation to adopt a mixed rule, this time based on the imitation of the ways of Marcus Aurelius. Schematizing the general structure of the chapter, we thus find that the counsel on the mixed constitution is put forward in the mid-section, flanked, or framed, by a two-fold scenario overtly, or covertly, emphasizing the vulnerable position of new princes ruling by cruel and fraudulent means. What we are suggesting here is that Machiavelli in *The Prince* 19, by bringing together what we, with reference to Aristotle, have defined as the rhetoric of confidence and the rhetoric of fear, has created a scenario that mimics the principal subject matter of the chapter, conspiracy.

THE TYRANT AND THE REPUBLIC

What are we to make of all this? Does our claim that Machiavelli fashioned his new prince as a tyrant still hold true, or should we now in the light of our reading of *The Prince* 19 conclude that he adopted Aristotle's strategy for converting tyranny into monarchy? At first glance, the difference between Machiavelli's and Aristotle's positions may not seem obvious. While the Greek philosopher's advice on feigning kingship leads the tyrant in the direction of monarchy, justice, and good government, Machiavelli's counsel in *The Prince* 19 exploits the same kind of scenario to induce his tyrannical new prince to establish an embryonic version of the mixed constitution. If this constitutional idea were to be understood in the traditional sense, as a system of checks and balances, it could be argued that there is little that distinguishes the two strategies. But this would most certainly be to misrepresent Machiavelli's position and to underestimate the originality of his thought.

To appreciate how radically Machiavelli's advice in chapter 19 breaks with the Aristotelian tradition, we need to consider it in relation to the former Secretary's general thought on the mixed regime. Machiavelli's most elaborate treatment of this constitutional ideal is to be found in *Discourses* I.2 and I.5–6, where he discusses the relative merits of the Roman, the Spartan, and the Athenian constitutions. Dismissing the popular regime Solon introduced in Athens in the sixth century BC as a misguided and short-lived experiment in democracy that ended in failure, because it neglected to provide for the interests of the great, or the aristocratic few, Machiavelli follows Polybius's lead in concentrating on the Roman and the Spartan alternatives.[82] When he first presents the Spartan constitution in *Discourses* 1.2, Machiavelli claims that Lycurgus, the lawgiver, had "ordered his laws so as to give their roles to the kings, the aristocrats, and the people."[83] This may sound as if he considered Lycurgus's state to have been perfectly mixed, well-balanced, and symmetrical, containing provisions for the one, the few, and the many.[84] However, when Machiavelli returns to the Spartan example in *Discourses* 1.5–6, he makes clear that the state Lycurgus founded was only partially mixed, combining elements of monarchy and aristocracy, being "governed by a king and by a narrow Senate," but giving no representation to the people.[85]

The ancient Roman republic offers a sharp contrast in this regard. While the Spartan constitution had been laid down at the foundation of the state, its Roman counterpart had evolved as the result of a long and tumultuous historical process, fueled by the class struggle between the Senate and the Plebs. Rome began as a monarchy, but Romulus, its founder, had from the very beginning, by reserving to himself only the right to command the armies and to convoke the Senate, imposed strict limits on the authority of the royal office.[86] Although Rome remained a monarchy for centuries, Romulus's orders proved so conformable to "a civil and free way of life" (*uno vivere civile e libero*) that when the city later became a republic, the only innovation needed was the replacement of the king by two annually elected consuls.[87] Later, the Tribunes of the Plebs were introduced to check the power of the Senate and to safeguard the interests of the people, a function previously performed by the king. Since this open and processual approach to constitutional development allowed Rome to increase her population,

[82] On the unmixed character of the Athenian constitution, see *Discorsi* 1.2, p. 206: "perché la non le mescolò con la potenza del principato e con quella degli ottimati."

[83] Ibid.: "il quale ordinò in modo le sue leggi in Sparta, che, dando le parti sue ai re, agli ottimati e al popolo, fece uno stato che durò piú che ottocento anni."

[84] Mansfield makes the point (*Machiavelli's Virtue*, p. 87) that Machiavelli treats Sparta as "an oligarchy made moderate by the presence of kings, not as a true mixed government with a share of power for prince, aristocracy, and people." Cf. Hulliung, *Citizen Machiavelli*, pp. 47–51; Parel, *The Machiavellian Cosmos*, pp. 133–34; Pocock, *The Machiavellian Moment*, pp. 188–99. Maurizio Viroli completely miscontrues Machiavelli's meaning by claiming (*Machiavelli*, p. 125) that his representation of the Spartan constitution in *Discorsi* 1.2 shows his "commitment to a well-ordered *popular* government" (my italics). Sullivan comes to the remarkable conclusion that Machiavelli prefers the Spartan constitution to the Roman. See Sullivan, *Machiavelli's Three Romes*, pp. 61–66 and 93–95.

[85] *Discorsi* 1.6, p. 214: "Sparta, come ho detto, era governata da uno re e da uno stretto senato."

[86] Cf. *Discorsi* 1.9, p. 224: "chi considerrà bene l'autorità che Romolo si riserbò, vedrà non se ne essere riserbata alcun'altra che comandare agli eserciti quando si era deliberata la guerra, e di ragunare il senato."

[87] Ibid.

to arm her citizens, to expand her borders, and to conquer the world, it is to be preferred, Machiavelli argues, to the Spartan policy of isolation, stability, and self-chosen weakness.[88]

To sum up Machiavelli's argument, the Spartan constitution, as a result of its failure to make provisions for the third order of society, the people or the many, did not qualify as an accomplished or full-grown mixed regime. In comparison to the Athenians, the Spartans had laid a firm foundation for their power by providing for the one and the few, but by refusing to arm the people and to allow foreigners into their state, they had refrained from taking the all-important third step in the Roman development.[89]

How does the constitutional argument of *The Prince* fit into this line of reasoning? As we have begun to see, the mixed regime Machiavelli insinuates in chapter 19, centered on a strong, acquisitive monarchic element and a broad popular base, bears an intriguing likeness to the constitution of the ancient Roman republic. When we arrive at *The Prince* 19, the role Machiavelli is fashioning for his princely reader has also begun to resemble that of Romulus, the founder of the Roman state, as Machiavelli later was to describe it in the *Discourses*. After having in chapter 6 advised the prince to found his state on force, and having in chapter 14 exhorted him to devote himself solely to military affairs, Machiavelli urges him now in chapter 19 to provide for his own security by withdrawing from internal affairs and its relentless antagonism between the great and the people. If we are to

88 Despite the Spartan republic's internal stability and the fact that it remained free for eight hundred years (*Discorsi* I.6, p. 215), Machiavelli does not hesitate to characterize it as a "weak republic" (*una republica debole*), with the motivation that it had proved unfit for expansion in the end. States of this type, and here Machiavelli also includes the modern example of Venice, ought to remain within their own limits and institute a law prohibiting expansion if they are to maintain themselves, since "expansion is the poison of such republics" (*l'ampliare è il veleno di simili republiche*) and "acquisitions founded upon a weak republic are completely ruinous" (*acquisti fondati sopra una republica debole, sono al tutto la rovina sua*).

89 If this all sounds remarkably familiar, it is because the internal logic of Machiavelli's argument on the mixed constitution in *Discorsi* I.2 and I.5–6 is literally identical to the principles underlying his discussion on expansionism and acquisition in ibid II.4, which we have discussed in chapter 4. While the former Secretary in *Discorsi* II.4 condemns the Athenians and the Spartans for having proceeded in a topsy-turvy manner by acquiring subjects before making companions, in chapter I.2 he reproaches Solon for having acted in a similar manner by extending power to the many before first having provided for the few. Similarly, Machiavelli's treatment of the Tuscan league as an intermediary stage in the Roman imperialist project replicates his view of Lycurgus's Spartan regime as an embodiment of the first two steps in the Roman constitutional development – foundation by one and extension of power to the few. The position Machiavelli takes on the ancient Tuscans and the ancient Spartans is thus complex: on the one hand, he approves of them for having proceeded in the right order; on the other hand, he criticizes them for having failed to go the whole distance. While no Tuscan city had succeeded in gaining the supremacy necessary for further acquisitions, the Spartans had, by refraining from incorporating the democratic element into their monarchic-aristocratic state, closed the door to territorial growth and lasting acquisitions.

believe Machiavelli, this was the same kind of power Romulus maintained for himself after founding the Roman state: "He who considers well the authority that Romulus reserved for himself will see that none other was reserved except that of commanding the armies when war was decided on and that of convoking the Senate."[90] And as we recall, Romulus founded a monarchy that conformed so well to *uno vivere civile e libero* that it later was able to evolve into a full-fledged, and perfect, mixed republic, *un republica perfetta.*

Upon close inspection, the French monarchy that Machiavelli in *The Prince* 19 holds up as an example of a "well-ordered state" corresponds remarkably well to this Roman model. Previously in the work, France has been classified as a feudal state, in which the king is "placed amidst a great number of hereditary lords, recognized in that state by their own subjects, who are devoted to them." These vassals, we are told, have their privileges, which "the king disallows only at his peril."[91] To judge from this account, there exists in contemporary France no apparent need to make provisions for the aristocratic order of the society, because its rights and its privileges are firmly established and respected by the king.[92] Against this background, the Parlement referred to in chapter 19 presents itself as a constitutional complement, or an amendment, to an already monarchic and aristocratic state. Through the introduction of this third judicial body (*iudice terzo*), safeguarding the interests of the people, or the many, the French constitution could be said to have attained the status of a mixed regime, however embryonic and imperfect. As it appears, then, the difference between the ancient Roman and the modern French constitutions should here be seen as being one of degree rather than kind.[93]

[90] *Discorsi* I.9, p. 224: "E chi considerrà bene l'autorità che Romolo si riserbò, vedrà non se ne essere riserbata alcun'altra che comandare agli eserciti quando si era deliberata la guerra, e di ragunare il senato." As Claude Lefort suggests (*Le travail de l'œuvre Machiavel* (Paris: Gallimard, 1972), p. 495), Machiavelli here judges Romulus's actions on the basis of their effects rather than on the basis of his intention.

[91] *Il principe* 4, pp. 127–28: "Ma il re di Francia è posto in mezzo di una moltitudine antiquata di signori, in quello stato, riconosciuti da' loro sudditi e amati da quegli: hanno le loro preminenze, non le può il re tòrre loro sanza suo periculo."

[92] For a different interpretation of Machiavelli's view of the social classes in France, see Giorgio Cadoni, *Machiavelli: Regno di Francia e "principato civile"* (Rome: Bulzoni, 1974), pp. 98–99. More recently, it would seem, Cadoni has approached the position taken in the current study, see Cadoni, *Crisi*, pp. 135–36. On the role of the French example in Machiavelli's thought, see also Alfredo Bonadeo, "The Role of the People in the Works and Times of Machiavelli," *Bibliothèque d'Humanisme et Renaissance* 32 (1970): 351–77, esp. 356–57.

[93] On the French constitution, see also *Discorsi* I.12, I.16, I.19, I.55, I.58 and III.1. In connection to discussing the ancient Roman republic's habit of repeatedly and successfully renewing itself through memorable executions of its rulers in ibid., III.1, Machiavelli expresses his approval of the harsh

The fact that Machiavelli in *The Prince* chooses to present the mixed regime from a monarchic perspective, and in the *Discourses* from a republican one, need not surprise us.[94] By doing so, students of classical rhetoric can tell us, he is simply heeding Aristotle's advice and adapting his argument and his rhetorical performance to the circumstances, the audience, and the constitutional context: appealing to security before the tyrant and to liberty in the popular assembly. In keeping silent about the republican intent of his political project in *The Prince* – a work addressed to a princely ruler, or to a Medici ruler with princely aspirations – it could be argued, Machiavelli was not only being prudent, but playing by the book as well.

It should now be obvious that Machiavelli's conception of the mixed regime represented a radical break with the traditional understanding, which had conceived of this constitutional ideal as a system of checks and balances. For the Florentine, it was instead an instrument for mobilizing the three orders of society, their contrasting viewpoints, and their desire for domination, within a constitutional framework designed for expansion and territorial growth. In Machiavelli's scheme, mobilizing the princely element means stimulating his lust for power and his tyrannical impulse, and turning it outward towards the republic's external end – growth, acquisition, and glory. What we witness in *The Prince* 19, and the work at large, is how Machiavelli transforms tyranny from being a destructive force that turns against and threatens to dissolve the other constitutional elements, into a dynamic, creative, and expansive power. Thus, while Aristotle had tried to disarm the tyrant by converting him into a good and just monarch, Machiavelli spurs him on and places him in the service of the republic.

But what are the implications of Machiavelli's view of the mixed regime as a means of fostering and containing the tyrannical element in relation

treatment to which the French Parlement subjects its monarchs. Thus, also in this regard, it would seem, the difference between the ancient Roman republic and the modern French monarchy is one of degree, rather than kind.

94 As Hans Baron has noted ("Machiavelli the Republican Citizen," pp. 116–17), the function Machiavelli in the *Discorsi* attributes to the Parlement of Paris contrasts sharply with the one he outlines in *Il principe* 19. Praising the Parlement in *Discorsi* III.1, Machiavelli claims that this institution, together with the other French parlements (*parlamenti*), was the prime reason that France – "the kingdom that lives under laws and orders (*sotto le leggi e sotto gli ordini*) more than any other kingdom" – had been able to maintain itself for such a long time. These laws and orders are renewed, he claims, every time the Parlement executes them against the nobility – or against the king himself. Thus, while Machiavelli in *Il principe* 19 presents the Parlement from a princely standpoint, describing it as an institution offering security for the king and the kingdom, he here treats it from the perspective of the people, and praises it for its ability to provide protection for the people *against* the king. Baron argues that this difference in perspective stems from the fact that *Il principe* and the *Discorsi* are based on two completely different political outlooks, or world-views. We hope in this chapter to have shown that this need not be the case.

to the political *here and now*? Although the former Secretary neither in *The Prince* nor in the *Discourses* explicitly applies his thoughts on the mixed regime to contemporary Florence, his discussions on the matter should in all likelihood be read as a contribution to Florentine constitutional debate.[95] In sharp contrast with the Florentine *ottimati*, who, inspired by the Spartan and the Venetian models, at the turn of the Cinquecento had begun to develop a theory of the mixed constitution that accentuated the role of the aristocratic middle element, Machiavelli followed the Roman example by emphasizing the two extremes, the one and the many. If the Medici had let themselves be persuaded to adopt his constitutional design in Florence, it would have brought about a considerable reinforcement of the regime's monarchic, or pseudo-monarchic, element, as well as a spectacular return of the people to the political scene. Instead of containing power and office-holding within a small and well-defined ruling class, as the *ottimati* proposed, this innovative scheme would have opened up popular participation and involvement under a strong military leadership. In Machiavelli's view, this arrangement would not only have given Florence a constitution resembling that of ancient Rome, but also have provided the city the necessary foundation for developing into a true republic fit for imperial greatness.

In the last two chapters we have seen how Machiavelli in a highly self-conscious way appropriates, refashions, and subverts Aristotle's political and ethical teaching. From what we have been able to discern, two basic principles underlie the elaborate strategy the Florentine employs vis-à-vis the Greek philosopher. The first consists in the bringing together and the combining of categories, policies, and practices that Aristotle had separated and kept apart. For Machiavelli, virtues and vices, rule by force and fraud, and the rhetoric of confidence and fear are not mutually exclusive, but interactive and complementary. The second strategy, which relates more directly to the general purpose of *The Prince*, aims at opening up Aristotle's closed, self-contained, and *polis*-centered republicanism to an expansive imperialist

[95] Cf. Alison Brown, *The Medici in Florence: The Exercise and Language of Power* (Florence: Olschki, 1992), pp. 300–02; Guidubaldo Guidi, "La teoria delle 'tre ambizioni' nel pensiero politico fiorentino del primo Cinquecento," *Il pensiero politico* 5 (1972): 241–59; Pocock, *The Machiavellian Moment*, p. 246–47 and *passim*. On the mixed constitution in Machiavelli, see also Roberto Esposito, *Ordine e conflitto: Machiavelli e la letteratura politica del Rinascimento italiano* (Naples: Liguori, 1984), pp. 184–87 and 191–92; Francesco Bausi, *I "Discorsi" di Niccolò Machiavelli: Genesi e strutture* (Florence: Sansoni, 1985), pp. 37–42, 75–79 and *passim*; Mansfield, *Machiavelli's Virtue*, pp. 82–85; John P. McCormick, "Addressing the Political Exception: Machiavelli's 'Accidents' and the Mixed Regime," *American Political Science Review* 87 (1993): 888–900; Paul Larivaille, *Les discours et l'évolution de la pensée politique de Machiavel* (Paris: Université Paris X-Nanterre, 1977), pp. 93–103 and 138. Cf. Lefort, *Le travail*, pp. 381 and 495–98.

development along Roman lines. As we have come to see, all the policies, strategies, and institutions emerging from Machiavelli's engagement with Aristotle in chapters 15 through 19 of *The Prince* – foreign acquisition, the combined rule of force and fraud, and a mixed regime based on strong monarchic and popular elements – are closely associated with the ancient Roman republic. Machiavelli's principal aim in absorbing and expanding the ethical, rhetorical, and political thought of his Greek predecessor, it would seem, is to expose its unresolved contradictions and to show that it contains the seed of the Roman development.

In reworking Aristotle's theory Machiavelli also reveals his intention in writing *The Prince*. By fashioning his princely reader as a tyrant in the classical sense of the term, and by creating a series of scenarios that play on the tyrant's desire for glory and greatness and his fear of assassination and loss of power, the Florentine creates a new prince who will unwittingly serve as an instrument for a Roman-inspired republican development, acting as founder and embodying the acquisitive spirit that will promote and fuel the future growth of the republic. This republican strategy emerges most clearly in chapter 19, where the former Secretary conducts his princely reader through a destabilizing discourse of fear and conspiracy in an attempt to sway him to institute an embryonic version of the mixed constitution, and to dedicate himself to the art of war and the pursuit of empire. In the next chapter we will see how Machiavelli in *The Prince* 25, the penultimate chapter of the work, employs a similar strategy to insinuate the necessity of adopting the principle of rotation in office, another cornerstone of the republican tradition.

CHAPTER 7

Sublunar writing

> For all their boasting, practical men do not know either men or the world; they do not even know the reality of their own works. [If they could return to life], the geniuses of pure politics, the *fatalia monstra* recorded in histories, would be astounded to learn what they have done without being aware of it, and they would read of their own past deeds as in a hieroglyph to which they had been offered the keys.
>
> Benedetto Croce

For many contemporary historians and political commentators, the French invasion of 1494 marked a turning point in Italian history. Taking this year as the starting point of his *History of Italy*, Francesco Guicciardini claimed that the French invasion had given rise to "innumerable calamities, horrible accidents, and variations of almost all things." Like "a sudden tempest," impossible to contain, it had upset Italy's peace and balance of power, and "turned everything upside down." Not only had the war caused the downfall of republics and principalities, forced people to leave the cities, and destroyed the countryside, it had also brought to Italy new fashions, new customs, new diseases, and new and crueler ways of waging war.[1] Contemporaries like Machiavelli and Vettori were of the same opinion. The vocabulary they used to describe the effects of the invasion bespeaks its rupturing influence and the velocity of cultural change they experienced: *movimento*, *perturbazione*, *varietà*, *accidenti*, *casi*, *instabiltà*, *variazioni*, *rinovazione*, *rovina*, *distruzione*, and *mutazione*.[2] In short, in these writers' view,

[1] Francesco Guicciardini, *Storia d'Italia* (5 vols., Bari: Laterza, 1929), I, pp. 67–68; Guicciardini, *Storie fiorentine dal 1378 al 1509* (Bari: Laterza, 1931), pp. 92–94. The disease Guicciardini refers to is syphilis, which by this time had become known as the Neapolitan or the French disease (*il male di Napoli* or *il male franzese*). Cf. Guicciardini, *Storia d'Italia*, I, pp. 204–05.

[2] Machiavelli employs metaphors traditionally used to denote the sublunar sphere when he argues that the war has thrown Italy into "un mar d'affanni tempestoso," bringing destruction and ruin of states and provinces, and when he compares the invasions to a "tempesta" and to "illuvioni esterne." See "Capitolo dell'ambizione," v. 87, in *Opere*, vol. IV, ed. L. Blasucci (Turin: UTET, 1989), p. 349; *Il principe* 24 and 25. Similarily, Guicciardini claims that the Italian wars show a "quanta instabilitá, né

the advent of the French marked a radical break in the continuity of Italian culture of a kind and suddenness never before known.[3]

In their attempts to render the war intelligible, Italian writers sought to contain its subversive potential within the religious and cosmological framework of the day, attributing its origin to either of the four major causal agents perceived by the pre-modern mind – man, fortune, Heaven (or the Heavens), and God.[4] Many put the blame on individual Italian rulers, whose imprudence, shortsightedness, and greed were alleged to have brought about the barbarian plague. The guilt seems in this regard to have been evenly divided up between the cunning duke of Milan, the treacherous Venetians, the imprudent king of Naples, the rash and cowardly Piero de' Medici, and Pope Alexander VI, who, if we are to believe Bernardo Rucellai, was "the most vicious of criminals whom our centuries have seen."[5] But most commentators agreed that human shortcomings could only give a partial explanation to the catastrophe. Girolamo Borgia was expressing a widespread opinion when he claimed that fortune and astrological conjuncture had had a hand in the disaster as well,[6] and Guicciardini himself in *History of Italy* attributes the changes alternately to the "impiety and meanness" of men, the variable character of *fortuna*, and "the just wrath of God."[7] Religious preachers and writers of strong Christian persuasion, like Savonarola, Bernardino Corio, and Girolamo Priuli, viewed

altrimenti che uno mare concitato da' venti, siano sottoposte le cose umane." According to him, the rulers of the peninsula had, by failing to make provisions for the "spesse variazioni della fortuna," become the principal cause of the "turbazioni" tormenting the province. See Guicciardini, *Storia d'Italia*, I, p. I. Francesco Vettori links the events of 1494 to the "rovina" of Florence, the "mutazione dello stato" in the city, and the general "distruzione" of Italy. See Francesco Vettori, *Scritti storici e politici* (Bari: Laterza, 1972), p. 254.

3 The view that the French invasion of 1494 marked a watershed in the history of Italy has been largely confirmed by modern historiography, albeit with some reservations. Ernst Breisach argues that Italian Renaissance historiography can be divided into two periods, with the year 1494 as the dividing line; see Ernst Breisach, *Historiography: Ancient, Medieval and Modern* (Chicago: University of Chicago Press, 1983), p. 154. Peter Burke claims that there is evidence to support the thesis that 1494 marks a "break in the history of Italian culture," see Peter Burke, *The Italian Renaissance: Culture and Society in Italy* (Cambridge: Polity, 1986), pp. 233–35. Felix Gilbert has claimed that the events beginning with the French invasion of 1494 gave rise to a new historical and political consciousness, see Felix Gilbert, *Machiavelli and Guicciardini Politics and History in Sixteenth Century Florence* (Princeton: Princeton University Press, 1965), pp. 255–70. Eric Cochrane maintains that although the change in historiography was not as dramatic and sudden as the events themselves might presuppose, the invasions had the long-term effect of revitalizing humanist historiography by providing it with "political and philosophical utility," see Eric Cochrane, *Historians and Historiography in the Italian Renaissance* (Chicago: University of Chicago Press, 1981), pp. 163–65.

4 On the Heavens, *cielo* or *cieli*, see Anthony J. Parel, *The Machiavellian Cosmos* (New Haven: Yale University Press, 1992), pp. 26–62.

5 Gilbert, *Machiavelli and Guicciardini*, p. 260. Cf. Breisach, *Historiography*, p. 157.

6 Gilbert, *Machiavelli and Guicciardini*, pp. 266–67.

7 Guicciardini, *Storia d'Italia*, I, p. I.

the foreign intervention as a divine punishment imposed on the Italians for their sins.[8] If Charles VIII was *flagellum Dei* and God's avenging sword, as many claimed, the whole episode could be safely accommodated within divine justice and the providential order. The Italians and the Florentines were to be punished for their avarice, their sodomy, and their other evil deeds, but through their repentance, their spiritual reformation, and the renovation of the Church, the wrath of God was eventually to be mitigated, and a new era of universal peace embarked upon.

The capability of containment and the explanatory potential of Aristotelian cosmology and the retributive system of divine justice can hardly be exaggerated. According to this world-view, the Earth belonged to the sublunar sphere, situated at the bottom tier of the harmonious and hierarchically ordered cosmos. At the top of the system, encompassing it, was the transcendental realm of the divine, where unmoving, incorporeal, and eternal beings, conventionally alluded to as *cose divine*, resided. Next came the celestial spheres, where the seven planets, generally referred to as *cose celeste*, revolved in flawless orbits, corporeal, but perfect and immune to change. Between these higher spheres and our sublunar world below there existed a sharp divide. In contrast to the beings of the higher levels, human bodies and sublunar things in general, variably referred to as *cose del mondo*, *cose terrene*, *cose inferiori*, *cose basse*, or *cose umane*, were perceived as corruptible, temporary, fluid, imperfect, and subject to change. So when the early Cinquecento writers, in commenting on the dramatic changes following the invasion of 1494, used terms and phrases drawn from the traditional Renaissance discourse on fortune and sublunar conditions, they were not only representing the war as an epitome of the human or the sublunar condition in general, but also, at least plausibly, indicating that these frightening and devastating events could be reassuringly contained within the providential and cosmological order.

However, this interpretation is complicated by the fact that medieval and pre-modern cosmology also offered, or contained, an alternative, radically different, and potentially more subversive understanding of the temporal world. The general topos was established by Dante Alighieri, when in the seventh song of the *Inferno* he let the figure of Vergil inform Dante, the pilgrim, that there exist two contrasting perspectives on fortune (*fortuna*). The first approach, which corresponds with the one we have outlined above, sees fortune as a minister of divine providence and an executor of

[8] Gilbert, *Machiavelli and Guicciardini*, p. 257; Weinstein, *Savonarola and Florence: Prophecy and Patriotism in the Renaissance* (Princeton: Princeton University Press, 1970), pp. 129 and 145.

God's will, in charge of the distribution and the constant redistribution of mundane goods (*i splendor mondani*). This is the Boethian and the accepted Christian view. The other perspective goes back to fortune's origin as the pagan goddess Fortuna, who, in analogy with the planetary gods, rules the sublunar sphere as her kingdom (*regno*). The change (*permutazion*) she imposes on this lowly world, Vergil explains, is fast and incessant, and her design is so seemingly irrational that it cannot be penetrated by the human intellect. The reason she rewards some and punishes others therefore remains obscure. Her power appears to be virtually limitless, and since she is deaf to blame and to flattery, she cannot be swayed by human desires.[9] In short, while the former view saw fortune from above, and from the privileged vantage point of the divine, this is fortune seen from below, and from a human or sublunar perspective. Following Dante's lead, Italian poets and humanists came to develop this dual approach to the universe into a relatively stable system with a rich repertoire of accompanying attributes and symbols.[10]

Needless to say, the fortune-oriented interpretation did not, in Dante's view, represent a true alternative to the providential perspective. Instead, he, and late medieval and early Renaissance thought in general, were careful to reconcile these sharply contrasting perspectives on the temporal world by subordinating the former to the latter. While the providential viewpoint was assumed to give a truthful and all-embracing perspective on God's creation, its sublunar counterpart was judged to offer an incomplete, or distorted, view of human existence and sublunar conditions in general. However, at

[9] Dante Alighieri, *Inferno*, canto VII, vv. 61–96. On the perspectivism of Dante's cosmology, see Alison Cornish, "Dante's Moral Cosmology," in *Cosmology: Historical, Literary, Philosophical, Religious and Scientific Perspectives*, ed. N. S. Hetherington (New York: Garland, 1993), pp. 201–15.

[10] The principal study of the medieval conception of fortune remains Howard Patch, *The Goddess Fortuna in Medieval Literature* (Cambridge, MA: Harvard University Press, 1927). On the theme of fortune in connection to the Fench invasion of 1494, see Mario Santoro, *Fortuna, ragione e prudenza nella civiltà letteraria del Cinquecento* (Naples: Liguori, 1978), pp. 15–26. For a discussion of the Renaissance view of fortune in relation to the concept *occasio*, see Frederick Kiefer, "The Conflation of *Fortuna* and *Occasio* in Renaissance Thought and Iconography," *Journal of Medieval and Renaissance Studies* 9 (1979): 1–27. Cf. Charles Trinkaus, *The Poet as Philosopher: Petrarch and the Formation of Renaissance Consciousness* (New Haven: Yale University Press, 1979), pp. 27–29; J. G. A. Pocock, *The Machiavellian Moment: Florentine Political Thought and the Atlantic Tradition* (Princeton: Princeton University Press, 1975), pp. 47–48. While being seen as the principal agent causing and controlling sublunar change, fortune was also believed to contain this change within her sphere. Thus, she could be conceived of both as the totality of sublunar change and as the principal agent causing this change. Renaissance writers could therefore simultaneously speak of the changes of fortune (*variazioni della fortuna*) and of fortune's great power over human affairs without committing a logical or conceptual fallacy. Iconographically, this double character of fortune meant that she could be identified both with the woman turning the wheel of Fortune and, alternately, with the wheel itself.

the same time as this dual and hierarchical approach allowed pre-modern thinkers to resolve the fundamental tension between the supralunary and the sublunary spheres built into the Aristotelian cosmological system, it opened up a Pandora's box of doubts and challenges. While an absolute and all-encompassing vision from above might be easy to envision in theory, it has proved more difficult to obtain in practice. Of course, Dante had during his ascent through the heavenly spheres experienced the reversal of perspective from human to divine, but this was a privilege that few could claim. How then were those who had never experienced the world from above to be persuaded that the transcendental perspective existed as a reality, and not only as a theoretical assumption, or as an imagined ideal? The simple truth of the matter was that if fortune were to be transformed into divine providence, faith was needed.[11] Or to put it differently, the subordination of fortune to providential truth was not to be argued before the tribunal of reason, but had to be accepted on authority from church or tradition.

At least, this seems to be the position Machiavelli takes when in the *Discourses* he slyly comments on the difficulty of forming an opinion on heavenly omens: "the cause of [such omens] I believe is to be discoursed of and interpreted by a man who has knowledge of things natural and supernatural, which we do not have."[12] Regardless of how we interpret this guarded statement, it is indicative of Machiavelli's categorical rejection of the providential perspective and of his equally radical emphasis on the sublunar world. In the *Discourses* and the *Istorie fiorentine*, we learn that men, states, and other sublunar things – which Machiavelli refers to as *mondane cose* ("worldly things"), *cose terrene* ("terrestial things"), *cose del mondo* ("things of the world"), *cose umane* ("human things"), and *stato mortale* ("mortal state") – rise and fall according to an immutable and preordained pattern of cyclical change.[13] Although the Florentine on various occasions evokes Heaven (*cielo*), the Heavens (*cieli*), and God (*Dio* or *Iddio*),[14] and uses rhetorical formulas that juxtapose phenomena belonging to the different orders of the Aristotelian universe – like "earthly or

[11] Cf. Pocock, *The Machiavellian Moment*, p. 43.

[12] *Discorsi* 1.56, p. 314: "La cagione di questo, credo sia da essere discorsa e interpretata da uomo che abbi notizia delle cose naturali e soprannaturali: il che non abbiamo noi."

[13] See above pp. 88–89. While Machiavelli depicts the natural order as constant and perpetual, all the objects, the bodies, the organisms, the states, and the religions that are born into it are seen to have a limited life-span allotted to them, and to undergo phases of birth, growth, maturity, decline, and death.

[14] On God as a causal agent in Machiavelli's thought, see Sebastian de Grazia, *Machiavelli in Hell* (London: Picador, 1992); Cary J. Nederman, "Amazing Grace: Fortune, God, and Free Will in Machiavelli's Thought," *Journal of the History of Ideas* 60 (1999): 617–38. By contrast, Anthony Parel

heavenly judgment," "remedies, human or divine," or "forces, natural or supernatural"[15] – he never abandons his sublunar point of view, or his focus on the temporal world. It is true that he depicts the sublunar world as governed by outside forces, but since their nature and the way in which they influence earthly life are inscrutable and beyond human understanding, it makes little difference whether he calls them God, the Heavens, Fortuna, nature, or chance. What matters is that man is denied access to the full vision, the insights, and the reassuring sense of containment promised by the providential perspective. In Machiavelli's world, man is left to himself, and whether or not he will succeed in his undertakings depends to a large extent, but not completely (since fortune or external forces may support or thwart his plans), on his ability to interpret the cycles of sublunar existence without understanding their origin or purpose.

The task of this chapter is to show how Machiavelli's radical focus on the sublunar sphere affects, and is reflected in, his rhetorical practice. Through a close reading of *The Prince* 25, where the Florentine openly and at length addresses the French invasion of 1494 and its effects on the Italian political situation, we will seek to demonstrate that Machiavelli's sublunar outlook was not just a vague and unarticulated notion, but a fundamental assumption that underlies his political theory as a whole, and a perspective that he actively, and with great technical bravura and panache, enacts in his

argues that Machiavelli cannot be considered a Christian writer, since God and divine providence are excluded from, or play no substantive part in, his theory. Instead, Parel claims that the Florentine entertained an astrological world-view. See Anthony J. Parel, *The Machiavellian Cosmos* (New Haven: Yale University Press, 1992); Parel, "The Question of Machiavelli's Modernity," in *The Rise of Modern Philosophy: The Tension between the New and Traditional Philosophies from Machiavelli to Leibniz*, ed. T. Sorell (Oxford: Clarendon, 1993), pp. 253–72. For an elaboration on Parel's position, see also Sammy Basu, "In a Crazy Time the Crazy Come Out Well: Machiavelli and the Cosmology of his Day," *History of Political Thought* 11 (1990): 213–39. The literature on Machiavelli's view of fortune is immense. See especially Hanna F. Pitkin, *Fortune is a Woman: Gender and Politics in the Thought of Niccolò Machiavelli* (Berkeley, CA: University of California Press, 1984), pp. 138–43; Skinner, *The Foundations of Modern Political Thought* (2 vols., Cambridge: Cambridge University Press, 1978), I, pp. 95–98; Wayne R. Newell, "How Original is Machiavelli? A Consideration of Skinner's Interpretation of Virtue and Fortune," *Political Theory* 15 (1987): 612–34; Thomas Flanagan, "The Concept of Fortuna in Machiavelli," in *The Political Calculus*, ed. A. Parel (Toronto: University of Toronto Press, 1972), pp. 127–35; Wayne A. Rebhorn, *Foxes and Lions: Machiavelli's Confidence Men* (Ithaca: Cornell University Press, 1988), pp. 170–83; Santoro, *Fortuna, ragione e prudenza*, pp. 235–90. In contrast to these scholars, Harvey Mansfield argues that Machiavelli, by opposing the cyclicity of the ancients and the transcendentalism of the Christians, and by playing out these two world-views against each other, demonstrates how man can conquer fortune. See Harvey C. Mansfield, *Machiavelli's Virtue* (Chicago: University of Chicago Press, 1996), pp. 109–22. Cf. Leo Strauss, *Thoughts on Machiavelli* (Chicago: University of Chicago Press, 1958), pp. 208–23; Oded Balaban, "The Human Origins of Fortuna in Machiavelli's Thought," *History of Political Thought* 11 (1990): 21–36.

[15] *Opere*, vol. IV, ed. Blasucci, p. 235: "iudicio o celeste o mondano"; *Discorsi* II.29, p. 405: "rimedio umano e divino"; *Istorie fiorentine* VI.34, p. 433: "forze, o naturali o soprannaturali."

writing. Indeed, Machiavelli's use of sublunar cyclicity in *The Prince* 25 is so inventive and so spectacular that it calls for the coining of a new concept. Sublunar writing is the term I propose for describing the textual strategy and the particular mode of discourse the former Secretary develops in the chapter in question. This interpretation will place us in a position to explain why Machiavelli in the famous last chapter of *The Prince* appears to revive the conventional framing categories – divine providence, the just war, and the desire for peace – which previously in the work he has either openly attacked, or implicitly called into question.

HUMAN NATURE AND THE QUALITIES OF THE TIMES

As we have begun to see, the late Middle Ages and the Renaissance understood the problem of temporality and contingency largely in terms of man's relation to fortune, or Fortuna, the unpredictable and unruly goddess who commands the conditions that regulate sublunar existence. Renaissance humanists from Petrarch onward excelled in composing lengthy treatises on the subject of fortune, her power over human affairs, and the tools, or remedies, that enable man to resist and oppose her capricious tyranny.[16] The general solution to the problem envisaged by the tradition that went back to the late Roman philosopher Boethius's *Consolation of Philosophy* consisted of the exercise of virtue (*virtus* or *virtù*), understood as a form of mental firmness and an unyielding commitment to the good.[17] According to Petrarch, there exist two paths of virtue by means of which man can oppose fortune: the active life (*vita activa*), which allows one to combat and to master her through strong and steadfast action, and the contemplative life (*vita contemplativa*), which requires that one rise above the lowly world of transient and uncertain things ("the goods of Fortune") and turn towards the unchanging, eternal realm and the unity experienced in God.[18] Later generations of humanists elaborated on these two positions – the active and the contemplative mode – and continued, almost without exception,

[16] See Skinner, *The Foundations*, 1, pp. 95–98.

[17] On Boethius's view on fortune and virtue, see Pocock, *The Machiavellian Moment*, pp. 36–43.

[18] The active aspect of Petrarch's thought is strongly emphasized by Quentin Skinner, see *The Foundations*, 1, pp. 92–94. Skinner's position has received criticism from Wayne Newell, who argues that in Petrarch the contemplative side dominates, see Newell, "How Original is Machiavelli?" For a catalogue of Petrarch's various statements on virtue and fortune, see Klaus Heitmann, *Fortuna und Virtus: Eine Studie zu Petrarcas Lebensweisheit* (Cologne: Istituto italiano di cultura, 1958). Heitmann's reading, which stresses the inconsistencies in Petrarch's treatment of the subject, has been opposed by Jerrold Siegel, who claims that Petrarch throughout his work enacted a classical Ciceronian debate between the Stoic and the Peripatetic positions, see Jerrold E. Siegel, *Rhetoric and Philosophy in Renaissance Humanism: The Union of Eloquence and Wisdom, Petrarch to Valla* (Princeton: Princeton University Press, 1968), pp. 31–62.

to define virtue as a stable and constant disposition, through which internal peace and serenity could be achieved, and an orderly and prosperous society created and maintained.

Machiavelli addresses the question of fortune for the first time in a letter to Giovan Battista Soderini of September 1506, the so-called *Ghiribizzi*, where he discusses the fact that contrary policies often produce the same result, while identical modes of proceeding often lead to radically different outcomes. He was to return to this issue on several occasions later in his work, most extensively in *The Prince* 25, book III of the *Discourses* and in his tercets on Occasion and Fortune. As we shall see, the solution to the problem of fortune and sublunar change he offers in these writings differs radically from those of his predecessors.

Machiavelli's views about human nature and sublunar reality are predicated on four basic assumptions, which he establishes repeatedly and with a clarity and a precision that can best be described as geometrical, or architectonic. First, he holds, like most classical writers before him, that the human character is constant. Since the nature (*natura*) of an individual is given once and for all, the person in question cannot change his nature (*mutare natura*), only develop its potential.[19] Second, according to Machiavelli, human beings fall within two contrary categories, each characterized by a specific quality and a specific mode of proceeding. In *The Prince* 25, he thus claims that men "proceed in different ways" to their common aim, glory, and riches: "one with caution, the other with impetuosity; one by violence, the other with art; one with patience, the other with its opposite."[20] Later in the chapter, he brings these two groups of qualities together under the contrasting categories of caution and impetuosity.[21] On the basis of this dichotomy, and his equally common distinction between "humane" and "cruel" modes, Machiavelli couples various rulers and captains in binary pairs: Scipio and Hannibal, Valerius Corvinus and Manlius Torquatus, Numa and Romulus, Piero Soderini and Julius II, Fabius Maximus and Scipio Africanus.[22] Third, Machiavelli assumes that neither of these two sets of qualities is good or bad in itself. Depending on how well they accord

[19] For Machiavelli's view of human nature, see Giulio Ferroni, "'Natura', 'qualità' e apparenza nella figura del politico," in *Il ritratto e la memoria: Materiali* III, eds. Augusto Gentili, Philippe Morel, and Claudia Cieri Via (Rome: Bulzoni, 1994), pp. 83–90; Cary J. Nederman, "Machiavelli and Moral Character: Principality, Republic and the Psychology of *Virtù*," *History of Political Thought* 21 (2000): 349–64.

[20] See note 31 below.

[21] Cf. Harvey C. Mansfield, Jr., "Introduction," in *The Prince*, p. xxiii.

[22] As the list suggests, the status of Scipio Africanus in Machiavelli's work is complex. In comparison with Hannibal, he is seen as an example of humanity and mercy, whereas in contrast to the cautious Fabius he represents impetuosity. See *Lettere*, pp. 136 and 138; *Il principe* 17, p. 164; *Discorsi* III.9 and III.21.

with the circumstances, they will bring either success and prosperity, or failure and ruin. This explains, for example, the neutral position he takes in the *Ghiribizzi* on the classical *disputa* between the humane Scipio and the cruel Hannibal. Fourth, Machiavelli presumes that human affairs are in a state of constant flux, and he defines the changing circumstances that influence the outcome of human enterprises by the term "the times" (*i tempi*). This concept, which has strong cosmological, if not astrological, implications, is in Machiavelli's thought intimately related to fortune (*fortuna*), and he often refers to it in connection to the human qualities, as in his frequently used phrase "the qualities of the times" (*le qualità de' tempi*).[23] To sum up, Machiavelli holds that the times are shifting according to a mysterious and impenetrable cosmic law in such a way that each temporal segment, defined as *tempo*, displays, or favors, a specific quality, analogous to the contrasting human dispositions commented on above. Consequently, in his view, periods congenial to impetuous or cruel action come to alternate cyclically with periods suited to a cautious or humane mode of proceeding.

Machiavelli's controversial position on sublunar reality, fortune, and human nature has far-reaching consequences for his cosmology, his ethics, and his ideological commitments. But before we can begin to pursue these questions in more depth, we need to take a closer look at *The Prince* 25.

In this chapter, Machiavelli takes us on a descent in four stages from the exalted heights of Renaissance cosmology towards the political *here and now*. In the opening, he addresses the widespread view that the sublunar world (*le cose del mondo*) is controlled "by fortune and by God" to such an extent that human prudence and human effort have no say in its governance. He takes issue with the defeatist attitude that contends that one should not worry too much about such things, but "let them be governed by chance (*sorte*),"[24] arguing that its current vogue in large part can be attributed to the contemporary state of worldly affairs: "This opinion has been more strongly held in our own times because of the great changes in affairs (*le variazione grande delle cose*) which have been seen and may still be seen, every day, beyond all human conjecture (*fuori di ogni umana coniettura*)."[25] At this point the argument enters its second stage, as Machiavelli goes on to

[23] On the astrological implications of the concept *tempi*, see Parel, *The Machiavellian Cosmos*, pp. 138 and 158.

[24] *Il principe* 25, p. 186: "E' non mi è incognito come molti hanno avuto e hanno opinione che le cose del mondo sieno in modo governate, da la fortuna e da Dio, che li uomini con la prudenza loro non possino correggerle, anzi non vi abbino remedio alcuno; e per questo, potrebbono iudicare che non fussi da insudare molto nelle cose, ma lasciarsi governare alla sorte."

[25] Ibid.: "Questa opinione è suta piú creduta ne' nostri tempi per le variazione grande delle cose che si sono viste e veggonsi ogni dí, fuora di ogni umana coniettura."

demarcate an area within which human agency and intentionality may still be viewed as viable notions: "Nevertheless, so as not to extinguish our free will, I judge it to be true that fortune is the arbiter of half of our actions, but that she leaves us to control the other half, or close to it."[26] As a consequence of this move, the categories that initially had shared the governance of the world – fortune and God – are transformed into an opposition between fortune and human free will, with human agency taking the place of divine providence.

The descent towards the human and the graspable reaches its third stage as Machiavelli brings up another humanist commonplace: the power of fortune represented by a raging river. Fortune, he claims, is like "one of these devastating rivers that, when they become enraged, flood the plains, destroy trees and buildings, move earth from one place and deposit it in another; everyone flees before them, everyone yields to their thrust without being able to hinder them in any way." Although such rivers are potent and potentially dangerous, they are not beyond human control. For if men are foresighted, Machiavelli argues, they can "when times are quiet . . . take precautions with dykes and dams so that when the river rises next time either the waters will be channeled off or its thrust will not be either so unrestrained or so damaging." The same applies to fortune, since she "shows her power where there is no organized virtue (*ordinata virtú*) to resist her, and therefore strikes in the places where she knows that no dykes or dams have been built to contain her."[27] This argument by metaphor has the effect not only of concretizing and visualizing the cosmological agent and the philosophical concept of fortune, but also of bringing her, and the forces she represents, closer to man. Arguably, it is easier to make provisions against a river, even a river as unpredictable as the flood-prone Arno, than to master an evasive cosmological and philosophical concept

[26] Ibid., pp. 186–87: "A che pensando io qualche volta, mi sono in qualche parte inclinato nella opinione loro. Nondimanco, perché il nostro libero arbitrio non sia spento, iudico potere essere vero che la fortuna sia arbitra della metà delle azioni nostre, ma che etiam lei ne lasci governare l'altra metà, o presso, a noi." Cf. Paul Oskar Kristeller, *Renaissance Concepts of Man and Other Essays* (New York: Harper and Row, 1972), pp. 1–21; Charles E. Trinkaus, Jr., "Valla: Introduction," in *The Renaissance Philosophy of Man*, eds. E. Cassirer, P. O. Kristeller, and J. H. Randall, Jr. (Chicago: University of Chicago Press, 1948), pp. 147–54.

[27] *Il principe* 25, p. 187: "E assomiglio quella a uno di questi fiumi rovinosi che, quando si adirano, allagano e' piani, rovinano li arbori e li edifizi, lievano da questa parte terreno, pongono da quella altra: ciascuno fugge loro dinanzi, ognuno cede all'impeto loro sanza potervi in alcuna parte ostare. E, benché sieno cosí fatti, non resta però che gli uomini, quando sono tempi queti, non vi potessino fare provedimento e con ripari e con argini: in modo che, crescendo poi, o eglino andrebbono per uno canale o l'impeto loro non sarebbe né si dannoso né sí licenzioso. Similmente interviene della fortuna, la quale dimostra la sua potenza dove non è ordinata virtú a resisterle: e quivi volta e' sua impeti, dove la sa che non sono fatti gli argini né e' ripari a tenerla."

like fortune. This is also to say that the human agent, following fortune's metaphorical transformation into a river, has come to acquire a greater say in worldly affairs than it previously enjoyed. At this point of the argument, the opposing categories are no longer fortune and human free will, but the river and human, or manly, virtue.

But the raging river is not the end point of Machiavelli's rhetorical descent towards the concrete, the contemporary, and the local. As the downward movement reaches its fourth stage, the river is, in its turn, metamorphosed into the foreign armies that from 1494 had been invading – or flooding – Italy: "And if you consider Italy, which is the seat of these changes, and which has set them in motion, you will see an open country without embankments or defenses. If it had been protected by proper virtue (*conveniente virtú*), like Germany, Spain, and France, this flood would not have caused such great changes or it would not have come at all."[28] This brings us back to Machiavelli's suggestion at the beginning of the chapter that the fatalistic opinion of the many, who hold that our lives are goverened "by God and by fortune," should be seen as an expression of the current sense of hopelessness and impotence. The argument has now gone full circle. By turning the river into the foreign troops overrunning Italy, the former Secretary not only inverts the traditional representation of the military invasion as a flooding river, but also reduces the abstract and metaphorical entities that allegedly determine our lives – that is, God, fortune, and the river – to their concrete and underlying reality, the invading foreign armies. As a consequence, we are back at the starting point, facing the original problem of how to overcome the defeatist attitude found among many of Machiavelli's contemporaries.

Machiavelli has in the course of his argument, in a studied and extremely effective way, shifted the opposing categories governing sublunar reality according to the following scheme:

fortune	God
fortune	free will
river	virtue
foreign invasions	Italian virtue

To signal that the descent from abstract universals and cosmological speculation to the political *here and now* has been completed, Machiavelli at this stage inserts a marker in the text: "And this I consider enough to say

[28] Ibid.: "E se voi considerrete la Italia, che è la sedia di queste variazioni e quella che ha dato loro il moto, vedrete essere una campagna sanza argini e sanza alcuno riparo: che, s'ella fussi riparata da conveniente virtú, come è la Magna, la Spagna e la Francia, o questa piena non arebbe fatto le variazioni grande che la ha, o la non ci sarebbe venuta."

about opposing fortune in general (*in universali*)." From here on, a different form of discourse will evolve: "But, limiting myself more to particulars (*a' particulari*), I say that . . ."[29] Machiavelli now turns to consider the question we addressed at the beginning of this section: to what extent do the success and the failure of a ruler depend on his nature (*natura*) or the qualities of the times (*le qualità de' tempi*)? Prosperous princes, the former Secretary claims, have often been seen to come to ruin without their natures or their personal qualities having undergone any noticeable change. On the basis of this observation, he concludes that "the prince who relies entirely upon fortune comes to ruin as it varies," and that "he will be prosperous who adapts his mode of proceeding to the qualities of the times."[30] At this point, two questions force themselves upon us: first, what can a ruler rely on, or literally, "lean on" (*si appoggia*), other than fortune; and second, how should a prince conduct himself in order to make "his mode of proceeding" harmonize with "the qualities of the times"? The traditional answer to the first question would be that he should "lean on" his virtue, but as we shall see, this is not the solution that Machiavelli's text offers.

Up to this point, Machiavelli has been adopting a theoretical and generalizing approach to the modes and the qualities of the times. But as we begin to descend from the level of abstract principles to the concrete political *here and now*, his prose starts to take on a swerving, almost dancing rhythm, mimicking the change of qualities caused by, or accompanying, the shifting times:

> For one sees that men, in the things which lead to the end that everyone seeks, that is, glories and riches, proceed in different ways: *one with caution, the other with impetuosity; one by violence, the other with art; one with patience, the other with its opposite* – and with these different modes each can succeed in reaching it. One also sees two cautious men, *one attaining his goal, the other not*; and similarly, two men equally succeed with two different methods, *one being cautious, the other impetuous*. This arises from nothing other than the quality of the times that either conform with, or do not conform with, their way of proceeding. From this follows what I have said, that two men, acting differently, may bring about the same effect; and of two men acting identically, *one may reach his end, the other not*. [italics added][31]

[29] Ibid.: "E questo voglio basti aver detto, quanto allo opporsi alla fortuna, in universali. [New paragraph]. Ma ristringendomi piú a' particulari, dico come . . ." For a different interpretation of this transitional sentence, see Anthony J. Parel, "Ptolemy as a Source of *The Prince* 25," *History of Political Thought* 14 (1993): 77–83.

[30] *Il principe* 25: "che si appoggia tutto in su la fortuna, rovina come quella varia. Credo ancora che sia felice quello che riscontra il modo del procedere suo con la qualità de' tempi: e similmente sia infelice quello che con il procedere suo si discordano e' tempi."

[31] Ibid., pp. 187–88: "Perché si vede gli uomini, nelle cose che gli conducono al fine quale ciascuno ha innanzi, cioè gloria e ricchezze, procedervi variamente: l'uno con rispetto, l'altro con impeto;

In this spectacular piece of writing, the repetitive use of the formula *one . . . the other*, *l'uno . . . l'altro*, seems designed to conjure up the incessant and rhythmical changes of sublunar reality. As the text makes us experience, in this lowly realm contrary qualities and the corresponding times follow up on each other in a constant, oscillating flux.

Theoretically speaking, the only way the individual can avoid being subdued by these never-ending variations, as Machiavelli will acknowledge later in the chapter, is to "change his nature with the times and with the affairs" (*si mutassi di natura con li tempi e con le cose*). If one were to attain such flexibility, one would also be able to enjoy a lasting good fortune.[32] But when Machiavelli back in 1506 brought up this hypothetical solution in the *Ghiribizzi*, he came to the conclusion that this kind of flexibility is not within the range of human possibility. Individual man, he then argued, can neither transcend nor appropriate sublunar cyclicity:

> And, truly, anyone so wise as to understand the times and the order of things and be able to accommodate himself to them would always have good fortune, or at least he would avoid the bad, and then it would become true that the wise man can command the stars and the fates. *But since such wise men cannot be found*, men being both shortsighted and unable to command their natures, it follows that fortune changes and commands men and keeps them under her yoke. [italics added][33]

Here, man's incapacity to govern his own nature and to foresee the changes ahead stands in the way of his mastery of fortune. External and internal forces, cosmology and psychology, stars and passions, what lies above and below politics, exert an insurmountable pressure on the individual and prevent him from exercising full control over his destiny.[34]

When Machiavelli readdresses the wise man solution in *The Prince* 25, he adduces two principal reasons why men cannot adapt themselves to the

l'uno per violenzia, l'altro con arte; l'uno con pazienzia, l'altro col suo contrario; e ciascuno con questi diversi modi vi può pervenire. E vedesi ancora dua respettivi, l'uno pervenire al suo disegno, l'altro no; e similmente dua equalmente felicitare con diversi studi, sendo l'uno rispettivo e l'altro impetuoso: il che non nasce da altro, se non da la qualità de' tempi che si conformano, o no, col procedere loro. Di qui nasce quello ho detto: che dua, diversamente operando, sortiscano el medesimo effetto, e dua equalmente operando, l'uno si conduce al suo fine e l'altro no."

32 Ibid., p. 188: "se si mutassi natura con e' tempi e con le cose, non si muterebbe fortuna."

33 *Lettere*, pp. 137–38: "E veramente chi fussi tanto savio, che conoscessi e' tempi e l'ordine delle cose et accomodassisi a quelle, arebbe sempre buona fortuna o e' si guarderebbe sempre da la trista, e verrebbe ad essere vero che 'l savio comandassi alle stelle et a' fati. Ma perché di questi savi non si truova, avendo li uomini prima la vista corta e non potendo poi comandare alla natura loro, ne segue che la fortuna varia e comanda a li uomini, e tiegli sotto el giogo suo." The translation is based on *The Portable Machiavelli*, eds. Peter Bondanella and Mark Musa (London: Viking Penguin, 1979), p. 64.

34 This aspect of Machiavelli's thought is well discussed in Parel, "The Question of Machiavelli's Modernity."

changing times: the power of habit and natural inclination: "Nor is there to be found a man so prudent that he knows how to accommodate himself to this, both because he cannot deviate from what nature inclines him to, and also because, having always prospered by acting in one way, he cannot be persuaded to depart from it."[35] Thus, Machiavelli in the *Ghiribizzi* as well as *The Prince* 25 claims that no one can be judged wise enough to be able completely to adapt himself to the changing circumstances. If such an individual were to exist, he argues, his virtue would not consist in a mental firmness or constancy, as the humanists had traditionally argued, but in an unlimited flexibility and capacity to imitate fortune. If the wise man solution were to work, the quality designed to provide stability – virtue – would have to fashion itself into its very opposite – fortune. But to look for this kind of virtue in an individual human being, Machiavelli's argument implies, would be contrary to the limitations that human nature and sublunar reality impose on men.[36] It would be tantamount to trying to square the circle, or, as Montaigne later was to put it: "it is folly to expect that fortune ever will arm us sufficiently against herself."[37]

SUBLUNAR WRITING

So far in *The Prince* 25, Machiavelli has been a model of lucidity. From a privileged vantage point outside the flux of time, he has, by depicting sublunar change as a closed self-balancing system, let us witness the workings of Fortune's wheel from the outside, or from above. This detached position, it could be argued, is equivalent to that of the Stoic sage whose very existence Machiavelli now has come to dispute. Following the rejection of

[35] *Il principe* 25, p. 188: "Né si truova uomo sí prudente che si sappia accomodare a questo: sí perché non si può deviare da quello a che la natura lo inclina, sí etiam perché, avendo sempre uno prosperato camminando per una via, non si può persuadere che sia bene partirsi da quella. E però l'uomo respettivo, quando e' gli è tempo di venire allo impeto, non lo sa fare: donde e' rovina."

[36] In *Il principe* 7 (pp. 138–39), Machiavelli describes Cesare Borgia in terms that seem to imply that it would be possible for an individual to combine the contrary qualities. Cesare is here said to know how to "vincere o per forza o per fraude; farsi amare e temere da' populi, seguire e reverire da' soldati" and to be "severo e grato, magnanimo e liberale." However, to judge from Machiavelli's subsequent argument, which includes his accusation against the duke for having allowed the election of Julius II to the Holy See, it is reasonable to assume that this idealized portrait is a rhetorical construct, rather than a description of the duke's true character. One of Machiavelli's main points in *Il principe* 7, it would seem, is to demonstrate that politics is an *ars* and not a *scientia*, and that therefore there can be no guarantee that political perfection will lead to political success. In this regard, the art of politics resembles the art of rhetoric as defined by Aristotle and Quintilian.

[37] Michel de Montaigne, *Oeuvres complètes*, ed. A. Thibaudet and M. Rat (Paris: Gallimard, 1962), p. 66: "Et est follie de s'attendre que fortune elle mesmes nous arme jamais suffisamment contre soy."

the wise man solution, his argument begins to grow increasingly obscure. This new mode of discourse opens with a conclusion: "And therefore the cautious man, when it is time to act impetuously, does not know how to do it, hence he is ruined: for if he would change his nature with the times and with affairs, his fortune would not change."[38] On the face of it, this comment may appear as a mere restatement of the principles established earlier in the chapter, but with *The Prince* 19 and its strategy of introducing new important elements under the cloak of repeating earlier statements in fresh memory, we are well advised to be on our guard. Upon closer examination, we also find that Machiavelli here, by treating one mode of proceeding – the cautious way – in isolation from its opposite, is stating only one side of the case against the wise man solution. In other words, while he argues that a cautious man will be unable to adapt his way of proceeding when the time for impetuosity comes, he strangely leaves out discussing the impetuous man. This omission is even more peculiar when one considers Machiavelli's normal routine of treating the contrary modes with impartiality and in conjunction. In the *Ghiribizzi, The Prince* 17, and previously here in chapter 25, he had taken great care to present the contrary modes symmetrically, either in general statements comprising them both, or in rhetorical constructions based on the formula *one . . . the other, l'uno . . . l'altro*.[39] While he there left us in no doubt as to the equal standing of the two qualities, his incomplete and asymmetrical treatment of them in the quoted passage forces us to wonder whether his conclusion applies evenly to both, as the premises of his argument have led us to believe. For is it not just as true that the impetuous man will come to ruin when a time requiring a cautious mode of proceeding arrives?

Possibly, the problem will be resolved when Machiavelli now turns to consider the impetuous ways of Julius II, who already in the *Ghiribizzi* had served as an example of the audacious and impulsive ruler. We are initially told that Julius "acted impetuously in all his affairs," and that he "found the times and circumstances conform so well with his mode of proceeding that he always met with success."[40] On this general statement, there follows

[38] *Il principe* 25, p. 188: "E però l'uomo respettivo, quando e' gli è tempo di venire allo impeto, non lo sa fare: donde e' rovina; che se si mutassi natura con e' tempi e con le cose, non si muterebbe fortuna."

[39] In the *Ghiribizzi*, the example of Julius follows on a series of contrasting examples of the arming and the disarming of the people, the building and the destroying of fortresses, the favoring and the disfavoring of the subjects. Even if Julius on this occasion is without a named counterpart, he is here contrasted with "many men." See *Lettere*, p. 137: "A molti, misurando e ponderando ogni cosa, riescono e disegni suoi. Questo papa, che non ha né stadera né canna in casa, a caso conseguita, e disarmato, quello che con l'ordine e con l'armi difficilmente li doveva riuscire."

[40] *Il principe* 25, p. 188: "Papa Iulio II procedé in ogni sua azione impetuosamente, e trovò tanto e' tempi e le cose conforme a quello suo modo di procedere che sempre sortí felice fine."

a detailed account of Julius's policy towards Bologna and the reactions of the other major powers to his various initiatives, which allowed him to accomplish "what no other pontiff . . . would ever have achieved."[41] At this point of the argument, however, Machiavelli appears to have become so captivated by Julius's impetuous maneuvers that he has completely forgotten whatever his example was intended to show or illustrate. Just like the Pope's political moves, which "made Spain and the Venetians stand still in suspense (*fece stare sospesi e fermi*),"[42] Machiavelli's lengthy account of them keeps us on tenterhooks as to whether Julius's mode of action represents a valid alternative to the savant and to the cautious man. Could it be that the Florentine here is beginning to question the general principles set forth earlier in the chapter? Julius's repeated and continuous success seems to suggest that princes, and men in general, by opting for the impetuous mode, can escape the constraints to which the cautious man is said to be subject.

But we are saved from this delusion, as Machiavelli at the end of his description of Julius's actions inserts a reminder about the general limitations that condition sublunar existence. If Julius had lived long enough to experience a change of times, we are told, he would have come to ruin as well, since nothing could have induced him to deviate from "those modes to which his nature inclined him."[43] After having made this observation, Machiavelli repeats, almost word for word, the general principle established earlier in the chapter: "I conclude, then, that since fortune varies and men remain fixed in their modes, they are successful when the two are in harmony, and unsuccessful when they are not in accord."[44]

If Machiavelli's intention had been to write a general treatise on the principles of statecraft, this theoretical and detached comment would have offered an appropriate conclusion to his discussion on fortune. But for some reason, at this point, he, inadvertently and with unexpected audacity, chooses to abandon his cautious and impartial way, and to side with impetuosity:

> I would certainly judge that it is better to be impetuous than cautious, because fortune is a woman; and it is necessary, if one wants to keep her down, to beat her and pound her. And one sees that she more often allows herself to be won by the

41 Ibid.: "Condusse adunque Iulio con la sua mossa impetuosa quello che mai altro pontefice, con tutta la umana prudenza, arebbe condotto."

42 Ibid.: "La qual mossa fece stare sospesi e fermi Spagna e viniziani."

43 Ibid., p. 189: "se fussino sopravvenuti tempi che fussi bisognato procedere con respetti, ne seguiva la sua rovina: né mai arebbe deviato da quegli modi alli quali la natura lo inclinava."

44 Ibid.: "Concludo adunque che, variando la fortuna e' tempi e stando li uomini ne' loro modi ostinati, sono felici mentre concordando insieme e, come e' discordano, infelice."

impetuous than by those who go to work more coldly. And so, being a woman, she is always the friend of the young, because they are less cautious, more ferocious, and command her with more audacity.[45]

How can Machiavelli possibly arrive at this conclusion? If we confront it with the premises set forth previously in the chapter, we find that it is questionable on several counts. First, it is made in complete disregard of the changing times, which Machiavelli throughout his argument endows with the power to determine which of the two qualties – impetuosity or caution – will reap success and failure, respectively. Second, as a consequence hereof, it comes to defy the fundamental impartiality towards caution and impetuosity that underlies Machiavelli's whole discussion. Third, as a piece of advice, it is utterly nonsensical, since it only applies to the impetuous man, who can be expected to act impetuously in any case, bound as he is to follow his natural inclination.

How then are we to understand Machiavelli's categorial statement that "it is better to be impetuous than cautious"? The many manifest discrepancies of *The Prince* 25 have induced scholars to argue that the work here enters an epistemological crisis. In a perceptive analysis of *The Prince*, Gennaro Sasso seeks to explain the contradictory end of chapter 25 in terms of an interrupted dialectic between the quest for intelligibility and the will to action characterizing the work as a whole. Although Machiavelli was well aware that the impetuous mode did not count for more than its cautious counterpart, his desire to inspire to action came in the end to take precedence over his ambition to create a meaningful and logically coherent text. According to Sasso, this choice was determined, at least in part, by Machiavelli's own personal and passionate preference for the active and impetuous approach. Dissatisfied with this improvised conclusion, Sasso goes on to argue, Machiavelli added a second ending at a later date in the form of the exhortative chapter 26, where the dramatic tension and the conceptual difficulties of the preceding chapter are resolved, or subsumed, under the all-embracing logic of divine providence.[46] Thomas Greene explores the chapter from a similar perspective, and comes to the conclusion that the epistemological failure of *The Prince* 25 constitutes the definitive breakdown of Machiavelli's intellectual project, the original aim

[45] Ibid.: "Io iudico bene questo, che sia meglio essere impetuoso che respettivo: perché la fortuna è donna ed è necessario, volendola tenere sotto, batterla e urtarla. E si vede che la si lascia piú vincere da questi, che da quegli che freddamente procedono: e però sempre, come donna, è amica de' giovani, perché sono meno respettivi, piú feroci e con piú audacia la comandano."

[46] Gennaro Sasso, *Niccolò Machiavelli: Storia del suo pensiero politico* (Naples L'Istituto italiano per gli studi storici, 1958), pp. 438–42.

of which had been to provide a reliable manual on princely government. Machiavelli's capitulation becomes manifest in the final chapter, where he abandons rational argumentation and cries out for a mythical savior, whose extraordinary qualities and redemptive virtue will bring future salvation to Italy.[47] John Najemy similarly argues that Machiavelli in chapter 25 fails to come up with an answer to the riddle of fortune and *variazione*, and that his argument offers an "unintended demonstration" of his inability to render politics intelligible. After having in vain tried out a series of hypothetical solutions to the problem of the changing times, Machiavelli embraces in the final chapter a redemptive form of princely virtue, which resolves the dilemma, but only "at a specific and recognizable moment of the historical project," associated with the decline of one's country into "apparent hopelessness and complete degradation."[48]

The observations Sasso, Greene, and Najemy make about the contradictory nature of *The Prince* 25 are undoubtedly of great importance and warrant the closest attention. But while there can be no denying that chapter 25 is riddled with inconsistencies and anomalies, the claim that these contradictions were unintended by the author, or should be seen to indicate an intellectual failure on his part, remains to be proved. Since the current study has revealed numerous occasions on which Machiavelli, writing for effect rather than for comphrehension, employs logical inconsistencies and discrepancies to achieve various rhetorical purposes, it would be rash to equate the manifest failure of his princely discourse with the failure of Machiavelli, the political analyst, without first having explored other options. As I hope to show, *The Prince* 25 is indeed open to a radically different reading, and there is, contradictions notwithstanding, an internal logic at work in the chapter, albeit not the one that we conventionally have come to expect from political or analytical texts.

To recapitulate what has emerged so far, Machiavelli at the beginning of chapter 25 adopts a theoretical and uncommitted point of view, treating the contrasting qualities of caution and impetuosity with impartiality. The

47 See Thomas M. Greene, "The End of Discourse in Machiavelli's *Prince*," in *Literary Theory/Renaissance Texts*, eds. P. Parker and D. Quint (Baltimore: The Johns Hopkins University Press, 1986), pp. 68–77.

48 John M. Najemy, *Between Friends: Discourses of Power and Desire in the Machiavelli–Vettori Letters of 1513–1515* (Princeton: Princeton University Press, 1993), pp. 209 and 207. For similar readings, see Andrew Mousely, "*The Prince* and Textual Politics," in *Niccolò Machiavelli's* THE PRINCE: *New Interdisciplinary Essays*, ed. M. Coyle (Manchester: Manchester University Press, 1995), pp. 161–71; Albert Russell Ascoli "Machiavelli's Gift of Counsel" in *Machiavelli and the Discourse of Literature*, eds. A. R. Ascoli and V. Kahn (Ithaca, NY: Cornell University Press, 1993), pp. 242–45; Victoria Kahn, *Machiavellian Rhetoric: From the Counter-Reformation to Milton* (Princeton: Princeton University Press, 1994), pp. 40–41; Charles D. Tarlton, "'Azioni in modo l'una dall'altra': Action for Action's Sake in Machiavelli's *The Prince*," *History of European Ideas* 29 (2003): 123–40.

general principle that men's success depends on how well their natures accord with the changing times, we learn, applies equally to both qualities. This view is endorsed as Machiavelli represents the oscillation between extremes and the non-simultaneity characterizing sublunar reality through the repetitive use of the formula *one . . . the other*. Men proceed in different ways and achieve their ends when their modes harmonize with the times – "*one with caution, the other with impetuosity; one by violence, the other with art; one with patience, the other with its opposite*." In this passage, written in elegant, rhythmic prose, the qualities of the times follow on each other, one after the other, but are still presented together and in a symmetrical fashion. Up to this point, Machiavelli can be said to have described the human conditions and the workings of fortune from a detached position outside, or above, sublunar flux.

However, at this juncture, an important shift occurs in the text, as Machiavelli begins to introduce us to sublunar writing, a literary practice perhaps unique to him. Leaving symmetry behind, he lets sublunar oscillation serve as the structuring principle for his argument, as he now starts to present the two qualities, and the two modes, in sequence instead of together. Contrary to his standard practice, he first states the case against the cautious man in isolation from his opposite, the impetuous man. As a consequence, we are left wondering whether the latter quality might be exempt from the restricting conditions formulated earlier in the chapter. The mystery thickens, as Machiavelli goes on to digress on the example of Pope Julius II, who by acting according to his impetuous nature succeeded in all his undertakings. For a brief moment, the impetuous mode appears to offer a solution to the problem. But when Machiavelli at the end of the lengthy digression bluntly observes that the reason why Julius never failed was because he died before encountering a change of times, it becomes clear that he has merely been playing with our expectations, perhaps with the intent of putting us through a test of judgment.[49]

As we have begun to see, the writing in the passages as the cautions man and Julius II mimics in an extremely effective way the succession of cautious and impetuous times on which it comments. To denote this mode of discourse, which seems to spring naturally from the conditions

[49] The idea of the text as a test of judgment is little explored in Machiavelli studies, but more thoroughly investigated in research on Montaigne. On this aspect of Montaigne's thought, see esp. David Lewis Schaefer, *The Political Philosophy of Montaigne* (Ithaca: Cornell University Press, 1990); Edwin M. Duval, "Lessons of the New World: Design and Meaning in Montaigne's 'Des Cannibales' (I:31) and 'Des coches' (III:6)," *Yale French Studies* 64 (1983): 95–112. For similar readings of Machiavelli, see John D. Lyons, *Exemplum: The Rhetoric of Example in Early Modern France and Italy* (Princeton: Princeton University Press, 1989), pp. 35–71; Kahn, *Machiavellian Rhetoric*, pp. 31–33 and *passim*.

characterizing sublunar existence, and which pretends loss of control and perspective, while in fact representing an extremely manipulative and self-conscious form of rhetoric, I propose that we use the term sublunar writing.[50]

Having reached the lowest and most concrete stratum of sublunar reality, the *here and now*, we find that the two contrary qualities, here conceptualized as caution and impetuosity, do not, and cannot, coexist. Although they follow upon each other incessantly, as Machiavelli's rhythmical prose, quoted above, suggests, they cannot be grasped or brought together in a single vision. When the time calling for impetuous action arrives, the period suited for the contrary mode of proceeding comes to an abrupt end. Henceforth, it will survive only in the recollection of a few men of learning, while for the large majority of people, who lack the ability to disengage themselves from the present and to contemplate sublunar existence from above, or from the outside, it will simply cease to exist. Sublunar writing, as practiced by Machiavelli, conveys what it means to experience the wheel of fortune and sublunar reality from within, without overview and without historical memory. To achieve this effect, Machiavelli presents the contrasting periods not simultaneously, but sequentially:

1 *Caution*: "And therefore the cautious man, when it is time to act impetuously, does not know how to do it, hence he is ruined . . ."
2 *Impetuosity*: "Pope Julius II acted impetuously in all his affairs . . . if times had come when he had needed to act with caution, his ruin would have followed . . ."

Following the juxtaposition of the cautious man and the impetuous Julius II, we seem to have returned to the starting point yet again, as Machiavelli for the umpteenth time hammers down the general truth about the incompatibility of men's inflexible natures and the constant mutability of the times. But in the course of the discussion, as we have seen, a new and radically different perspective on sublunar reality has emerged. This point of view, which, roughly speaking, corresponds to the perspective on fortune from below that we outlined at the outset of this chapter, Machiavelli has introduced in stages, or, as he himself might have said, little by little, or *poco a poco*. As he now is about to bring the chapter to closure, he repeats this move at a stroke, or *ad un tratto*.

[50] Sublunar writing, as defined here, can be understood in relation to the automatic writing of the surrealists. Whereas the surrealists sought to achieve spontaneity and concreteness by withdrawing the writing process from the control of consciousness, Machiavelli's aim in chapter 25, as well as on other occasions, is to create the impression of such a loss of control. Sublunar writing, as I define it here, is premised on, and requires, a cyclical framework, characterized by a never-ending oscillation between the two extremes.

1 *Perspective from above*: "I conclude, then, that since fortune varies and men remain fixed in their modes, they are successful when the two are in harmony, and unsuccessful when they are not in accord."
2 *Perspective from below*: "I would certainly judge that it is better to be impetuous than cautious, because fortune is a woman . . ."

Universal truth and partial advice directed at the *here and now* are in this passage juxtaposed in a singularly confusing way. But having uncovered the cosmological assumptions underlying Machiavelli's practice of sublunar writing, we can see that this seemingly contradictory textual maneuver is in fact extraordinarily well prepared and highly consistent with the intrinsic logic of the chapter. We can also see how well the Florentine's position in favor of impetuosity agrees with his general view of the political situation in and around Florence at the time he composed *The Prince*. Extremely critical of the Italian rulers' failure to exercise caution during the period preceding the French invasion, he castigates in chapters 24 and 25 "these princes of ours," who believed that the "quiet times" in which they were living never would come to an end, and therefore failed to take precautions against "the storm during the calm," and to build dykes against the coming flood.[51] With the alien invaders already in the country, Machiavelli now judges that the time for cautious and preventive action is over, and that the moment for impetuous deeds has arrived.[52]

However, the fact that Machiavelli, in giving concrete advice adapted to circumstance, merely is applying the general principles of the chapter to the immediate political context of *here and now*, does not explain why he states his preference for the impetuous mode in categorical terms. This one-sided conclusion is not only unwarranted, but, as we have seen, directly

[51] *Il principe* 24, p. 186: "questi nostri principi, e' quali erano stati molti anni nel loro principato, per averlo di poi perso, non accusino la fortuna, ma la ignavia loro perché, non avendo mai ne' tempi quieti pensato ch'e' possino mutarsi . . . il che è comune difetto degli uomini, non fare conto nella bonaccia della tempesta."

[52] That Machiavelli considered it necessary to adopt an impetuous and cruel mode of action at the time is also suggested by the view that he takes of Florentine and Italian affairs in the *Discorsi*. See especially his discussion in *Discorsi* III.9 of Piero Soderini and Julius II, the Medici family's immediate predecessors as heads of Florence and the Church respectively. According to Machiavelli (p. 449), Piero Soderini, after his election as Gonfalonier for life in Florence in 1502, proceeded "in tutte le cose sue con umanità e pazienza." As long as the times were in accordance with this mode of proceeding, he and his fatherland (*patria*) flourished, but when the times changed and "bisognava rompere la pazienza e la umiltà, non lo seppe fare; talché insieme con la sua patria rovinò." Soderini's cautious and humane mode is here contrasted to the impetuous and furious ways of Pope Julius II. Since the qualities of the times throughout Julius's reign (from 1503 to 1513) remained consonant with his impetuous ways, he enjoyed constant success and never suffered any reversals of fortune. On the basis of this evidence, we may conclude that Machiavelli, at the time he composed *Il principe*, viewed the political situation in the twin cities of Florence and Rome to be suited more to strong, impetuous, and ferocious action, than to a cautious and humane mode of proceeding.

contrary to the premises of his argument. As to why he chose to speak in this way, we may only speculate, but perhaps Machiavelli is here giving us a demonstration of how he thought that the political adviser, the truly wise man, should present his advice when addressing the *here and now* – with confidence, without undue reservations, and without bringing up other times and other contexts.

FABIUS AND SCIPIO

The argument on political action, human nature, and the qualities of the times in chapter 25 is an important key to Machiavelli's ideological position in *The Prince*. But to unpack its ideological implications, we need to consider it in the context of the related discussions in the *Ghiribizzi* and the *Discourses*.[53] In the *Ghiribizzi* of 1506, Machiavelli claims that a ruler or military commander who displays qualities contrary to the customary ways of the region will gain a great following there: "Cruelty, perfidy, and contempt for religion help to increase the reputation of a new ruler (*un dominatore nuovo*) in a province where humanity, faith, and religion have long abounded; in like manner, humanity, faith, and religion are efficacious where cruelty, perfidy, and contempt for religion have reigned for a time." Just like an excess of bitter or sweet things makes us develop a taste for the contrary flavor, Machiavelli argues, too much good and too much evil make men desire the opposite extreme. The cruel Hannibal enjoyed success in Italy, and the humane Scipio in Spain, not because they adapted to circumstances, but because their natures and "manners of proceeding" corresponded with "the times and the order of things." If they had changed places, neither of them would have been successful.[54]

As we have already seen, in the *Ghiribizzi* Machiavelli rejects the idea of the wise man, who, by accommodating himself to the changing times, would be able to enjoy permanent good fortune. However, it is intriguing to note that in connection to this letter he toyed with a different solution to

[53] Stephen M. Fallon, "Hunting the Fox: Equivocation and Authorial Duplicity in The Prince," *Publications of the Modern Language Association of America* 107 (1992): 1181–95, esp. 1189.

[54] *Lettere*, p. 138: "Giova a dare reputazione ad uno dominatore nuovo la crudeltà, perfidia et irreligione in quella provincia dove la umanità, fede e religione è lungo tempo abbundata, non altrimenti che si giovi la umanità, fede e religione dove la crudeltà, perfidia et irreligione è regnata un pezo; perché, come le cose amare perturbano el gusto e le dolci lo stucano, cosí li uomini infastidiscono del bene, e del male si dolgono. Queste cagioni, infra le altre, apersono Italia ad Annibale e Spagna a Scipione, e cosí ognuno riscontrò el tempo e le cose secondo l'ordine del procedere suo. Né in quel medesimo tempo arebbe fatto tanto profitto in Italia uno simile a Scipione, né uno simile ad Annibale in Spagna, quanto l'uno e l'altro fece nella provincia sua." It is important to realize that "to accord with" here should be understood as "to be contrary to."

the problem of the mutability of the times. In a marginal note of uncertain date, he implies that lost fortune can be recovered by a change in the mode of proceeding: "When fortune has been worn out, the individual, the family, and the city come to ruin; everyone has his fortune founded on his mode of proceeding, and each one of them wears out, and when fortune is worn out, one must regain her with another mode."[55] While this possibility is denied the individual, whose fixed nature prevents him from changing his mode of proceeding, it might still be open to families and cities that consist of men of different natures and dispositions.[56] In this marginalia, Machiavelli seems thus to suggest that a city, or a state, that has found a way of alternating between the modes of Hannibal and Scipio, between cruelty and humanity, may continue to enjoy a lasting good fortune.

Machiavelli develops these ideological ramifications further in *Discourses* III.9, entitled "How it is necessary to change with the times in order to always have good fortune." Posing the by now familiar question why contrary modes of proceeding often bring about the same result, and why similar ways frequently lead to different outcomes, he follows the line of argument developed in the *Ghiribizzi* and *The Prince* 25, but is now more explicit about its bearing on the constitutional question. While a principality will enjoy success only as long as the fixed nature of its prince accords with the times, he argues, a well-ordered republic can extend its good fortune by changing rulers according to circumstance. To demonstrate this point, Machiavelli brings up the example of the Roman republic's epochal triumph over Carthage in the Second Punic War. When Rome during the initial phases of the war suffered from the assault of Hannibal, it was able to bring forth the naturally cautious Fabius, who managed to withstand the attack by using a temporizing tactic, which later earned him the epithet the *Cunctator*, "il Temporeggiatore," or "the Delayer."

55 Ibid., p. 137n: "Come la fortuna si straca, cosí si ruina l'uomo, la famiglia, la città; ognuno ha la fortuna sua fondata sul modo del procedere suoi, e ciascuna di loro si straca e quando la è straca bisogna racquistarla con un altro modo."

56 The mentioning of the family in this context may suggest the influence from Leon Battista Alberti's *Della famiglia*. In this work, Alberti discusses the changing fortunes of families and states in a proto-cyclical manner, see Leon Battista Alberti, *I primi tre libri della famiglia* (Florence: Sansoni, 1946), pp. 1–17, esp. 14. On the subject of the family Machiavelli is relatively silent in the *Discorsi*, but in III.46 he claims that the fact that different families display different modes of proceeding, some being harder and others more effeminate, can be attributed only in part to inheritance, since intermarriages constantly supply new blood. Therefore, he concludes, education must be an important factor in the shaping of a family's character. In the *Discorsi* III.43 (p. 517), he makes a similar case about cities, arguing that different peoples exhibit different characteristics over time "secondo la forma della educazione."

Everyone knows that Fabius Maximus proceeded hesitantly and cautiously with his army, far from all impetuosity and from all Roman audacity, and good fortune made this mode of his match well with the times. For when Hannibal, young and with fresh fortune, had come into Italy and had already defeated the Roman people twice, and when that republic was almost deprived of its good military and was terrified, better fortune could not have come than to have a captain who held the enemy at bay with slowness and caution.[57]

At a later date, when the tides of the war turned to Rome's favor and victory was within her reach, the republic, against the advice of Fabius, placed the young and impetuous Scipio at the head of its armies. By unexpectedly bringing the war over to Africa, the latter succeeded in conclusively defeating the Carthaginians, thus ending the war in victory. Had it not been for the cautious Fabius, Machiavelli concludes, Rome would not have survived Hannibal's attack, but if Fabius had been king of Rome, "he could easily have lost that war; for he did not know how to vary his procedure as the times varied." But since Fabius lived in a republic, "where there were diverse citizens and diverse humors," his ways, being "the best in times proper for sustaining war," could be complemented, or substituted, by those of the impetuous Scipio, which were apt "in times suited for winning it."[58] In Machiavelli's eyes, these two stages of the Hannibalic war demonstrate in an exemplary manner how a well-ordered republic, like the ancient Roman one, by adapting itself to the varying times, can overcome the limitations of the principality, and attain power, longevity, and constant good fortune.[59]

How do Machiavelli's various accounts of the relation between human nature and changing circumstance in the *Ghiribizzi*, *The Prince*, and the *Discourses* fit together? One possibility to consider is that the Florentine's position underwent a development from its early articulation in the *Ghiribizzi* to the republican teaching of the *Discourses*, and that he first, after having written himself into a corner in *The Prince* 25, began to work

[57] *Discorsi* III.9, p. 449: "Ciascuno sa come Fabio Massimo procedeva con lo esercito suo rispettivamente e cautamente discosto da ogni impeto e da ogni audacia romana, e la buona fortuna fece che questo suo modo riscontrò bene con i tempi. Perché sendo venuto Annibale in Italia, giovane e con una fortuna fresca, ed avendo già rotto il popolo romano due volte, ed essendo quella republica priva quasi della sua buona milizia e sbigottita, non potette sortire migliore fortuna che avere uno capitano il quale con la sua tardità e cauzione tenessi a bada il nimico."

[58] Ibid.: "E se Fabio fusse stato re di Roma, poteva facilmente perdere quella guerra, perché non arebbe saputo variare col procedere suo secondo che variavono i tempi; ma essendo nato in una republica dove erano diversi cittadini e diversi umori, come la ebbe Fabio, che fu ottimo ne' tempi debiti a sostenere la guerra, cosí ebbe poi Scipione ne' tempi atti a vincerla."

[59] Cf. Fallon, "Hunting the Fox," pp. 1191–92; Nederman, "Machiavelli and Moral Character," pp. 361–63.

out the republican solution of *Discourses* III.9.[60] However, a more reasonable interpretation, given the elaborate and carefully planned discourse of chapter 25, would be to assume that this conclusion is already implicit in *The Prince*. It is only if the state founded by the new prince is transformed into a republic capable of changing with the times, Machiavelli insinuates, that it will be able to achieve continuous growth and lasting good fortune. But for reasons too obvious to elaborate, he here refrains from openly stating this conclusion. Leaving the inference unspoken, suspended in the air, for the analytical reader to work out, he resorts instead to a call to action, addressed to his princely reader.

If we adopt the latter interpretation, we will at this point witness a bifurcation of Machiavelli's readership occur, leaving us with the two different types of intended readers of *The Prince*. On the one hand, the princely reader, who here will be only too grateful to Machiavelli for ending his intellectual torment and for offering him an easy way out of his conceptual entanglement; on the other, the analytical reader, whose dual perspective on the text we have been tracing in our analysis of the chapter. Having seen Machiavelli's general teaching undergo a gradual adaption to the *here and now*, this reader will understand that the advice to adopt the impetuous approach at the end of the chapter can offer no more than a temporary solution to the dilemma facing the prince and his state. A humanist by training, well versed in Livy and Roman history, the analytical reader could also be expected to tease out the republican conclusion that Machiavelli has planted in the chapter, and which he later, writing under less constraint, will make explicit in the *Discourses*.[61] Hereby, we have also come up with an answer to the remaining question of what a prince might "lean on" other than his fortune. As the implicit teaching of the chapter suggests, he should lean on a republican constitution based on the principles of rotation in office and the mixed regime.

To conclude our discussion of *The Prince* 25, we have with Sasso, Greene, and Najemy argued that the solution Machiavelli offers to the dilemma of man's inflexible nature and the changing times at the end of the chapter is

[60] Najemy argues that Machiavelli "without being fully aware of what he was doing" wrote a series of "disruptions and contradictions" into chapter 25 that undermined his attempt at providing a solid foundation for princely government. According to Najemy, Machiavelli's conversion to republicanism took place under the influence of the criticism he received from Francesco Vettori, see Najemy, *Between Friends*, pp. 209n and 328–34. Kahn maintains that Machiavelli's view of republicanism as superior to monarchy "emerges out of a rhetorical and dialectical analysis of principalities." Even though it is not altogether clear whether this should be taken to mean that Machiavelli's analysis in *Il principe* led him to develop the republican position of the *Discorsi*, this seems to be the burden of Kahn's argument. See Kahn, *Machiavellian Rhetoric*, pp. 19 and 44.

[61] Cf. ibid., p. 40.

logically unsatisfactory. But where these critics discern only "an arbitrary choice" marking the failure of Machiavelli's "rationalist program" (Sasso), the impossibility of "any meaningful statement" following the implosion of "conceptual space" (Greene), or an "unintended demonstration" of the inability to impose meaningful rules of conduct and discursive categories "on a world reluctant to recognize [them]" (Najemy), we have uncovered a calculated and extremely refined discursive strategy of republican intent.[62] By bringing to light the sublunar and republican underpinnings of Machiavelli's advice, we have been able to conclude that the collapse of the princely discourse taking place in chapter 25 is an intended effect of Machiavelli's argument, and the logical end-point of his intellectual enterprise in *The Prince*.

MYSTERY RECOVERED

Machiavelli's argument in *The Prince* 25, which took us down from the lofty heights of cosmological speculation and timeless universals to the practical sphere of political action, where partial and one-sided choices often must be made, sets the scene for the exhortation to seize and liberate Italy in the final chapter, *The Prince* 26.[63] While the former chapter began on a fatalistic note, the latter opens in contrary fashion. In Italy, we are told, an enormous arena for achieving glory, honor, and greatness is awaiting a new prince capable of introducing novel classical orders in the peninsula: "Considering, then, all of the things discussed above, and thinking to myself about whether at the present time in Italy (*al presente in Italia*) it is propitious to honor a new prince, and whether there is matter that provides an opportunity for a prudent and virtuous man to introduce a form that would bring honor to him and good to the people of this community, it seems to me that so many things concur to favor a new prince that I never knew a time more appropriate."[64] In short, we are here about to enter the final stage of the

[62] Sasso, *Niccolò Machiavelli*, p. 439; Greene, "The End of Discourse," p. 74; Najemy, *Between Friends*, p. 209.

[63] On the relationship between chapters 25 and 26, see Hans Baron, "The *Principe* and the Puzzle of the Date of Chapter 26," *Journal of Medieval and Renaissance Studies* 21 (1991), p. 88. While Baron has a point when he claims that *Il principe* 26 cannot have been written after the French victory over the Swiss at Marignano in September 1515, his attempt to fix the date of its composition to early 1515 is less convincing. The argument presented here suggests that chapters 25 and 26, at least from a rhetorical or compositional point of view, belong together.

[64] *Il principe* 26, p. 189: "Considerato adunque tutte le cose di sopra discorse, e pensando meco medesimo se al presente in Italia correvano tempi da onorare uno nuovo principe, e se ci era materia che dessi occasione a uno prudente e virtuoso d'introdurvi forma che facessi onore a lui e bene alla università delli uomini di quella, mi pare concorrino tante cose in benefizio di uno principe nuovo, che io non so qual mai tempo fussi piú atto a questo."

rhetorical descent initiated in *The Prince* 25, with the definite shift of focus from a discourse on principles and generalities to one directed at the *here and now* being marked by the phrase, "at the present time in Italy" (*al presente in Italia*).

The Prince 26 is remarkable for several reasons. In this chapter most of the legitimatory devices discussed previously in this study – divine providence, the just war, liberty, and peace – return with unexpected force. The monumental undertaking the former Secretary announces in the chapter heading – the conquest and the liberation of Italy – is not only a source of honor, glory, greatness, and reputation for a new prince, we learn, but also divinely sanctioned and just.[65] The Medici, who are now being directly addressed for the first time since the dedicatory letter, are said to enjoy the favor of God and of the Church over which they currently rule, and their mission is described as a "redemption" (*redenzione*). How can this justificatory language be explained? The fact that several of the legitimizing principles adduced in the chapter are dependent upon a transcendental grounding outside, or above, sublunar flux makes the question of their reemergence all the more perplexing. If we thought that we had demonstrated that Machiavelli has no, or little, regard for such categories, and that his principal aim is to demystify political and military discourse, it now seems that we may have to reconsider our position.

While there is universal agreement that Machiavelli's ardent invocation of the divine and the *patria* in *The Prince* 26 conflicts with the cold pragmatism and the unembellished language of the rest of the work, critics disagree as to the nature and the function of Machiavelli's rhetoric in the final chapter. A time-honored reading claims that its call to liberate Italy is the true rationale of the whole work, the good purpose justifying the use of evil means advocated earlier in the work.[66] Other scholars, among them Sasso, Greene, and Najemy, see in the final chapter an attempt to cover up for the intellectual failure of chapter 25.[67] De Grazia believes that Machiavelli actually is serious when he speaks of God and his elect and claims that the chapter contains "significant metaphysical and theological statements."[68]

[65] Ibid.: "Exhortatio ad capessendam Italiam in libertatemque a barbaris vindicandam." Price, as well Bondanella and Musa, omit the part of the heading that indicates that Italy should be not only liberated but also seized. See *The Prince*, eds. Q. Skinner and R. Price, p. 87: "Exhortation to liberate Italy from the barbarian yoke"; and *The Portable Machiavelli*, eds. P. Bondanella and M. Musa, p. 162: "An Exhortation to liberate Italy from the Barbarians."

[66] For a survey of this literature, see Baron, "The *Principe* and the Puzzle," pp. 85–86.

[67] See Najemy, *Between Friends*, pp. 213–14; Sasso, *Niccolò Machiavelli*, pp. 438–42; Greene, "The End of Discourse."

[68] De Grazia, *Machiavelli in Hell*, pp. 58–70, 379, 385, and *passim*; quote from p. 31.

Zupan and Ascoli similarly argue that the Florentine here is allowing his "subterranean," or "hidden," identification with Savonarola to surface.[69] By contrast, Lefort discerns in *The Prince* 26 a move from a discourse on knowledge and meaning to one on political propaganda. According to him, Machiavelli, by dissimulating the role of the innocent prophet, is here presenting the Medici with the themes and the self-image they should project in order to win the hearts and the minds of their subjects.[70]

Before anything else is said, it is important to note that the ambiguous, or complex, way in which *The Prince* 26 is composed virtually invites such conflicting interpretations. A brief survey of how Machiavelli treats the justificatory devices of divine providence, the just war, and peace will bear this out. When first introduced, the Christian God is presented as a product of popular imagination, desires, and longings. In the past, we are told, there have appeared men in whom "some glimmer of light" has shone, and who seem to have been "ordained by God" for Italy's redemption. But they have all proved to be false redeemers, who "at the height of their careers" have been "rejected by fortune."[71] Still, the Italians continue to hope for a redemptive, divinely inspired intervention, and to yearn for their providentially destined savior: "Look how Italy now prays to God to send someone to redeem her from these barbarous cruelties and insolencies."[72] They now place their hopes in the Medici: "At the present, there is no one to be seen in whom she can place more hope than in your illustrious house, which with its fortune and virtue, favored by God and by the Church of which it is now prince, could make itself the head of this redemption."[73] The notorious slipperiness of this passage prevents us from determining whether Machiavelli here assumes the objective existence of God as the supreme authority upholding the Church, or continues to refer to the

[69] See Patricia Zupan, "Machiavelli and Savonarola Revisited: The Closing Chapter of *Il Principe*," *Machiavelli Studies* 1 (1987): 43–64; quotation from p. 45. Cf. Ascoli, "Machiavelli's Gift of Counsel," p. 256; Timothy Hampton, *Writing from History: The Rhetoric of Exemplarity in Renaissance Literature* (Ithaca: Cornell University Press, 1990), p. 74. On Savonarola as the chief source of inspiration behind *Il principe*, see also J. H. Whitfield, *Discourses on Machiavelli* (Cambridge: W. Heffer, 1969), pp. 87–110.

[70] Claude Lefort, *Le travail de l'œuvre Machiavel* (Paris: Gallimard, 1972), pp. 447–49.

[71] *Il principe* 26, p. 190: "E benché insino a qui si sia mostro qualche spiraculo in qualcuno, da potere iudicare ch'e' fussi ordinato da Dio per sua redenzione, tamen si è visto come di poi, nel piú alto corso delle azioni sua, è stato da la fortuna rebrobato."

[72] Ibid.: "Vedesi come la priega Iddio che li mandi qualcuno che la redima da queste crudeltà e insolenzie barbare."

[73] Ibid.: "Né ci si vede al presente in quale lei possa piú sperare che nella illustre Casa vostra, la quale con la sua fortuna e virtú, favorita da Dio e da la Chiesa, della quale è ora principe, possa farsi capo di questa redenzione."

people's belief in him.[74] Machiavelli invokes divine providence again after having exhorted the Medici to emulate the ways of the great pagan, or quasi-pagan, heroes of the past, Cyrus, Theseus, and Moses: "And although they were exceptional and marvelous men, yet they were men, and each of them had less opportunity than the present one; for their undertaking was not more just than this one, nor easier, nor was God more of a friend to them than to you."[75] Yet again, Machiavelli indulges in ambiguity. For at the same time as this statement can be seen as evidence of his belief in the divine support for the Medici and their ancient predecessors, it can also be taken to mean that the Medici should not let their *lack* of electedness stop them from undertaking their historical task. The legendary heroes of the past, this other reading contends, acheived glory and greatness *without* having any greater claim to justice on their side, and *without* God being more of a friend to them than to the Medici. According to de Grazia, Machiavelli is here affirming that the cause of the Medici is just and divinely sanctioned, but as we can see, the passage supports the diametrically opposite reading as well.[76]

Great justice surrounds the Medici's mission, Machiavelli goes on to claim, quoting from Livy in Latin: "for war is just which is necessary, and arms are pious when there is no hope but in them."[77] To bring out the implications of this citation, we need to read it back into its Livian context. In the beginning of the ninth book (IX.I), Livy relates how a small group of "ambitious" Samnites made a raid into Roman territory with the intent of provoking war between the two peoples. The strategy was successful, for when the Samnites later sent an embassy to Rome to negotiate a new peace agreement, the Romans flatly declined their offer. Consequently, the Samnite ambassador, Claudius Pontius, could upon his return home inform his people that the Romans wanted war at all costs. To call his compatriots to arms, he invoked the just war in the memorable speech from which Machiavelli quotes in *The Prince* 26, and refers to again in *Discourses* III.12 and *Florentine Histories* V.8. The Samnites went to war, the former Secretary argues in the *Discourses*, building their hope of victory on this alleged, but

[74] As we recall, Machiavelli had in *Il principe* 11 (p. 149) claimed that the Church had arrived at its temporal power not through divine intervention and support, but "col danaio e con le forze." See above p. 183.

[75] Ibid. 26, p. 190: "e benché quelli uomini sieno rari e maravigliosi, nondimeno furno uomini, ed ebbe ciascuno di loro minore occasione che la presente perché la impresa loro non fu piú iusta di questa, né piú facile, né fu Dio piú amico loro che a voi."

[76] De Grazia, *Machiavelli in Hell*, p. 31 and *passim*. Cf. Kahn, *Machiavellian Rhetoric*, p. 42; Pocock, *The Machiavellian Moment*, p. 171.

[77] *Il principe* 26, p. 190: "Qui è iustizia grande: iustum enim est bellum quibus necessarium et pia arma ubi nulla nisi in armis spes est." Cf. Livy IX.I.

fabricated, necessity and the self-proclaimed righteousness of their cause.[78] Having unpacked the implications of Machiavelli's Livian quotation, we are yet again left with a choice between two radically different interpretations. Should we take the statement at face value, and consider it dislodged from its original context, or should we, as the humanist reader, familiar with Livy's narrative, could be expected to do, understand it according to its original meaning?

The four verses Machiavelli quotes from Petrarch's *Italia mia* at the end of the chapter are subject to a similar change in meaning resulting from contextual dislocation.

> Virtue will take up arms against fury,
> and make the battle short,
> because the ancient valor in Italian hearts
> is not yet dead.
>
> *Virtú contro a furore*
> *prenderà l'armi, e fia el combatter corto,*
> *che l'antico valore*
> *nelli italici cor non è ancor morto.*[79]

In Petrarch's original, these lines refer to an inner battle raging within the soul of the Italian people, a struggle seen as analogous to the civil war that at the time was tearing the country apart. They are directly related to the final verses of the poem, where the despairing poet, addressing the "magnanimous few who love the good" (*magnanimi pochi a chi 'l ben piace*), famously exclaims: "Peace, peace, peace" (*Pace, pace, pace*).[80] Wrenched from their original context, however, they come in *The Prince* to convey a completely different message. Reifying Petrarch's military metaphor, the former Secretary, who offers his advice to a tyrannical, or semi-tyrannical, prince instead of to the virtuous few, transforms what in *Italia mia* had been an inner struggle against unruly passions into a military crusade against the fury of the foreign invaders. In the process, Machiavelli also uncovers, beneath Petrarch's Christian and Aristotelian definition of *virtù*, a Roman form of spiritedness still burning in the hearts of the Italian peoples. In short, while Petrarch's *Italia mia* closes with a passionate call to peace and moderation, Machiavelli's *Prince* ends with an equally ardent call to war.

78 *Discorsi* III.12, p. 458: "sopra la quale necessità egli fondò con gli suoi soldati la speranza della vittoria."

79 *Il principe* 26, p. 192. English translation from Machiavelli, *The Prince*, trans. H. Mansfield, p. 105.

80 Francesco Petrarch, *Italia mia*, vv. 119–22: "Proverai tua [addressing the poem itself] ventura / fra' magnanimi pochi a chi 'l ben piace; / di' lor: 'Chi m'assicura? / I' vo gridando: Pace, pace, pace.' " Quotation from *Petrarch's Lyric Poems: The* Rime sparse *and Other Lyrics* (Cambridge, MA: Harvard University Press, 1976), p. 263.

As this discussion shows, Machiavelli's discourse in *The Prince* 26 is fraught with ambiguity and open to conflicting interpretations. His use of conventional legitimatory devices such as divine providence and the just war can be read, on the one hand, naïvely as "significant metaphysical and theological statements," reflecting his own personal views, and on the other, suspiciously as mere pretexts, or covers, for taking up arms. While the first reading contradicts everything that has been said in this study, the second reading fits well into the pattern we have been seeking to establish throughout our analysis of Machiavelli's major works, *The Prince* and the *Discourses*. If we opt for the second reading, we are led to conclude that Machiavelli here performs a double act, by simultaneously surrounding the Medici expansionist project with a legitimazing frame of imperial mystery, and teaching his analytical readers the arcane art of framing war. Metaphorically speaking, he acts like the master illusionist, who satisfies his general audience by performing the trick they have come to see, leaving them in bewilderment, while at the same time allowing his most perceptive spectators – his disciples, the magicians of the future – to see what they need to see in order to be able to figure out how the trick is done, and to repeat it themselves.

But if we have reason to suspect that Machiavelli's appeals to divine providence and the just war are rhetorical devices designed to promote Medicean expansionism, what about his passionate appeal to Italian patriotism in *The Prince* 26? Are we now to retreat to De Sanctis's more than century-old claim that Machiavelli elevated the *patria*, understood as a strong and unified Italian national state, above ethical, legal, and religious concerns, and made her into his divinity?[81]

The term Italy, or *Italia*, is undeniably one of the most divisive in Machiavelli's lexicon, and scholars have come up with many conflicting interpretations of its meaning in *The Prince* 26.[82] The former Secretary was anticipating the unification of Italy by envisaging a unified nation-state on the model of contemporary France and Spain.[83] He was merely thinking of some form of temporary military alliance or a loosely organized federation

[81] Francesco De Sanctis, *Storia della letteratura italiana*, ed. B. Croce (2 vols, Bari: Laterza, 1958), 1, p. 151.

[82] On Machiavelli's patriotism in general, see Felix Gilbert, "The Concept of Nationalism in Machiavelli's *Prince*," *Studies in the Renaissance* 1 (1954): 38–48; Vincent Ilardi, "'Italianita' among Some Italian Intellectuals in the Early Sixteenth Century," *Traditio* 12 (1956): 339–67; reprinted in Ilardi, *Studies in Italian Renaissance Diplomatic History* (London: Variorum Reprints, 1986). Cf. Paolo Margaroli, "L'Italia come percezione di uno spazio politico unitario negli anni cinquanta del XV secolo," *Nuova rivista storica* 74 (1990): 517–36. See also note 84 below.

[83] De Sanctis, *Storia della letteratura italiana*, 1, pp. 142, 145, 149–55, and 183.

of states in central Italy.[84] He originally intended his advice to serve the creation of a small duchy in the Romagna, but then added, when the political situation changed, the final chapter in which he exhorts the Medici to throw out the invaders and to unify Italy.[85] His appeal to patriotism is merely a means of providing the tyrannical methods recommended in the rest of the work with an appearance of legitimacy and justification. Interpretations point in many directions, but Machiavelli's invocation of *Italia* is with no, or few, exceptions viewed as an expression of his Italian nationalism, or proto-nationalism, which is seen to surpass the parochialism of the city-state and the region.[86] In other words, when Machiavelli says Italy, he means Italy, a geographical and cultural entity that is more or less identical to the one referred to by this term today.

What evidence is there for this reading? As we have seen, Machiavelli begins in *The Prince* 26 to appeal to Italian patriotism already in the chapter heading, where he exhorts his addressee "to seize Italy and to free her from the Barbarians."[87] As the wording suggests, Machiavelli wants us to believe that the conquest and the liberation of Italy will go hand in hand. But who should then conquer Italy? The obvious answer is the Medici family, headed

[84] Frederico Chabod, *Scritti su Machiavelli* (Turin: Einaudi, 1964), pp. 66–67. Cf. Chabod, *L'Idea di Nazione* (Bari: Laterza, 1961), pp. 6–7; Luigi Russo, *Machiavelli* (Bari: Laterza, 1969), p. 212. According to Chabod, Machiavelli's notion of "Italy" did not refer to a tightly knit cultural and historical unity. Instead, it consisted of a limited number of independent provinces: Lombardy, Tuscany, the kingdom of Naples, Rome, and the Romagna. Also Felix Gilbert argues (*Machiavelli and Guicciardini*, p. 183) that the policy Machiavelli proposes in the concluding chapter of *Il principe* did not aim at a united Italy, but at "a temporary alliance of the existing Italian rulers and city-states in order to get rid of the *oltramontani*."

[85] Hans Baron claims that nothing in the first twenty-five chapters of *Il principe* suggests that Machiavelli composed the work with Italian unification in mind. According to Baron, the former Secretary's dream of a militarily strong and independent Italy must therefore have arisen at a later date. On the basis of his dating of the final chapter to between January and March 1515, Baron concludes that the treatise originally had a more limited scope and was intended to serve as a handbook for princely rule of a minor principality in central Italy. See Baron, "The *Principe* and the Puzzle." For a similar reading, see Cecil Clough, *Machiavelli Researches* (Naples: Istituto universitario orientale, 1967), pp. 42–60. Humphrey Butters opposes this reading, arguing that *Il principe* was neither intended to serve as a "practical guide [. . .] for the Medici regime in Florence," nor as "a manual to help Giuliano rule the Romagna," H. C. Butters, *Governors and Government in Early Sixteenth-Century Florence 1502–1519* (Oxford: Clarendon Press, 1985), p. 224. However, Butters's own conclusion does little to shed light on the mystery of *Il principe* (p. 225): "What Machiavelli's precise intentions in writing the *Prince* were, apart from the desire to secure employment, remains unclear."

[86] For Florentine readings of *Il principe* 26 and the work as a whole, see Sergio Bertelli, *Introduzione all'Opera Omnia di Niccolò Machiavelli* (Milan: Feltrinelli, 1968), pp. xxix–xxx; Fallon, "Hunting the Fox"; Robert Grundin, "Sequence and Counter-Sequence in Il Principe," *Machiavelli Studies* 3 (1990): 29–42. Mario Martelli, "Machiavelli e Firenze dalla repubblica al principato," in *Niccolò Machiavelli: Politico, storico, letterato*, ed. J.-J. Marchand (Rome: Salerno, 1996), pp. 15–31, esp. 25–26. However, none of these scholars argues, as I shall do in the following, that Machiavelli in the final chapter uses the Papacy and the notion of "Italy" as covers for Florentine imperialism.

[87] See note 65 above.

by Leo and Lorenzo, to whom the chapter is addressed. Drawing freely on the episode from Exodus, or possibly Psalm 77 in the Vulgata, where the march of the Israelites towards the promised land under Moses' leadership is described, Machiavelli presents the Medici as the God-ordained and long-awaited saviors of Italy: "Besides this, here may be seen extraordinary things without precedent, brought about by God: the sea has opened; a cloud has shown you the way; the rock has poured forth water; it has rained manna here; everything has concurred in your greatness."[88] After this remarkable passage, a long account of the present state of Italian military affairs follows, during which numerous appeals are made to the patriotic pride invested in the *patria*, ending with Machiavelli exhorting the Medici to institute a native militia. The bellicosity of the chapter heading, where Machiavelli had exhorted the Medici not only to liberate, but also to seize Italy, is now mitigated as the whole project is recast as a defensive war against foreign aggression. Since all Italians presently regard the Medici as their providentially destined liberators, seizing and defending Italy amounts to one and the same thing:

> This opportunity, therefore, must not be allowed to pass, so that Italy, after such a long time, may see her redeemer. Nor can I express with what love he would be received in all those provinces that have suffered from these foreign floods; with what thirst for revenge, with what obstinate faith, with what devotion and with what tears. What gates would be closed to him? What peoples would deny him obedience? What envy would oppose him? What Italian would deny him homage?[89]

If we are to believe Machiavelli, the historic feat awaiting the Medici is to be conceived not as an extension of Florentine or papal power, nor as the beginning of a new Medicean empire in central Italy, but as a triumphal procession, flanked by crowds of rejoicing Italians, full of ancient mystery, newborn faith, love, and obedience. Upon Medicean success, Machiavelli insists, general approval, gratitude, and peace will follow. For what Italian would refuse to obey a ruler who has saved and liberated his country?

[88] *Il principe* 26, p. 190: "Oltre a di questo, qui si veggono estraordinari sanza esemplo, condotti da Dio: el mare si è aperto; una nube vi ha scorto el cammino; la pietra ha versato acque; qui è piovuto la manna. Ogni cosa è concorsa nella vostra grandezza." On the source of this passage, see Machiavelli, *The Prince*, trans. H. C. Mansfield, p. 103; Hugo Jaeckel, "What is Machiavelli Exhorting in his Exhortatio? The Extraordinaries," in *Niccolò Machiavelli: Politico, storico, letterato*, ed. Marchand, pp. 59–84.

[89] *Il principe* 26, p. 192: "Non si debba adunque lasciare passare questa occasione, acciò che la Italia vegga dopo tanto tempo apparire uno suo redentore. Né posso esprimere con quale amore e' fussi ricevuto in tutte quelle provincie che hanno patito per queste illuvioni esterne, con che sete di vendetta, con che ostinata fede, con che pietà, con che lacrime. Quali porte se li serrerebbono? Quali populi gli negherebbono la obbedienza? Quale invidia se li opporrebbe? Quale italiano gli negherebbe lo ossequio?"

This is indeed a rosy picture of the future lying ahead for the Medici and the Italian peoples, but it leaves plenty of thorny questions unanswered. First, in what capacity are Pope Leo and his family to seize and liberate Italy, as rulers of the Church, or of Florence? Second, since the liberation will be a military undertaking, the new prince would have to raise soldiers, but from where are these to be drawn? Third, how is the opposition that can be expected from the Venetians, the Milanese, the duke of Ferrara, the Aragon king of Naples, the republic of Siena, and various other regional powers to be overcome? And finally, we learn that the Medici's seizure and liberation of Italy will ennoble or glorify their fatherland, but what does Machiavelli actually mean when he refers to "this fatherland" (*questa patria*)?[90]

To explain and elucidate the meaning of Machiavelli's reference to Italy in *The Prince* 26, we need to evolve a larger view of his Italian project. According to Vincent Ilardi, Machiavelli develops in *The Prince* and the *Discourses* three separate schemes for creating a strong, unified state in Italy capable of withstanding foreign aggression. This unification can be accomplished first through princely conquest along the lines drawn up in *The Prince*; second, through subjugation by a hegemonial republic following the example of the ancient Romans, who began by acquiring allies whom they later subdued and reduced to subjects; and third, through the forming of a league of independent republics modeled on that of the ancient Etruscans. The last two methods are identical to the ones we discussed above when dealing with *Discourses* II.4.[91] While Ilardi claims that all three methods aimed at "a new political and military settlement in the peninsula," and that this was to be achieved through subjugation rather than through integration, he insists on viewing them as distinct and separate solutions to Italy's political dilemma.[92] Italian liberty and unity are Machiavelli's overriding aims, he maintains, but whether they are achieved through the agency of the Medici, Cesare Borgia, Florence, or some other Italian state is of secondary importance to him. In Ilardi's view, the fact that the former Secretary invoked the *patria* at the end of *The Prince* did not mean that his "local patriotism led him to advocate that only Florence should [be] the dominant state in Italy."[93]

But are the three strategies Ilardi identifies really so different from each other after all? When we in chapter 4 of this study discussed Ilardi's third

90 Ibid.: "A ognuno puzza questo barbaro dominio. Pigli adunque la illustre Casa vostra questo assunto, con quello animo e con quella speranza che si pigliono le imprese iuste, acciò che, sotto la sua insegna, e questa patria ne sia nobilitata e, sotto e' sua auspizi, si verifichi quel detto del Petrarca, quando disse . . ."

91 See above pp. 134–39.

92 Ilardi, "'Italianita,'" pp. 359–63.

93 Ibid., p. 363. Still, as Ilardi points out, Machiavelli as a rule uses the term *patria* to denote not Italy, of which he rarely speaks, but his native Florence, about which he always has a lot to say.

strategy, the Etruscan way of expanding through a league, we came to the conclusion that to Machiavelli this method merely represented the first stage in the Roman imperialist development, that is, Ilardi's second strategy, and not a valid alternative way of empire- or state-building. Later, in chapters 5 and 6, we have seen the embryo of a Roman-inspired republic gradually emerge from within the discourse of *The Prince*, with Machiavelli's rhetorical manipulation of the fear of his princely reader in *The Prince* 19 setting the stage for his recommendation to introduce a rudimentary form of the mixed regime. In *The Prince* 25, the former Secretary placed the aspiring new prince in the untenable position of having to adapt his inflexible nature to the changing times, insinuating the ephemerality of his future success and the necessity of founding a classically inspired republic, based on the principle of rotation in office. While in the *Discourses* the Florentine depicts the Spartan constitution and the Etruscan league as embryonic versions of the Roman ideal, in *The Prince* he treats the French monarchy in a similar way, using it as a stepping stone for his advice on how to imitate, or emulate, Roman modes and orders. This leads us to conclude that Ilardi's first method – the princely and the Medicean project of *The Prince* – should also be seen as part of a step-by-step strategy predicated on Machiavelli's processual view of Roman history, aimed at the founding of an expansionist republic, a *republica perfetta*.

This interpretation makes *The Prince* into a fundamentally republican and imperialist work, but does it also mean that the expansionist program it contains is designed to serve Florentine purposes, like the one we have uncovered in the *Discourses*? Our analysis in chapter 4 of Machiavelli's stance on the Pisan issue in *The Prince* 5 suggested that an unstated Florentine point of view underlies the use of persuasive strategies in the work. While this reading seems to be contradicted by the appeal to Italian patriotism in *The Prince* 26, we should do well at this point to recall Machiavelli's own account in the *Discourses* of how the ancient Romans in the course of their rise to world domination concealed their true intentions behind protestations of friendship, good faith, and the pursuit of the common good of Italy. In the course of the present chapter we have come to suspect that the former Secretary engages in a similar form of deception himself, when in *The Prince* 26 he adduces divine providence, the just war, and the quest for peace to justify Medicean expansion. Against this background, I submit, we have strong reason to believe that his repeated invocation of *Italia* in this final chapter serves as a façade for Florentine imperialist aspirations. If we adopt this reading, the unique opportunity Machiavelli refers to in the opening of *The Prince* 26 takes on a new and more precise meaning.

What he is alluding to here, it would seem, is the fact that Florence after the Medici's elevation to the Papacy, for the first time since the breakdown of the Guelf league back in the Trecento, is in a position to pursue her long-standing aim of liberty and empire under a different name than her own. With the Medici having at their disposal the money and the forces that in the recent past had made Alexander VI and Julius II great, the Arno city should seize the opportunity to liberate Italy under papal banners instead of those of the hateful Marzocco, and to spread her power throughout the peninsula, covertly and secretly, without fanfare or boasting.[94] Later in the *Discourses*, Machiavelli would address the same basic program to the Florentine leadership of the future, the young aristocrats of the Orti Oricellari circle, private citizens, whom he judged worthy of being the princes of the strong and expansive Florentine republic of his imagination.[95] But as we all know, neither they, nor the Medici, were destined to become the historical agents that would bring this ambitious project, which has continued to haunt the Western mind well into the new millennium, to completion.

94 Cf. *Discorsi* II.21, p. 383, where Machiavelli praises the ancient Romans for having ruled the towns of Italy without leaving "in them any sign of the empire of the Roman people (*non lasciavano alcuno segno d'imperio per il popolo romano*)."

95 Cf. ibid., dedication, p. 196.

Conclusion: cui bono?

> When television has shown a fine picture and explained it with a brazen lie, idiots believe that everything is clear. The demi-elite is content to know that almost everything is obscure, ambivalent, "constructed" by unknown codes. A more exclusive elite would like to know what is true, hard as it is to distinguish in each particular case, despite all their access to special knowledge and confidences. Which is why they would like to get to know the method of truth, though their love usually remains unrequited.
>
> Guy Debord

Machiavelli's theoretical work resembles a Florentine Renaissance palazzo in its unique mixture of sophistication and self-imposed austerity. The difficulty in interpreting him is to no small extent due to the fact that his texts, openly or obliquely, simultaneously operate on several different levels, of which at least three can be distinguished here. The first, and the most widely recognized, level is that of principle, or theory. Machiavelli's writings are replete with generalizing statements, rules, axioms, and maxims that taken together form the core of his realist theory of political action, which in many quarters has earned him the title of the founder of modern political science. Second, there is the level of ideology. As recent scholars have been able to demonstrate, and as we have seen in the course of this study, Machiavelli's work draws on, and engages, many of the main themes of classical and Renaissance political thought and contemporary Florentine political debate. While adhering to the general doctrine of liberty and empire permeating the Florentine republican tradition, Machiavelli also questions several of the ideological tenets of Florentine foreign policy and offers a radically new view of the justification of war. This engagement with the local and contemporary context points to the third level, which we in our introductory chapter have defined as the rhetorical level. Machiavelli in his theoretical work not merely attempted to redefine the ways in which his contemporaries talked about politics, but also addressed the political *here and now*, giving advice, at times openly, but more often in indirect and subtle ways. Any attempt to interpret and to understand Machiavelli's intellectual and political project must take each of these three levels into account and explain how they relate, interact, and overlap.

Machiavelli's universalism, or claim to universalism, rests in part on his precepts, rules of action, and mottos, and in part on the paradigmatic status he attributes to his Roman model.[1] The main focus of his political theory, it could be argued, is on the principles underlying the foundations of power and the workings of government. Whatever else they are, his main works, *The Prince* and the *Discourses*, are manuals on how to achieve political success. They give advice on how to gain, preserve, and increase political power, expounding the political and military measures by which states may acquire strength and expand their territory, and by contrast, how to avoid the errors that lead to decay and ruin. This universalizing discourse, which includes sweeping unsupported generalizations on human nature, the laws of history, and sublunar or human conditions in general, extends well beyond the limited sphere of politics and carries profound scientific and philosophical implications. Although Machiavelli's presentation is far from systematic, his method based on observation and his cool and analytical style of argumentation bring him close to the modern political scientist. A chill of abstraction pervades the Florentine's work, blending his tight-lipped advice, his basic premises of power politics, and his literary style into a cohesive and highly orginal approach to, and vision of, the world.

Since the universalizing tendency of Machiavelli's theory is balanced by great flexibility and pragmatism, it never runs the risk of lapsing into rigid or dogmatic thinking. The political actor, the adviser, and the analyst, he insists, should always be sensitive to the particular aspects of the social contexts and the political situations within which they operate. In his view, political prudence requires not only a firm grasp of the political realities, but also an ability to adapt to the contingencies of place, time, and person, the political *here and now*. The seeming contradiction between Machiavelli's emphasis on adaptability and his teaching of power politics, which, as a rule, favors strong action over weak and adaptive policies, can be easily reconciled in his Roman model.

[1] On Machiavelli's use of maxims and maximatic discourse, see Barbara Spackman, "Machiavelli and Maxims," *Yale French Studies* 77 (1990): 137–55. On the relationship between rules and examples in Machiavelli, see Jean-Jacques Marchand, "L'interprétation de l'histoire chez Machiavel," *Études de Lettres* 4 (1978): 31–47, esp. 38–39. Cf. John D. Lyons, *Exemplum: The Rhetoric of Example in Early Modern France and Italy* (Princeton: Princeton University Press, 1989), esp. pp. 43–50 and 58.

In Machiavelli's eyes, the history of ancient Rome, by incorporating every possible political situation, provided a complete set of precedents for future republics and empires. By studying the rise and fall of the Roman republic, one could therefore gain a detailed understanding of the political development in all its stages, and by extrapolating from it, one could extract examples illustrating and embodying the principles of political prudence. As we have seen, the political model resulting from this study consists in a step-by-step approach to republican government and empire-building. The Roman state had been founded by one strong man, Romulus, who had instituted the Senate, representing the few, to which he had delegated some of his power. After the expulsion of the kings, the republic was established and the Tribunes of the Plebs instituted, giving representation also to the many. At this point, Machiavelli claims, the Roman republic became perfectly mixed, *una republica perfetta*, as it realized its internal aim, liberty. Its other, external aim, empire, it achieved in a similar way. After having initially relied on the assistance of their allies, or companions, to speak with Machiavelli, the Romans had gradually come to head a powerful league of Italian peoples, enabling them to acquire subject territories also outside Italy. When the time was ripe they had also subjugated their allies and established themselves as lords of Italy and rulers of an ever-growing empire. Far from being linear, the Roman development, internal as well as external, had evolved by a process of trial-and-error. The Romans, having no model to follow themselves, had learnt by their mistakes and shown great flexibility and imagination by inventing and reinventing their modes and orders as they went along.[2] In the process, they had, at least in Machiavelli's view, created a universal model for political action. As a rule choosing policies and strategies that contributed to the growth of their power, the Romans made a fundamental distinction between acting and negotiating from a position of strength and from one of weakness. Since temporization and other weak policies to them were merely provisional strategies to be used while strengthening one's power base and one's political foundation, they never came to view adapting to circumstance as an end in itself.

In commenting on his native Florence, his beloved *patria*, Machiavelli states time and again that her current plight is due to her failure to follow the Roman path, or to be more precise, her refusal to enter the cycle of

[2] *Discorsi* II.4, p. 341: "non ce n'era innanzi a Roma esemplo." On the Romans acting without example, see Lyons, *Exemplum*, pp. 35–71, esp. 45, 52, and 71. On the question of agency in Machiavelli's account of Roman history, see Claude Lefort, *Le travail de l'œuvre Machiavel* (Paris: Gallimard, 1972), pp. 593–96.

development inscribed in the Roman model.[3] It is against this background that Machiavelli's unrelenting inquiry into the foundation of Florence – evident from his writings on the militia of 1506, *The Prince*, the *Discourses*, the *Discursus Florentinarum Rerum*, his proposal for Florentine constitutional reform of 1520, as well as the *Istorie fiorentine* – takes on its full significance.

In his treatment of the founding of Florence in the introduction to the *Discourses*, Machiavelli departs from the civic humanist tradition by emphasizing not the city's republican orgins, but the fact that she began her history as an unfree colony under Roman domination. Cities that have had an unfree beginning, he claims, rarely "make great strides" and are therefore rarely counted among the great capitals, or "the leaders of kingdoms." Because Florence was built "under the Roman empire, it could in its beginning not make any gains (*augumenti*) other than those conceded to it by courtesy of the prince."[4] Returning to Florence's early history later in the *Discourses*, Machiavelli adds that the city for a long time had lived abjectedly, without regard for herself, used to enduring the rule of others. When she finally was able to breathe freely, she began to "make her own orders, which could not have been good, since they were mixed with the ancient that were bad." In this way Florence had governed herself during the past two hundred years, Machiavelli continues, "without ever having had a state for which it could truly be called a republic."[5] To judge by these passages, Machiavelli conceives of Florence as an unfounded, or at least insufficiently founded, city or state. This reading is supported by the opening of his *Discursus Florentinarum Rerum* of 1520, where the former Secretary claims that Florence, as a result of her many and frequent changes

3 Felix Gilbert argues that the Roman model was central to Machiavelli, because it "demonstrated to him the possibility of the rise of a city-republic to world power, and therefore was for him the embodiment of an ideal republic," "Machiavelli: The Renaissance of the Art of War," in *Makers of Modern Strategy from Machiavelli to the Nuclear Age*, eds. P. Paret, G. A. Craig, and F. Gilbert (Oxford: Clarendon Press, 1986), pp. 21–22. But it would not be unfair to say that Gilbert did not follow up or fully develop this insight in his many studies on Machiavelli's work.

4 *Discorsi* I.1, p. 200. "E per non avere queste cittadi la loro origine libera, rade volte occorre che le facciano processi grandi, e possinsi intra i capi dei regni numerare. Simile a queste fu l'edificazione di Firenze, perché . . . si edificò sotto l'imperio romano: né poté, ne' principii suoi, fare altri augumenti che quelli che per cortesia del principe gli erano concessi." In the omitted passage, Machiavelli relates two different theories on the founding of Florence – on the one hand, Salutati's and Bruni's view that it was the work of Sulla's veterans; on the other, Poliziano's later claim that it occurred when the mountaineers of Fiesole moved down to the Arno plain during Augustus's reign – as if to suggest that it is of little consequence whether the city was founded under the republic or the principate.

5 Ibid., I.49, p. 299: "cominciò a fare suoi ordini; i quali sendo mescolati con gli antichi, che erano cattivi, non poterono essere buoni: e cosí è ita maneggiandosi per dugento anni, che si ha di vera memoria, sanza avere mai avuto stato per il quale la possa veramente essere chiamata republica."

of government, never has been either a republic or a principality worthy of the name.[6]

The thwarted quest for a Florentine foundation is a recurrent theme in *The Prince* as well. Here Machiavelli treats in turn Girolamo Savonarola, Cesare Borgia, and Piero Soderini as failed founders of a Florentine or Tuscan state. Contrasting Savonarola, the unarmed prophet, in chapter 6 to the great founders of antiquity, Moses, Cyrus, Theseus, and Romulus, Machiavelli claims that the Dominican failed to impose his "new orders" (*ordini nuovi*) in Florence because he was unable to defend them with force when the people stopped believing in him as divinely elected. The detailed discussion in chapter 7 of Cesare Borgia's abortive attempt to conquer Florence and make himself "Lord of Tuscany" (*signore di Toscana*) is followed in chapter 9 by an oblique reference to Piero Soderini, Machiavelli's former employer, who had ruled Florence as Gonfalonier for life in the years 1502–12.[7] Speaking in general terms of "a private citizen, who becomes prince of his fatherland . . . with the support of his fellow citizens," Machiavelli argues that such a ruler should build his foundation on the people (*popolo*) while suppressing the nobles (*grandi*).[8] Soderini had failed to give Florence a strong foundation, Machiavelli insinuates, because he had relied too much on the city's civic institutions and failed to use harsh measures against the supporters of the old regime, or to "kill the sons of Brutus," as he was later to say when discussing his former employer in less guarded terms in the *Discourses*.[9]

While illustrating the inherent dangers of weak and ambiguous policies, the Florentine examples in *The Prince* take on added importance from the fact that the treatise is addressed to the Medici, the new rulers of Florence and the successors of Savonarola and Soderini, who in the final chapter also are exhorted to found a new principality in Italy. The question of Florence's lack of foundation can therefore not be dismissed merely as an example among others. From beneath Machiavelli's discussion of the

[6] *Opere*, ed. C. Vivanti, (3 vols., Turin: Einaudi, 1997–), I, p. 733: "La cagione perché Firenze ha sempre variato spesso nei suoi governi, è stata perché in quella non è stato mai né repubblica né principato che abbi avute le debite qualità sue."

[7] According to Sergio Bertelli, there existed at the beginning of the Cinquecento a "pro-Borgian movement" in Florence, consisting of oligarchs who were "ready to support [Cesare Borgia's] claim against the Great Council." See Sergio Bertelli, "Machiavelli and Soderini," *Renaissance Quarterly* 28 (1975), pp. 6–7. On Piero Soderini and his rule as the oblique subject of *Il principe* 9, see Roslyn Pesman Cooper, "Machiavelli, Pier Soderini and *Il Principe*," in *Altro Polo: A Volume of Italian Renaissance Studies*, eds. C. Condren and R. Pesman Cooper (Sydney: University of Sydney, 1982), pp. 132–38.

[8] *Il principe* 9, p. 143: "quando uno privato cittadino . . . con il favore delli altri sua cittadini diventa principe della sua patria."

[9] See *Discorsi* III.3.

principles underlying the foundation of states in general, his anguished and impatient concern with the fate of his native city constantly resurfaces.

When Machiavelli returns to the foundation theme in the *Discourses*, he claims that a city of Florence's type, where there are no feudal lords (*signori di castella*) and where an extreme degree of equality reigns, can easily be given a free, republican form of government (*uno vivere civile*) by "a prudent man having knowledge of the ancient civilization."[10] While in *The Prince* he had implied that Savonarola, as well as Soderini, had failed to provide a strong and lasting foundation for Florence, because they were either ignorant of, or neglected, the Roman model, which we have seen being insinuated into the work, he now claims that a ruler, or a statesman, who has learned the lessons of the past would be able to put Florence back on track, allowing her to enter the Roman development and to initiate a new cycle of power.[11]

The difference in emphasis between the *Discourses* and *The Prince* on this point should not be mistaken for a sudden reversal of values or ideological allegiance.[12] The fact that Machiavelli in the *Discourses* comments on the possibility of founding a republic (*uno vivere civile*) in Florence, and in *The Prince* gives general advice on how to found a new principality (*un principato nuovo*), does not contradict this reading. On the contrary, since according to the Roman example, as described in the *Discourses*, Rome's constitutional development and territorial expansion began with Romulus's founding of the city as a monarchy capable of developing in the direction of *uno vivere civile*. If Florence is to follow in the footsteps of her ancient forebear, Machiavelli teaches, she needs to be founded, or refounded, by "a prudent man" as *uno vivere civile* (the *Discourses*), or as a principality capable of developing in this direction (*The Prince*).

On this general level of discourse, Florence's historical failure can be attributed alternatively to her inability to grasp the principles of power politics, or to her unwillingness to follow Roman precedents. Portraying his native city as a yet unfounded, or inadequately founded, state, lacking the strong underpinnings needed for territorial growth, Machiavelli turns the civic humanists' triumphalist notion of Florence as the New Rome

[10] Ibid., I.55, p. 312: "uno uomo prudente e che delle antiche civilità avesse cognizione."

[11] Girolamo Savonarola and Piero Soderini figure as failed founders of Florence in Ibid., I.7, I.45, I.52, I.56, III.3, III.9, and III.30.

[12] The contrary position has been taken notably by Hans Baron, who, in his article "Machiavelli the Republican Citizen and Author of *The Prince*," argues that the *Discorsi* and *Il principe* are "different in basic attitudes" and that the former work contains "a republican message irreconcilable" with the latter. See *In Search of Florentine Civic Humanism: Essays on the Transition from Medieval to Modern Thought* (2 vols., Princeton: Princeton University Press, 1988), II, pp. 101–51; quotes from p. 143.

on its head. But the former Secretary's awareness of Florence's current weakness did not mean, as has often been claimed, that he thought that the city-state had played out its historical role and had been superseded by the emerging absolute or national monarchies of France and Spain.[13] This reading is anachronistic and without textual foundation, since Machiavelli's chancery writings, theoretical works, and private correspondence show that throughout his political and literary career he was thinking in terms of city and empire, not of emerging nation-states, judging his native Florence in the context of the Roman model and viewing the French monarchy, and other positive modern examples, as bleak reflections of the glorious ancient Roman republic.[14]

In this regard, Machiavelli was firmly anchored in the Florentine republican tradition. But in contrast to, for example, Leonardo Bruni, who in the *Laudatio* had happily inscribed Florence in his version of the Roman model, Machiavelli drew other, less than flattering, conclusions from this comparison. While Bruni's Florence was on the rise, Machiavelli's had yet to enter the cycle of historical development perfected by ancient Rome. Consequently, Florence comes on the level of principle to serve as Machiavelli's negative counterpart to the positive Roman example, which frequently makes it into an object of derison, and its history into a storehouse of negative examples and lessons on what to avoid.[15] But it would be a mistake to assume on the basis of this observation that Machiavelli viewed his native city merely as an abstract entity and a specimen for study, or that he was indifferent to its fate. Instead, we have compelling reason to believe that it was his concern with Florence's current malaise, evident from his chancery writings and his private letters, that induced him to move beyond the ideological level of the civic humanists and to embark on his general inquiry into republican government and to formulate his universal theory of power politics. As we have argued throughout this study, the levels

[13] For readings that view Machiavelli as an early prophet, or promoter, of Italian nationalism, see for example Francesco De Sanctis, *Storia della letteratura italiana*, ed. B. Croce (2 vols., Bari: Laterza, 1958), 1, pp. 141–92; Myron P. Gilmore, *The World of Humanism, 1453–1517* (New York: Harper & Row, 1952), pp. 132–36; Sebastian de Grazia, *Machiavelli in Hell* (London: Picador, 1992), pp. 146–56. See also above pp. 258–60.

[14] Cf. Pierre Manent, *An Intellectual History of Liberalism*, English trans. (Princeton: Princeton University Press, 1994), pp. 3–19; Elena Fasano Guarini, "Machiavelli and the Crisis of the Italian Republics," in *Machiavelli and Republicanism*, eds. G. Bock, Q. Skinner, and M. Viroli (Cambridge: Cambridge University Press, 1990), pp. 17–40, esp. 30–32 and 38–40.

[15] Cf. Mark Hulliung, *Citizen Machiavelli* (Princeton: Princeton University Press, 1983), pp. 61–98. As Hulliung points out (pp. 92–93), the difference between the civic humanists and Machiavelli can also be described in stylistic terms, as a contrast between the latter's "unconventional tone of irony" and "the conventional humanist tone of eulogy."

of general principles and applied politics should in Machiavelli's thought be seen as intimately related. For although his theory is cast in general terms, it always points to and calls for implementation in the particular context of contemporary politics, that is, the Florentine *here and now*. This is also, we submit, how Machiavelli expected the implied audience of the *Discourses*, the young republican aristocrats of the Orti Oricellari, who for their "infinite good parts" deserved to be princes, to read his work.[16]

Machiavelli's contrasting of ancient Rome and contemporary Florence on the level of general principles need to be complemented by a more detailed discussion of how this dichotomy is played out on the ideological level. The ideological aspects of Machiavelli's work, which in recent years have attracted increasing attention from scholars, raise the question of the Florentine's place within the Western tradition and of the puzzling relationship between the monarchic teaching of *The Prince* and the republican theory of the *Discourses*. In separate studies, Quentin Skinner and Maurizio Viroli have, by situating *The Prince* in the genres of Quattrocento advice-books for princes and early Cinquecento Florentine treatises on *arte dello stato*, and the *Discourses* in that of classical and medieval republicanist theories of political liberty, given authoritative accounts of ideological conventions and vocabularies in which Machiavelli's work participates.[17] According to their interpretation, the alleged conflict between *The Prince* and the *Discourses* can be understood largely in terms of the two works belonging to, or depending on, different ideological traditions. The current study has taken issue with this view by arguing that the primary context of Machiavelli's work is not the mirror-for-princes genre or medieval and Renaissance republicanism in general, but the ideological writings of the Florentine civic humanists and the Florentine tradition at large.[18] In this tradition dating back to the late Dugento, comprising medieval Guelfism, early Quattrocento civic humanism, and the political

[16] On Machiavelli's influence on Zanobi Buondelmonti, one of the addressees of the *Discorsi*, and the other participants in the republican conspiracy of 1522, see Iacopo Nardi, *Istorie della città di Firenze*, ed. L. Arbib (2 vols., Florence, 1838–41), II, p. 77. The fact that Machiavelli expects the implied readers of the *Discorsi* to be familiar with *Il principe* as well is evident from a series of cross references in the former to the latter. See *Discorsi* II.20, p. 381; III.19, p. 472; III.42, p. 516.

[17] The principal studies on the ideological aspects of Machiavelli's work are Skinner, *The Foundations of Modern Political Thought* (2 vols., Cambridge: Cambridge University Press, 1978), I, pp. 113–89; Maurizio Viroli, *From Politics to Reason of State: The Acquisition and Transformation of the Language of Politics 1250–1600* (Cambridge: Cambridge University Press, 1992), pp. 126–77. Cf. Felix Gilbert, *Machiavelli and Guicciardini: Politics and History in Sixteenth Century Florence* (Princeton: Princeton University Press, 1965), p. 188.

[18] While it is true that there existed two dominant ideological traditions in late medieval and early Renaissance Italy, one princely, or monarchic, and one republican, which both drew on ancient Roman history for propagandistic and legitimizing purposes, it remains unclear to what extent

thought of Savonarola, Florence was seen as an elect city, designated to become alternately the new Rome and the new Jerusalem. Celebrating their city's ancient origins and using her Roman heritage to bolster her republican form of government and her claim to territorial rule, Florentine propagandists and humanists created a powerful ideology based on the twin notions of liberty at home and empire abroad. Throughout his chancery career and later in his theoretical works, Machiavelli shared this patriotic outlook and sought out ways to promote Florence's longstanding aspirations to become a great and expanding empire, modeled on the example of the ancient Roman republic.

Although this understanding of the ideological context of Machiavelli's work is far from being original, it places us in a position to better appreciate the novelty of his political thought. For while Machiavelli draws on the same language of classical republicanism and the same Roman imperial ideology as the Florentine tradition in general, he extends, through his combined emphasis on first principles and the political *here and now*, the scope of political discourse to a general level of theory, as well as to a rhetorical level of application, which we rarely, if ever, encounter in the writings of Bruni, Palmieri, and the other civic humanists. This is why there is no paradox in saying that Machiavelli's work, in comparison to those of his Florentine predecessors, is at one and the same time less confined to its local and contemporary context, and more directly aimed at the *here and now* of Florentine politics.

This dual emphasis on the universal and the local also allows us to understand better how Machiavelli's ideological position on the relationship between modern Florence and ancient Rome differed from those of Bruni and the other civic humanists. While Machiavelli shared his predecessors' Roman-inspired view of the Republic as having two aims or ends – to preserve its liberty internally and to expand its empire externally – he did not, in contrast to them, regard the republican and imperial legacy of the ancient Roman republic as an exclusive Florentine birthright. To him, the Roman heritage was instead to be seen as a political and strategic model, which any state, or any ruler, could adopt and use as a blueprint for success. In Machiavelli's theoretical work, diplomatic reports, and private correspondence, there is a deep and genuine fear that some other modern

Machiavelli's work can be defined in relation to them. Rather than saying that Machiavelli combined elements from these two ideological vocabularies, it would be more accurate to say that he, by going back to the original Roman source, created a dynamic model of political development that contains ideological elements, notions, and concepts which can also be found in the works of medieval and Renaissance princely ideologues and republican theorists.

state will bring about this Roman revival before the Florentines.[19] In the *Discourses*, and later in *The Art of War* (1518), he claims that the Venetians have had the ambition to create a new "world monarchy like the Roman" – *una nuova monarchia nel mondo* – but that they have failed to seize the opportunity because they had refrained from arming their own citizens.[20] In his letters to Francesco Vettori, written while, and shortly after, he was composing *The Prince*, the former Secretary expressed his apprehension about the Swiss, who at the time were in the process of ousting the French from Lombardy and establishing control over the strategically important city of Milan. Since the Swiss in their militia consciously imitated the ancient Romans, Machiavelli feared that they would before long emerge as the new lords or arbiters of Italy.[21] The general assumption underlying this imagined scenario Machiavelli makes explicit in *The Art of War*, where he argues that the first Italian ruler who "starts down this road [i.e. adopts the Roman-inspired miliary system presented and promoted in the work] before anyone else, will become lord of this province (*signore di questa provincia*)."[22] Although these fears may have been unfounded, they go a long way to explain the sense of urgency and the burning desire for political

19 Patrick Coby, who claims that Machiavelli is "not a patriot," but "a technician of statecraft, an adviser without loyalties, happy to offer his knowledge to any who understand," mistakes the universalizing tendency of Machiavelli's work for a lack of attachment to his *patria*, his native Florence; see *Machiavelli's Romans: Liberty and Greatness in the Discourses on Livy* (Lanham, MA: Lexington, 1999), p. 27. When Coby writes that the former Secretary's "advice, written down and soon to be published, respects no national boundaries," he seems to be implying that Machiavelli was intent on having his major works, *Il principe* and the *Discorsi*, published and disseminated also to audiences outside Florence. Of course, there is nothing to support this claim, and from what we know Machiavelli never made any effort to have these works made available outside Florentine circles. See chapter 1, note 43 above, and note 23 below. Machiavelli's love of *patria* is a constant theme in his work, see Yves Charles Zarka, "L'amour de la patrie chez Machiavel," *Archives de Philosophie* 62 (1999): 269–80; and pp. 258–63 above.

20 *Discorsi* III.31, p. 495 and *Opere*, ed. Vivanti, I, p. 549. On the term "world monarchy," *monarchia nel mondo* or *monarchia universalis*, see Franz Bosbach, *Monarchia universalis: Ein politischer Leitbegriff der frühen Neuzeit* (Göttingen: Vandenhoeck & Ruprecht, 1988); Anthony Pagden, *Lords of All the World: Ideologies of Empire in Spain, Britain and France, c. 1500–c. 1800* (New Haven: Yale University Press, 1995), pp. 29–62. The accusation that Venice was aspiring to the "monarchia d'Italia" was commonplace in Italian diplomatic discourse from the mid-fifteenth century onwards, see Paolo Margaroli, "L'Italia come percezione di uno spazio politico unitario negli anni cinquanta del XV secolo," *Nuova rivista storica* 74 (1990), pp. 529–30.

21 On Machiavelli's view of the Swiss, see John M. Najemy, *Between Friends: Discourses of Power and Desire in the Machiavelli–Vettori Letters of 1513–1515* (Princeton: Princeton University Press, 1993), pp. 157–65, 170–75, 180–84, 300–04, and *passim*; Mikael Hörnqvist, "*Perché non si usa allegare i Romani*: Machiavelli and the Florentine Militia of 1506," *Renaissance Quarterly* 55 (2002), pp. 185–86. Machiavelli had as early as 1500, or thereabouts, been impressed by how the Swiss in their militia were attempting to revive the infantry orders and military virtue of the ancient Romans.

22 *Arte della guerra*, p. 689: "E io vi affermo che qualunque di quelli che tengono oggi stati in Italia prima entrerrà per questa via, fia, prima che alcuno altro, signore di questa provincia."

change that pervade most, if not all, of Machiavelli's writings from *Del modo* of 1503 to *The Art of War* of 1518.[23]

The fact that Florence had no hereditary right to the title of the new Rome, or to the pragmatic Roman model, in Machiavelli's view did not diminish the importance of the Roman example for his native city. On the contrary, it merely meant that the ideological language of the Florentine tradition had to be recast into a rhetorical mold, and given a more practical and process-oriented articulation. The centrality of the Florentine context for Machiavelli's work is evident from how he on the ideological level labored to influence, and to change, the ways in which the Florentine elites, present and future, not men in general, thought and talked about politics.[24] As we have seen, the main target of criticism in his theoretical writings, *The Prince* and the *Discourses* included, are the *savi*, the wise men of Florence, whom he reproaches for having elevated their weak policy of half-measures and compromise to the level of political wisdom. To win acceptance for his own radical views, and to pave the way for a policy based on the Roman model in Florence, Machiavelli found it necessary to expose the ideological nature of this received wisdom, and to contest the ideological foundation of the Florentine republican tradition and the established Florentine foreign policy doctrine, based on notions such as the middle way, temporization, and neutrality.

Machiavelli's attack on the ideological conventions of Florentine political culture took added historical importance from the fact that the middle way (*via del mezzo*) was not only a central tenet of Florentine foreign policy, but also a key element in Aristotelian ethics. As is well known, Aristotle had defined virtue as a mean, or a middle way, between extremes. By turning Aristotle's notion on its head and by redefining virtue as the ability to encompass and to make complementary use of the extremes, Machiavelli, inspired by the Roman imperial strategy, came to effect a

[23] The fact that this sense of urgency gradually begins to fade from Machiavelli's work should be seen in relation to John Najemy's observation that his writings from *Il principe* to the *Istorie fiorentine* show a "progressively deepening interest in the history of his city." See "Machiavelli and the Medici: The Lessons of Florentine History," *Renaissance Quarterly* 35 (1982), p. 555. Cf. Nicolai Rubinstein, "Machiavelli and the World of Florentine Politics," in *Studies on Machiavelli*, ed. M. P. Gilmore (Florence: Sansoni, 1972), p. 23.

[24] This is also to say that Machiavelli's work is not adressed, at least not primarily, to a disembodied political analyst existing outside time and space, as Mansfield seems to suggest. See Harvey C. Mansfield, *Machiavelli's Virtue* (Chicago: University of Chicago Press, 1996), pp. x, 50, 109–10, 182–83, and 277–78. Cf. Anthony Parel, "Why did Machiavelli Write The Prince?" *Machiavelli Studies* 3 (1990): 154–61, esp. 157–58. Mansfield claims that "Machiavelli does not speak only to Florentines or to Italians but to all men." See *Machiavelli's Virtue*, p. 277. Perhaps, it would here be more correct to say that the author of *Il principe* and the *Discorsi* speaks to men in general, but to Florentines more specifically.

minor revolution in the history of ethics. To repeat Roman success and to achieve republican liberty and imperial greatness, Machiavelli implies, the modern Florentines would have to break with the Aristotelian and the Christian definitions of virtue. For him, to be "good" or to be "virtuous" includes displaying the conventional virtues, but also being able to make calculated and dispassionate use of vice, or to "enter into evil," as he puts it in *The Prince*. The ancient Romans displayed love of liberty, patriotism, and an admirable commitment to the civic culture of their city, but, as Machiavelli was quick to add, they also showed a great capacity for deceit and cruelty. These combined qualities, embodied by military commanders such as Manlius Torquatus and Furius Camillus, had enabled the Romans to remain free for centuries and to pursue a policy of continuing conquest that had made their republic mighty and glorious.

The strategic and ethical considerations underlying the Roman policy of conquest Machiavelli makes explicit when discussing the destruction of Alba and the pacification of Latium, two episodes belonging to a crucial stage in the Roman development that the modern Florentine republic had yet to reach. In *Discourses* II.3, Machiavelli, by quoting Livy's famous dictum "Meanwhile Rome grew from the ruin of Alba" (*Crescit interea Roma Albae ruinis*),[25] invites his Florentine readers to consider how destruction and growth were related in the rise of Roman power. The fate of the ancient city of Alba had been sealed, we learn from Livy, when the Roman king, Tullus, after its conquest in *c.* 650 BC, had ordered it to be razed and the Alban people transfered to Rome to dwell there. After the destruction, however, great benefits followed for the vanquished. Appearing before them, Tullus solemnly proclaimed that the Roman people were now ready to welcome them into their city.[26] The king made good on his promise. To encourage further settlements in the part of Rome allotted to the Albans, he chose it as the site for his new palace. The foremost among the new settlers he elevated to Roman senators, and many others were recruited to the Roman army, where they were given ranks according to their social status. Since these favors must be seen as excessive and extraordinary, considering that they were bestowed by a conqueror on a vanquished people, it would be simplistic or reductive to claim that the Albans were destroyed, pure and

[25] See Livy I.30.I.

[26] Ibid., I.28.7. In his rendering of Tullus's speech before the Albans, Livy conveys the vision of a growing Roman empire (English trans. B. O. Foster from *Livy in Fourteen Volumes* (Cambridge, MA: Harvard University Press, 1919–59), I, p. 103): "May prosperity, favour, and fortune be with the Roman people and myself, and with you, men of Alba! I purpose to bring all the Alban people over to Rome, to grant citizenship to their commons, to enrol the nobles in the senate, to make one city and one state."

simple. Perhaps, it would be more correct to say that they were destroyed as Albans, before being recreated and benefited as Romans.[27]

Another example illustrating how Rome used a combined policy of destruction and benefits to increase in size and strength is provided by Furius Camillus's conquest of Latium in 338 BC, related by Livy and discussed by Machiavelli in *Del modo* and the *Discourses*. In his speech before the Senate, Camillus sets out two radical options for how to deal with the defeated Latins – cruel punishment or kind forgiveness – of which he himself seems to favor a policy of clemency and the extension of citizenship to the vanquished.[28] This latter policy, Camillus argues, had been made possible through military victory, which had reduced the Latins to an impressionable state and made them susceptible to molding. He therefore urges the Senate to "resolve [their] own anxiety" and make up their minds regarding the fate of the vanquished, who are said to be awaiting their decision in "dull amazement," and with their "spirits suspended betwixt hope and fear."[29]

By repeatedly drawing his Florentine compatriots' attention to this important episode in Roman history, Machiavelli makes them witness a ritual of subjugation and becoming, staged by the conqueror with the purpose of rendering the vanquished more susceptible to the imposition of his new modes and orders. What the Roman art of empire in general, and the conquest of Latium in particuler, teaches, Machiavelli implies, is that people are most likely to allow themselves to be molded into obedient subjects, and potential citizens, after having undergone the purgatorial and liminal

[27] Machiavelli's reference to the Alban example in the *Discourses* II.3 is far from straightforward, and may need some clarification. The chapter opens with the above-mentioned quotation from Livy (see note 25 above), and continues with an account of how Rome promoted her own growth by use of force (*forza*) and of love (*amore*) – that is, on the one hand, the destruction of conquered cities and the compulsory resettlement of their inhabitants in Rome; and on the other, the encouragement of foreigners to come and settle in the city. This is followed by a comparison of this Roman strategy with the less effective policies of Sparta and Athens, before the chapter ends with the citation from Livy being repeated. Although Machiavelli does not discuss the conquest of Alba explicitly in the chapter (Alba is, in fact, only mentioned in the quotations from Livy at the beginning and the end), its function as a framing device suggests its importance for the argument as a whole. Although Machiavelli in the chapter defines *forza* and *amore* as two different methods (*vie*) for growth, his way of presenting them gives us reason to question how distinct they really are. The hospitality the Romans demonstrated towards the vanquished Albans, whose city they shortly before had destroyed, was no less generous than the welcome they normally bestowed on those who out of free choice came to live in their city.

[28] Livy VIII.13.16. According to Livy, Camillus addressed the Senate in these words (English trans. B. O. Foster, IV, p. 57): "Would you follow the example of your fathers, and augment the Roman state by receiving your conquered enemies as citizens? You have at hand the means of waxing great and supremely glorious. That government is certainly by far the strongest to which the subjects yield obedience gladly."

[29] Ibid., VIII.13.17 (English trans. B. O. Foster, IV, p. 57).

experience of being torn between the extremes of life and death.[30] Before being recreated as Romans, the Albans and the Latins had been put through this experience and the mental confusion and the loss of identity that go with it. By a spectacular use of force and terror, the Romans had purged them of their former selves and their former allegiances, before recreating them as Romans, equipping them with Roman arms, and investing them with Roman civic rights.

There were thus, if we are to believe Machiavelli, two sides to Rome's successful imperialism. On the one hand, it involved a policy of destruction that included the razing of cities, mass executions, and the deportation of peoples; on the other hand, it included a policy of benefits, such as the granting of citizenship, spectacular displays of mercy, and the resettlement of the vanquished in Rome. This two-sided imperial strategy enabled Rome to expand in population, territory, and military might. Its success was clearly visible, when Romans, Albans, and Latins soon could be seen fighting side by side in the Roman army for their common benefit and for the increase of Roman power.

The modern Florentines, with their parochial assumptions, their insistence on the policy of the middle way, and their inability to encompass and to combine the extremes, had never been able to achieve this reshaping of political identities. Whereas the rulers of the Roman monarchy and the early Roman republic had cultivated and developed the complex strategy of destroying *and* benefiting into a veritable imperialist art, the wise men of contemporary Florence had, because of "their weak education and their slight knowledge of things," failed to transcend the suffocating limits of the city-state.[31] After a promising start back in the Trecento, when the city had adopted a Roman-like strategy of fraternization vis-à-vis its closest neighbors, she had resorted to an ambiguous policy of hesitant suppression and

[30] The interesting case of the Pivernates, which Machiavelli refers to in *Discorsi* II.23 (pp. 348–49), does not contradict this inference. When a representative of the vanquished Pivernates appeared before the Roman Senate and was asked about what kind of peace the Romans could expect from his people, if they were to refrain from punishing them, he answered: "If you give us a good one, both faithful and perpetual; if a bad one, not long-lasting" (translation adapted from *Discourses on Livy*, p. 183). The Senate, or the wiser part of it, as Machiavelli remarks, appreciated the answer and decided to grant the Pivernates Roman citizenship. Through his brave statement, it would seem, the Pivernate had placed himself in the liminal position of the conquered. By disclosing to the Romans that his people were not going to accept a peace on bad terms, he had in fact imposed onto himself and his people the policy of the two extremes. The message conveyed by his statement could be summed up thus: either you let us live in liberty or you are welcome to destroy us. Since the wise among the Romans recognized themselves in this brave attitude, they decided to bestow the title of Roman citizen on a man, and on a people, who, mentally speaking, were already Romans.

[31] *Discorsi* III .27, p. 487: "Ma la debolezza de' presenti uomini, causata dalla debole educazione loro e dalla poca notizia delle cose."

uncommitted friendship. As a result, Florence had come to be surrounded by peoples animated by anti-Florentine sentiment, which had left her with no choice other than to rule her own territories and the neighboring cities by force and open repression. But instead of drawing the inevitable conclusion and destroying the city of Pisa politically, thus severing once and for all the attachment of the Pisans to their ancient communal liberty and the Pisan name, the Florentines had persisted in holding this notoriously rebellious and unruly people by means of fortresses. As a consequence, they had failed to convert their neighbors into loyal Florentine subjects willing to fight for the common cause of Florentine, or Tuscan, liberty and empire.

To achieve their longstanding aims of liberty and empire, and to found a true republic, Machiavelli contends, his compatriots would have to gain a better understanding of the dynamics of the ancient Roman republic, rethink their foreign policy doctrine based on appeasement and containment, and subject Aristotelian and Christian virtue to a radical redefinition. But Machiavelli's aim in *The Prince* and the *Discourses*, as elsewhere, is not merely to challenge and to manipulate the ideological conventions and the political language of his day, but also to influence policy-making and political action in a more concrete sense. To remain within the realm of political discourse would in his view be a sign of the very weakness and the corruption, political as well as intellectual and moral, that his work was intended to combat and remedy. The theoretical insights and the historical lessons it contains would remain ineffective and immaterial, he would have argued, if they were not implemented or applied to the *here and now*, where political decisions are made and the fates of nations decided. This observation leads us to address the rhetorical level of Machiavelli's work.

In this study, we have explored the meaning of Machiavelli's work mainly on two of the three levels of interpretation outlined above: on the one hand, the ideological level, focusing on how it draws on, challenges, and seeks to reshape a number of entrenched ideological and intellectual conventions, beliefs, and practices at the heart of Florentine political culture; on the other hand, the rhetorical level, inquiring into how Machiavelli in his principal works, *The Prince* and the *Discourses*, rhetorically addresses and interacts with his intended, or original, audiences with regard to the particularities of time, place, and circumstances. To this end, we have developed a dual, or double-layered, form of reading that encompasses the contrasting viewpoints of the author and his implied audience. To uncover Machiavelli's authorial intention, or intentions, and to bring out his text's intended intellectual and emotional effects on its designated reader, we have let it assert its power over us, and allowed our responses to be controlled by its arguments and its rhetorical devices. Differently put, we have through identification with Lorenzo de' Medici the younger, and the Medici family in general, inquired into what Machiavelli's *Prince* does, or attempts to do, to its princely reader. To grasp the intention of the *Discourses*, we have in a similar way read the treatise with a view to how the work was intended to be read and used by its young Florentine addressees, the republican readers of the Orti Oricellari. By so doing, we have favored the rhetorical approach over the theoretical and the ideological, but not to the exclusion of these other levels of interpretation. For as we have already made clear, Machiavelli's emphasis on the local and the contemporary context of early Cinquecento Florence does not by any means imply that his work is of no more than parochial interest. The articulation of his principles and their intended application might be directed toward the Florentine *here and now*, but, as Machiavelli himself was keenly aware, their character is generic and therefore applicable to any context, past, present, or future. His status as a modern classic and a lasting influence within the Western tradition would not have surprised the man, who in the preface to the *Discourses* claimed to have entered "a path as yet untrodden by anyone."[32]

This type of rhetorical reading requires a broad and multi-faceted contextual approach. To achieve this aim, we have situated our interpretations of *The Prince* and the *Discourses* in a great variety of political and cultural contexts: the contemporary theories of the justification of war, the Florentine foreign policy doctrine of the middle way and temporization, the republican love of liberty, the call for a return to the form of government associated with Lorenzo the Magnificent, the absenteeism of the Medici from Florence following Giovanni de' Medici's election to the Papacy, the recovery of Pisa and the pacification of the Florentine dominion, the classical Roman triumph, Aristotelian cosmology, and the pre-modern views on the sublunar world. We have also argued that Machiavelli's intellectual development and political project need to be understood in relation to the general ideological climate and the changing attitudes to the ancient Romans in early Cinquecento Florence. As we have seen, Machiavelli's overt and covert use of the Roman model and his repeated adaptations to the changing ideological, political, and moral landscape of contemporary Florence go a long way to explain his perplexing mixture of studied silences, insinuating remarks, and outspoken advice on subjects such as the connection between contemporary Florence and ancient Rome, and the republic's dual aim of

[32] Ibid., I preface, p. 197: "ho deliberato entrare per una via, la quale, non essendo suta ancora da alcuno trita."

liberty and empire. Our focus on how Machiavelli fitted his Roman example and his rhetorical strategies to suit the time, place, and circumstances has contributed to shedding new light on some of the major interpretative difficulties surrounding his work, and most importantly, offered a plausible explanation for the much-debated difference between *The Prince* and the *Discourses*.

As we have seen, Machiavelli's first elaborate use of the Roman expansionist model occurred in his memorandum on the Aretine question, *Del modo di trattare i popoli della Valdichiana ribellati*, of 1503. This oration, in which the Secretary of the Second Chancery explicitly argues that Florence in dealing with the Aretine rebellion should imitate the Roman policy of the two extremes, rule by destruction and by benefits, can be studied on the three levels of interpretation oulined above. On the level of principle, Machiavelli sets forth his theory of cyclical change and historical repetitiveness, restated later in the *Discourses*, while contrasting the positive Roman example to its negative Florentine counterpart. On the ideological level, these premises translate into criticism of the Florentine middle way and praise of the Roman imperial strategy of benefits and destruction. But as becomes abundantly clear toward the end of the extant draft of the oration, these general principles and ideological statements have in *Del modo* been adduced, on the rhetorical and practical level of discourse, merely to drive home the need for the pacification of the Aretine region, and to support the call to action.[33] If interpreted in this way, *Del modo* provides us with an early model for how Machiavelli's multi-dimensional rhetoric works when set forth in an open and undisguised manner.

Del modo can be seen as a brave, but perhaps injudicious, attempt on the part of the Secretary of the Second Chancery to exhort his employers to take a firm stand on the Aretine issue and to reshape Florentine attitudes toward territorial rule in general. The failure of the oration's Roman-inspired advice, it would seem, was due not only to it taking issue with the Florentine foreign policy doctrine of the middle way, but also to the fact that it conflicted with contemporary opinions on the ancient Romans. As we have seen, Machiavelli's proposal to imitate Roman imperial strategy was not favorably received in the governing circles of Florence, and the leading citizen Piero Guicciardini, in a *pratica* of January 1506, dismissed the idea of using the two extremes against Arezzo, because he judged it to be a "Roman thing." As this *pratica* and other contemporary sources, as well as Machiavelli's own retrospective comments in the *Discourses* and *The*

[33] For a fuller treatment of *Del modo*, see above pp. 103–06 above.

Art of War, indicate, the ancient Romans had in early Cinquecento Florence, for ideological, moral, and religious reasons, come to be viewed with suspicion, if not outright hostility. In the face of these anti-Roman sentiments, it seems reasonable to assume, Machiavelli later came to revise his rhetorical strategy and to renounce the combative rhetoric of *Del modo*. If correct, this assumption would explain the remarkable silence Machiavelli and his associates observed on the Roman model and the military system of the ancient Roman republic, a humanist commonplace, in their official writings on the new Florentine militia ordinance, initiated in 1506.[34] If this military and political project were to stand a chance of gaining the support of the Florentine leadership, Machiavelli seems to have realized, its Roman inspiration would have to be suppressed and kept secret.

After the return of the Medici in 1512, the ideological climate of Florence underwent a profound change and the ancient Romans regained their former symbolic role within the artistic, ritual, and political culture of the city. During St. John's Day of 1513, the new regime staged four triumphs with Roman imperial motifs – featuring Julius Caesar, Pompey, Caesar Augustus, and Trajan – accompanied by scrolls and tablets. As we have suggested, this choice of Roman triumphators, as well as a series of more practical measures taken during their first year back in Florence, indicated that the Medici were more inclined to princely power than to maintaining the city's republican tradition.[35] Machiavelli's references to ancient Roman examples in *The Prince*, which was begun around this time, reflect, comment on, and obliquely subvert the political message of these Medicean manifestations. In chapters 3 to 5 of the treatise, ancient Rome is explicitly cited as the prime model for expansionist warfare and imperialist strategy, and in chapter 16 the imposing figure of the Roman triumphator emerges from behind the enigmatic term the "big giver," or *gran donatore*. The internal, liberty-oriented implications of the Roman model are insinuated into *The Prince* 19 and 25, where Machiavelli, by intimating the necessity of the mixed constitution and the republican principle of rotation in office, advocates modes and orders that we have reason to believe were inspired by the processual view of the Roman development described above.

In our analysis of *The Prince*, we have come to witness how the former Secretary, by shaping his *principe nuovo* into part-classical tyrant and part-Roman triumphator, creates a vehicle for the foundation of a strong and expansive republic. Having freed his self-interest and his thirst for reputation, honor, glory, and greatness from conventional constraints, Machiavelli

[34] See Hörnqvist, "*Perché*." [35] See above pp. 159–60 above.

goes on to cut away the ground under his princely reader's feet to make him susceptible to rhetorical manipulation and to the advice that he has no other remedy at his disposal than to introduce an embryonic form of civil government. The strategy of exploiting the self-serving and power-seeking character of a tyrannically inclined ruler for a good end, we have argued, follows naturally from Aristotle's assumptions that a tyrant, who primarily sees to his own utility, is more likely to let himself be persuaded and moved if exhorted to do so for the sake of his own security, or personal gain, than for some other, more noble end. It also seems to stem from Machiavelli's general view of human nature. According to the Florentine most men are wicked, shortsighted, selfish, governed by appearances, fears, and hopes of short-term gains.[36] Such persons, it could be argued, can only be persuaded to serve a good end, or to pursue good effects, unwittingly, and in spite of themselves, through appeals to their selfish desires or aspirations.

In this rhetorical strategy, it is of secondary importance whether the prince is aware of the part he has been assigned to play in the overall scheme and whether he understands the full ramifications of his actions. What matters in Machiavelli's political script, as in his comedy *La mandragola*, is that each of the involved parties plays its role effectively, contributing to the happy outcome of the operation and to the satisfaction of all. It could even be argued that the success of the plot of *The Prince* depends upon, or at least is greatly facilitated by, the princely agent being ignorant of the republican motivations governing the project as a whole. Such a princely reader could be assumed to happily mistake the personal glory and the greatness Machiavelli promises him for the ultimate purpose of *The Prince*.

The absolute, or next to absolute, silence Machiavelli in *The Prince* observes on the Florentine and republican dimensions of his project needs little explanation. For openly to advocate a program of Florentine expansionism in a manuscript set to circulate at the Roman curia would have been naïve in the extreme, and to speak frankly about republican motives in a treatise addressed to a family aspiring to princely power equally imprudent.[37] Instead of committing such uncharacteristic and novice-like blunders, we are now in a position to argue, Machiavelli made a virtue of necessity, and overcame the external constraints under which he was writing, by making them into an integral aspect of his rhetorical mode of expression.

[36] In *The Prince* 17 (p. 163), for example, he states that men in general, princes not excluded, are "ingrati, volubili, simulatori e dissimulatori, fuggitori de' pericoli, cupidi del guadagno."

[37] As we recall, Machiavelli on 10 December 1513 entreated his friend Francesco Vettori, the Florentine ambassador to Rome, to show the original version of *Il principe* to Giulano de' Medici. On this occasion, Machiavelli also expressed misgivings about the treatise falling into the hands of Piero Ardinghelli, one of Giuliano's Florentine secretaries. See *Lettere*, pp. 296–97.

Addressing his republican friends of the Orti Oricellari later in the *Discourses* and *The Art of War* (begun in 1518 and published in 1521), Machiavelli cast off the courtier's mask to offer extensive analysis of the political and military system of the ancient Roman republic, and the love of liberty and the acquisitive mentality which he regarded as the driving forces behind Rome's unprecedented territorial expansion and empire-building.[38] These works attest to the continuity of Machiavelli's intellectual and political project and his long-term commitment to the idea of a Florentine empire based on the principles of power politics embodied by the ancient Roman republic. In the *Discourses*, the reader is invited to participate in Machiavelli's own investigations into Roman history, ancient and modern republicanism, the general principles of power politics, the instrumental use of religion, the causes of political and moral corruption and decay, and so forth. By means of spectacular examples and other rhetorical strategies, the reader is led to conceive of, and to evaluate, various historical situations, examples, and political modes and orders. Machiavelli's primary concern in this work, it would seem, is to promote his readers' understanding and judgment of statesmanship and worldly things in general. Instead of presenting his advice in a candid and straightforward manner, Machiavelli takes his readers on a long quest for the secrets behind Rome's rise to greatness, assigning them a role as co-participants in the text, leaving many things to be inferred and many conclusions precariously suspended along the way. This strategy is evident, for example, in *Discourses* II.4, where Machiavelli implicates his readers in a series of interpretative choices, designed to make them detect the deceptive Roman imperial strategy of expanding through alliances, conquest, and assimiliation.[39] This exploration is followed by direct advice, addressed to his Florentine compatriots, to revive the Tuscan league of the past, which on closer inspection reveals itself to be a thinly disguised version of the first step in the Roman method.[40]

But as we have seen, the Florentine and the republican reader of the *Discourses* is addressed in *The Prince* as well, where he, in various subtexts beneath the princely discourse of the work, is conjured into being through a series of conspiratorial winks and subtle innuendos. By reading between

[38] On the Florentine context of *The Art of War*, see Hörnqvist, "*Perché*," pp. 169–70.

[39] This strategy anticipates not only the rhetorical performance of Ligurio in Machiavelli's *La mandragola*, but also those of Michel de Montaigne in his *Essais* and of Iago in Shakespeare's *Othello*. On the two latter examples, see David Lewis Schaefer, *The Political Philosophy of Montaigne* (Ithaca: Cornell University Press, 1990), and Brian Vickers, *Appropriating Shakespeare: Contemporary Critical Quarrels* (New Haven: Yale University Press, 1993), pp. 74–91.

[40] For a fuller treatment of *Discourses* II.4, see above pp. 133–39 above.

the lines, an ability Machiavelli's text actively encourages us to develop, and by investigating purposeful irregularities and intentional ambiguities, the analytical reader of *The Prince* is led to discover the work's Florentine bias and the embryonic stages of the republican development, described more fully and openly in the *Discourses*. From the elevated and privileged vantage point of this discerning reader, many of Machiavelli's iron laws, axiomatic convictions, and other absolutes come to assume a somewhat dubious and ironic character. Rather than being unconditional statements of truth, they reveal themselves to be rhetorical constructs of a more temporary or provisional application. Machiavelli's irony and the tongue-in-cheek tone of his text can in large part be explained as an effect of his double-layered form of discourse, which allows two conflicting perspectives to coexist without loss of textual integrity: on the one hand, the limited understanding of the princely reader; on the other, the more farsighted and synoptic point of view of the republican counselor or political analyst. Since the former perspective is contained within the latter, the ideologies and the constitutional ideals they represent cannot be considered to be of equal or comparable value. As we have been able to conclude, there is in *The Prince*, as well as in the *Discourses*, internal textual evidence to support the notion that the republic is superior to the principality, and that the latter is to be seen as nothing more than a preparatory, or preliminary, stage in a constitutional development based on the Roman model. This is also to say that the contrast between *The Prince* and the *Discourses* should be understood as a difference in audience, strategy, and emphasis, but not in aim.

How, then, is Machiavelli's subtle and elaborate way of writing to be explained? While it is easy to see the reasons for him engaging in secret writing in *The Prince*, where he speaks directly to the hostile, or potentially hostile, audience of a tyrannical ruler, and only indirectly to the good, it is more difficult to see why he should continue to write in this guarded, or indirect, manner also in the *Discourses*, where he explicitly addresses good men, who for "their infinite good parts" deserve to be princes.[41] The intricate form of discourse that Machiavelli develops in the latter work, we may speculate, stems not from external constraints, but from the insight that a teaching based on implicatures and implied meanings is more effective, and more congenial to the cultivation of political prudence, than the open and direct form of education contained in the traditional mirror-for-princes and the humanist treatises on republican government. In any case, through this rhetorical invention, Machiavelli took political discourse to new, unprecedented heights, and developed a radically new form of strategic thinking

[41] *Discorsi*, dedication, p. 196: "per le infinite buone parti loro."

that was later to find its way on to the Elizabethan stage, as well as into the secret chambers of Whitehall, Quay d'Orsay, and Washington.

But as we all well know, Machiavelli's own imperial dreams and his imagined Florentine republic of the future were never to materialize. The Medici's intention of becoming newborn Romans, it soon became clear, did not extend beyond the ritual arena of Florence, and Machiavelli's hope of seeing them use the moral and financial backing of the Church to pursue Florence's longstanding aspirations to become a new Rome, not only culturally, but also politically and militarily, would rapidly begin to fade. Admittedly, there were moments of renewed hopes, as when, for example, in January 1515 rumors had it that Paolo Vettori, Francesco's brother, was about to be made Medicean governor of Parma, Piacenza, Modena, and Reggio, and possibly to appoint Machiavelli as his personal adviser.[42] Perhaps a second such instance was the election of Lorenzo the Younger as captain of the revived Florentine militia in August 1515, which, as we have seen, in the official documents was said to take its inspiration from the ancient Roman practice of placing one of their own citizens at the head of their army.[43] Another moment occurred in 1520, when Cardinal Giulio de' Medici, the future Pope Clement VII, in examining the possibility of reforming the government of Florence, requested constitutional proposals from Machiavelli and a number of other Florentine intellectuals. In his contribution to this debate, *Discursus Florentinarum Rerum*, the former Secretary outlined a reform program which, in the vein of *The Prince* and following his Roman model, would have reordered the city as a true republic, while giving princely, or monarchic, authority to the childless cardinal during his lifetime. Like a modern-day Romulus, Giulio de' Medici would "command the army, exercise full control over the criminal courts, and

42 On this episode, see Najemy, *Between Friends*, pp. 330–34. However, I cannot agree with Najemy's conclusion that Machiavelli's letter to Francesco Vettori of 31 January 1515 shows that the former Secretary by this time had given up his hopes of playing an advisory role in Medicean politics. On the contrary, in my view, the letter clearly indicates that he not only hoped but expected that Paolo Vettori would employ him and make use of his advice from *Il principe*. Having in the letter outlined how the program of *Il principe* could be applied to the task facing Paolo, Machiavelli added (*Lettere*, p. 350): "Io ne parlai seco [i.e. Paolo Vettori]; piacqueli, e penserà d'aiutarsene." For interpretations of this letter similar to the one adopted here, see Hans Baron, "The *Principe* and the puzzle of the date of chapter 26," *Journal of Medieval and Renaissance Studies* 21 (1991): 83–102, esp. 98–100; Sergio Bertelli, *Introduzione all'Opera Omnia di Niccolò Machiavelli* (Milan: Feltrinelli, 1968), pp. xxviii–xxix.

43 See above, p. 161 above. It is generally assumed that the dedicatory letter accompanying *Il principe* dates from the first half of 1515. On the date of the dedication, see Carlo Dionisotti, "Machiavelleria ultima," *Rivista storica italiana* 57 (1995): 20–28; Giorgio Inglese, "Introduzione," in Niccolò Machiavelli, *De Principatibus* (Rome: Istituto storico italiano per il Medio Evo, 1994), pp. 8–9; Corrado Vivanti, "Introduzione," in *Opere*, ed. Vivanti, 1, pp. 831–32; see also Baron, "The *Principe* and the puzzle of the date of chapter 26."

have the laws in [his] breast."[44] The arrangement thus would not only have provided Florence with her long-awaited republican constitution, but it would also have given the cardinal the best of both worlds: security and power in this life, and the eternal glory and fame that pertain to founders of republics in the next.[45] As we can see, this was an exceptionally cheeky proposal, and Machiavelli can hardly have been surprised when it became clear that Cardinal Giulio had no intention of adopting his scheme.

In this context it is of more than passing interest to confront Machiavelli's political project with the views of Francesco Guicciardini, the former Secretary's distinguished friend and his most perceptive contemporary reader, whom he in a letter, in a rare gesture of recognition, describes as someone who "understands the secrets" and "knows the world."[46] According to Guicciardini, who had come to accept Machiavelli's general view that states undergo cycles of birth, rise, maturity, and senescence, Florence was unfit for radical reforms and constitutional innovations, since the city was aging and already on her way down. For the aristocratic Guicciardini, the aim of Florentine politics should instead be to save what could be saved, and to remedy what was not beyond repair. In his *Dialogo* of 1520, he has the elderly Bernardo del Nero, the main voice of the dialogue, warn his *ottimati* audience of the difficulties involved in changing the government of Florence:

Consider, too, that our city is now old, and as far as one can conjecture from its development, the nature of things and past examples, it is now declining rather than growing. It's not like a new-born or a young city, which is easy to form and set up, and receives the habits given to it without any difficulty. When cities are old, it is difficult to reform them; and once they have been reformed, they soon lose their good set-up and always remember their original bad habits.[47]

44 *Opere*, ed. Vivanti, 1, p. 743: "ella è una monarchia, perché voi comandate all'armi, comandate a' giudici criminali, avete le leggi in petto". On the *Discursus Florentinarum Rerum*, see Guidubaldo Guidi, "La teoria delle 'tre ambizioni' nel pensiero politico fiorentino del primo Cinquecento," *Il pensiero politico* 5 (1972): 241–59, esp. pp. 244–53; Viroli, *From Politics to Reason of State*, pp. 169–73; Wayne A. Rebhorn, *Foxes and Lions: Machiavelli's Confidence Men* (Ithaca: Cornell University Press, 1988), pp. 225–26; Alison Brown, *The Medici in Florence: The Exercise and Language of Power* (Florence: Olschki, 1992), pp. 239 and 297–98; Giovanni Silvano, "Florentine Republicanism in the Early Sixteenth Century," in *Machiavelli and Republicanism*, eds. G. Bock, Q. Skinner, and M. Viroli (Cambridge: Cambridge University Press, 1993), pp. 56–61; Theodore A. Sumberg, *Political Literature of Europe: Before and After Machiavelli* (Lanham, MD: University Press of America, 1993), pp. 52–62. See also Guidubaldo Guidi, "Niccolò Machiavelli e i progetti di riforme costituzionali a Firenze nel 1522," *Il pensiero politico* 2 (1969): 580–90.

45 See *Opere*, ed. Vivanti, 1, p. 744.

46 *Lettere* (Machiavelli to Francesco Guicciardini on 22 May 1526), p. 427: "Io direi piú oltre, se io parlassi con uomo che non intendesse i segreti o non conoscesse il mondo."

47 Francesco Guicciardini, *Dialogo e discorsi del reggimento di Firenze* (Bari: Laterza, 1932), pp. 81–82; English trans., *Dialogue on the Goverment of Florence*, trans. Alison Brown (Cambridge: Cambridge University Press, 1994), p. 79. Cf. J. G. A. Pocock, *The Machiavellian Moment: Florentine Political*

It is tempting to take this admonition as being addressed to Machiavelli and his Florentine readership, and to read Bernardo's argument as a refutation of the former Secretary's view that Florence is an unfounded and unborn city with a promising bright future.[48] This reading, which would suggest that Machiavelli's ideas by this time had come to gain a certain following in Florence, is supported by the fact that Guicciardini shortly afterwards sat down to compose a critical commentary on the *Discourses*. Objecting to his friend's cult of the Roman republic, Guicciardini here argued that Machiavelli in idealizing the ancients had turned a blind eye to their manifest shortcomings, and omitted to mention several valuable modern political and military innovations of which they had been ignorant.[49] It is a mistake, Guicciardini states in his *Ricordi*, to "quote the Romans at every turn," since following the Roman example in all situations would require a city that lived under identical conditions. In the same way as it would be foolish to "expect an ass to race like a horse," he implies, it is ridiculous to believe that tired old Florence could follow in the footsteps of ancient Rome.[50] The success of the Roman republic, Guicciardini contends, is beyond replication.

When Machiavelli in his *Istorie fiorentine* (1520–25) looks back upon more than three centuries of Florentine internal and external development, he appears to have absorbed his friend's criticism and come around to share his view on Florence's past history and future destiny. In any case, Machiavelli now claims that the Florentines had emerged on the historical scene back in mid-Dugento, when they had founded "their liberty" (*la loro libertá*), and within a short time acquired such "authority and force" that they had emerged not only as "head of Tuscany," but also as one of the leading cities of Italy.[51] After the enactment of the Ordinances of Justice in 1295, the city had arrived at the peak of her historical cycle, or as Machiavelli puts it: "Never was our city in a greater or more happy state than at that time." Her riches and reputation were formidable in the eyes of others, and her military might great. The fact that she could muster 30,000 men at arms, a number that could be increased to a staggering 70,000 by the

Thought and the Atlantic Tradition (Princeton: Princeton University Press, 1975), pp. 240–41 and 247.

[48] Cf. Pocock, *The Machiavellian Moment*, p. 232.

[49] Francesco Guicciardini, "Considerazioni intorni ai Discorsi del Machiavelli sopra la prima deca di Tito Livio," in Giucciardini, *Scritti politici e ricordi* (Bari: Laterza, 1993), p. 57.

[50] Guicciardini, *Ricordi*, 2nd series, n. 110 in Giucciardini, *Scritti politici e ricordi*, p. 308: "volere che uno asino facessi el corso di uno cavallo." English translation in Guicciardini, *Dialogue on the Government of Florence*, p. 173.

[51] *Istorie fiorentine* II.6, p. 350: "Né si potrebbe pensare quanto di autorità e forze in poco tempo Firenze si acquistasse; e non solamente capo di Toscana divenne, ma intra le prime città di Italia era numerata."

raising of additional troops in the countryside, had, in conjunction with her internal unity and social harmony, enabled her to extend her empire over the whole of Tuscany, which now obeyed her "in part as subject, in part as friend."[52] However, from here on, Machiavelli's Florentine history is the unfolding narrative of a gradual decline, the main theme of which is the Arno republic's chronic inability to grasp the opportunities that come her way. Although there are moments of regained vitality and ingenuity, of which we have seen an example in connection to the expulsion of the Duke of Athens in 1343, the lessons offered are as a rule of a purely negative kind.[53] As we approach Machiavelli's own time, the tone becomes more resigned and disparaging. The conflict-ridden and defensively minded Medicean republic of the Quattrocento, in which the greed of merchants has taken the place of civic values, and where hired mercenaries have been substituted for the communal militia, offers a sharp contrast to the young, vigorous Florentine commune of the late Dugento. On the few occasions Machiavelli raises his argument to the theoretical and ideological levels of *The Prince* and the *Discourses*, it is merely to rehearse his usual juxtaposition of ancient Rome, that timeless key to political success, and modern Florence, the sorrowful city of wasted opportunities.[54] The Florence of Machiavelli's *Istorie fiorentine* is indeed a tired old city, a humble ass unfit to run with the horses, and most definitely not the stuff of which glorious empires are made.

With no Florentine founder and no new, vigorous republic visible on the horizon, the aging Machiavelli seems to have resigned himself to the fact that his beloved Florence would not, after all, become the historical stage for the implementation of his project. Perhaps he took some consolation in the thought that others, as he had predicted in the preface to the *Discourses*, would come after him and bring his enterprise to fruition in other places

[52] Ibid., II.15, p. 363: "Né mai fu la città nostra in maggiore e più felice stato che in questi tempi, sendo di uomini, di ricchezze e di riputazione ripiena; i cittadini atti alle armi a trentamila e quelli del suo contado a settantamila aggiugnevano; tutta la Toscana, parte come subietta parte come amica, le ubbidiva." These figures should be compared with Machiavelli's remark in *Discourses* II.3, where he claims that ancient Rome, by employing *forza* and *amore*, grew so rapidly that the city already at the time of her sixth king was able to raise an army of 80,000 men.

[53] See above pp. 140–41.

[54] The essential scholarship on Machiavelli's *Istorie fiorentine* includes Felix Gilbert, "Machiavelli's *Istorie Fiorentine*: An Essay in Interpretation," in *Studies on Machiavelli*, ed. Gilmore, pp. 83–95; Hulliung, *Citizen Machiavelli*, pp. 68–92; Najemy, "Machiavelli and the Medici"; Salvatore di Maria, "Machiavelli's Ironic View of History: The *Istorie Fiorentine*," *Renaissance Quarterly* 45 (1992): 248–70; Mansfield, *Machiavelli's Virtue*, pp. 137–75; Riccardo Fubini, "Machiavelli, i Medici, e la storia di Firenze nel Quattrocento," *Archivio Storico Italiano* 155 (1997): 127–41; Mark Jurdjevic, "Machiavelli's Sketches of Francesco Valori and the Reconstruction of Florentine History," *Journal of the History of Ideas* 63 (2002): 185–206.

and at other times.[55] Needless to say, in this respect, history was to prove him right, for there has over the centuries certainly been no lack of candidates, eager to listen to his advice, and to pick up his theory, or what they have taken to be his theory, and to apply it to their own *here and now*.

For his many disciples and followers, Machiavelli's work would come to serve as an inexhaustible source of worldly wisdom, a storehouse of cynical maxims, and a fundamental link back to classical political philosophy. It offered an antidote to wishful thinking and a rite of initiation into the *arcana imperii* and the art of rhetorical manipulation. These new Machiavellians would in his overall theory also find many things on which to improve. While they accepted his general premises, the rise of capitalism, the discoveries of modern science, and the continuous progress in technology allowed them to draw other conclusions from them. The insight that trade, technical innovations, and capital investments may lead to global economic growth made obsolete the Florentine's zero-sum view of the world, but at the same time strengthened his claim that the pursuit of self-interest may contribute to the public good. Important advances in the applied sciences and in military technology made outmoded his all-inclusive Roman model, but at the same time provided the moderns with new powerful means to realize the time-honored aims of the Roman republican tradition, liberty and empire. In a similar way, the physics of Galileo Galilei, by establishing the unity of matter and by eliminating the division between the sublunar and the supralunar spheres, not only tore to pieces the Aristotelian cosmology, to which Machiavelli and most of his contemporaries had subscribed, but also gave added weight to the Florentine Secretary's focus on the mundane, sublunar realm and on worldly affairs in general.

As the traditional and pre-modern framework of Machiavelli's theory fell away, almost like a cardboard stage set, dissolved and vanished, it became apparent that many of his general assumptions, stereotypes, and preconceptions did carry surprisingly little weight in his thought. Dislodged from its Florentine context and its contemporary trappings, the core of Machiavelli's theory – his exclusive focus on *cose del mondo*, his view of human nature as desiring, acquisitive, and expansive, and his uncompromising rejection of the status quo in all respects and in all areas – revealed itself to constitute a dynamic, emerging, and ever-developing historical force, which has later come to be known by the name of modernity. By unchaining man's

[55] *Discorsi*, preface, pp. 198–99: "E benché questa impresa sia difficile, nondimanco, aiutato da coloro che mi hanno, ad entrare sotto questo peso, confortato, credo portarlo in modo, che ad un altro resterà breve cammino a condurlo a loco destinato."

desire for acquisition and love of liberty, his *desiderare di acquistare* and his *affezione del vivere libero*, Machiavelli had created a power destined to put an end to centuries of backwardness, obscurantism, and oppression. By tearing asunder veils of political and religious illusion, and by impressing itself upon hearts and minds, embracing those who want to join in its progress, and uprooting and devouring all that comes in its way, or opposes its principles and interests, it has transformed, and is in the process of transforming, the lives of millions of people. Its advances have been cheered by many and left others standing in shock and awe. It has given rise to resentment and hatred, and fueled a clash of identities and of civilizations. Is it a destructive or benevolent force? A new form of imperialism disguised as democracy and globalization, while in reality relying on naked, shameless, and brutal exploitation? Or is it a liberator that will bring justice and benefit to mankind? Perhaps it is still too early to say. What is beyond doubt, though, is that the aim of this power is to conquer the world, and to do so in the name of liberty.

Index

IDEAS IN CONTEXT

Edited by QUENTIN SKINNER (*General Editor*), LORRAINE DASTON, DOROTHY ROSS and JAMES TULLY

1 RICHARD RORTY, J. B. SCHNEEWIND and QUENTIN SKINNER (eds.)
Philosophy in History
Essays in the historiography of philosophy
pb: 0 521 27330 7

2 J. G. A. POCOCK
Virtue, Commerce and History
Essays on political thought and history, chiefly in the eighteenth century
pb: 0 521 27660 8

3 M. M. GOLDSMITH
Private Vices, Public Benefits
Bernard Mandeville's social and political thought
hb: 0 521 30036 3

4 ANTHONY PAGDEN (ed.)
The Languages of Political Theory in Early Modern Europe
pb: 0 521 38666 7

5 DAVID SUMMERS
The Judgment of Sense
Renaissance nationalism and the rise of aesthetics
pb: 0 521 38631 4

6 LAURENCE DICKEY
Hegel: Religion, Economics and the Politics of Spirit, 1770–1807
pb: 0 521 38912 7

7 MARGO TODD
Christian Humanism and the Puritan Social Order
hb: 0 521 33129 3

8 LYNN SUMIDA JOY
Gassendi the Atomist
Advocate of history in an age of science
hb: 0 521 30142 4

9 EDMUND LEITES (ed.)
Conscience and Casuistry in Early Modern Europe
hb: 0 521 30113 0

10 WOLF LEPENIES
Between Literature and Science: The Rise of Sociology
pb: 0 521 33810 7

11 TERENCE BALL, JAMES FARR and RUSSELL L. HANSON (eds.)
Political Innovation and Conceptual Change
pb: 0 521 35978 3

12 GERD GIGERENZER *et al.*
The Empire of Chance
How probability changed science and everyday life
pb: 0 521 39838 x

13 PETER NOVICK
That Noble Dream
The 'objectivity question' and the American historical profession
pb: 0 521 35745 4

14 DAVID LIEBERMAN
The Province of Legislation Determined
Legal theory in eighteenth-century Britain
hb: 0 521 24592 3

15 DANIEL PICK
Faces of Degeneration
A European disorder, c.1848–c.1918
pb: 0 521 45753 x

16 KEITH BAKER
Inventing the French Revolution
Essays on French political culture in the eighteenth century
pb: 0 521 38578 4

17 IAN HACKING
The Taming of Chance
pb: 0 521 38884 8

18 GISELA BOCK, QUENTIN SKINNER and MAURIZIO VIROLI (eds.)
Machiavelli and Republicanism
pb: 0 521 43589 7

19 DOROTHY ROSS
The Origins of American Social Science
pb: 0 521 42836 x

20 KLAUS CHRISTIAN KOHNKE
The Rise of Neo-Kantianism
German Academic Philosophy between Idealism and Positivism
hb: 0 521 37336 0

21 IAN MACLEAN
Interpretation and Meaning in the Renaissance
The Case of Law
hb: 0 521 41546 2

22 MAURIZIO VIROLI
From Politics to Reason of State
The Acquisition and Transformation of the Language of Politics 1250–1600
hb: 0 521 41493 8

23 MARTIN VAN GELDEREN
The Political Thought of the Dutch Revolt 1555–1590
hb: 0 521 39204 7

24 NICHOLAS PHILLIPSON and QUENTIN SKINNER (eds.)
Political Discourse in Early Modern Britain
hb: 0 521 39242 X

25 JAMES TULLY
An Approach to Political Philosophy: Locke in Contexts
pb: 0 521 43638 9

26 RICHARD TUCK
Philosophy and Government 1572–1651
pb: 0 521 43885 3

27 RICHARD R. YEO
Defining Science
William Whewell, Natural Knowledge and Public Debate in Early Victorian Britain
hb: 0 521 43182 4

28 MARTIN WARNKE
The Court Artist
The Ancestry of the Modern Artist
hb: 0 521 36375 6

29 PETER N. MILLER
Defining the Common Good
Empire, Religion and Philosophy in Eighteenth-Century Britain
hb: 0 521 44259 1

30 CHRISTOPHER J. BERRY
The Idea of Luxury
A Conceptual and Historical Investigation
pb: 0 521 46691 1

31 E. J. HUNDERT
The Enlightenment's 'Fable'
Bernard Mandeville and the Discovery of Society
hb: 0 521 46082 4

32 JULIA STAPLETON
Englishness and the Study of Politics
The Social and Political Thought of Ernest Barker
hb: 0 521 46125 1

33 KEITH TRIBE
Strategies of Economic Order
German Economic Discourse, 1750–1950
hb: 0 521 46291 6

34 SACHIKO KUSUKAWA
The Transformation of Natural Philosophy
The Case of Philip Melancthon
hb: 0 521 47347 0

35 DAVID ARMITAGE, ARMAND HIMY and QUENTIN SKINNER (eds.)
Milton and Republicanism
pb: 0 521 64648 0

36 MARKKU PELTONEN
Classical Humanism and Republicanism in English Political Thought 1570–1640
hb: 0 521 49695 0

37 PHILIP IRONSIDE
The Social and Political Thought of Bertrand Russell
The Development of an Aristocratic Liberalism
hb: 0 521 47383 7

38 NANCY CARTWRIGHT, JORDI CAT, LOLA FLECK and THOMAS E. UEBEL
Otto Neurath: Philosophy between Science and Politics
hb: 0 521 45174 4

39 DONALD WINCH
Riches and Poverty
An Intellectual History of Political Economy in Britain, 1750–1834
pb: 0 521 55920 0

40 JENNIFER PLATT
A History of Sociological Research Methods in America
pb: 0 521 64649 9

41 KNUD HAAKONSSEN (ed.)
Enlightenment and Religion
Rational Dissent in Eighteenth-Century Britain
hb: 0 521 56060 8

42 G. E. R. LLOYD
Adversaries and Authorities
Investigations into Ancient Greek and Chinese Science
pb: 0 521 55695 3

43 ROLF LINDNER
The Reportage of Urban Culture
Robert Park and the Chicago School
hb: 0 521 44052 1

44 ANNABEL BRETT
Liberty, Right and Nature
Individual Rights in Later Scholastic Thought
hb: 0 521 56239 2

45 STEWART J. BROWN (ed.)
William Robertson and the Expansion of Empire
hb: 0 521 57083 2

46 HELENA ROSENBLATT
Rousseau and Geneva
From the First Discourse *to the* Social Contract, *1749–1762*
hb: 0 521 57004 2

47 DAVID RUNCIMAN
Pluralism and the Personality of the State
hb: 0 521 55191 9

48 ANNABEL PATTERSON
Early Modern Liberalism
hb: 0 521 59260 7

49 DAVID WEINSTEIN
Equal Freedom and Utility
Herbert Spencer's Liberal Utilitarianism
hb: 0 521 62264 6

50 YUN LEE TOO and NIALL LIVINGSTONE (eds.)
Pedagogy and Power
Rhetorics of Classical Learning
hb: 0 521 59435 9

51 REVIEL NETZ
The Shaping of Deduction in Greek Mathematics
A Study in Cognitive History
hb: 0 521 62279 4

52 MARY MORGAN and MARGARET MORRISON (eds.)
Models as Mediators
pb: 0 521 65571 4

53 JOEL MICHELL
Measurement in Psychology
A Critical History of a Methodological Concept
hb: 0 521 62120 8

54 RICHARD A. PRIMUS
The American Language of Rights
hb: 0 521 65250 2

55 ROBERT ALUN JONES
The development of Durkheim's Social Realism
hb: 0 521 65045 3

56 ANNE McLAREN
Political Culture in the Reign of Elizabeth I
Queen and Commonwealth 1558–1585
hb: 0 521 65144 1

57 JAMES HANKINS (ed.)
Renaissance Civic Humanism
Reappraisals and Reflections
hb: 0 521 78090 x

58 T. J. HOCHSTRASSER
Natural Law Theories in the Early Enlightenment
hb: 0 521 66193 5

59 DAVID ARMITAGE
The Ideological Origins of the British Empire
hb: 0 521 59081 7 pb: 0 521 78978 8

60 IAN HUNTER
Rival Enlightenments
Civil and Metaphysical Philosophy in Early Modern Germany
hb: 0 521 79265 7

61 DARIO CASTIGLIONE and IAIN HAMPSHER-MONK (eds.)
The History of Political Thought in National Context
hb: 0 521 78234 1

62 IAN MACLEAN
Logic, Signs and Nature in the Renaissance
The case of Learned Medicine
hb: 0 521 80648 8

63 PETER MACK
Elizabethan Rhetoric
Theory and Practice
hb: 0 521 81292 5

64 GEOFFREY LLOYD
The Ambitions of Curiosity
Understanding the World in Ancient Greece and China
hb: 0 521 81542 8 pb: 0 521 89461 1

65 MARKKU PELTONEN
The Duel in Early Modern England
Civility, Politeness and Honour
hb: 0 521 82060 6

66 ADAM SUTCLIFFE
Judaism and Enlightenment
hb: 0 521 82015 4

67 ANDREW FITZMAURICE
Humanism and America
An Intellectual History of English Colonisation, 1500–1625
hb: 0 521 82225 4

68 PIERRE FORCE
Self-Interest before Adam Smith
A Genealogy of Economic Science
hb: 0 521 83060 5

69 ERIC NELSON
The Greek Tradition in Republican Thought
hb: 0 521 83545 3

70 HARRO HOPFL
Jesuit Political Thought
The Society of Jesus and the state, c.1540–1640
hb: 0 521 83779 0

71 MIKAEL HÖRNQVIST
Machiavelli and Empire
hb: 0 521 83945 9